Adirondack Mountain Club

Central Trails

Adirondack
ADK
Mountain Club

Fourth Edition
Forest Preserve Series (4th ed.), Volume 3

Editor, Michael N. Kelsey

Adirondack Mountain Club, Inc.
Lake George, New York

Published by the Adirondack Mountain Club, Inc.
814 Goggins Road, Lake George, NY 12845-4117
www.adk.org

The Adirondack Mountain Club is dedicated to the protection and responsible
recreational use of the New York State Forest Preserve and other parks, wild
lands, and waters vital to our members and chapters. The Club, founded in 1922,
is a member-directed organization committed to public service and stewardship.
ADK employs a balanced approach to outdoor recreation, advocacy, environmental education, and natural resource conservation.

ADK encourages the involvement of all people in its mission and activities;
its goal is to be a community that is comfortable, inviting, and accessible.

Library of Congress Cataloging-in-Publication Data

Adirondack mountain club central trails / / Michael N. Kelsey, editor. -- 4th ed.
    p. cm. -- (Forest preserve series ; volume 3)
    Rev. ed. of: Adirondack trails. Central region / by Laurence T. Cagle, 3rd ed.,
c2004.
    ISBN 978-0-9896073-2-2 (guidebook alone) -- ISBN 978-0-9896073-3-9 (cen-
tral trails guide & map pack) 1. Hiking--New York (State)--Adirondack Mountain Region--Guidebooks. 2. Adirondack Mountain Region (N.Y.)--Guidebooks.
I. Kelsey, Michael N., 1978- II. Adirondack Mountain Club.
    GV199.42.N652A35 2012
    796.5109747'5--dc23
                                2012044629

ISBN 13-digit: 978-0-9896073-2-2

Printed in the United States of America
25 24 23 22 21 20 19 18 17 16 15 14   1 2 3 4 5 6 7 8 9 10 11 12 13 14

In Memory Of

Norman John Kelsey
June 9, 1944–November 6, 1993

Every trail has its start, every summit its rewards, every journey its lasting memory.

My 15-year life journey with my father introduced me to the location, spirit, and endless opportunities of the Adirondack Park, in particular the *Central Trails* region. Together, on our third attempt, we reached the summit of then-trailless Moxham Mt. in the month preceding his diagnosis with cancer. There, high atop the mountain we nicknamed "Scarface," we celebrated our achievement by unfurling a homemade flag with our names and the date of our climb.

My father's death less than four months later altered my life. Equally life-changing were the seeds of exploration and the thirst to achieve goals that he planted deep within.

I have undertaken each subsequent trek in his memory.

—Michael Norman Kelsey

Adirondack
ADK
Mountain Club

WE WELCOME YOUR COMMENTS

Use of information in this book is at the sole discretion and risk of the hiker. ADK, makes every effort to keep its guidebooks up-to-date; however, trail conditions are always changing.

In addition to reviewing the material in this book, hikers should assess their ability, physical condition, and preparation, as well as likely weather conditions, before a trip. For more information on preparation, equipment, and how to address emergencies, see the introduction.

If you note a discrepancy in this book or wish to forward a suggestion, we welcome your comments. Please cite book title, year of most recent copyright and printing (see copyright page), trail, page number, and date of your observation. Thanks for your help!

Please address your comments to:
Publications
Adirondack Mountain Club
814 Goggins Road
Lake George, NY 12845-4117
518-668-4447
pubs@adk.org

24-HOUR EMERGENCY CONTACTS

In-town and roadside: **911**

Backcountry emergencies in the Adirondacks: DEC dispatch, **518-891-0235**

Backcountry emergencies elsewhere: **518-408-5850**, or toll-free, **877-457-5680**

(See page 25 for more information.)

Contents

Overview Map 6

Preface 7

Introduction 11

Olmsteadville–Minerva Section 27

Siamese Ponds Wilderness Area 41

    From the South 41

    From the East 59

    From the North 75

    From the West (Kunjamuk Section) 89

Indian Lake Section 95

Lewey Lake and West Canada Lakes Section 109

Blue Mountain Lake and Sargent Ponds Section 135

The Great Camps, Pigeon Lake Wilderness Area, and

    Moose River Recreation Area 151

Piseco–Powley Road Vicinity 185

New York 10 Corridor 203

Silver Lake Wilderness Area 235

Appendices 247

    I. Glossary of Terms 247

    II. State Campgrounds in or near the Central Trails Region 248

Acknowledgments 249

About the Editor 250

Adirondack Mountain Club 251

Index 254

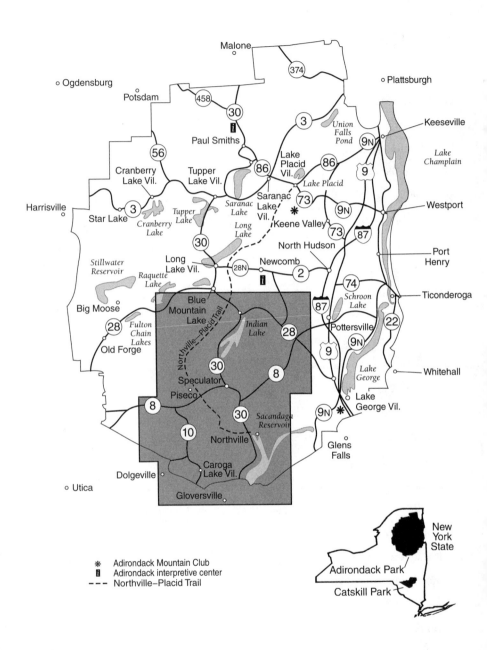

* Adirondack Mountain Club
ℹ Adirondack interpretive center
--- Northville–Placid Trail

Preface

The *Central Trails* region encompasses some of the best recreational opportunities the Adirondack Park has to offer. Its low peaks and wooded forests are coveted as much for their serenity as for their rejuvenating powers. It is possible many times over to escape out of cell phone range to experience true solitude. For those with navigation skills, there are ample opportunities to explore the pristine backcountry wilderness off-trail.

The region is perhaps best known for its countless backcountry lakes, rivers, and streams, perfect for fishing, wading, or photographing. Vast lakes, including Indian, Blue, Raquette, Piseco, and the Great Sacandaga Lake, are as popular with boaters today as they were to the railroad tycoons and barons of the previous century.

Now in its fourth edition, the scope of this guidebook has grown to include territory previously detailed in the Forst Preserve Series' West-Central and Southern Region guides. Thus this edition comprises significantly more trail descriptions, and revisions include the renumbering of all trails, with corresponding numbers on the National Geographic Trails Illustrated map. That map, titled *744 Northville/Raquette Lake*, also bears grid coordinates that correspond to each trail description.

The region's newly defined boundaries include five designated wilderness areas: Siamese Ponds, Blue Ridge, West Canada Lakes, Pigeon Lake, and Silver Lake. Wilderness Areas are governed by the Adirondack Park's strictest regulations, thereby affording hikers the least intrusive experiences in nature. The region's eight Wild Forests are less regulated and allow in some parts snowmobiles, mountain bikes, and floatplanes. Nevertheless, the region's serenity overpowers. Two Primitive Areas lie within, including the picturesque Hudson River Gorge, which beckons rafters, kayakers, and hikers alike.

In the south and in the west the terrain is gradual to flat. This makes it attractive to cross-country skiers in the winter and families of hikers of all ages in other seasons. In the north there are mountains with views and climbs comparable to those found in the High Peaks, but without the crowds. The highest mountain in the region, Snowy Mountain, misses the 4000 ft mark by only 101 ft. An additional twelve mountains reside on the Adirondack Hundred Highest list, most accessible only by bushwhack. Numerous other summits sport fire towers.

More than half of the 132 mi Northville–Placid Trail meanders its way through the region, including the trail's southern terminus in Upper Benson, just north of its formal start in Northville. Snaking through the northwest corner is the 90 mi Adirondack Canoe Classic route from Old Forge to Saranac Lake. Eventually the 4600 mi North Country Trail, conceived as the nation's longest long-distance trail, traversing seven states, will also meander east–west through New York State's

Northville-Placid Trail. Joanne Kennedy

Forest Preserve almost entirely on trails within this guidebook's purview.

Paddlers and anglers come for the area's abundant rivers, and rock climbers and cavers for the rock formations at Chimney Mt. as well as the cliffs of Good Luck Mt. The region's many bald summits lure hikers year-round. Thirteenth Lake is popular with the disabled community owing to its wide, gravel-lined shoreline trail and wheel-chair accessible latrines.

Particularly in the southern section, hiking trails follow former logging roads, off-season snowmobile trails, or stagecoach routes that led to settlements now abandoned, the product of the region's booming logging and tanning industries. The region enjoys past and present claims on the world's garnet mining industry, providing inspiring day trips to the abandoned Hooper Mine and Humphrey Mountain, where intrepid garnet hunters can still be rewarded with backcountry gemstone finds.

Many trails pass beaver dams and follow the shores of lakes inhabited by loons. Moose activity has been on the rise. Fish ponds beckon. A few miles north of Warrensburg, in the Charles Lathrop Pack Demonstration Forest, is the tallest recorded white pine in the state: 175 feet high and at least 135 years old. Additional old-growth trees line the Powley-Piseco Road and elsewhere, along more than a few trails. Lumbering and tanning were once big industries, but now the

West Canada Lakes. Joanne Kennedy

forest has grown back. Here are trails that see minimal human use, as well as untouched acres ripe for exploration.

The area had its share of personalities, including the colorful trapper and guide, Adirondack French Louie, who was most active in the West Canada Lakes region. The Durants and the Vanderbilts entertained the rich and powerful at their wealthy estates, the Sagamore, Uncus, and Pine Knot "camps" surrounding Raquette Lake. By far and away, the area's most historic moment was the September 13–14, 1901, carriage ride by Vice President Theodore Roosevelt upon learning that a shot fired by an anarchist in Buffalo, N.Y., had imperiled the life of President William McKinley. Roosevelt, who had just finished a hike up Mt. Marcy, was sworn in as President of the United States at the North Creek train depot.

Just as important are those of us who visit frequently to blend in and go unnoticed, and then return to our lives refreshed. It is to you for whom this guidebook will prove its greatest value. Trek with care.

—Michael N. Kelsey
Salt Point, New York
January 2014

View of Blue Mt. Chris Murray

Introduction

The Adirondack Mountain Club Forest Preserve Series

The Forest Preserve Series of guides to Adirondack and Catskill trails covers hiking opportunities on the approximately 2.5 million acres of Forest Preserve (public) land within the Adirondack Park and close to 300,000 acres in the Catskill Park. The Adirondack Mountain Club (ADK) published its first guidebook, covering the High Peaks and parts of the Northville–Placid Trail, in 1934. In the early 1980s, coinciding with the decade-long centennial celebration of the enactment of the Forest Preserve legislation in 1885, ADK set out to achieve its goal of completing a series of guides that would cover the two parks. This series now includes the following guidebooks:

1 Adirondack Mountain Club High Peaks Trails
2 Adirondack Mountain Club Eastern Trails
3 Adirondack Mountain Club Central Trails
4 Adirondack Mountain Club Western Trails
5 Adirondack Mountain Club Northville–Placid Trail
6 Adirondack Mountain Club Catskill Trails

The public lands that constitute the Forest Preserve are unique among all other wild public lands in the United States because they enjoy constitutional protection against sale or development. The story of this unique protection begins in the 1800s and continues today as groups such as ADK strive to guard it. This responsibility also rests with the public, who are expected not to degrade the Forest Preserve in any way while enjoying its wonders. The Forest Preserve Series of trail guides seeks not only to show hikers, skiers, and snowshoers where to enjoy their activities, but also to offer guidelines whereby users can minimize their impact on the land.

THE ADIRONDACKS

The Adirondack region of northern New York is unique in many ways. It contains the only mountains in the eastern United States that are not geologically Appalachian. In the late 1800s it was the first forested area in the nation to benefit from enlightened conservation measures. At roughly the same time it was also the most prestigious resort area in the country. In the twentieth century, the Adirondacks became the only place in the Western Hemisphere to host two winter Olympiads. In the 1970s the region was the first of significant size in the nation to be subjected to comprehensive land use controls.

Geologically, the Adirondacks are a southern appendage of the Canadian

Shield. In the United States the Shield bedrock, which is over one billion years old, mostly lies concealed under younger rock, but it is well exposed in a few regions. Upward doming of the Adirondack mass in the past few million years—a process that is still going on, resulting in the mountains rising a few millimeters every century—is responsible for erosional stripping of the younger rock cover. The stream-carved topography has been extensively modified by the sculpting of glaciers, which, on at least four widely separated occasions during the Ice Age, completely covered the mountains.

Ecologically, the Adirondacks are part of a vegetation transition zone, with the northern, largely coniferous boreal forest (from the Greek god Boreas, owner of the north wind, whose name can be found on a mountain peak and series of ponds in the High Peaks region) and the southern deciduous forest, exemplified by beech-maple stands, intermingling to present a pleasing array of forest tree species. Different vegetation zones are also encountered as one ascends the higher mountains in the Adirondacks; the tops of the highest peaks are truly arctic, with mosses and lichens that are common hundreds of miles to the north.

A rugged and heavily forested region, the Adirondacks were generally not hospitable to Native Americans, who used the region principally for hunting. Remnants of ancient campgrounds have been found in some locations. The native legacy survives principally in place names.

The first European to see the Adirondacks was likely the French explorer Jacques Cartier, who on his first trip up the St. Lawrence River in 1535 stood on top of Mont Royal (now within the city of Montreal) and discerned high ground to the south. Closer looks were had by Samuel de Champlain and Henry Hudson, who came from the north and south, respectively, within a few weeks of each other in 1609.

For the next two centuries the Champlain Valley to the east of the Adirondacks was a battleground. Iroquois, Algonquin, French, British, and eventually American fighters struggled for control over the valley, and with it, supremacy over the continent. Settlers slowly filled the St. Lawrence Valley to the north, the Mohawk Valley to the south, and somewhat later, the Black River Valley to the west. Meanwhile the vast, rolling forests of the interior slumbered in virtual isolation, disturbed only by an occasional hunter, timber cruiser, or wanderer.

With the coming of the nineteenth century, people discovered the Adirondacks. Virtually unknown as late as the 1830s (the source of the Nile River was located before the source of the Hudson), by 1850 the Adirondacks made New York the leading timber-producing state in the nation. This distinction did not last for long, though, as the supply of timber was quickly brought close to extinction. Meanwhile, mineral resources, particularly iron, were being exploited. After the Civil War, people began to look toward the Adirondacks for recreation. At the same time, resource conservation and wilderness preservation ideas began to take hold, sometimes conflicting with the newfound recreational interests. Conservation and preservation concepts were given legal standing in 1885, when the New York State legislature created the Adirondack Forest Preserve and directed that "the lands now or hereafter constituting the Forest Preserve shall be forever kept as wild forest lands." This action marked the first time a state government had set aside a significant piece of wilderness for reasons other than its scenic uniqueness.

In 1892, the legislature created the Adirondack State Park, consisting of Adirondack Forest Preserve land plus all privately owned land within a somewhat arbitrary boundary surrounding the Adirondacks, known as the "blue line" because it was drawn in blue on a large state map when it was first established. In 1894, in response to continuing abuses of the Forest Preserve law, the state's voters approved the inclusion of the "forever wild" portion of that law in the constitution of New York State, thus creating the only preserve in the nation that has constitutional protection. Today the Forest Preserve (the lands owned by the people of the State of New York) includes 2.5 million acres within the 6-million-acre Adirondack Park, the largest park in the nation outside of Alaska.

After World War I, tourism gradually took over as the primary industry in the Adirondacks. The growth of the second-home industry spurred implementation of land use plans and an Adirondack Park Agency to manage them. While the plans and the Agency have remained controversial, they indicate the need to address the issues facing the Adirondacks boldly and innovatively.

STATE LAND UNITS AND CLASSIFICATIONS

Since 1972, most Forest Preserve lands in the Adirondacks have been classified as either Wilderness, Primitive, or Wild Forest, depending on the size of the unit and the types of use thought to be desirable for that unit. The largest and most remote units are generally Wilderness, with only foot travel permitted and minimum facilities, such as lean-tos.

Primitive areas are similar, but with a nonconforming "structure" such as a fire tower, road, or private inholding. Wild Forest areas are generally smaller but potentially more intensively used, with snowmobiles and mountain bikes permitted on designated trails. Management of each unit is prescribed in a unit management plan (UMP), which determines what facilities, such as trails or shelters, will be built and maintained as well as any special regulations needed to manage each unit effectively.

USING THIS GUIDEBOOK

Like all the volumes in the Adirondack Mountain Club Forest Preserve Series of guides to Adirondack and Catskill trails, this book is intended to be both a reference tool for planning trips and a field guide to carry on the trail. All introductory material should be read carefully; it contains important information regarding current camping and hiking regulations as well as numerous suggestions for safe and proper travel.

The guide is divided into geographic sections. The introduction to each of these sections gives hikers an idea of the opportunities available in that area as well as information on facilities and regulations common to that section. Each section's

LEGEND

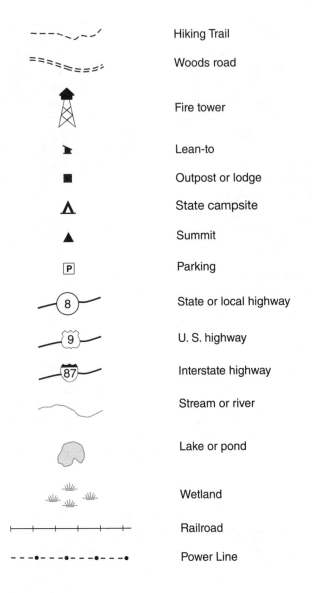

Hiking Trail

Woods road

Fire tower

Lean-to

Outpost or lodge

State campsite

Summit

Parking

State or local highway

U. S. highway

Interstate highway

Stream or river

Lake or pond

Wetland

Railroad

Power Line

introduction also provides recommended hikes in the "short," "moderate," and "harder" categories. Many of these recommended hikes incorporate lesser-used trails in an attempt to make hikers aware of the many beautiful and seldom-visited places aside from the most popular hiking, climbing, and camping areas.

MAPS

Every guidebook is this series matches trail information provided on National Geographic Trails Illustrated maps covering the Adirondack and Catskill Parks. These large-format, two-sided, folding, waterproof maps were created in partnership with ADK. Together the guides and maps are vital hiking tools, the latter also serving as road maps within the Adirondack and Catskill Parks. The following list identifies each map and the Forest Preserve Series guide to which it corresponds. All are available from ADK.

ADK Guide	Trails Illustrated Map	Additional Information
High Peaks Trails	742 Lake Placid/High Peaks	
	746 Saranac/Paul Smiths	Eastern side covers northern High Peaks
Eastern Trails	743 L. George/Great Sacandaga	
Central Trails	744 Northville/Raquette Lake	
Western Trails	745 Old Forge/Oswegatchie	
	746 Saranac/Paul Smiths	Western side covers NW portion of Western region
Catskill Trails	755 Catskill Park	
Northville–Placid Trail	744 Northville/Raquette Lake	
	742 Lake Placid/High Peaks	Western side covers northern N-P Trail

These maps are letter-number coded, with letters running up and down the right and left borders, and numbers running horizontally along the top and bottom. Each trail's coordinate appears with the corresponding description in this book (sample coordinate: A4), and each trail is numbered on the map and in the book. These numbers are not used on any signs on the trails.

A few hike descriptions are supported by page maps located nearby within the text. See the map legend on p. 14 for symbols used on the page maps.

All of the maps discussed in the preceding are available from ADK. Other maps, guidebooks, and information also can be obtained from ADK's Member Services Center in Lake George and the High Peaks Information Center on ADK's Heart Lake Property near Lake Placid.

ABBREVIATIONS AND CONVENTIONS

In each of the books in the Forest Preserve Series, R and L, with periods omitted, are used for right and left. The R and L banks of a stream are determined by look-

MORE ON N–P TRAIL AND HIGH PEAKS MAPS

ADK also offers two folded pocket-sized maps, one sold in the back of the Northville–Placid Trail guidebook and another sold separately for the High Peaks. Both are based on USGS quadrangles with updated overlays of trails, shelters, campsites, and private land boundaries.

The High Peaks pocket-sized map also shows the boundary between the Eastern and Western zones of the High Peaks Wilderness Area, an important distinction because there are different regulations for each zone. Additional important symbols indicate junctions with private trails and roads that serve as landmarks with which to locate one's position and a reminder that hikers are not to use these roads or trails.

ing downstream. Likewise, the R fork of a stream is on the R when one faces downstream. N, S, E, and W, again without periods, are used for north, south, east, and west. Compass bearings are given in degrees. N is 0 degrees, E is 90 degrees, S is 180 degrees, and W is 270 degrees.

The following abbreviations are used in the text:

ADK	Adirondack Mountain Club
AMR	Adirondack Mountain Reserve
APA	Adirondack Park Agency
ATIS	Adirondack Trail Improvement Society
DEC	New York State Department of Environmental Conservation
GPS	Global Positioning System
PBM	permanent benchmark
USGS	United States Geological Survey
4WD	four-wheel-drive vehicle
ft	foot or feet
jct.	junction
km	kilometer or kilometers
m	meter or meters
mi	mile or miles
yd	yard or yards

TRAIL SIGNS AND MARKERS

Marked and maintained DEC trails for Adirondack hikers, cross-country skiers, snowshoers, and snowmobilers tend to have signs posted at trailheads and major trail junctions. Trail signs usually give the distance to named locations on the trail.

Trail markers are plastic disks placed on trees or posts along the trails and on the signs at trailheads and junctions. The color and type of marker used on a trail is included in the descriptions in this book. (Painted blazes on trees generally indicate property boundaries and should not be confused with trail markers.)

With normal alertness to one's surroundings and exceptions made for lightly traveled trails, most marked trails are easy to follow. Although this guidebook does mention particularly tricky turns or trails that might pose special difficulties, each hiker must remain alert at all times for changes of direction. Group leaders have a particular responsibility not to let inexperienced members of their party travel by themselves. A trail that seems obvious to a more experienced person may not be that way at all to an inexperienced member of the group.

It should go without saying that one should never remove any sign or marker. Hikers noticing damaged or missing signs should report this to the DEC.

All trails described in this guide are on public land or public rights-of-way that cross private land. The continued goodwill of public-spirited landowners is directly dependent upon the manner in which the public uses this land. The "posted" signs occasionally found on rights-of-way serve to remind hikers that they are on private land over which the owner has granted permission for hikers to pass. In most cases, leaving the trail, camping, fishing, and hunting are not permitted on these lands. Hikers should respect the owner's wishes.

DISTANCE AND TIME

Trails in this guidebook have been measured with a professional surveyor's wheel and in some cases using GPS devices. Distances are expressed to the nearest tenth of a mile. Shorter distances are expressed as yards, and the number of yards has usually been derived from a wheel measurement in the field.

NOTE: In cases where there is disagreement between a sign and the guide's stated distance, the latter can be assumed to be correct. DEC has been informed of these discrepancies.

The start of each section of this guide includes a list of trails in the region, the mileage unique to the trail, and the page on which the trail description begins. All mileages given in the trail description are cumulative, the beginning of the trail being the 0.0 mile point. A distance summary is given at the end of each description, with a total distance expressed in kilometers as well as miles. If a trail has climbed significantly over its course, its total ascent in feet and meters is provided.

MOBILE PHONES

Mobile phones can't always be relied upon in case of an emergency in the backcountry. Despite many highly publicized stories, their use is limited by terrain, distance from communication towers, battery life, and other factors. Those who carry them should, out of consideration for their fellow hikers, use them only when necessary—and should have alternative plans for handling emergencies in case they do not operate.

If you must use your mobile phone in an emergency it is sometimes possible to obtain better range and reception by moving to a higher elevation and/or an area where you are not blocked by steep cliffs or other obstructions.

To the inexperienced hiker, distances are likely to seem longer on the trail, depending on the weight of the pack, the time of day, and the frequency and degree of ascents and descents. He or she will quickly learn that there is a significant difference between "sidewalk miles" and "trail miles."

No attempt has been made to estimate travel time for these trails. A conservative rule to follow in estimating time is to allow an hour for every one and one-half miles, plus one half hour for each one thousand feet of ascent, letting experience indicate how close the individual hiker is to this standard. Most day hikers will probably go a little faster than this, but backpackers will probably find they go somewhat slower. Some quickening of pace usually occurs when descending, though this may not be true on steep descents.

DAY HIKING and WILDERNESS CAMPING

It is not the purpose of this series to teach one how to hike or camp. The information below should, however, serve to make hikers aware of the differences and peculiarities of New York's backcountry while giving strong emphasis to currently recommended procedures for reducing environmental damage—particularly in heavily used areas. Users who intend to hike or camp for the first time are urged to consult a current book on the subject, attend one of the many workshops or training sessions available, or at least join a group led by someone with experience.

Except for Johns Brook Lodge, 3.5 miles up the Marcy Trail from Keene Valley (see *Adirondack Mountain Club High Peaks Trails*), there are no huts in the Adirondacks or Catskills for public use, such as are common in the White Mountains of New Hampshire. There are many lean-tos at convenient locations along trails and also many possibilities for tenting. The regulations regarding tenting and the use of lean-tos are simple and unrestrictive compared to those of other popular backpacking areas in this country and Canada. It is important that every backpacker know and obey the restrictions that do exist because they are designed to promote the long-term enjoyment and protection of the resource.

The following page lists some of the most important Forest Preserve regulations, many of which pertain to day hikers as well. Complete regulations and recent updates can be found online at the DEC website (www.dec.ny.gov).

- Except where marked by a "Camp Here" disk, camping is prohibited within 150 feet of roads, trails, lakes, ponds, streams, or other bodies of water.
- Groups of ten or more persons (nine in the High Peaks Region) or stays of more than three days in one place require a permit from the New York State Forest Ranger responsible for the area.
- Lean-tos are available in many areas on a first-come, first-served basis. Lean-tos cannot be used exclusively and must be shared with other campers.
- Use pit privies provided near popular camping areas and trailheads. If none are available, dispose of human waste by digging a hole six to eight inches deep at least 150 feet from water or campsites. Cover with leaves and soil.
- Do not use soap to wash yourself, clothing, or dishes within 150 feet of water.
- Fires should be built in existing fire pits or fireplaces if provided. Use only dead and down wood for fires. Cutting standing trees is prohibited. Extinguish all fires with water and stir ashes until they are cold to the touch. Do not build fires in areas marked by a "No Fires" disk or sign. Camp stoves are safer, more efficient, and cleaner.
- At all times, only emergency fires are permitted above 4000 feet in the Adirondacks and 3500 feet in the Catskills.
- Carry out what you carry in. Use Leave No Trace practices (see p. 22).
- Keep your pet under control. Restrain it on a leash when others approach. Collect and bury droppings away from water, trails, and campsites. Keep your pet away from drinking water sources.
- Observe and enjoy wildlife and plants, but leave them undisturbed.
- Removing plants, rocks, fossils, or artifacts from state land without a permit is illegal.
- Do not feed any wild animals.
- Store food properly to keep it away from animals—particularly bears.
- No camping is permitted above 4000 feet (1219 meters) at any time of the year in the Adirondacks.
- Except in an emergency or between December 21 and March 21, camping is prohibited above an elevation of 3500 feet in the Catskills.

LEAN-TOS

Lean-tos are available on a first-come, first-served basis up to the capacity of the shelter—usually about eight persons. Thus a small party cannot claim exclusive use of a shelter and must allow late arrivals equal use. Most lean-tos have a fireplace in front (sometimes with a primitive grill) and sanitary facilities. Most are located near some source of water, but each camper must use his or her own judgment as to whether or not the water supply needs purification before drinking. It is in very poor taste to carve or write one's initials in a shelter. Please try to keep these rustic shelters in good condition and appearance.

Because reservations cannot be made for any of these shelters, it is best to carry a tent or other alternate shelter. Many shelters away from the standard routes,

James Bullard

however, are seldom used, and a small party can often find a shelter open in the more remote areas.

The following regulations apply specifically to lean-tos, in addition to the general camping regulations listed above:

- No plastic may be used to close off the front of a shelter.
- No nails or other permanent fastener may be used to affix a tarp in a lean-to, but it is permissible to use rope to tie canvas or nylon tarps across the front.
- No tent may be pitched inside a lean-to.

GROUPS

Any group of ten or more persons or smaller groups intending to camp at one location three nights or longer must obtain a permit before camping on state land. A permit is also required for group events, including day hikes, involving more than twenty people. This system is designed to prevent overuse of certain critical sites and also to encourage groups to split into smaller parties.

Permits can be obtained from the New York State forest ranger closest to the actual starting point of one's proposed trip. The local forest ranger can be contacted by writing directly; if in doubt about whom to contact, send a letter to the DEC Lands and Forests Division Office address for the county in which your trip will take place. They will forward the letter to the proper ranger, but write early enough to allow a response before your trip date.

One can also make the initial contact with the forest ranger by telephone (see p. 25, bottom of sidebar). Note that forest rangers' schedules during the busy summer season are often unpredictable. Forest rangers are listed in the white pages of local phone books under "New York, State of; Environmental Conservation, Department of; Forest Ranger." Bear in mind when calling that most rangers operate out of their private homes; observe the normal courtesy used when calling a private residence. Contact by letter is much preferred. Camping with a large group requires careful planning with a lead time of several weeks to ensure a happy, safe outing.

FOREST SAFETY

The routes described in this guidebook vary from wide, well-marked DEC trails to narrow, unmarked footpaths that have become established through long use. With normal alertness and careful preparation the hiker should have few problems in land navigation. Nevertheless, careful map study and route planning are fundamental necessities. Hikers should never expect immediate help should an emergency occur. This is particularly true in winter, when fewer people are on the trails and weather is a more significant factor.

In addition to a map, all hikers should carry a compass and know at least the basics of its use. In some descriptions, the Forest Preserve Series uses compass bearings to differentiate trails at a junction or to indicate the direction of travel above timberline. More important, a compass can be an indispensable aid in the event that you lose your way.

Winter trips, especially, must be carefully planned. Travel over ice on ski and snowshoe trips must be done with caution. The possibility of freezing rain, snow, and cold temperatures should be considered from early September until late May. True winter conditions can commence as early as November and last well into April, particularly at higher altitudes. It is highly recommended that hikers travel in parties of at least four people, be outfitted properly, rest when the need arises, and drink plenty of water. Leave trip plans with someone at home and then keep to your itinerary.

DRINKING WATER

For many years, hikers could trust almost any water source in the backcountry to be pure and safe to drink. Unfortunately, as in many other mountain areas, some water sources have become contaminated with a parasite known as *Giardia lamblia.*

This intestinal parasite causes a disease known as giardiasis—often called "beaver fever." It can be spread by any warm-blooded mammal when infected feces wash into the water; beavers are prime agents in transferring this parasite because they spend so much of their time in and near water. Hikers themselves have also become primary agents in spreading this disease because some individuals appear to be unaffected carriers of the disease, and other recently infected individuals may inadvertently spread the parasite before their symptoms become apparent.

Prevention: Follow the guidelines for the disposal of human excrement as stated above. Equally important, make sure that every member of your group is aware of the problem and follows the guidelines as well. In addition, practicing good hygiene on the trail can help prevent the spread of this and other diseases. The health of a fellow hiker may depend on your consideration.

LEAVE NO TRACE

ADK supports the seven principles of the Leave No Trace program:

1. Plan Ahead and Prepare
Know the regulations and special considerations for the area you'll visit.
Prepare for extreme weather, hazards, and emergencies.
Travel in groups of less than ten people to minimize impacts.

2. Travel and Camp on Durable Surfaces
Hike in the middle of the trail; stay off of vegetation.
Camp in designated sites where possible.
In other areas, don't camp within 150 feet of water or a trail.

3. Dispose of Waste Properly
Pack out all trash (including toilet paper), leftover food, and litter.
Use existing privies, or dig a cat hole five to six inches deep,
    then cover hole.
Wash yourself and dishes at least 150 feet from water.

4. Leave What You Find
Leave rocks, plants, and other natural objects as you find them.
Let photos, drawings, or journals help to capture your memories.
Do not build structures or furniture or dig trenches.

5. Minimize Campfire Impacts
Use a portable stove to avoid the lasting impact of a campfire.
Where fires are permitted, use existing fire rings and only collect downed
    wood.
Burn all fires to ash, put out campfires completely, then hide traces of fire.

6. Respect Wildlife
Observe wildlife from a distance.
Avoid wildlife during mating, nesting, and other sensitive times.
Control pets at all times, and clean up after them.

7. Be Considerate of Other Visitors
Respect other visitors and protect the quality of their experience.
Let natural sounds prevail; avoid loud sounds and voices.
Be courteous and yield to other users on the trail.

For further information on Leave No Trace principles, log on to
www.lnt.org.

Water Treatment: No water source can be guaranteed to be safe. Boil all water for 2 to 3 minutes, utilize an iodine-based chemical purifier (available at camping supply stores and some drug and department stores), or use a commercial filter designed specifically for giardiasis prevention. If after returning from a trip you experience recurrent intestinal problems, consult your physician and explain your potential problem.

HUNTING SEASONS

Unlike the national park system, public lands within the Adirondack and Catskill state parks are open to sport hunting. There are separate rules and seasons for each type of hunting (small game, waterfowl, and big game), but it is the big-game season, i.e., deer and bear, that is most likely to concern hikers. Confrontations can occur when hikers and hunters are inconsiderate of the needs and rights of each other. Problems can be greatly reduced by careful planning.

It is advisable to avoid heavily hunted areas during big-game seasons. Consult the DEC website (www.dec.ny.gov) for the latest season schedules. Because it is difficult to carry a deer or bear carcass long distances or over steep terrain, hikers will find few hunters more than a mile from a roadway or in rugged mountain country. Lower slopes of beech, maple, and hemlock have much more hunting pressure than cripplebush, spruce, and balsam fir on upper slopes. Motorized vehicles are not allowed in areas designated as Wilderness, so hike there; most areas designated as Wild Forest have woods roads where vehicles can be used, so avoid these areas, which are likely to be favored by hunters. Try to avoid the opening and closing day of regular deer season. For safety, wear a bright-colored outer garment; orange is recommended.

ADK does not promote hunting as one of its organized activities, but it does recognize that sport hunting, when carried out in compliance with the game laws administered by the DEC, is a legitimate sporting activity.

Big-game seasons in the Adirondacks are usually as follows:
- Early Bear Season: Begins the first Saturday after the second Monday in September and continues for five weeks.
- Archery Season (deer and bear): September 27 to opening of regular season.
- Muzzle-loading Season (deer and bear): The seven days prior to opening of the regular season.
- Regular Season: Last Saturday in October through the second Sunday in December.

BEAR SAFETY

Most wildlife in the Adirondacks and Catskills are little more than a minor nuisance around the campsite. Generally, the larger the animal the more timid it is in the presence of humans. Some animals are emboldened by the aroma of food, however, and bears, the most intimidating of these, quickly habituate to human food sources.

BEAR CANISTERS

Bears in many parts of the Adirondacks have figured out the long-popular campers' technique of hanging food from a rope strung between two trees. Thus the DEC is now recommending—in some cases requiring—the use of bear-resistant, food-storage canisters.

- Bear canisters are required in the Eastern High Peaks Wilderness Area April 1 through November 30.
- The canisters can be obtained from many outdoor retailers, borrowed from many ADK chapters, or rented or purchased at ADK's Heart Lake or Lake George facilities. The canisters also protect food from many smaller forest creatures.
- The DEC's current management goal with respect to bears is to educate campers about proper food storage. Bears unable to get food from campers will, it is hoped, return to their natural diet. Thus campers play an important role in helping to restore the natural balance between bears and humans. Losing one's food to a bear should be recognized as a critical failure in achieving this goal.

The following tips will reduce the likelihood of an encounter with a bear.
- Never keep food in your tent or lean-to.
- Bear-resistant canisters are required in the Eastern High Peaks Wilderness Area April 1 through November 30.
- In other areas, use a canister or hang food at least fifteen feet off the ground from a rope strung between two trees that are at least fifteen feet apart and one hundred feet from the campsite. (Hangs using a branch have a high failure rate.) Using dark-colored rope tied off five or more feet above the ground makes it less likely that a foraging bear will see the line or find it while sniffing along the ground.
- Wrap aromatic foods well.
- Plan carefully to keep trash and leftovers to a minimum. Wrap in sealed containers such as large Ziploc bags, and hang or place in canister.
- Hang your pack, along with clothing worn during cooking.
- Keep a garbage-free fire pit away from your camping area.
- Should a bear appear, do not provoke it by throwing objects or approaching it. Bang pots, blow a whistle, shout, or otherwise try to drive it off with sharp noises. Should this fail, leave the scene.
- Report bear encounters to a forest ranger.

RABIES ALERT

Rabies infestation has been moving north through New York State. Although it is most often associated with raccoons, any warm-blooded mammal can be a carrier.

Although direct contact with a rabid animal in the forest is not likely, some precautions are advisable:

- Do not feed or pet any wild animals, under any circumstances.
- Particularly avoid any wild animals that seem to be behaving strangely.
- If bitten by a wild animal, seek medical attention immediately.

INSECT-BORNE DISEASES

Although not unique to the Adirondacks and Catskills, two insects found in these areas carry potentially lethal diseases. Deer ticks can spread Lyme disease, and mosquitoes can transmit West Nile virus. These are issues of particular concern in the Catskills.

In both instances, protection is advisable. Wear long pants and long-sleeved shirts and apply an insect repellent with the recommended percentage of N, N-diethyl-meta-toluamide (commonly known as DEET). On returning home, thoroughly inspect yourself, and wash yourself and your clothing immediately. Seek immediate attention if any early symptoms (rash, long-term fatigue, headache, fever) arise.

View from Moxham Mt. Michael N. Kelsey

Olmstedville–Minerva Section

 The Olmstedville–Minerva section is one of those seldom-traveled parts of the Adirondack Park, seemingly unknown to the general hiking public. Hikers bypass it on the E as they head up the Adirondack Northway (I-87) to the High Peaks. Campers miss it on the W as they travel up NY 30 through the lake country. All of this has resulted in an island of noncommercial Adirondack country treasured by those who know it for its beauty, solitude, and true Adirondack atmosphere.

This has always been timber country. It was state Assemblyman Wesley Barnes of Olmstedville who championed the legislative bill that created the Forest Commission in 1885. The Forest Commission became the Conservation Department, which in turn became today's Department of Environmental Conservation.

The destinations in this section range from Blue Ledges on the Hudson River, to the waters of Stony Pond country, to the vistas of the High Peaks from Vanderwhacker Mt. There are many private clubs in this section. Their private trails appear on topographic maps. The hiker is cautioned to obtain permission before walking private trails that are not described in this guide.

Recommended hikes in this section include:

SHORT HIKES
Hewitt Eddy–Boreas River: 2.4 mi (3.8 km) round trip. A charming walk along the Boreas River.

Rankin Pond: 0.8 (1.3 km) round trip. A scenic stroll to a lake with many attractive features.

MODERATE HIKE
Blue Ledges: 5 mi (8 km) round trip. A woods walk to one of the most beautiful parts of the Hudson River.

HARDER HIKES
Hewitt Pond to Irishtown: 15.8 mi (25.3 km) round trip. Travel from pond to pond through magnificent forest, on the Stony Pond from Hewitt Pond and Stony Pond from Irishtown Trails.

Vanderwhacker Mt.: 5.6 mi (9 km) round trip. Climb a mountain for a panoramic view of the High Peaks.

Trail Described	Total Miles (one way)		Page
Stony Pond Country			28
1 Stony Pond from Hewitt Pond	4.0	(6.4 km)	28
2 Center Pond	0.2	(0.3 km)	29
3 Stony Pond from NY 28N	2.1	(3.4 km)	30
4 Stony Pond from Irishtown	3.9	(6.2 km)	31
5 Blue Ledges	2.5	(4.0 km)	33
6 Rankin Pond	0.4	(0.6 km)	34
7 Linsey Marsh	2.0	(3.2 km)	34
8 Hewitt Eddy–Boreas River	1.2	(1.9 km)	35
9 Moxham Mt.	2.3	(3.7 km)	36
Vanderwhacker Mt.	2.8	(4.5 km)	37

Stony Pond Country

Stony Pond is actually a lake. It has an irregular shoreline of immense length. Green Mt., to the E, is a good bushwhack trip and an even better snowshoe destination in winter.

The collection of small ponds and lakes north of Irishtown offers a great variety of opportunities to the hiker. A day trip to Stony Pond can begin at any of three trailheads: Irishtown, NY 28N, or Hewitt Pond. A through trip from Hewitt Pond S to Irishtown can be a long day hike or a more leisurely backpack or fishing trip. The trail to Stony Pond from NY 28N makes a pleasant afternoon outing or can be the beginning of an interesting day hike to Irishtown.

1 Stony Pond from Hewitt Pond

Trails Illustrated Map 744: R23

The trail from Hewitt Pond to Stony Pond is lightly used and overgrown in places. Be sure to keep track of the last trail marker while searching for the next one. However, persistence is amply repaid by the nice combination of ponds, a bog, and open woods along the route.

▶Trailhead: Hewitt Rd. to the trailhead turns E off NY 28N at Aiden Lair. (While the club refers to itself as the Hewitt Lake Club, the USGS map refers to the body of water as Hewitt Pond and its neighboring mountain as Hewitt Pond Mt.) This is 6.6 mi N of the intersection of NY 28N and Olmstedville Rd. in Minerva and 1.9 mi S of the Boreas River bridge. The level dirt road leads 0.5 mi to a large parking area on the S side of the road, just before the gateway to the Hewitt Lake Club. ◀

The trail leaves the corner of the parking area, following red DEC trail markers. A gentle down slope leads 100 ft to a 400 ft boardwalk over a wet area. The Hewitt Lake Club property line appears on the L at 0.2 mi. The posted shoreline of Hewitt Pond is visible through the trees.

At 0.3 mi, the trail climbs a small grade to a height of land. Dropping down more steeply, it reaches the shoreline of Hewitt Pond again at 0.6 mi. The trail follows the shoreline, which at this point is part of the state-owned Forest Preserve. Hewitt Pond Mt. can be seen N across the pond.

Gradually pulling away from the pond, at 0.8 mi the trail turns R and crosses a brook at the remains of a small bridge at 1mi. The route follows the brook for a short distance, and then turns from S to SE as it leaves the brook and ascends a gradual grade.

The trail reaches the thickly tree-lined E shore of Barnes Pond at 1.7 mi. A fast-moving inlet stream is crossed and soon the trail leaves the pond to begin the long upgrade that terminates at the beginning of the Stony Pond watershed. Height of land is at 2.3 mi, after an ascent of 370 ft.

The descent is less steep than was the climb. At 2.7 mi a bog meadow with a small pond at its far end comes into view. The trail follows its E border to a jct. at 3.1 mi. Here, a DEC trail with yellow markers goes L and cuts 0.2 mi E over a low ridge, dropping down to Center Pond (see trail 2).

The trail follows the outlet of the pond to the NE corner of Stony Pond at 3.3 mi. Crossing the brook, the trail heads back upstream 40 yd before turning sharply N and climbing a ridgeline. From the height of land the trail descends SW and crosses a brook at 3.6 mi. The route follows an open woods road from this point and pulls away from Stony Pond to bypass a peninsula.

Stony Pond Brook, the outlet of Stony Pond, is reached at 4 mi, where it cuts through a rock zone. The Stony Pond lean-to is just out of sight on the opposite bank.

Beavers may have added to the natural dam at the outlet, making its crossing somewhat difficult. If so, a drier crossing may be found over one of the smaller beaver dams downstream. After crossing, find a woods road from NY 28N and follow it uphill to the lean-to, which occupies a very picturesque setting.

❋ Trail in winter: This is a very difficult trail for skiers.

🚶 Distances: To Hewitt Pond, 0.2 mi; to Barnes Pond, 1.7 mi; to top of ridge, 2.3 mi; to Center Pond Trail jct., 3.1 mi; to NE end of Stony Pond, 3.3 mi; to Stony Pond lean-to, 4 mi (6.4 km).

2 Center Pond

Trails Illustrated Map 744: R23

Center Pond is an attractive body of water surrounded by a fairly open forest and shoreline. A trail from Little Sherman Pond appears to have been abandoned with the development of the trail to Stony Pond from Hewitt Pond.

▶Trailhead: Follow the directions for the Stony Pond from Hewitt Pond Trail (trail 1) to a trail jct. at the 3.1 mi point.◀

The trail is not identified by a sign and is overgrown in places. However, yellow DEC trail markers are plainly visible at the jct. and can be followed easily to the pond. They lead L (E) up a moderately steep ridge. The grade soon levels. A few minutes' walk brings you to a steep downgrade and the shore of Center Pond at 0.2 mi.

❊ Trail in winter: This is very difficult to ski, but might be a short snowshoe trip for campers at the Stony Pond lean-to.

🐾 Distances: To Center Pond, 0.2 mi (0.3 km). Total distance from trailhead, 3.3 mi (5.3 km).

3 Stony Pond from NY 28N

Trails Illustrated Map 744: R23

This is the shortest route to Stony Pond. The trail follows an old woods road over easy up-and-down grades. Its course is part of a snowmobile trail to Irishtown. In summer, it makes a delightful afternoon hike.

▶Trailhead: Access is off NY 28N, 3.9 mi N of the Olmstedville Rd.-NY 28N intersection in Minerva and 2.8 mi S of Hewitt Rd. in Aiden Lair. A long curve in the road has an equally long pullout area on its E side. A DEC signpost marks the spot.◀

The woods road wends its way up a slight grade, leveling at 0.1 mi. On a curve, at 0.3 mi, a side trail R leads to an open campsite. (From the campsite, a footpath descends 0.1 mi to the shore of Twentyninth Pond. The N half of the shoreline is state-owned.)

The trail continues up a minor grade. At 0.4 mi, the trail bears L and an old woods road ascends a hill R. From a height of land at 0.5 mi, a long downgrade leads to a brook, which is crossed on corduroy at 0.8 mi. Still descending, the trail reaches the valley bottom at 1 mi, where it crosses another brook immediately downstream from a high beaver dam on the N side of the trail.

The trail traverses one more minor hill line. Corduroy and minor rerouting at 1.8 mi mark the site of previous beaver activity. Then the final upgrade to Stony Pond commences, parallel to the S of Stony Pond Brook.

Stony Pond with its lean-to is reached at 2.1 mi. The lean-to sits at a slight elevation above the pond level. An open area offers a gentle breeze and many wildflowers. It's a beautiful location.

❊ Trail in winter: This is an excellent ski trail. Combined with the Stony Pond from Irishtown trail (trail 4) and the ponds, an excellent day of backcountry skiing is available. The ponds are generally frozen by January, but care should always be taken when on ice.

🐾 Distances: To Twentyninth Pond side trail, 0.3 mi; to beaver dam on trail, 1 mi; to Stony Pond, 2.1 mi (3.4 km).

4 Stony Pond from Irishtown

The hike from Irishtown makes a nice day trip. However, be prepared to gain 930 ft in elevation to the ridge beyond Little Sherman Pond on the way. A through trip from NY 28N, with vehicles at both ends of the trail, is a less difficult way to see this land.

▶Trailhead: Access is off John Brannon Rd. in Irishtown. From the flashing light in Olmstedville, head N on the Minerva Rd. At 0.3 mi, at the Olmstedville village road sign, turn R. Travel 1.8 mi to Irishtown. Turn L at the ball field onto CR 37, passing St. Mary's Church and cemetery. Pass the Minerva transfer station and then cross Minerva Stream bridge at 0.4 mi. Turn R at the John Brannon Rd. T intersection. Drive another 0.4 mi to the trailhead. A cable barrier at the W side of the road marks the location. There is room on the shoulder of the road to park.◀

Stony Pond Lean-to. Bruce C. Wadsworth

The first part of the hike is over private land. Care should be taken to stay on the trail. The woods road heads N following red trail markers and yellow snowmobile trail markers. Avoid all side roads in this section.

At 0.2 mi the trail crosses Falls Brook. The remains of an old dam can be seen downstream. A large waterfall is downstream. Informal side trails lead to it; it is especially interesting in the springtime. Cascades of water pour down the brook on the L as elevation is gained.

At a fork at 0.3 mi, the trail continues straight over a knoll; the road L leads to a private camp. A Forest Preserve sign at 0.6 mi indicates that the trail is entering state land. Rushing water can be heard from deeper in the woods. The steady upgrade continues to 1.3 mi, where the trail steepens sharply for a short distance before moderating.

At a fork at 2 mi, a sign on a tree points the way to Sherman Pond. Bear R. An old woods road crosses the trail at 2.1 mi. Red tape to the R marks a snowmobile bypass of a muddy area.

A major trail jct. is reached at 2.5 mi. The red-marked foot trail to Stony Pond turns abruptly L and heads W. (The yellow-marked trail N is part of the original Stony Pond trail, which once continued along the E side of Big Sherman Pond and crossed the neck between Big Sherman and Little Sherman Ponds until it was flooded by beaver activity. The first tenth of a mile is still used to provide snowmobile access to Big Sherman Pond, but the remainder of the old trail has disappeared.)

At 2.6 mi the trail crosses Falls Brook, the outlet of Big Sherman Pond, just below a beaver dam. (The trail from here to the end of Little Sherman Pond is overgrown in places. Note the location of the previous trail marker while scouting the next one.) The trail climbs away from the water, but returns twice before the end of Big Sherman Pond is reached at 3.1 mi. Here the beginning of the crossover trail (now flooded) is seen cutting back R to the shoreline.

The trail continues N and reaches Little Sherman Pond at 3.2 mi. A jct. is reached at the end of Little Sherman Pond. (The trail R once went to the E corner of Stony Pond and then NW to Center Pond; it no longer is used.) The trail turns L and climbs steeply to 3.4 mi. It then gradually descends, turning L above the shoreline as it approaches the S end of Stony Pond at 3.5 mi. (The yellow-marked trail directly to the shore provides snowmobile access to the pond.) At 3.8 mi, the trail crosses a brook in a small cove of the pond and bears R as it parallels a rock wall. The Stony Pond lean-to is at 3.9 mi. Here the trails from NY 28N and Hewitt Pond (trail 1) merge.

❄ Trail in winter: Refer to Stony Pond from NY 28N (trail 3).

🐾 Distances: To Forest Preserve land, 0.6 mi; to Stony Pond Trail jct., 2.5 mi; to Big Sherman Pond outlet, 2.6 mi; to Little Sherman Pond, 3.2 mi; to Stony Pond lean-to, 3.9 mi (6.2 km).

5 Blue Ledges

Trails Illustrated Map 744: R21

Blue Ledges, where the Hudson River makes a horseshoe bend at the base of gigantic cliffs, is a unique place. The trail to Blue Ledges is very pleasant to walk and the grades are relatively easy, with the exception of the last few hundred yards' descent to the river.

The river run from below the Lake Abanakee dam on the Indian River through the Hudson River Gorge to North River is very popular among canoeists, kayakers, and private and commercial rafters (see ADK's *Canoe and Kayak Guide: East-Central New York State*). Commercial rafting on the river is heavy in the spring and fall when water is released from the dam on Lake Abanakee. Under the terms of an agreement between the Town of Indian Lake and DEC, there is a daily limit of 1000 people on commercial rafts. That many have been known to sweep by Blue Ledges on a spring Saturday.

▶Trailhead: Access to the trailhead is from the North Woods Club Rd. off NY 28N, 1.7 mi N of the intersection of Minerva Lake Rd. and NY 28N in Minerva. The North Woods Club Rd. forks W near the height of land on a curve. (If approaching from the S on NY 28N, it is easy to drive by without noticing it.) The macadam strip soon becomes a narrow but generally smooth dirt road. The road crosses the Boreas River 3.7 mi from NY 28N and shortly thereafter crosses an abandoned railroad track as it winds and climbs steeply up a grade. After a descent, a large DEC signpost on the S side of the road marks the trailhead, 6.7 mi from NY 28N. There is a large parking area on each side of the road. This road is plowed in winter, but be advised that it should not be used without 4WD and a taste for danger.◀

The blue-marked DEC trail immediately crosses an inlet brook of Huntley Pond on a bridge and heads S. At 0.1 mi, it reaches Huntley Pond. The trail follows the shoreline of this attractive pond for a short distance, then turns SW up a small grade. At a height of land the trail descends to a brook crossing at 0.6 mi. Turning W, the trail parallels the stream, passing several sites of beaver activity. At 1.6 mi, the route moves away from the stream and gradually gains elevation. The trail swings around the end of a ridge and then heads SE. The roar of the Hudson River can be heard in the valley below, though one cannot see the river at this point.

A small rock lookout ledge is reached at 2 mi. In autumn, the view of the ridge across the river from here is beautiful. The descent to the river now begins. Gradual at first, but then moderate, the slope is not difficult.

The trail drops down more steeply at 2.4 mi and ends at the river's edge directly across from the Blue Ledges. The sheer cliffs rise over 300 ft into the sky. Rapids are downstream, but good swimming is upstream during low-water periods in summer.

This section of river is one of the finest paddling waters in the Northeast. It is evident that the commercial users of the river have been doing an excellent job keeping this area attractive.

If backpacking, please camp at least 150 ft away from the river. Collect and carry out all litter that accumulates during your stay.

❄ Trail in winter: Not recommended for skiing because of the steep descent to the river.

🚶 Distances: To Huntley Pond, 0.1 mi; to brook crossing after height of land, 0.6 mi; to lookout ledge, 2 mi; to Blue Ledges at Hudson River, 2.5 mi (4 km).

6 Rankin Pond

Trails Illustrated Map 744: R22

Rankin Pond is like any of hundreds of little ponds in the Adirondacks. It is, however, so easily accessible that it can be visited without using a whole day. Anyone with a few minutes to spare can take a pleasant respite from a road trip and have a relaxing interlude or lunch break.

▶Trailhead: A DEC signpost (sometimes missing in early spring) marks the trailhead on the W side of NY 28N, 4.3 mi NW of Minerva and 4.3 mi S of the Boreas River bridge. There is parking for a few cars across the road from the trailhead.◀

The trail follows blue DEC trail markers and heads W from the parking area, parallel with the highway. It soon turns NW and a gradual descent into a hardwood forest commences. It crosses a small opening at 0.1 mi. Then a small climb up a rise must be achieved before Rankin Pond comes into view. A minor descent leads to the shore of the pond at 0.4 mi.

A small clearing presents an excellent view of the pond. A large rock makes a nice seat for enjoying the view of the water. There are yellow pond lilies, purple irises, and many other water flowers at this quiet spot in the wilderness.

❄ Trail in winter: This is a very short trail for winter use.

🚶 Distance: To Rankin Pond, 0.4 mi (0.6 km).

7 Linsey Marsh

Trails Illustrated Map 744: S22

Linsey Marsh is an elongated depression N of Hewitt Pond Mt. The trail travels over gradual grades on dry ground through a mixed-wood forest.

▶Trailhead: The trailhead is off the E side of NY 28N, 1.1 mi S of the Boreas River bridge. A small DEC signpost marks the spot. A parking area is on the W side of the road.◀

The trail follows yellow markers up a bank from the road. The direction changes from NE to N at 0.3 mi. After a height of land at 0.5 mi, there is a short jog E at 0.8 mi, but the general direction is NNE.

The trail crosses a brook on a dilapidated bridge at 1.1 mi. It ascends a moderate grade between close trees for 100 ft before gradual grades again become the norm. The route swings E at 1.2 mi. Slightly rolling terrain continues to 1.4 mi, where the route again heads N. A long, gradual downhill slope to Linsey Marsh begins here.

Linsey Marsh is reached at 2 mi. It is impossible to get near the water, but the marsh is very interesting. Open water in its center is bordered by marsh grasses and flowers.

❋ Trail in winter: This is a little-used but quite pleasant trail for both snow-shoers and skiers.

🐾 Distances: To height of land, 0.5 mi; to bridge over creek, 1.1 mi; to Linsey Marsh, 2 mi (3.2 km).

8 Hewitt Eddy–Boreas River

Trails Illustrated Map 744: S22

The Boreas River was alive with French-Canadian river runners every spring a hundred years ago. More than one lumberjack lost his life getting the logs down to the chain boom on the Hudson River at Glens Falls. Today, a footpath provides a beautiful little walk into Hewitt Eddy. If two vehicles are available, a 2 mi loop hike can be done by combining the two DEC-labeled trails (Hewitt Eddy Trail and Boreas River Trail). The preferable direction for walking, described here, is from the Hewitt Eddy trail to the Boreas River bridge.

▶Trailhead: Access is on the W side of NY 28N, at the S end of the Boreas River bridge. This is 8.7 mi N of Minerva and 5.2 mi S of the NY 28N-Tahawus Rd. intersection. (The remains of an old public campsite are evident on the old bridge road, across the road from the trail. It has several open campsites, fire-places, and picnic tables.) Parking is available on the old bridge road opposite the trail.◀

Blue DEC trail markers indicate the route along the E bank of the river. Attractive conifers and vibrant water sounds keep your interest. The trail stays close to the water, crossing occasional tributaries. Hewitt Eddy, a wide spot in the Boreas River, is at 1.2 mi. Here, a wide, placid pool circles on itself below the turbulent waters upstream. The eddy is where the waters rejoin in a long, lazy arc after a rock forces the Boreas River to split its flow.

The trail continues for another 0.8 mi to NY 28N, 0.8 mi S of the Boreas River bridge. The trail here is an especially nice woods walk along the Boreas River. A variety of ferns, flowers and trees are intriguing. The trail passes Stony Pond Brook at 1.5 mi and begins a slow grade descent at 1.8 mi. NY 28N is reached at 2 mi.

❋ Trail in winter: This trail is not suitable for skiing. Although suitable for snowshoeing, it is not particularly interesting in winter.

🐾 Distances: To Hewitt Eddy, 1.2 mi (1.9 km); to NY 28N via Hewitt Eddy trail, 2 mi (3.2 km).

9 Moxham Mt. Trail

The relatively new trail to Moxham Mt (2012) confirms what locals have known for decades: views from the open Moxham ridge make this 2.3 mi hike very worthwhile.

▶Trailhead: On Fourteenth Road 2 mi from its intersection with Route 28N, just S of Minerva. The Fourteenth Road intersection with Route 28N is 7 mi from the NY 28-NY 28N intersection just outside North Creek, or about 2.6 mi from the Warren County-Essex County border. The first 1.8 mi of Fourteenth Rd. is paved, and the last 0.2 mi on a narrow dirt/gravel road descends rapidly to a low point where there is trailhead parking for a few cars. Currently (early 2014), there are no trailhead signs, so ignore the blocked woods road straight ahead and look for surveyor's tape on the trees at the R (S) end of the parking area. After 50 ft, yellow DEC trail markers indicate the trail.◀

Leaving Fourteenth Rd., the trail begins to climb immediately to the top of a small ridge at 0.5 mi. The trail follows the ridge SE and descends into a valley. An outlet stream of a small wetland and beaver habitat is soon crossed. The trail then contours around the hill, crossing the inlet stream, and ascends to a col. Here, the trail bends L and ascends to the extended ridge of the Moxham Range at 1.3 mi. The first of numerous views to the S and W is found here. Prominent in the center is Gore Mt.'s groomed ski trails, and adjacent Pete Gay Mt. hovering over the hamlet of North Creek. The active garnet mines on Ruby Mt. are identifiable, as is the Hudson River in the foreground. On a clear day the fire towers on Blue Mt. and Snowy Mt. are also visible.

View from Moxham Mt. Michael N. Kelsey

The trail turns here and follows the Moxham ridge high above the NY 28N valley. Beneath the cliffs and parallel to the ridge are three ponds in succession: Mud, Long, and Clear. At 1.8 mi. the trail reaches the imposing view of Moxham's high point, referred to by some as Signal Mountain. Owing to a geological survey disc misspelling sometimes attributed to nineteenth century surveyor

View from Vanderwhacker Mt. Richard Nowicki

Verplank Colvin, the mountain is sometimes also referred to as "Maxam" or "Maxham."

The trail continues ahead along the open ridge amid constant mountainous views. The final 300 ft ascent leads to the 2464 ft summit at 2.3 mi. Three surveying bolts attest to the mountain's past. Legend has it that Robert Moxham fell to his death while surveying Dominick's patent in 1798. The mountain, then known as Jones Mt., was renamed in his memory.

Although the ascent from the parking lot is only about 930 ft, a tally of all the trail's ups and downs, both coming and going, yields a total of almost 1500 ft.

❋ Trail in winter: Note that Fourteenth Rd. is plowed only as far as the road is paved. Add 0.2 mi to your journey each way to avoid getting a car stuck on the unplowed road. This trail makes for a delightful snowshoe trek.

🐾 Distances: To top of small ridge 0.5; to first view on ridge 1.8 mi; to summit, 2.3 mi (3.7 km). Ascent, 930 ft (283 m). Elevation, 2,464 ft (751 m).

Vanderwhacker Mt. Trail

Trails Illustrated Map 744 and 742: S22 / P. 38

The summit of Vanderwhacker Mt. provides perhaps the finest panorama of the High Peaks to be seen from the southern Adirondacks. Its fire tower is in good condition and is being maintained by the DEC.

▶Trailhead: Access to the trailhead is on a gravel road, posted as Moose Pond Way, off the W side of NY 28N, immediately N of the Boreas River bridge. There is a signpost at the jct. The initial grade from the highway is on loose hardscrab-

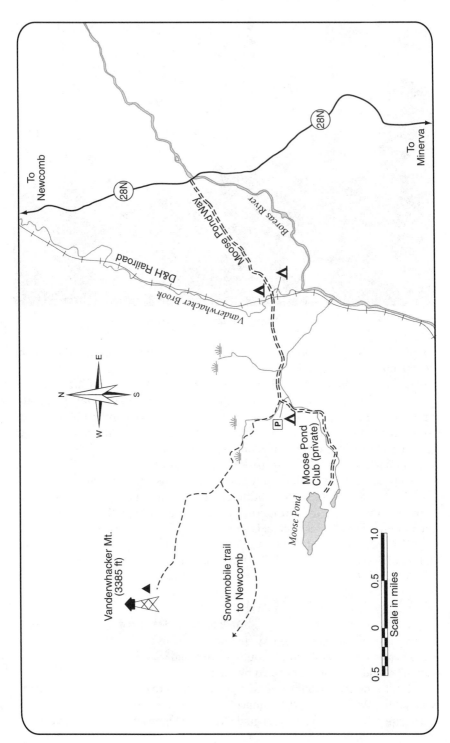

ble stone, but the road is satisfactory beyond this point if speed is controlled. There is a campsite on the R at 1.5 mi just before crossing Vanderwhacker Brook and another campsite on the L between the brook and the abandoned railroad tracks. At 2.6 mi, a small sign indicates the trailhead to the R. The trailhead and parking area are 20 rough yd from the road, and there is space to park safely on the road. (Just past this turn, there is another campsite on the R, but beyond there the road leads to the private Moose Pond Club.)◄

From the register (0.0 mi.) the wide trail, with red DEC hiking trail markers, climbs gradually NW through a hardwood forest. Soon leveling off, it swings N along the L bank of a brook, which it crosses at 0.3 mi.

A beaver dam on the R at 0.6 mi has flooded the trail, forcing its relocation to the L. A long marsh is on the L at 0.7 mi, with Little Beaver Mt. in the distant W. At 0.9 mi, a second beaver dam can be seen to the L and the trail begins to climb away from the marsh as it weaves in and out of the snowmobile trail.

The snowmobile trail, now barely evident, turns L at 1.3 mi, bearing around the base of the mountain, while the hiking trail continues straight ahead. The grade becomes moderate just before the fire observer's cabin at 1.4 mi. The trail climbs up, through a large opening with grass and berry bushes, to the cabin and outbuildings.

The trail continues uphill between the buildings, the slope becoming moderate as the trail follows a series of switchbacks. At 1.9 mi, the grade eases appreciably as the trail passes through a small hollow. The remaining distance to the summit at 2.8 mi is extremely attractive with gradual upgrades.

The summit is closed in on three sides, but magnificent open views can be obtained to the N. Algonquin and Avalanche Pass stand out. Colden, Redfield, Marcy, Haystack, Allen, Gothics, Sawteeth, Nipple Top, Dix, and Macomb, as well as the Boreas Range and many minor peaks, can be seen. A 360° view is gained from the fire tower. Moose Pond is below to the S. Beaver Ponds and Split Rock Pond are more distant in the SW.

❋ Trail in winter: The access road is not plowed in winter and is excellent for skiing to the observer's cabin. The skier can then switch to snowshoes and continue to the summit.

🐾 Distances: To marsh, 0.7 mi; to fire observer's cabin, 1.4 mi; to end of switchbacks, 1.9 mi; to summit, 2.8 mi (4.5 km). Ascent, 1650 ft (503 m). Elevation, 3385 ft (1032 m).

Sacandaga River. Mark Bowie

Siamese Ponds Wilderness Area

 The Siamese Pond Wilderness Area (SPWA) comprises more than 114,000 acres and includes thirty-six ponds and lakes, most of which drain into the East Branch Sacandaga River. Elevations range from 1280 ft to 3472 ft, and most grades are gradual, following aquatic tributaries through valleys.

Many trails provide access to the region, which has been divided into four parts in this guidebook: the SPWA from the South, East, North, and West (Kunjamuk section).

FROM THE SOUTH

Trails in this section all enter the Siamese Ponds Wilderness Area from NY 8. Access to NY 8 from the W in this section is off NY 30, 3 mi N of Wells. From the E, drive SW on NY 8 from Wevertown, where it crosses NY 28.

The SW part of the Siamese Ponds Wilderness Area is one of the last truly remote portions of the Forest Preserve. Only hunters' and anglers' trails probe up the tributaries of the East Branch Sacandaga River, leaving the interior a true wilderness. The first half of this section begins N of Wells, where NY 8 and NY 30 intersect. Its trails branch off NY 8/30 as it passes through the Sacandaga River valley to Speculator. This relatively narrow valley gains nearly 400 ft elevation in about 5 mi between Auger Falls and Christine Falls. A very nice easy day's outing can be had by combining Griffin Falls (part of trail 10, page 43), Auger Falls (West), and Austin Falls.

At one time Christine Falls and Whiskey Falls could have been added to the outing, however, the reopening of a hydroelectric facility at Christine Falls has closed that area to public access. The raising of the road level when NY 30 was rebuilt N of Speculator has made the stop at Whiskey Falls somewhat hazardous and probably not advisable.

The most used marked trail described in this chapter is the East Branch Sacandaga Trail. It is a trunk trail for several other trails in the region.

This is a region where hiking is enjoyable, fishing is good, and wildlife is plentiful. Since many of the trails are unmarked hunters' paths, hikers should study their maps well and carry a compass.

Following are some recommended hikes in this section:

SHORT HIKES:
Auger Falls (East): 2.6 mi (4.2 km) round trip. A hike along an old woods road to a charming waterfall.

Auger Falls (West): 2.4 mi (3.8 km) round trip. An attractive series of waterfalls in a hemlock gorge awaits the hiker.

Austin Falls: 0.4 mi (0.6 km) round trip. Unusual formations in the rock shore-line make this an interesting place.

East Branch Sacandaga Gorge and Square Falls: 2.4 mi (3.8 km) round trip. An unmarked footpath leads through a narrow gorge to a small waterfall and swimming hole.

MODERATE HIKES
Shanty Brook and Mud Ponds: 7.6 mi (12.2 km) round trip. Shanty Brook is a pleasant route through the forest to two attractive bodies of water. Note this is an unmarked, unmaintained trail.

Second Pond: 5.4 mi (8.6 km) round trip. Rolling terrain and open forests make for a delightful trip to an attractive lake.

HARDER HIKES
Siamese Ponds: 4.6 mi (7.4 km) round trip. A variety of terrains, ranging from crossing a ridge to strolling along the East Branch, can make for a long day.

Curtis Clearing: 3.4 mi (5.4 km) round trip. A bit of careful observation is nec-essary to find your way into one of the least traveled parts of the region. Note this is an unmarked, unmaintained trail.

	Trail Described	Total Miles (one way)		Page
10	Auger Falls (east side)	1.3	(2.1 km)	43
11	Auger Falls (west side)	1.2	(1.9 km)	45
	Austin Falls Walk	0.2	(0.3 km)	45
	County Line Brook	4.8	(7.7 km)	46
	Shanty Brook and Mud Ponds	3.8	(6.1 km)	48
	Fox Lair Walk	1.0	(1.6 km)	50
	East Branch Sacandaga Gorge and Square Falls	1.2	(1.9 km)	51
12	East Branch Sacandaga to Old Farm Clearing (from S)	9.6	(15.4 km)	52
12	Old Farm Clearing to East Branch Sacandaga (from N)	9.6	(15.4 km)	53
	Curtis Clearing	1.7	(2.7 km)	54
13	Siamese Ponds	2.3	(3.7 km)	56
	Bog Meadow	2.5	(4 km)	56
14	Second Pond	2.7	(4.3 km)	58

10 Auger Falls *(East Side)*

The hike to Auger Falls can be expanded many ways to make a delightful day hike. The falls is unusual. Its twisting course among rugged boulders and cliffs is intriguing.

▶Trailhead: Access is off NY 8 at the abandoned village of Griffin. From the jct. of NY 8 and NY 30, N of Wells, proceed 2.6 mi NE along NY 8. At this point, there is a DEC signpost for Cod Pine and Willis Lake. Across the road to the L is a dirt road (easy to miss). The bridge over the East Branch Sacandaga River 0.2 mi down the dirt road has been reopened to vehicular traffic, but parking on the far side of the bridge is limited and access to private camps should not be restricted. Ample parking is available near NY 8. The trail bears L once across the bridge.◀

From the bridge (0.0 mi), a gently rolling narrow dirt road heads W. At 0.5 mi, it passes a camp on the L. Red snowmobile markers begin at a barrier gate immediately beyond the camp. The old road becomes a grassy lane through a mixed wood forest.

At 1.3 mi, a DEC warning sign on a tree states, "Warning—Hazardous Gorge Area—Sheer Cliffs—Swift Water—Slippery Footing." A side trail L leads to the river above Auger Falls. Informal paths branch off from this trail and head downstream to the falls. Good views of the cascading water are found from the paths that wind along the top of the cliffs above the water. Hikers are encouraged to be careful.

The trip can be extended by continuing along the old road. It is well worth considering because the route is very attractive. Macomber Creek is reached at 1.5 mi. (A bushwhack up this creek provides another way into the extremely wild southern portion of the Siamese Ponds Wilderness Area.) A snowmobile bridge crosses the creek.

The route soon becomes a grassy footpath along the river. It then bears R, away from the water, gaining slight elevation. Lush ferns make the next half-mile extremely nice. Beyond this point is land leased by the International Paper Co. and closed to the general public.

Upon the return to the bridge over the East Branch at Griffin, a short trip to Griffin Falls is in order. Cross the bridge (heading toward NY 8) and follow the road around a bend. At a large boulder R, a very steep informal path drops down the bank to the river and Griffin Falls. High cliffs border the falls. The raging water forces its way through sharply angular layers of rock. It is a geologist's dream spot. This is a perfect place to take photos or have lunch.

❄ Trail in winter: Excellent cross-country skiing is possible along the old road described in this trip. For another trip, the skier can also continue 3 mi E of NY 8 to the virgin pines at Old Pine Orchard near Wells.

🐾 Distances: To camp, 0.5 mi; to side trail (Auger Falls), 1.3 mi (2.1 km); to Macomber Creek, 1.5 mi (2.4 km).

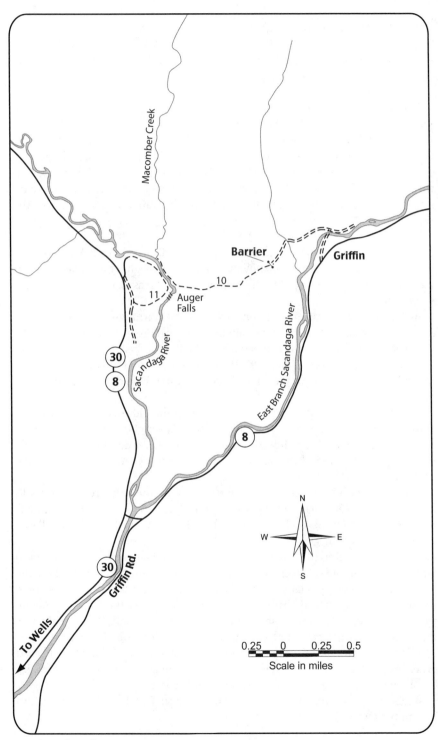

Scale in miles

11 Auger Falls (West Side)

Trails Illustrated Map 744: J19 / P. 44

The Sacandaga River cuts sharply through the rock of a narrow gorge at Auger Falls. It is a magnificent spectacle and a place of great natural beauty. A loop trip showing the many moods of the river is possible.

▶Trailhead: Access to the trailhead is off the E side of NY 8/30, 1.7 mi N of the NY 8 and NY 30 intersection N of Wells. Turn R into the gravel road entrance, and then immediately turn R again onto a narrow dirt road heading S. Follow this road a little over 0.1 mi to the unmarked DEC trailhead on the L, just before the road becomes a grassy lane. (The dirt road may be too rutted for a vehicle without 4WD. An alternative is to park on a widened area of the gravel road just beyond the turnoff for the dirt road. This adds 0.1 mi to the reported distance to the falls, but the distance for the loop as a whole remains the same.)◀

A DEC sign at the trailhead states: "Warning—Hazardous Gorge Area—Sheer Cliffs—Swift Water—Slippery Footing." A trail register is located 100 ft into the woods; past it, yellow DEC trail markers become evident.

The wide, level trail swings N toward the river. At 0.3 mi, the attractive forest gives way to the river as the trail approaches the rim of the gorge. Three distinct cataracts are below, as the trail continues N through a very handsome stand of hemlocks. A large stone masonry fireplace at 0.4 mi is in view of the upper cataract. This is a good spot to have lunch.

The official trail ends here, but informal paths continue upstream, weaving around blowdown and paralleling the river as it changes to rocky rapids. At 0.9 mi, the river becomes quiet, as the trail ends at a large clearing L. (Farther upstream is a good launching site for canoeing.) The road out of the clearing leads S to the trailhead at 1.2 mi, completing the loop.

❊ Trail in winter: This could be a short snowshoe trip, but parking on NY 30 is not very safe. Visiting the falls via Auger Falls (East Side) (trail 10, p. 43) would be advisable.

❋ Distances: To Auger Falls fireplace, 0.4 mi; to open clearing, 0.9 mi; to return to trailhead at end of loop, 1.2 mi (1.9 km).

Austin Falls Walk

Trails Illustrated Map 744: K18

In contrast to the raging torrent of Auger Falls, Austin Falls presents a small but broad waterfall. The charm of this section of river is in the potpourri of geological ocean-bottom evidence in the rock, potholes, rock channels, polished rock, and glacial striae (grooved bedrock) evident as one walks beside the fast-flowing water upstream from the falls. Both photographer and geologist will find much of interest. The falls are at roadside, so the only hiking is along the river.

▶Trailhead: Access to Austin Falls is off Old NY 8. Turn E off NY 8/30, 6.5 mi N of the NY 8 and NY 30 intersection N of Wells. Cross the steel bridge over the

Sacandaga River and drive S beside the E side of the river. Austin Falls is 2.6 mi S along this road (Old NY 8). There is a rough pullout parking space. The falls can't be seen from the road, so you must be careful to observe the exact mileage. International Paper has a public picnic area 0.3 mi farther along this road. ◄

The falls is just a few feet off the road, but easily missed if one is not seeking it. Interesting features extend about 0.2 mi upstream from the falls.

❄ Trail in winter: Not recommended for a winter outing.

🚶 Distance: To falls, 50 ft; upstream walk, 0.2 mi (0.3 km).

County Line Brook

Trails Illustrated Map 744: K20

County Line Brook roughly parallels the boundary line between Hamilton County and Warren County. The footpath along its W bank follows an old woods road to its terminus far back in the hills of the Siamese Ponds Wilderness Area. The variation in scenery makes this a very pleasant day hike. The trail is neither marked nor maintained.

►Trailhead: Access to the footpath is off NY 8, 0.2 mi SW of the Hamilton-Warren County boundary line road signs. There is a small pullout on the R. A steep path drops off the bank, descending 50 ft to the East Branch Sacandaga River. A short way downstream, two cables span the river; however, it is easier to rock-hop to the opposite bank by going slightly upstream. The County Line Brook footpath begins on the opposite bank at the cables (0.0 mi). A large DEC "Rules and Regulations" sign is nailed to a tree at this point. There is a fire ring nearby. ◄

The footpath leads inland from the river approximately 100 yd, where it intersects another path. Turn R (NE), and follow this path. County Line Brook is reached at 0.2 mi, just upstream from its confluence with the East Branch. The path now parallels the brook's W bank along a well-defined woods road running N.

The route moves back from the brook after a few minutes. At 0.8 mi, a long grade climbs high above the brook, which continues to be visible downslope. Eventually, the gradient of the brook rises to meet the path's elevation.

The trail reaches a vlei at 2 mi. The sizeable outlet stream of Buckhorn Pond cuts across the path. (County Line Brook Falls is near here. Turn around and walk back along the path until you are on dry ground at the edge of the wet area. Then walk 200 yd E into the woods, staying on dry ground along the edge of the vlei to the falls. The falls drops 7 ft into a deep pool. This is a nice place to swim.)   The path skirts the vlei on higher dry ground. To the R, the vlei is studded with small beaver dams, alders, and open stretches. Both the route and the change of scenery are pleasant.

The trail gradually moves away from the brook, but after dropping down a short grade at 2.5 mi comes alongside the brook again at the jct. of its E and W branches. The E branch extends toward Mud Ponds to the NE, while the W

Austin Falls. Richard Nowicki

branch heads N and then NW. The brook runs wide and deep here.

As the trail continues along the W branch, at 2.6 mi a huge erratic can be seen to the L. The stream is noticeably more narrow and rocky; the valley more closed in. The route is beside the brook, occasionally moving away from and then returning to the water.

The trail arrives at Lost Creek at 3.7 mi. The path is lightly used beyond this point and inexperienced hikers might consider turning around. The trail parallels the W bank of the brook to a large clearing; as long as that fact is remembered and the brook is kept within sight or sound, the chances of getting lost are slim. A large beaver dam is on the R at 4 mi. Almost immediately, the path changes direction sharply, looping W in a horseshoe before heading NW again.

At 4.3 mi, the valley narrows considerably and the grade becomes moderate. The route climbs away from the stream on an eroded section of the old road and soon the sound of a rushing stream is noted. A brief side trip will reveal that the brook's course falls through a narrow, deeply vertical rock gorge.

Height of land at 4.6 mi features another vlei. The slowly moving water is in a deep channel. The trail crosses another small tributary near the end of this attractive vlei at 4.7 mi, then passes through the forest to a clearing at 4.8 mi. This is the location of a former hunters' campsite, evident in 1998, when a large set of tiered bunks stood in the open, an incongruous sight deep in the woods.

❄ Trail in winter: The County Line Brook footpath has ideal grades and width for cross-country skiing. It makes a nice day trip or can be combined with the Shanty Brook–Mud Ponds Trail (see below) for a very rugged outing. As with many NY 8 trails, one must find a frozen ice bridge across the East Branch before it is possible to enjoy a winter outing.

🐾 Distances: To County Line Brook, 0.2 mi; to long grade, 0.8 mi; to vlei, 2 mi; to jct. of E and W branches, 2.5 mi; to Lost Creek, 3.7 mi; to height of land, 4.6 mi; to clearing at end of trail, 4.8 mi (7.7 km).

Shanty Brook and Mud Ponds

Trails Illustrated Map 744: L20

The hike up Shanty Brook into the Mud Ponds region is a trip into one of the most beautiful sections of the Siamese Ponds Wilderness Area. The grades are negligible. As in all unmarked trail travel, the hiker should carry and use both map and compass.

In the heyday of guiding in the Adirondacks, many of the nicest bodies of water were unfortunately called Mud Pond or Mud Lake. There are over thirty such bodies of water in the mountains with this uninspiring appellation. It is said this was done by the guides themselves, to make other guides believe those ponds were not good for fishing. The ponds in this case should perhaps have been called the Blue Hills Lakes to do them justice. They are jewels in the forest.

▶Trailhead: Access is from NY 8 at the large DEC Shanty Brook parking area. This is 10.1 mi NE of the jct. of NY 8 and NY 30 N of Wells and 4.7 mi SW of the large parking area at the Siamese Ponds Wilderness Area trailhead. ◀

A dirt road slants L (NW), from NY 8 toward the East Branch Sacandaga River, slightly more than 0.1 mi N of the parking area. About 100 ft along this road, several rough paths lead down a steep bank to the water's edge. Look for the start of the Shanty Brook footpath on the opposite bank (0.0 mi). This is downstream from the place where Shanty Brook enters the East Branch. At times of low water in the summer and fall, the East Branch is wide but very shallow at this point. Rock-hop or wade across the stream.

Climb the opposite bank and locate the beginning of the path. It is well traveled and easy to follow. It soon heads inland away from the river in a generally N direction. The path reaches the W bank of Shanty Brook at 0.2 mi and follows it for a short distance. The route then angles up a slope away from the water, though you can still see the brook for a while. At 0.7 mi, a 75 ft long wet section is reached, where you cannot see the brook. The trail bends just beyond this point.

Approximately 100 yd into the woods to the R (E), Shanty Brook Falls is located. A faint path leads to the falls. The water tumbles over a 12 ft rock ledge into a deep pool below. The stream cuts through the sheer walls of the gorge as it flows downstream. This is a lovely spot and an ideal place for a swim. Extremely interesting curves and cuts through the rock channel are visible for a long distance upstream from the falls.

Returning to the main trail, the route continues N. The path makes a brief swing E at 1.3 mi, crosses a rocky tributary brook, and then crosses to the E side of Shanty Brook at 1.4 mi. For the next half-mile, the sounds of the gurgling brook entertain you as you walk along its E side.

A large but somewhat empty vlei is reached at 1.9 mi. There is some evidence beaver may be returning to fill the vlei again. The Blue Hills ridge is to the W; Black Mt. can be glimpsed over the trees to the NE. Stay to the E side of the vlei and head in a straight line to its NE corner. Here, the path becomes obvious again.

After another short wet section, the valley begins to narrow against the ridge L. The brook cuts between the path and the ridge, but is not generally visible. The vlei becomes a series of beaver meadows, visible at L.

The path continues N until it is along Shanty Brook again. A large beaver meadow at 2.7 mi is where Stockholm Brook merges with Shanty Brook. Big Hopkins Mt. can be seen in the distant NE.

Cross Shanty Brook on the large rocks at the edge of the meadow. Once across, find the narrow rock channel that runs along the W edge of the meadow. Follow it until you pick up the faint path that continues along the edge of the meadow. Continue to the NW edge of the meadow, where the path again becomes easy to follow. It angles upward away from the meadow.

The route swings W at 2.8 mi. The low, rolling terrain is easy to walk and the trail is obvious.

The E end of the first Mud Pond is reached at 3.5 mi. The path extends along its S shore. A prominent rock formation can be seen across the pond at its midpoint. Open campsites are found at the midpoint and at the far end of the pond. The footpath winds over a small ridge at the end of the lake and terminates at 3.8 mi. Here a huge beaver dam divides the two ponds. Gigantic logs have drifted up against the dam. They provide an ideal spot to sit and eat lunch.

The view W down the second Mud Pond is one of the best in the Siamese Ponds Wilderness Area. Nearly a half-mile of water pierces the forest here. A view of Buckhorn Mt., with Macomber Mt. behind its R shoulder, completes the scene.

❊ Trail in winter: In late winter, when the East Branch Sacandaga is frozen over, this is a fine cross-country ski trip. Follow the trail to the first vlei and then ski right up snow-covered Shanty Brook to the Mud Ponds. Good map navigators then ski the ponds, swing SW around the Blue Hills, and ski down County Line Brook's E branch back to NY 8. This trip requires good backcountry skiing capabilities.

🐾 Distances: To Shanty Brook, 0.2 mi; to Shanty Brook crossing, 1.4 mi; to vlei, 1.9 mi; to fork, 2.5 mi; to beaver meadow, 2.7 mi; to first Mud Pond, 3.5 mi; to end of route, 3.8 mi (6.1 km).

Fox Lair Walk *(unmaintained)*

Trails Illustrated Map 744: L21

Fox Lair is the name Alexander Hudnut gave his estate, which is now state property. Its ruins, along with those of the old Oregon Tannery, provide points of interest for a short walk of up to a mile over the roads and paths of this land. It is a good place for a stroll, lunch, and a swim in the East Branch.

▶Trailhead: The N end of the estate is accessed via two dirt roads that head W across a meadow 2.2 mi SW of the Siamese Ponds Wilderness Area parking lot and 2.5 mi NE of the Shanty Brook parking area on NY 8. At the S end, a grassy road slants toward the river 3 mi SW of the Siamese Ponds Wilderness Area parking lot and 1.7 mi NE of the Shanty Brook parking area. The grassy road is within sight of a more obvious pullout and of a dirt road that dead-ends a few yards into the woods.◀

Both ruins are most easily found from the S end. A faint trail drops down the bank L toward the river about 100 yd from the rock barrier across the grassy road. The remains of the tannery can be found in the undergrowth. Continuing on, the grassy road soon passes steps leading down to a swimming hole L and then a more elaborate set of steps heading obliquely R up a knoll to the Fox Lair ruins.

The hiker who enjoys a bit more challenge can find the Fox Lair ruins from the N end of the estate by following a dirt road paralleling NY 8 until it turns into a grassy path. After crossing two old bridges with iron railings, a search through the undergrowth toward the river will reveal the knoll and ruins.

❊ Trail in winter: Winter use of the area could be fun, especially as a beginning snowshoe outing for children. Stay away from the river ice, however.

🚶 Distance: Approximately 1 mi (1.6 km).

East Branch Sacandaga Gorge and Square Falls *(unmaintained)*
Trails Illustrated Map 744: L21

This exquisite little trip is for the nimble-footed and light at heart. The camera buff will find it fascinating; the lover of wildflowers will not be disappointed. The trip is best done in summer or fall, when the water of the East Branch is low. The water is swift, and your rock-hopping skills must not fail you if you wish to stay dry.

▶Trailhead: Access is off NY 8, where an unmarked abandoned dirt road angles NW into the woods toward the East Branch. This dirt road is 2.1 mi S of the large DEC parking area at the Siamese Ponds Wilderness Area trailhead and 2.8 mi N of the DEC Shanty Brook parking area. There is a wide, sandy shoulder at the N end of a small grassy field where the road begins (0.0 mi).◀

The winding road dead-ends at 0.1 mi. A path extends onward a short distance to a crossing of a small stream. On the opposite side, the path heads L for 20 yd and then abruptly turns R and climbs a little grade. A few more yards of travel and the East Branch can be seen L below. The route continues N (upstream). The trail splits briefly, but soon rejoins.

At 0.3 mi, a side trail branches L 30 yd to the rocky riverbank, where a double cable stretches across the creek. (It is for use in times of high water, but is a very risky venture at best.) Go upstream until you find a suitable spot to rock-hop to the opposite bank.

Once across the stream, climb to the top of the riverbank. Find the informal path that heads upstream. Beautiful large hemlocks give shade as you gaze down into the rock-walled gorge.

The valley wall steepens greatly at 0.5 mi. While there is no significant difficulty, it is clear that one should not rush through the next section. The path contours the slope. Walk carefully.

The gorge widens again at 0.8 mi. The remainder of the trip is relatively flat and easy to walk. Square Falls at 1.2 mi, while not high, is quite broad. Water spills over the crest at several points, channeling into a deep pool at its base. It is a rare person who can resist a swim here.

Myriad wildflowers are found along the bank of the stream. A short walk beyond the falls is an immersion in lush ferns and flowers. Plan to spend some time here before the short return trip.

❋ Trail in winter: This is not a good winter route; the river and grades are not easy on snowshoes in places.

🚶 Distances: To side trail, 0.3 mi; to falls, 1.2 mi (1.9 km).

12 East Branch Sacandaga to Old Farm Clearing

(from the south)   **Trails Illustrated Map 744: M21**

This truck trail is the primary DEC trail into the Siamese Ponds Wilderness Area from the S. It runs NW to the beginning of the Siamese Ponds Trail (trail 13) and then swings N to Old Farm Clearing near Thirteenth Lake. Once you have climbed the shoulder of Eleventh Mt., the trail follows the old stagecoach route from North Creek to Bakers Mills for most of its course.

The East Branch Sacandaga trail is often used by hikers, skiers, and snow-shoers for through trips, with a car waiting for them at the other end of the trail.

▶Trailhead: The Eleventh Mt. trailhead is located on the W side of NY 8, 4 mi W of Bakers Mills. A large parking area, trail sign, and trail register are found here.◀

The trail leaves the rear of the parking area, passes a trail register, and quickly steepens. Elevation increases 240 ft before the col across the ridge of Eleventh Mt. at 0.3 mi. Here, the old stagecoach route enters from the L and the grade moderates. Walking is level through the col, but steepens again as you start the descent on the far side of the ridge. Views of the cliffs of Eleventh Mt. on the R are interesting.

A long, gradual descent brings you to Diamond Brook at 1.5 mi. (Diamond Brook intersects the Bog Meadow Trail 3.5 mi to the N.) This tributary of the East Branch is both shallow and broad. Spring freshets sometimes wash out the bridge here, but it generally isn't needed in the summer. These washouts may also make the trail unclear. Once across the brook, walk downstream several yards to the confluence with the East Branch. Here the trail is clear again, following the river upstream along its N bank.

A beaver meadow is soon reached, from which Diamond Mt. can be viewed to the N. The trail is essentially level here and closely parallels the river. Farther on, it alternately wanders away from the river and back again. A ford across the river to the Curtis Clearing Trail (p. 54) at 2.6 mi is followed by Burnt Shanty Clearing at 2.7 mi. A few apple trees growing here are all that is left to indicate where the clearing once existed.

Still on the level, the trail moves farther from the river, coming to a trail jct. at 3.5 mi. The newer marked trail heads L toward the East Branch; the R fork is the original trail. The suspension bridge across the East Branch is reached at 4 mi. The Sacandaga lean-to can be found not far off the trail. (The trail across the suspension bridge leads 2.3 mi to the Siamese Ponds; see trail 13.) From the suspension bridge, the trail heads upstream beside the E bank of the river. It rejoins the original trail at 4.3 mi.

At Big Shanty Flow, at 4.6 mi, a large, rustic sign on a tree states, "Big Shanty River Driving Camp 1890s." A large boulder R of the trail at 5.2 mi has a USGS benchmark in its center at eye level. The trail passes the cut made by Cross Brook on a bridge wide enough for skiers at 5.7 mi.

The route crosses a much shallower East Branch section at 6.6 mi. A single-strand cable was once here, but in 1992, a bridge, suitable for skiing, was built. The stream is easily rock-hopped at low-water periods. About 200 ft of elevation will be gained between here and Old Farm Clearing. At 7.7 mi, the trail begins to ascend, alternately climbing moderate and more gradual grades. It peaks at 8.8 mi, levels, and then gradually descends.

The marked trail from Kings Flow and Puffer Pond (trail 23, p.72) enters from the L at 9.5 mi. There is a signpost at this jct. A small spring on the R at 9.6 mi announces that the large clearing at Old Farm Clearing is just ahead.

❄ Trail in winter: For good skiers this is an excellent ski trail. Arranging vehicles for a through trip is time-consuming, however. Some short stretches require good control. Most people prefer skiing this trail from N to S.

🐾 Distances: To col, 0.3 mi; to Diamond Brook, 1.5 mi; to Curtis Clearing ford, 2.6 mi; to lean-to fork, 3.5 mi; to Sacandaga Lean-to, 4 mi; to Big Shanty Flow, 4.6 mi; to Cross Brook, 5.4 mi; to East Branch crossing, 6.6 mi; to Puffer Pond Trail jct., 9.5 mi; to Old Farm Clearing, 9.6 mi (15.4 km). It is another 1.2 mi to a summer parking area at the E access point.

12 Old Farm Clearing to East Branch Sacandaga

(from the north)   Trails Illustrated Map 744: O21

▶Trailhead: Access to the trailhead is from Old Farm Clearing (trail 21, p. 70). From the S end of the clearing (0.0 mi), the trail follows blue markers S. The way is over an open woods road through a pine plantation. ◀

The trail passes a spring on the L immediately after the clearing. At 0.1 mi, it reaches a signpost jct. Continue straight ahead. (The R turn leads to Puffer Pond, trail 23, p. 72.)

The trail climbs a gentle grade, levels, and at 0.8 mi begins a rolling descent toward the bridge over the East Branch Sacandaga River. The slope is moderate. From 1 to 1.4 mi, the trail is badly eroded. At 1.9 mi, the descent slackens and the trail traverses a number of small humps as it approaches and then parallels the East Branch Sacandaga River at L. Rushing water from spillage over a beaver dam can be heard at 2.9 mi. The dam can be seen near the trail at L.

A small grade brings you to the East Branch Sacandaga River at 3 mi, some 200 ft lower in elevation than Old Farm Clearing. In 1992 a bridge, suitable for skiing, was built across the East Branch at this point.

The now level trail passes through hardwoods. A wide bridge carries it over Cross Brook at 3.9 mi. A large boulder on the L side of the trail is seen at 4.4 mi. It has a brass USGS BM 1677 embedded in its center at eye level.

A large rustic sign on a tree at the R side of the trail marks arrival at Big Shanty Flow at 5 mi. It states, "Big Shanty River Driving Camp 1890s."

The route forks R at 5.3 mi. (The L fork is the original trail and is better skiing, however, it bypasses the lean-to.) The trail soon parallels the bank of the East Branch Sacandaga River. The East Branch Sacandaga Trail lean-to and suspension bridge are reached at 5.6 mi. (The trail across the suspension bridge leads 2.3 mi to the Siamese Ponds, trail 13).

From the lean-to, the trail leaves the stream and rejoins the original trail at 6.1 mi. Burnt Shanty Clearing is passed at 6.9 mi, but only a few old apple trees and a slight widening of the trail indicate the location of this old landmark site. The ford across the East Branch Sacandaga River to the Curtis Clearing Trail is passed at 7 mi, though it cannot be seen from the trail.

Pleasant trail walking takes you to a clearing at 8 mi where Diamond Mt. can be seen to the N, L of the trail. Diamond Brook bridge is reached at 8.1 mi. Not long after, the climb over the shoulder of Eleventh Mt. begins, with a gain of almost 300 ft in elevation. The route is uniform in grade. It levels for a short while at 9.2 mi at the col of the ridge. At the end of the col, the trail leaves the old stagecoach road it has been following and, bearing L, drops steeply down to NY 8. (Skiers should be expert to do this last section with speed.) At 9.6 mi, a DEC trail register announces the large NY 8 parking area.

❄ Trail in winter: This trail is an excellent ski trail. Care and control must be exercised from 0.8 mi to the river and from 9.2 mi to the end of the trail. Allow plenty of time for placing vehicles for point-to-point trips.

🐾 Distances: To Puffer Pond Trail jct., 0.1 mi; to East Branch Sacandaga River, 3 mi; to Cross Brook, 3.9 mi; to Big Shanty Flow, 5 mi; to East Branch Sacandaga Trail lean-to, 5.6 mi; to Curtis Clearing Trail jct., 7 mi; to Diamond Brook, 8.1 mi; to Eleventh Mt. col, 9.2 mi; to NY 8 trailhead, 9.6 mi (15.4 km).

Curtis Clearing (unmaintained)

Trails Illustrated Map 744: M20

Curtis Clearing is the site of an abandoned farm. There is little reason for going there, except to muse over occasional artifacts as you wander around the clearing. Getting there is the interesting part. If you wish to be in a little-traveled forest, where evidence of bears is much more abundant than evidence of humans, you'll enjoy this trip.

▶Trailhead: Access is from the East Branch Sacandaga Trail (trail 12) starting at NY 8. The Curtis Clearing Trail follows a well-defined old woods road. Once located, it is easy to hike. Some care is required to locate it.◀

The hiker leaves the East Branch Sacandaga Trail 2.6 mi from NY 8. This is 1.1 mi from the Diamond Brook bridge. After being close to the East Branch for several minutes, this level trail edges away from and out of sight of the river. In a shallow dip, a small section of corduroy is crossed. Approximately 100 paces beyond this point is a large old blaze on a tree at the R side of the trail. "CC" is carved on the opposite side of the tree. This is where you must leave the East Branch Trail (0.0 mi). (Burnt Shanty Clearing is 0.1 mi farther on, with several old apple trees.)

Turning L, follow a faint path 200 ft to the bank of the East Branch. Large rock

East Branch Sacandaga River. Mark Bowie

formations are on both sides of the river here. A small sandbar and a very large dead gray birch are on the opposite side of the stream. Rock-hop or ford the river. The Curtis Clearing trail begins on the opposite bank and heads W upstream.

At 0.1 mi, turn L, staying E of and above a marshy area near the river. Soon an old woods road is visible heading SW. The road is generally clear from this point to Curtis Clearing. The level route passes through mostly deciduous forest.

After crossing a brook at 0.3 mi, the path passes through a tiny circular clearing at 0.7 mi before heading W again. Soon thereafter it parallels Curtis Brook above the brook's E bank. The route crosses Curtis Brook at the outlet of a large beaver meadow and pond at 1 mi. (The road is easier to find if the lower of the two beaver dams is used as a reference point.) A visible and well-traveled trail crosses the brook shortly before the beaver pond. Turning sharply NW, the path curves around the beaver meadow. Turning W again, it heads up a long gradual grade.

At height of land the first of several large rock piles is seen. Soon after, the path reaches the first of several small clearings that comprised the Curtis Clearing farm. It continues beyond for 0.3 mi and ends in another old clearing. This is 1.7 mi from the East Branch.

❈ Trail in winter: Once across the river, this trail could be an interesting part of a day's outing.

🚶 Distances: To East Branch, 200 ft; to Curtis Brook, 1 mi; to end of trail, 1.7 mi (2.7 km). Total distance from NY 8, 4.3 mi (6.9 km).

13 Siamese Ponds

Trails Illustrated Map 744: M20

Siamese Ponds makes a good day's hike from NY 8 or an interesting exploration if one is camped at the lean-to on the East Branch Sacandaga River.

▶Trailhead: The Siamese Ponds Trail begins at the lean-to where the suspension bridge crosses the East Branch Sacandaga River (0.0 mi). It is reached via side trails to the lean-to from the East Branch Sacandaga Trail (trail 12). The lean-to and trailhead are 4 mi from NY 8 and 5.7 mi from Old Farm Clearing. The course of the trail is over the N shoulder of Siamese Mt., ascending 525 ft before reaching the ponds.◀

From the suspension bridge the trail heads W. Beaver have been active R of the trail, but their effects won't interfere with your hiking. At 0.4 mi the grade begins to increase.

The trail crosses Siamese Brook at 1.1 mi and reaches height of land at 2.1 mi. Here the trail descends briefly. It passes informal campsites, both L and R, at 2.2 mi before the final drop to the lower pond shoreline at 2.3 mi. A designated campsite can be found here.

Paths have been made by anglers and hikers around both sides of the ponds. The most actively used one crosses a small beaver dam and skirts the S shoreline. It eventually reaches the upper pond after another 1.3 mi.

❇ Trail in winter: For those adept in backcountry skiing, Siamese Ponds makes a long trip but a very interesting place to visit.

🚶 Distances: To Siamese Brook, 1.1 mi; to height of land, 2.1 mi; to lower Siamese Pond, 2.3 mi (3.7 km). Total distance from NY 8, 6.3 mi (10.1 km).

Bog Meadow

Trails Illustrated Map 744: N21

The route follows a 180-year-old woods road over gentle grades and level stretches. The destination is an exquisite bog meadow where a rippling brook provides a very enjoyable lunch spot. In recent years, maintenance decline and summer growth have made this trail sometimes difficult to use. In places, nettles make long trousers a must. Most of the trail is obvious; however, a few places in the early part of the trip require care. Take a compass and map and remember that the course is generally W.

▶Trailhead: To reach the trailhead, turn N off NY 8 onto Edwards Hill Rd. in the hamlet of Bakers Mills. Travel 1.5 mi, then pass on the L a large red farmhouse, a red home, and finally a white house. The hike begins at a narrow unmarked road on the L, immediately past the white house (0.0 mi). Park cars on the shoulder of Edwards Hill Rd., beyond this point. ◀

Follow the access road 0.1 mi over private land to a point where it begins to curve toward a white summer home. Here, the hiking route branches L onto a grassy woods road.

You soon pass an old log cabin and a well. At 0.3 mi, avoid a L turn with a chain barrier. Continue straight ahead on the less-used grassy path. Five minutes more walking brings you to denser forest and soon thereafter to state Forest Preserve land.

A gentle grade winds its way upward through the woods. Avoid a side trail R at 0.7 mi. At 1 mi, height of land is reached, 370 ft above the trailhead. Partway down the next slope, a tree on the R contains the mysterious carving "WVH DIED HERE OCT 1979." About 100 ft beyond the tree, the road turns L, and the Bog Meadow Trail continues straight ahead (NW) over a small hump of land. A gradual descent then brings you to Diamond Brook at 1.3 mi. The trail angles L across the brook. From this point onward the route becomes much easier to follow. Conifers are numerous and the trail is level.

Ten minutes later a low ridge comes into view at R, and soon thereafter the land begins to drop off on the L. The trail continues at a gradual decline, leveling just before reaching Round Pond Brook and Bog Meadow at 2.5 mi. An open campsite is just across the brook, upstream from the meadow.

A walk on the meadow is impressive. The dense forest surrounds it; the brook meanders through it. The trail circles around the meadow and crosses Round Pond Brook again, skirting L around blowdown on the opposite bank.

The hike can be extended beyond this point, but the trail isn't as pleasant and is more difficult to follow. Most hikers would end the hike here.

The trail continues to a jct. at 3.4 mi. An unclear path drops off to the R. A compass bearing of due N along this path takes you past an old hunters' open campsite. Just beyond, the way levels but is blocked by water due to beaver activity. Second Pond Flow can be seen through the trees ahead. Maneuvering around to the R will take you past the water and out onto the open meadow of the flow at 3.7 mi. It is many times larger than Bog Meadow, but not as easy to walk. It is well worth seeing, however, if you don't mind some discomfort hiking over from Bog Meadow.

The L path from the jct. at 3.4 mi is obvious for about a half-mile, but then becomes extremely difficult to follow. It leads to a clearing at a stream crossing 0.9 mi from the jct. This section should not be attempted except by those with good compass, map-reading, and off-trail hiking experience.

❄ Trail in winter: In winter, with summer growth flattened, this trail is a fine ski route. Just upstream from the bog, there are lovely ponds to explore on skis or snowshoes. The user must be cautious and good with maps and compass.

🐾 Distances: To Diamond Brook, 1.3 mi; to Mud Pond trail, 2.1 mi; to Bog Meadow, 2.5 mi (4 km).

14 Second Pond

The hike to Second Pond makes an extremely nice day trip. It has few grades and passes through magnificent open forests. Second Pond is over half a mile long and is very attractive.

▶Trailhead: Access is off NY 8, along Chatiemac Rd. This road is 0.5 mi S of Black Mt. Ski Lodge and 1.5 mi N of Bakers Mills. Turn W onto Chatiemac Rd. and gain about 600 ft elevation as you drive 2.3 mi to the trailhead. The unmarked trailhead (0.0 mi) is on the R (N) side of the road, but is easily found. (If you happen to pass the trailhead and reach Chatiemac Club and Chatiemac Lake, turn around and drive 0.3 mi back to the trailhead.)◀

The yellow-marked trail heads generally N. At 0.1 mi a pond can be seen L. Crossing a brook at the pond's dammed outlet, the level route continues onward. At 0.4 mi a meadow is visible far downslope through the trees to the R.

The path climbs very gradually. Its course remains generally N until before Height of Land Mt. to the W. At 0.8 mi the grade increases as the trail ascends a spur. Excellent views of the open woods and large boulders are R of the path. Height of land is attained at 1.1 mi, only 190 ft above the trailhead elevation of 2320 ft.

The trail now swings W until it hugs the steeper sides of Height of Land Mt. A slight loss of elevation occurs at 1.2 mi. The path then stays mostly on contour for the next mile.

At 2.2 mi, the trail begins to descend off the shelf. A gradual swing N and then NE occurs over the next half-mile. A final gradual descent leads to the S shore of Second Pond at 2.7 mi. An open campsite with fire ring is located a short distance back from the shore.

This is an attractive sheet of water about a half-mile in length. An island and hills in the distance draw your interest. The water spreads out in equal expanses both to the R and L. Anglers' paths follow the edge of the shore. With enough time, a walk around the pond would be enjoyable.

❄ Trail in winter: The grades of this trail are very suitable for intermediate skiers. Map skills and some care as to route location are necessary, but the woods are generally so open that navigation is relatively easy.

🐾 Distances: To beaver pond, 0.1 mi; to height of land, 1.1 mi; to descent, 2.2 mi; to Second Pond, 2.7 mi (4.3 km).

Siamese Ponds Wilderness Area

FROM THE EAST

Old Farm Clearing and Thirteenth Lake provide trailhead access to the Siamese Ponds Wilderness Area from the NE and, owing to new trail extensions to Botheration Pond (trail 22), also afford entry to the network of trails surrounding Garnet Hill Lodge. The latter are especially popular with cross-country skiers. The road from North River generally follows the stagecoach route of the 1800s to Old Farm Clearing. From there the stagecoach road to Indian Lake went past Puffer Pond and Kings Flow. Another route went to Bakers Mills. Today, these old roads are hiking trails.

Access is via Thirteenth Lake Rd. off NY 28 at the Hamilton County line just N of North River and S of where the unused (2013) railroad crosses the highway. A DEC sign indicates this is the way to the Siamese Ponds Wilderness Area. Turn S onto Thirteenth Lake Rd. and follow the macadam up the hill.

There is a road jct. at 3.3 mi. The dirt road to the R is Beach Rd. It leads 0.5 mi to the parking area at Thirteenth Lake. An Americans with Disabilities Act-compliant campsite with four wheelchair accessible tents sites, hardened roads, wide latrines, and elevated fire rings can be found here.

The main road continues across a concrete bridge and leads 0.8 mi to a jct. with a small DEC sign. The R fork (Old Farm Rd.) leads another 0.5 mi to a winter parking area L. A summer parking area is another 0.3 mi ahead, at a trail register and vehicle barricade. Old Farm Clearing is 1.2 mi along a woods road from this point.

Recommended hikes in this section include:

SHORT HIKES

William Blake Pond on the Halfway Brook trail: 1.6 mi (2.6 km) round trip. A short walk to a pretty pond.

Hooper Mine and William Blake Pond: 1.8 mi (2.9 km) round trip. A step back into history to look at an abandoned garnet mine and a serene body of water on a loop hike.

Elizabeth Point: 1.8 mi (2.9 km) round trip. A nice lunch spot on Thirteenth Lake.

MODERATE HIKES

Peaked Mt. Pond and Peaked Mt.: 7.2 mi (11.5 km) round trip. A day trip to a pretty pond with an option to climb a rocky summit.

Balm of Gilead Mt.: 1.8 mi (2.9 km) round trip. A short climb for a panoramic view of the Siamese Ponds Wilderness Area.

HARDER HIKES
Puffer Pond: 11 mi (17.6 km) round trip from parking area. Reaching this pond requires climbing a ridge, but it is worth the effort.

Gore Mt.: 9.4 mi (15 km) round trip. A strenuous uphill climb to fantastic views.

	Trail Described	*Total Miles (one way)*		*Page*
15	Gore Mt. via Schaefer Trail	4.7	(7.5 km)	60
16	Peaked Mt. Pond and Peaked Mt.	3.6	(5.8 km)	62
17	Halfway Brook	3.3	(5.3 km)	64
18	Raymond Brook	3.5	(5.6 km)	66
19	Balm of Gilead Mt.	0.9	(1.4 km)	67
20	Hooper Mine	0.4	(0.6 km)	68
21	Old Farm Clearing	1.2	(1.9 km)	69
	Elizabeth Point	0.9	(1.4 km)	69
22	Botheration Pond	2.1	(3.4 km)	70
23	Puffer Pond	4.2	(6.7 km)	71
24	Hour Pond	1.6	(2.6 km)	72
25	Hour Pond–Peaked Mt. Connector	1.6	(2.6 km)	73

15 Gore Mt. via the Schaefer Trail

Trails Illustrated Map 744: O22

The Schaefer Trail (rerouted in 2010) starts up Gore Mt. at the North Creek Ski Bowl area. Much of the trail ascends steeply up or along the R bank of Roaring Brook, with views of waterfalls, and later, the High Peaks. At 3583 ft, Gore Mt. ranks 84 on the list of Adirondack Hundred Highest.

This trail, which leads to the summit of Gore, is named in honor of the Schaefer brothers, Carl, Paul, and Vincent. Paul was a renowned conservationist and writer; Carl and Vincent were major figures in developing skiing on the mountain before the present state-run downhill facility was constructed. The brainchild of Paul's son-in-law Don Greene, the original trail was designed, cut, and marked by Greene and other volunteers. DEC Forest Ranger Steve Ovitt is responsible for the subsequent rerouting of the trail.

▶Trailhead: The trailhead is located at the North Creek Ski Bowl. It is reached by driving north along NY 28 from Warrensburg. Cross NY 8 at a four-way stoplight at Wevertown. Proceed 4.8 mi farther on NY 28, passing a Stewarts Shop and the road L to the Gore Mountain downhill ski area. Turn L on the gravel Ski Bowl Rd., then shortly after, turn L again at a sign to "Grunblatt Memorial Beach" and "trailhead." Park on the L in the beach parking lot, and begin hiking at the

Schaefer Trail sign. ◀

From the DEC sign, the trail slants diagonally L across the hillside on an obvious footpath, following blue DEC hiking trail markers. Cross the gravel road to the town dump and proceed through an open gate to resume the footpath. A short distance from the gate, in an open clearing, is the trail register.

Beyond the register, enter hemlock woods and continue uphill following blue DEC markers. A small creek is on the R. Do not cross the creek, but look for a blue marker, which signals a hard L turn. At 0.3 mi, the trail crosses an old woods road with a view L into a clearing. Continue straight on the mostly level terrain of a town trail now marked with blue DEC signs, which then begins to climb again. The trail passes moss-covered erratic boulders on the L.

At 0.4 mi, the trail reaches an intersection where the town trail branches L and the Schaefer Trail veers R. At 0.9 mi, the trail takes a hard R and follows the old North Creek Reservoir trail. At 1 mi, it crosses a tributary to Roaring Brook, then passes a picturesque spring on the R, and just beyond, a little cave. The trail then reaches the base of a series of waterfalls on Roaring Brook at 1.1 mi. Leaving the first waterfall, the trail climbs steeply up the hillside and follows along Roaring Brook in sight of many other waterfalls. At times the trail approaches the stream close enough for hikers to rest on the bedrock of the streambed.

At 1.3 mi the Schaefer Trail approaches the bridge for the new connector ski trail between the North Creek Ski Bowl and Gore Mountain Ski Area. There is a high boulder wall on your R just before the bridge. Ignore the blue trail marker near the bridge and look for the switchback that leads up and around the right end of the wall. The trail follows along the top of the wall and crosses the ski trail (but not the bridge), before continuing, still on the R bank of Roaring Brook.

In the next 0.1 mi, there is a very nice place to get out on the bedrock of the brook. Shortly after, the trail intersects a maintenance road on a second bridge (again, do not cross the bridge) which carries the water supply from the Hudson River across Roaring Brook to Gore Mountain's snowmaking system. After its intersection with the road, the trail continues on the same side of Roaring Brook and becomes much gentler because it now follows the reconstituted Nordic ski trail of many years ago.

At 1.6 mi the route finally leaves the streamside and continues to climb up to the edge of the North Creek Reservoir at 1.8 mi. Here you will find a comfortable rock bench on which to rest and enjoy the beauty of the reservoir and the surrounding hills. Beyond this point, the trail turns N, away from the reservoir, and then circles farther W.

At 2 mi, there is a jct. with the red-marked Rabbit Pond trail on the right. At 2.5 mi, the trail crosses a power line as it continues a gentle ascent to the W. At 3.2 mi, the trail enters a large clearing known as Ives Dam, where it turns sharply to the L, crosses Roaring Brook, now a very small stream, and enters the woods again heading almost SE.

At this point the trail stops being part of the old Nordic ski trail and resumes being a footpath that climbs quickly up to the Woodout ski trail at Gore. At 3.4 mi, the hiking trail crosses the Woodout ski trail and proceeds up through the forest between ski trails to cross the Lower Woodin ski trail. From here the trail continues to ascend until it exits the woods by converging with the summit maintenance road/ski trail called Lower Cloud at 3.8 mi. Follow the ski trail and the blue markers down a small dip and then up a steep section to an open area with good views to the NE at 4.1 mi.

Beyond this point the trail continues on a road under the High Peaks Chair all the way to the summit. At 4.5 mi the trail passes the top of the High Peaks chairlift on the L and reaches the summit at 4.7 mi. The opening leading to the closed tower is just beyond. The open portion of the summit is to the L (E) with good views N to the High Peaks and E toward the mountains around Lake George.

❋ Trail in winter: During downhill ski season, the trail is likely to be open for snowshoeing only to the first bridge, which serves the connector ski trail between the North Creek Ski Bowl and Gore Mountain Ski Area. Gore Mountain Ski Area does not allow snowshoeing on their downhill ski trails during ski season.

❧ Distances: To Roaring Brook, 1.1 mi; to North Creek Reservoir, 1.9 mi; to power line, 2.5 mi; to convergence with Woodout Ski Trail, 3.4 mi; to summit and fire tower, 4.7 mi (7.5 km). Ascent, 2560 ft (780 m). Elevation, 3583 ft (1092 m).

16 Peaked Mt. Pond and Peaked Mt.

Trails Illustrated Map 744: P21

The trail to Peaked Mt. Pond offers a day hike that is about as perfect as it gets. Seldom does so much variety occur in such a short distance. The pond is lovely, and its setting in the shadow of the bold rocky face of Peaked Mt. provides a photographer's picnic. A connector trail with Hour Pond (trail 25) allows for a loop overnight trip or a long day-hike.

▶Trailhead: The trailhead is at the boat launching area and wheelchair-accessible campsites at the N end of Thirteenth Lake (see section opening, p. 59). A trail register and trailhead sign are located at the lakeshore. The trail is marked with a combination of red DEC trail markers and circular red blazes.◀

The trail hugs the W edge of Thirteenth Lake. At times it climbs high above the water only to return to the shore again. At a fork at 0.2 mi, a sign points the way to a camping area down the L fork, while the trail bears R up a knoll and around the camping area. A private beach is seen across the lake at 0.5 mi.

When Peaked Mt. Brook enters Thirteenth Lake at 0.8 mi, the trail turns W and follows the N side of the brook upstream. In the next 0.8 mi it gains nearly 300 ft elevation, however, the grade is so uniformly gradual and the views along the cascading brook so interesting that the ascent seems easy.

At 1.6 mi the trail levels and crosses the brook, soon arriving at the first of three vleis. From here to Peaked Mt. Pond the trail winds around the vleis and

Peaked Mt. from Balm of Gilead Mt. Michael N. Kelsey

crosses the brook several times. The first view of Peaked Mt. is partway around the first vlei.

Beaver activity is evident at all three vleis. The beaver lodge and dam just off the trail on the R at 1.9 mi are hard to miss. Another set is to the L at 2.1 mi. A long curving dam floods a large area just before the brook is crossed for the last time at 2.8 mi.

Climbing a moderate grade, the trail reaches the shore of Peaked Mt. Pond at 2.9 mi. A trail leads R around the S edge of the pond, where a few open campsites are found. A fine view of the mountain is obtained a short distance along this trail.

The trail to this point has been easy and pleasant. Those interested in no more than such a walk may wish to have lunch and enjoy the view of the mountain across the water. The remaining ascent to the summit is far more rugged and very steep in places.

The path around the E end of Peaked Mt. Pond almost immediately crosses the outlet of the pond. The trail parallels the shoreline, though a ways back from the water in most places. At 3 mi, the trail reaches the NE corner of the pond, where a narrow cove is found.

The trail skirts the end of the cove and steeply climbs the shoulder of the mountain. At one time, garnet was mined on this part of Peaked Mt. The route often changes direction as it ascends.

At 3.5 mi, the trail breaks out onto open rock for a short distance. Distant peaks and ponds can be seen. Then the path plunges back into the woods for the short remaining distance to the summit at 3.6 mi.

Summit elevation is 2919 ft, 669 ft above the pond. By moving to various open rocky sections of the summit, one can find extremely fine views. Open pit garnet mines can be seen on Ruby Mt. to the NE and on Gore Mt. to the SE. Peaked Mt. Pond is directly below. The mountains of Vermont are farther E. The High Peaks of the Adirondacks unfold to the N. Big, flat-topped Blue Mt. is on the horizon to the NW. Gazing past the flat expanses to the W brings you to Snowy Mt. and the Blue Ridge.

❄ Trail in winter: This is a delightful snowshoe trip in winter, especially in late winter. Crampons are suggested once beyond Peaked Mt. Pond.

🐾 Distances: To Peaked Mt. Brook, 0.8 mi; to first brook crossing, 1.6 mi; to Peaked Mt. Pond, 2.9 mi; to summit, 3.6 mi (5.8 km). Ascent, 1245 ft (379 m); summit elevation, 2919 ft (890 m).

17 Halfway Brook

Trails Illustrated Map 744: O21

This trail was created in 2005 mainly as a cross-country ski trail to extend the existing William Blake Pond trail. Hikers may enjoy the trail all year long, but should be attentive to skiers in the winter months. William Blake Pond was originally dammed to provide water for running the Hooper Mine. Today, it is a small pond whose depth varies depending upon the degree of beaver activity. It makes a nice day hike past several vleis and through remote forests. A shorter circuit loop is also available by starting at the Garnet Hill Lodge and hiking towards William Blake Pond, returning via the Hooper Mine connecting trail (see Hooper Mine trail description, trail 20).

▶Trailhead: Access is off Barton Mine Rd., 3.9 mi S from NY 28 at North River, and 0.6 mi N from the Barton Garnet Mine barrier. The trail leaves Barton Mine Rd. to the W at a small grassy entranceway where the road crosses a small brook. The trail starts just before the paved road begins an ascent. A sign indicates the start of the trail and blue markers can be seen ahead. A pull-out for parking can be seen 0.1 mi ahead. ◄

Heading SW at first, the trail quickly veers W and descends gently through a wooded forest. At 0.3 mi the first glimpses of a bog becomes visible to the N as the grade levels. The trail soon reaches open views to The Vly where a beaver dam and lodge can be studied. Amphibians dawdle in The Vly's outlet.

Halfway Brook is crossed at 0.4 mi and the fern-lined trail continues N briefly, past white birch and occasional signs of bear. The trail soon descends slightly heading W and crosses a stream at 0.7 mi where a marsh comes into view to the SE. As the trail begins to climb, an arrow on a tree announces an abrupt right turn N followed by a sharp left turn W, the latter also marked by an arrow disc. Two seasonal streams are crossed before a steep hill rises on the right at 1.2 mi. Rock piles and old growth trees capture the eye. Soon the inlet of William Blake Pond is reached. Wrapping around the pond's perimeter an open view is reached at 1.6 mi, where an old beaver dam acts as a border.

The trail soon leaves the pond and passes a trail jct. where a yellow-marked trail heads N 0.4 mi to Hooper Mine (trail 20). Stay to the left and William Blake Pond soon comes back into view at its western bank at a spot conducive to meditation. The next half-mile is unmarked, but the trail is obvious. Pay close attention as blue markings resume at 2.3 mi where a faint path leaves the beaten path heading W. Follow this blue trail 0.1 mi to its intersection with the Overlook Trail at a stream crossing. A sign for the Balm of Gilead Trail is located here. For those wishing to lengthen their hike, Balm of Gilead Mt. (trail 19) makes a pleasant side trip.

The blue trail continues to the right of the Balm of Gilead Mt. sign and is occasionally marked by blue cross-country ski markers. At 3.2 mi the trail ends at a trail register on the East Branch Sacandaga Trail (trail 12). A right turn onto East Branch Sacandaga Trail (which is also marked with blue trail markers) will lead 0.1 mi, to Old Farm Clearing parking area.

❄ Trail in winter: This trail could make a decent snowshoe trek. Skiers should reverse the trail, parking at the Garnet Hill Mine or at Old Farm Clearing and ski E to Barton Mine Rd to best take advantage of the Halfway Brook Trail's ups and downs. Skiers seeking a full day trip may choose to extend the trip across Barton Mine Rd to Raymond Brook Trail (trail 18). Skiers crossing the Garnet Hill Lodge property should purchase a cross-country ski ticket.

🎿 Distances: To The Vly, 0.3 mi; to jct. with yellow Hooper Mine trail, 1.7 mi; to W bank of William Blake Pond, 1.9 mi; to intersection with Balm of Gilead trail, 2.4 mi; to East branch Sacandaga River Trail, 3.2 mi; to Old Farm Clearing parking area, 3.3 mi (5.3 km).

18 Raymond Brook

Trails Illustrated Map 744: O22

As with Halfway Brook Trail (trail 17), the Raymond Brook Trail is a partial re-vival of a section of the ski trail network that was once frequented in the mid-twentieth century in and around Gore and Pete Gay Mountains. Owing to private landowner permission, these revitalized trails now link up with Little Gore (also known as the North Creek Ski Bowl). Combined with the Halfway Brook Trail, the Raymond Brook Trail makes a nice one-day ski or hike across the shoulders of Pete Gay and Gore Mountains.

From its start high up on Barton Mine Rd, Raymond Brook Trail takes the hiker through a deciduous forest and past numerous streams before descending 1160 ft. to a parking area on NY 28.

Raymond Brook Trail is best hiked in a southeastern direction so as to avoid a constant ascent if hiked in reverse. In winter months, hikers should steer clear of cross-country skiers.

▶Trailhead: Access is the same as for Halfway Brook Trail (trail 17). There is no sign for Raymond Brook Trail, but there is a sign across the road for Halfway Brook Trail. A small parking area is on the R 0.1 mi above the trailhead.

The southern parking lot is accessible at mile marker 1040 off of NY 28, 1.3 mi N of the intersection of NY 28 and NY 28N in the hamlet of North Creek. A gravel road angles off the W side of the road to a circular gravel parking lot. Al-though a DEC sign there prohibits snowmobiling, there are no signs announcing the trailhead.◀

Leaving Barton Mine Rd., the trail leads E on a flat stretch of land dotted with blue cross-country ski blazes. Halfway Brook can be heard babbling in the dis-tance. The trail crosses on a bridge made of natural materials at 0.1 mi, and be-gins a slight ascent as it follows the stream, crossing more bridges at 0.3 and 0.4 mi. Here, the trail turns S leaving Halfway Brook behind. Climbing steadily over the next tenth of a mile, a height of land is soon reached. A steep descent begins at 0.7 mi as the trail zigzags to soften the grade. The forest is young and decid-uous owing to blowdown caused by heavy ice storms in 2008.

The trail levels at 1 mi and a series of four stream crossings are required with and without aid of bridges over the course of the next 0.2 mi. At 1.3 mi the trail passes close to an old metal ski shed. From here, the trail begins a long, steep descent and follows the Raymond Brook Creek for the next mile with scenic vis-tas from high above on a narrow ridgeline at 1.8 mi. Given the steep drop-off here, snowshoers need to be especially alert to fast-moving skiers while hiking on this ridge.

At 2.2 mi the trail crosses a third creek on a bridge and begins a series of gradual ascents. The scenery has now changed. Birch, beech, and pine trees are every-where. A bog is passed at 2.5 mi. An interesting blue rock wall outcrop borders the trail at 2.7 mi before ascending slightly and passing through a pine grove.

The trail, now a wide roadbed, descends steeply at 3 mi, curving as it goes.

Follow the trail markers closely because at 3.2 mi the trail will veer L while the roadbed continues ahead down a steep embankment. Turning L, the trail now weaves back and forth downhill before flattening in a beautiful grove of birch at 3.4 mi. Paralleling the trail, NY 28 is now distinguishable through the trees, as is the Hudson River behind it. The parking lot off NY 28 is reached at 3.5 mi.

❄ Trail in winter: Raymond Brook Trail's constant downhill travel and its proximity to the Halfway Brook Trail make this sure to be a favorite among cross-country ski enthusiasts. Snowshoeing is possible, but practice extreme caution to avoid collisions with skiers on the steep grades of this shared trail.

🏃 Distances: To first bridge, 0.1 mi; to start of steep descent 0.7 mi; to old ski shed, 1.3 mi; to steep ridge overlooking creek, 1.8 mi; to blue rock wall, 2.7 mi; to NY 28 parking area, 3.5 mi (5.6 km). Total descent from trailhead: 1160 ft (354 km).

19 Balm of Gilead Mt.

Trails Illustrated Map 744: O21

Balm of Gilead Mt. is a small mountain, but its view is well worth the climb. It provides an excellent vista into the Siamese Ponds Wilderness Area.

▶Trailhead: Access is via Thirteenth Lake Rd. off NY 28 at North River, near the Hamilton County line road sign. Turn at the DEC signpost marking the route to the Siamese Ponds Wilderness Area.◀

Follow Thirteenth Lake Rd. SW. At a jct. at 3.3 mi, continue across a concrete bridge. Avoid the R turn onto Beach Rd. Bear L up the hill at 4 mi, avoiding the R fork (Old Farm Rd.) that continues on toward Old Farm Clearing. The L fork has a small sign pointing the way to Garnet Hill Lodge. Continue straight through the jct. at 4.4 mi, instead of going L up the hill to the lodge. A cross-country ski shop is at 4.6 mi from NY 28. Park off the road. Remember, you are on private land at the courtesy of Garnet Hill Lodge.

From the L side of the tennis court (0.0 mi), head S on a dirt road for a short distance. As the road begins to climb a grade, bear R, where a trail has been brushed out. Almost immediately, bear R again onto the Overlook Trail. This trail winds through the woods, coming to a jct. behind a camp at 0.2 mi. Continue straight ahead SW. Ignore the blue trail that intersects after 200 ft, but take the well-worn unmarked Balm of Gilead path that bears L (S). The trail is not well maintained, but receives enough use to be followed easily. It climbs gradually through a climax forest. Shortly after crossing a brook at 0.3 mi, the trail turns L. Red paint blazes mark the way from here.

At 0.5 mi, a red diamond-shaped metal marker is found on a large sugar maple. From here climbing becomes moderate.

At 0.9 mi, the trail runs R up to a large boulder and circles L around its base to an open cliff face and fire ring at the summit.

The view is striking. The S end of Thirteenth Lake, with its marshy inlet, dominates the scene. Bullhead Mt. parallels the lake's W shore. Puffer Mt. is to the SW. Bare-topped Peaked Mt. is on the extreme R to the NW. The second bump of Balm of Gilead Mt. is directly to your L in front (S), and the shoulder of Eleventh Mt. can be seen in the distance to the L of the bump. A more complete view of Thirteenth Lake can be had by heading N another 100 yd from this spot.

❋ Trail in winter: This is a short but interesting snowshoe trip in the winter. This trail begins on the private land of the Garnet Hill Lodge. A ski ticket should be purchased in winter.

🐾 Distances: To first brook, 0.3 mi; to red metal marker, 0.5 mi; to summit, 0.9 mi (1.4 km). Ascent, 425 ft (130 m). Elevation, 2345 ft (715 m).

20 Hooper Mine

Trails Illustrated Map 744: O21

The Hooper Mine is an abandoned open pit garnet mine on state land. The short walk to it is well worth the effort. The high walls of the open pit and the garnet-rich rock are very unusual.

▶Trailhead: Access is the same as that for Balm of Gilead Mt. Trail (trail 19, p. 67). The trail begins at the L side of the tennis court. Follow the dirt road a short distance until it begins to climb a grade. Bear R onto a path, which after another 50 ft reaches a second jct. Avoid the R turn to the Overlook Trail. Instead, go straight ahead to the SSE. ◀

The trail parallels the dirt road as it bends around. At 0.2 mi, within sight of a house at the end of the road, the trail to the mine abruptly turns R. It climbs a gradual grade S, but soon makes a large horseshoe bend to the N. The mine is reached at 0.4 mi.

The best view is gained by climbing the rock outcrop to the L of the pit entrance. The bright orange oxidized rock of the pit wall stands out. The pit itself forms a 200 yd diameter amphitheater. The active Ruby Mt. Mine can be seen in the distance to the N.

A discernible footpath starts to the E (L) of the pit entrance, wraps around the tall oxidized rock, and climbs it steeply from behind. Abandoned foundations can be found in the forest just behind the pit.

A well-defined herd path can be seen to the L at about 100 ft as one leaves the mine entrance. This easy-to-follow unmarked pathway wraps around most of the mine with short side trails to overlooks and past some interesting abandoned structures. A yellow trail leading to William Blake Pond begins off the herd path 0.5 mi from the pit entrance, and gives the option of making a 1.8 mi loop trip back to the parking area. An old abandoned "magazine explosives shed" sits in the woods at the start of the yellow trail. The yellow trail heads E and then S 0.4 miles where it intersects with the Halfway Brook Trail (trail 17). Stay R (W), and William Blake Pond quickly appears on the L. Follow the unmarked trail N as it winds through the woods 0.5 mi until it reaches the Overlook Trail at a point where it passes behind a camp. Turn R on the Overlook Trail and follow it until you are once again at the dirt road that leads L to the tennis courts and your car.

❈ Trail in winter: This is a very short but worthwhile snowshoe trip, with interesting photographic opportunities. Because the trail begins on the private land of Garnet Hill Lodge, skiers should purchase a ski ticket.

⚐ Distances: To abrupt R turn, 0.2 mi; to mine, 0.4 mi; to yellow trail, 0.9 mi; to William Blake Pond, 1 mi; to Overlook Trail, 1.6 mi; to tennis courts, 1.8 mi (2.9 km).

21 Old Farm Clearing

Trails Illustrated Map 744: O21

Only stone foundations amidst the trees provide clues to the character of the old farm that once occupied this clearing. A tree plantation covers most of what must have been open land in the late 1800s.

One used to be able to drive into this spot, where several trailheads are found. Now that the land is classified as Wilderness, the road is closed to vehicles.

▶Trailhead: Refer to section opening, p. 59, for access directions.◀

The dirt road that leads to Old Farm Clearing begins at a stone barrier and trail register at the rear of the summer parking area. From here, rolling grades lead S, high above the E shore of Thirteenth Lake.

Elizabeth Point Trail is on the R at 0.6 mi. This pleasant route through deciduous forest reaches Old Farm Clearing at 1.2 mi. Several trails lead from the far end of the clearing and informal campsites are found in the trees on the periphery. There is a spring 50 ft S of the clearing.

❈ Trail in winter: Perhaps no short trail is skied as often as this one. Feeder trails from Garnet Hill Lodge to the parking area bring many weekend guests to here and then beyond into the Siamese Ponds Wilderness Area. Because of the relatively high elevation (1800 ft), there is often snow here when none can be found in the lower valleys.

⚐ Distances: To Elizabeth Point trailhead, 0.6 mi, to Old Farm Clearing, 1.2 mi (1.9 km).

Elizabeth Point

Trails Illustrated Map 744: O21

Elizabeth Point is a small projection of the E shoreline of Thirteenth Lake. It has a picnic table and fireplace, and shallow water tempts the swimmer. It can be reached easily by canoe from the N end of the lake, but makes a very nice walk from the parking area for a picnic.

▶Trailhead: The trail is unmarked, but easy to find and follow. The trailhead is 0.6 mi along the Old Farm Clearing Trail (trail 21). Here (0.0 mi) the trail gradually descends a narrow footpath W to the shore of Thirteenth Lake, where two informal campsites are found. ◀

At 0.2 mi, the grade steepens before leveling again at 0.3 mi at a campsite that sits slightly above the water. A short path leads down to a small sandy beach.

The trail continues up a knoll 120 ft to a larger campsite and fireplace. Side trails from this site lead approximately 100 ft to another small sandy beach. Large white pines and birches give way to a view across the lake toward Peaked Mt.

❋ Trail in winter: In deep snow this little trail provides access onto Thirteenth Lake. It requires good control by skiers and may be icy.

🚶 Distances: Old Farm Clearing trail to Elizabeth Point., 0.3 mi (0.5 km); from parking area, 0.9 mi (1.4 km).

22 Botheration Pond

Trails Illustrated Map 744: O21

This is a cross-country ski trail crossing the East Branch of the Sacandaga River on a very ornate log bridge. It later passes along the W side of Botheration Pond, starting at Old Farm Clearing from the East Branch Sacandaga Trail (trail 12), and ending at the jct with the Halfway Brook Trail. It permits access to the interior area S and E of Balm of Gilead Mountain.

▶ Trailhead: Access is from Old Farm Clearing trailhead (see section opening, p. 59). This trail starts at Old Farm Clearing along the East Branch Sacandaga Trail (trail 12). A trail kiosk and sign-in register is encountered 0.1 mi from the Old Farm trailhead parking lot. ◀

The red-blazed Botheration Pond Trail begins by a DEC sign 1 mi from the kiosk. This is just before two boulders on either side of the trail. The Botheration Pond Trail, L (0.0 mi), starts up a gradual grade through a conifer plantation, and may be wet for the first 0.2 mi. Beyond this first wet section, the trail is generally dry and a pleasant walk through the forest. Height of land is reached at 0.4 mi. The descent to the East Branch of the Sacandaga River at 1 mi is steeper than the first part of the trip. A clearing on the bank of the river includes a fire ring.

The trail crosses the rushing river on an exceptionally ornate log bridge. Soon after crossing, the trail begins a winding ascent up and around the hillside, leaving the river behind. The sound of the river is a constant companion for much of the next 0.5 mi. Crossing a log bridge over a side tributary at 1.5 mi the trail continues to contour up and around the hillside. It rock hops across a second tributary at 1.9 mi and crosses the river on a second ornate bridge at the outflow of Botheration Pond (2.1 mi).

The trail continues NE to pass along the W side of Botheration Pond. The pond is often visible through the woods to the right. There are several places where the trail comes close enough to the pond to bushwhack over to its shore for a better look. You may spy the summit of Gore Mt. to the SE in the distance.

At 2.8 mi the trail turns E and crosses the inflow to Botheration Pond on a couple of log bridges. It then traverses up and across the hillside to reach the blue-blazed Halfway Brook Trail at 3.6 mi. One sign indicates Barton Mines Road 1.4 mi to the R. A second sign indicates the Garnet Hill intersection at 1.7 mi and, to the L at 2.6 mi, the Old Farm Rd. trailhead.

❄ Trail in winter: Snowshoers must be prepared to share trail on this popular cross-country ski trail.

🏃 Distances: To East Branch Sacandaga River, 1 mi; to the Botheration Pond outflow, 2.1 mi; to Halfway Brook Trail, 3.6 mi (5.8 km).

23 Puffer Pond

Trails Illustrated Map 744: O20

This is a primary trail leading to the interior of the Siamese Ponds Wilderness. Its branch trails offer many fine alternatives for extended backpacking trips.

▶Trailhead: Access is off NY 28 in North River. See the section opening (p. 59) for directions to the parking lot of the Old Farm Clearing Trail (trail 21). From the rear of the parking area, follow the woods road 1.2 mi to Old Farm Clearing. Pass through the clearing and continue S 0.1 mi on the East Branch Sacandaga Trail from Old Farm Clearing (trail 12) to a jct. This is the Puffer Pond trailhead (0.0). The R fork heads for Puffer Pond. (The L fork continues to NY 8 via the East Branch Sacandaga Ttrail.◀

Follow blue trail markers through a tree plantation. Native growth is soon reached and a long gradual descent begins. The trail is wide and crosses three small streams at 0.3 mi, 0.8 mi, and 0.9 mi. It crosses a major inlet on a wood bridge at Buck Meadow Creek to Thirteenth Lake at 1 mi. From this low point of elevation (1700 ft), 484 ft elevation will be gained to reach Puffer Pond.

A moderate upgrade soon brings you to the sounds of cascading water. Shortly after, the trail passes a series of small waterfalls. It parallels the R side of Hour Pond Brook, crossing to the L side on a bridge at 1.3 mi. Turning L, the trail on a bridge climbs a small grade to the Hour Pond Trail jct. (trail 24) at 1.5 mi.

Continuing straight ahead, the Puffer Pond Trail crosses Hour Pond Brook again. The trail now gradually ascends rolling terrain. There is a short, wet section at the end of a clearing at 1.9 mi. After paralleling a beaver meadow, the trail turns R and crosses a stream at 2.3 mi. (If coming from the opposite direction, be sure to turn L here. The trail R is a false herd path.)

The gradually rolling terrain eventually becomes almost level. The Twin Ponds footpath jct. is passed, perhaps unnoticed, at 3.6 mi, followed by a short descent to level trail. A somewhat wet section occurs just before Puffer Pond at 4 mi.

A side trail L leads 50 yd to a lean-to on the shore of

Ann Hough

Puffer Pond. Another side trail leads back to the main trail, which continues 0.2 mi along the N shoreline to a second lean-to. It sits above the water level at the jct. of the Kings Flow (trail 27) and Puffer Pond Brook (trail 28) Trails. Several open campsites are located between the two lean-tos. Puffer Pond is sometimes used as a base camp for climbers seeking to bushwhack up trailless Puffer Mt. At 3472 ft elevation, Puffer Mt. ranks 92 on the list of the Adirondack Hundred Highest.

Siamese Ponds Wilderness, Thirteenth Lake

❄ Trail in winter: If snow conditions are good, this can be an enjoyable trail, which can be extended via the Puffer Pond Brook Trail to Kings Flow. There is often crusty ice from the 0.1 mi point to 0.3 mi.

🚶 Distances: To Thirteenth Lake inlet, 1 mi; to Hour Pond Trail jct., 1.5 mi; to Twin Ponds jct., 3.6 mi; to Puffer Pond jct., 4.2 mi (6.7 km). This is 5.5 mi (8.8 km) from the parking area.

24 Hour Pond

Trails Illustrated Map 744: O20

Hour Pond is one of the most attractive of the 67 ponds in the Siamese Ponds Wilderness Area. Its sandy bottom and open shoreline provide a fine setting for a short backpack trip. The trail winds its way over gentle knolls and easy grades. The pond is 3.1 mi from Old Farm Clearing. It is possible to make a loop trip over the Hour Pond Connector Trail (trail 25) to Peaked Mt. PondTrail (trail 16) for a day hike or overnight trip.

▶Trailhead: The beginning of the trail is where Puffer Pond Trail (trail 23) crosses Hour Pond Brook for the second time, 1.5 mi from Old Farm Clearing. Circular yellow discs with black arrows indicate the trail is unmarked. However, it is in excellent condition and very pleasant to walk. ◀

Branching R from the Puffer Pond Trail (0.0 mi), the route parallels Hour Pond Brook and gradually gains elevation. The brook is heard but seldom seen. At 0.7 mi, the trail drops down briefly to cross a brook. The trail jct. with the Hour Pond–Peaked Mt. Connector Trail (trail 25) is found here.

A large marsh floods the trail at 0.8 mi, just after it descends a short moderate grade. This is easily circumvented by crossing the outlet on the L side of the pond and then walking across the beaver dam. A designated campsite can be found here just before crossing over the dam. Turning L (W), the trail skirts a marsh. A second beaver dam is to the L at 1 mi.

The trail continues up another gradual grade and circles around to the N. A metal sign prohibiting camping is found at 1.2 mi. At 1.4 mi, Hour Pond can be seen below and to the L through the trees. The trail turns L, passing a lean-to sign at 1.4 mi that leads 0.1 mi to an otherwise hidden lean-to built in 2008. At 1.6 mi, the trail reaches an open campsite at the pond's edge.

Several open campsites are found along the E shoreline. Bullhead Mt. is across the pond. Hour Pond Mt. is seen in the distance beyond the N end of this very large pond. The view N from the outlet is particularly nice.

❄ Trail in winter: Hour Pond Trail is popular with skiers and snowshoers alike.

𝐌 Distances: To first beaver dam, 0.8 mi; to Hour Pond, 1.6 mi (2.6 km). Total distance from the parking area is 4.3 mi (6.9 km).

25 Hour Pond–Peaked Mt. Connector

Trails Illustrated Map 744: O20

A short wooded climb over the shoulder of a mountain connects two popular destinations, making it possible to visit both in a day, or enticing the weekend hiker to spend adequate time at both.

▶Trailhead: The beginning of the trail is found along the Peaked Mt. Trail (trail 16) by a wooden bridge over Peaked Mt. Brook, 0.1 mi W of the shoreline of Thirteenth Lake. The trailhead is clearly marked with a sign, and both trails are blazed with red trail markers.◀

Cross the bridge over Peaked Mt. Brook and follow the red-blazed trail as it parallels Thirteenth Lake shoreline for the next 0.3 mi. The trail reaches a perplexing area at 0.3 mi, at which point it appears to diverge in two different directions. The Hour Pond–Peaked Mt. Connector trail turns R here and begins to ascend. The blazed trail ahead leads to two designated campsites at the lake's shore and then terminates. The ground is particularly muddy here.

Turning R the trail climbs gradually, crossing a stream at 0.4 mi. The trail follows the stream over the next mile, ascending steeply at times. At 0.7 mi the trail is very narrow and overlooks a pool several feet deep. The beaver pond is reached at 0.8 mi. At 1.2 mi, height of land is reached. In winter and leafless spring, this location provides views of the Moxham Range to the S, followed by views of Bullhead Mt. to the N. The trail begins its long descent at 1.3 mi until it joins the Hour Pond Trail (trail 24) at 1.6 mi. The last 0.1 mi is particularly scenic as tall fir trees dot the trail. Hour Pond is 0.8 mi to the R.

❄ Trail in winter: This is a popular ski destination. This connector trail provides options, but is steep and particularly narrow in sections.

𝐌 Distances: to start of the ascent, 0.3 mi; to height of land, 1.2 mi; to Hour Pond Trail jct., 1.6 mi (2.6 km).

Kings Flow. Glen Marsh

Siamese Ponds Wilderness Area

FROM THE NORTH

Kings Flow is in the NW corner of the Siamese Ponds Wilderness Area. A dam, constructed to back up water needed for logging in the late 1880s, created the flow.

There are several ways to enter this northern part of the wilderness area. The most commonly used access is across private land at Kings Flow. A small daily parking fee is required. A second access is over Lyme Timber Company land from Big Brook Rd. where the public enjoys recreation rights under a State of New York conservation easement. Be respectful of private property rights if accessing trails from this entry point. The John Pond trailhead, which avoids private land, is a third entry point.

The Kunjamuk Trail is the major N–S route in this area. It follows the old stagecoach route from Speculator to Indian Lake. The upper end crosses Lyme Timber land. No camping or building of fires is allowed.

Chimney Mt. has unique geological characteristics that have yet to be fully explained. This is a section of the Adirondacks rich in history and lore.

The state land W of Kings Flow and E of Indian Lake is excellent hiking and skiing country. It has been underutilized because of the difficulty of access. Some of the trails are unmaintained and receive only sporadic use by hunters and anglers. Nevertheless, this is an area of great beauty. The hiker who is tired of crowding in more popular areas of the Adirondacks will enjoy the opportunities for solitude here.

Recommended hikes in this section include:

SHORT HIKES
Chimney Mt.: 2 mi (3.2 km) round trip. This truly remarkable geological oddity will draw the curious hiker back to its summit many times.

Clear Pond: 2.2 mi (3.5 km) round trip. A pretty little pond in an attractive setting.

MODERATE HIKES
John Pond: 4.4 mi (7 km) round trip. The cliffs beyond this exquisite pond beckon the climber.

HARDER HIKES
Kunjamuk Trail: 15.6 mi (25 km) round trip. The farther you walk, the wilder it becomes. Over 30 mi of routes can be combined in a trip down this old road.

	Trail Described	Total Miles (one way)		Page
26	Chimney Mt.	1.0	(1.6 km)	76
27	Puffer Pond from Kings Flow	2.1	(3.4 km)	77
28	Puffer Pond Brook	1.9	(3.0 km)	78
29	Kings Flow East	2.8	(4.5 km)	79
	Humphrey Mt.	1.4	(2.2 km)	80
30	Kunjamuk Trail	7.8	(12.5 km)	81
	Round Pond from the Kunjamuk Trail	1.5	(2.4 km)	83
	Kunjamuk Mt.	1.1	(1.8 km)	84
31	John Pond	2.2	(3.5 km)	84
32	John Pond Crossover	3.2	(5.1 km)	85
33	Clear Pond	1.1	(1.8 km)	86
	Center Pond	0.1	(0.2 km)	87

26 Chimney Mt.

Trails Illustrated Map 744: O19

Chimney Mt. is a geologic oddity. Its structure illustrates a complex tectonic origin that has left not only an interesting chimney but also myriad caves around its upper reaches. Fascinating as a short day trip, it can also form the foundation for many years of study for the caver and amateur geologist.

▶Trailhead: Access begins at the intersection of NY 28 and NY 30 in Indian Lake village. Drive S, 0.6 mi, on NY 30. Turn L onto Big Brook Rd. After 1.2 mi, drive over an extensive bridge at Lake Abanakee. Bear R at the fork 2.1 mi past Lake Abanakee. At the crossroads intersection with Hutchins and Moulton Rds., turn R. The Kunjamuk Trail (trail 30) access bridge across Big Brook is on the R at 6.1 mi. Finally, 7.8 mi after leaving NY 30, at Chimney Mt. Wilderness Lodge on Kings Flow there is a specified parking area with a small daily use fee. Hikers are reminded that this private landowner is permitting access across his property to the Siamese Ponds Wilderness Area as a courtesy to the public. Continuation of this privilege is dependent upon how the public uses it.◀

Walk E down a dirt road across a mowed field to the DEC trail register at the edge of the woods, R (0.0 mi). Bear L from there to another sign indicating the direction of the blue-marked trail up the mountain.

State land begins at 0.2 mi. From there, the route crosses a brook and begins to climb, moderately at first and then steeply. At 0.8 mi, the first of several herd paths heads L. (The herd paths lead to caves and views W of Kings Flow and Round Pond; the higher ones ascend to a ridge opposite the chimney. From there, the chimney can be seen in full profile.)

The trail ascends steeply up a rock massif and breaks out of the trees into the open at 0.9 mi. A small dip in the trail precedes the final rocky ascent to the chimney. Snaking through a narrow rock passage leads to an enclosure of high rocks.

To the L it is possible to drop down under huge overhanging rocks to a lookout.

Straight ahead the trail drops briefly. Sidling around to the L of the trail brings you face-to-face with the huge chimney-like formation that gives Chimney Mt. its name. Elevation here is 2500 ft, some 760 ft above the trailhead. The large flat-topped mountain to the N horizon over the chimney's L shoulder is Blue Mt. The path that descends to the N circles around to the cut between the chimney and the ridge next to it. This is a hazardous route.

The chimney is below the true summit of the mountain, which has an elevation of 2721 ft. The summit can be reached via a 0.2 mi herd path that begins to the R of the trail just before it enters the narrow rock passage to the chimney. The herd path drops into a hollow and heads E on an easy grade. The summit is rocky and provides a 360° panorama. Blue Mt. is N; the High Peaks, NE; Bullhead Mt., E; Puffer Mt., S; Humphrey Mt., SW; and Snowy Mt., W.

❄ Trail in winter: This is a nice snowshoe trail. Steep sections require care.

🏃 Distances: Trailhead to state land, 0.2 mi; to first herd path, 0.8 mi; to clearing, 0.9 mi; to chimney, 1 mi (1.6 km). Ascent, 760 ft (232 m). Elevation, 2500 ft (762 m).

27 Puffer Pond from Kings Flow

Trails Illustrated Map 744: O19

This is the primary route to Puffer Pond from the N, although two other routes are possible.

▶Trailhead: Access to the trailhead is the same as that for Chimney Mt. (trail 26).◀

Follow red trail markers from the DEC signpost 0.1 mi E of the Kings Flow parking area. The route heads SE on a wide, grassy road, soon crossing a minor brook on a bridge. At 0.1 mi, the trail leaves the road, forking R at a small sign. (Avoid the L branch, which curves up a grade.) State land begins at 0.3 mi.

Trending E, the route crosses a tributary of Carroll Brook at 0.6 mi. The trail circles the N edge of a beaver meadow and crosses Carroll Brook itself at 0.7 mi. Bullhead Mt. can be seen upstream to the E.

Once across the brook, turn L and follow the trail along the L bank of Carroll Brook. Signs of beaver activity are obvious along the brook. At 1.1 mi the trail leaves Carroll Brook and gradually climbs to higher elevations over a col SE of Bullhead Mt.

The jct. of the John Pond Crossover Trail (trail 32), at 1.3 mi, is surrounded by huge hemlocks at a wide point of the trail. A few trees have indistinct gray paint spots and there are several cut logs. (The blue-marked John Pond Crossover Trail drops down a grade to the N; see trail 32.)

The red-marked Puffer Pond Trail curves R and climbs steadily to height of land in the col, some 460 ft higher than Carroll Brook. After a brief level stretch, the 176 ft descent to Puffer Pond begins. It is moderately steep, except for one

In the chimney of Chimney Mt. Robert Meyer

minor leveling at 2 mi, just after a brook crossing.

One more dip and a slight upgrade lead, at 2.1 mi, to a three-way jct. and a lean-to at Puffer Pond. The lean-to sits on a bank 15 ft above water level. To the L, another 0.2 mi NE along the shoreline trail, is a second lean-to, sitting close to the water off a small side trail. Between the two lean-tos are several informal open campsites.

A blue-marked trail heads NE to Old Farm Clearing and Thirteenth Lake (trail 21; see opening of Siamese Ponds from the East, p. 59). The trail W along Puffer Pond Brook leads to a jct. with the Kings Flow East Trail (trail 29). Puffer Mt. dominates the scene across the pond to the S.

❄ Trail in winter: This is a good snowshoe trail. The ridge beyond the John Pond Crossover Trail (trail 32) is not suitable for most skiers.

🚶 Distances: To Carroll Brook, 0.7 mi; to John Pond Crossover Trail jct., 1.3 mi; to Puffer Pond, 2.1 mi (3.4 km).

28 Puffer Pond Brook

Trails Illustrated Map 744: O19

The Puffer Pond Brook Trail connects Puffer Pond with the Kings Flow East Trail (trail 29). The trail is no longer maintained by DEC, but it is used regularly and is relatively easy to follow. The most enjoyable direction of travel is W from Puffer Pond. (Originally a stagecoach route, its grade is superb for cross-country skiing.)

▶Trailhead: The trailhead (0.0 mi) begins at the lean-to on the N shore of Puffer Pond where there is a three-way trail jct. (see trail 27, p. 78). ◀

The trail heads W and then SW, closely following the shoreline of Puffer Pond. At the end of the pond, it swings W away from the water.

At 0.5 mi, the trail reaches the R bank of Puffer Pond Brook and parallels it for the next mile. As the brook cuts deeper into the valley floor, the trail retains its constant grade. Consequently, the stream is often heard, but not seen, below to the L. At other times, cascading waters rush close by the hiker.

The route leaves the brook at 1.5 mi as the brook's gradient increases. At the first short incline since leaving Puffer Pond, the trail turns N and then NW, away from the stream. The way is almost level to 1.7 mi, where the route passes through a narrow gully cut by years of wagon use. Here, at a jct., continue straight ahead. (If you turn L, a steep grade leads to Puffer Pond Brook and ascends again. Eventually, a jct. with Kings Flow East Trail, trail 29, is reached.) Soon after passing a second wagon-worn narrow gully, the trail drops to the jct. with the Kings Flow East Trail at 1.9 mi.

❄ Trail in winter: The gradual grades of an old stagecoach route make this a good winter ski trail, especially for through trips from Old Farm Clearing to Kings Flow.

🏃 Distances: To end of Puffer Pond, 0.4 mi; to Puffer Pond Brook, 0.5 mi; to turn from brook, 1.5 mi; to Kings Flow East Trail jct., 1.9 mi (3 km).

29 Kings Flow East

Trails Illustrated Map 744: N19

The Kings Flow East Trail heads S along the E shore of Kings Flow. The region it penetrates is less traveled than many sections of the Siamese Ponds Wilderness Area. The walk along the flow is generally level, and views of the water are extensive.

▶Trailhead: Access is the same as that for Chimney Mt. (trail 26). From the parking area, head W across the open field to the flagpole in the direction of the water. One hundred yards S of the flagpole, at 150°, cross a small bridge. Continue along the field edge a short distance to a grassy road on the L. This is the beginning of the Kings Flow East trail (0.0 mi). ◀

The unmarked, wide, grassy lane heads straight S for 0.4 mi to Carroll Brook. Once across the brook the route becomes a path through thick brush. The woods soon open up and Kings Flow is clearly seen R of the trail. The Flow remains visible for the next 1.5 mi.

The Puffer Pond Brook Trail (trail 28) branches L at 1.1 mi. The route continues along the flow, becoming a more rolling course. At 1.3 mi, the flow is lost from view. The trail continues S along the base of Puffer Mt., just E of the wet lowlands that drain into Kings Flow.

A brief descent brings the trail to the Puffer Pond Brook crossing at 1.5 mi. An unmaintained spur of the Puffer Pond Brook Trail (trail 28) comes in L. One hundred yd farther on, the trail crosses a smaller stream coming off Puffer Mt.

Several red and silver bottle caps on trees at the R of the trail at 2.2 mi mark the jct. of the abandoned Wakely Brook trail to Round Pond. The trail continues S to a second jct. at 2.4 mi. Here, the Humphrey Mt. Trail branches R (see below). The East Trail dips slightly and makes a sharp L turn at the jct. It continues S another 0.4 mi before terminating at 2.8 mi.

❄ Trail in winter: This trail is excellent in conjunction with other local trails for cross-country skiing or snowshoeing.

🐾 Distances: To Carroll Brook, 0.4 mi; to Puffer Pond Brook Trail jct., 1.1 mi; to Puffer Pond Brook, 1.5 mi; to Humphrey Mt. Trail, 2.4 mi; to end of Trail, 2.8 mi (4.5 km).

Humphrey Mt. *(unmaintained)*

Trails Illustrated Map 744: N19

Humphrey Mt. is the twin-peaked mountain seen to the S as you look down Kings Flow. It makes a nice climb. Most hikers don't bushwhack to the summit. Instead, they try to locate the old garnet mine, which operated during World War I. The trail generally is clear except for some short stretches in its upper reaches. Examine your map well and have your compass ready.

▶Trailhead: The trailhead (0.0 mi) is located on the R side of the Kings Flow East Trail (trail 29) at the 2.4 mi point (see p. 79). There is a little dip in the otherwise level trail just before the jct. The Humphrey Mt. Trail bears R at the jct., while the Kings Flow East Trail makes a L turn.◀

Leaving the trailhead, the route follows red plastic disks and, in places, red tape. The trail soon aligns to 230°. At 0.2 mi, the trail drops down at a gradual grade. Thick conifers line the trail as it approaches Humphrey Brook at an angle and crosses it at 0.3 mi.

The route winds around a bit before climbing a short steep slope at 0.4 mi. The woods then open up and the trail heads SW. At 0.6 mi, the trail enters a large clearing of brush and downed trees. A lumber camp once operated in this area.

The trail leaves the clearing at 0.8 mi and generally heads S. The grade steepens. The trail turns W at 1 mi, now climbing steeply. Then it turns sharply S at 1.1 mi. Markers are sometimes hard to spot as the trail continues its steep ascent.

Curving around to the SW, the trail reaches a conical pile of mine tailings at 1.4 mi. The tailings pile has become overgrown over the years, so much so that it is possible to reach the top before realizing what it is. A narrow, shallow valley leads S from the pile. The mine was a narrow vein and the exact location is difficult to discern, though garnet-bearing rocks from the mining process can be spotted.

Hikers continuing to the summit must bushwhack from this point.

✳ Trail in winter: This trail is a good climb for experienced winter snowshoers.

👣 Distances: To Humphrey Brook, 0.3 mi; to clearing, 0.6 mi; to garnet tailings pile, 1.4 mi (2.2 km). Total from Kings Flow parking area, 3.8 mi (6.1 km). Ascent from trailhead, 720 ft (220 m).

30 Kunjamuk Trail

Trails Illustrated Map 744: O18

The Kunjamuk Trail presents a few challenges that need not deter experienced hikers. Blowdown on Petes Hill slows progress, but needn't stop it. On a through trip, the Kunjamuk River must be waded. In dry weather, this is more fun than challenging. In wet weather, each hiker must make up his or her own mind before trying it. Regardless, those who are looking for an enjoyable walk through wilderness will find that gradual grades and the beauty of the woods amply compensate for any obstacles.

▶Trailhead: Access is from Indian Lake village via Big Brook Rd. Follow the same access route as for the Chimney Mt. trailhead (see p. 76) to the 6.1 mi point. Turn R at the road intersection and cross Big Brook on a wooden bridge. There is a pullout on the R at 0.2 mi, just before the road turns R and ascends a hill. This is the recommended parking area.◀

The first unmarked 1.6 mi of this route cross Lyme Timber land. No camping is allowed until state land has been reached.

The trail, marked with blue DEC trail markers after the 1.6 mi point, begins on a wide dirt road that heads S into the woods (0.0 mi) as the main road turns R and ascends a hill. (The main road goes to Crotched Pond, but has been privately leased and is no longer open for public use.) A camp is visible L at 0.4 mi. The route changes to a grassy lane at a log collection area at 0.5 mi.

The next approximately three-fourths of a mile often is rutted and muddy from ATV use. At 0.7 mi, a stony road angles R up a hillside. Continue straight. (The road to the R is an alternate route to the T intersection mentioned below.) Avoid woods roads angling L at 0.8 and 0.9 mi. As the trail ascends a moderate grade, two more woods roads angle L at 1.1 mi. Bear R.

The trail then levels as it reaches a T intersection at 1.2 mi. A camp is on the R. Turn L and avoid all side roads. As the main route curves R at 1.3 mi, the Round Pond from Kunjamuk Trail (see p. 83) cuts back to the L.

Care must be taken at 1.4 mi, where the trail makes a L turn off the grassy road into the woods. ATVs have churned up the trail and made a loop around a mud hole a short distance into the woods. Continue straight through the loop.

At 1.6 mi, avoid climbing a moderate grade. (This leads to a timber collection area and large turnabout.) Instead, turn L onto a narrower, level woods road. State land and a barrier cable are found 150 ft along this road. The contrast between lumbered land and wilderness land is great. The way is shaded and far more enjoyable underfoot. The grassy trail winds around from S to SW.

Kunjamuk Creek. Michael N. Kelsey

Round Lake is soon seen through the trees, just before a trail jct. at 2.1 mi. An open campsite and path to the lake are L. The R turn leads 0.2 mi to a private camp. The Kunjamuk Trail continues straight ahead, staying in sight of the lake. Magnificent white birches line the shore. The trail gains slight elevation and the higher contour provides excellent viewing of the water. As many as four beaver lodges can be seen at one time. The trail is excellent.

The trail crosses a creek at 2.8 mi near the end of the lake. It makes a sharp L turn with a camp in view and ascends a minor grade at 3.2 mi. The unmarked Kunjamuk Mt. Trail (see p. 84) begins on the R at a trail jct. at 3.8 mi, just after a creek crossing. The trail narrows somewhat, but is easy to follow. At 4.1 mi, a large bog meadow is visible, L, and the trail crosses another creek at 4.4 mi. At 5.2 mi, spruces close in on the trail, which crosses a very minor, wet mossy spot at 5.3 mi. The route opens up again and crosses Wakely Brook on an old beaver dam. The source of Wakely Brook is the marsh upstream.

Now the long gradual climb over the E shoulder of Petes Hill begins. Tape markers on trees are very common from this point to the Kunjamuk River. Petes Hill was severely affected by a microburst storm in 1995, and blowdown is still encountered on this section of trail. However, with a bit of persistence and careful attention to the red tape markers, the route can be followed without much difficulty. Height of land at 6.2 mi is hardly evident. Elevation loss is gradual at first as the route descends Petes Hill, but increases more rapidly toward the bottom.

A stream can be heard at 7.6 mi and soon East Brook comes into view 50 ft L through the trees. The wide but shallow brook angles its way through tilted rock joints. The trail makes a sharp R turn and at 7.7 mi reaches a very wide, open meadow. In summer, this meadow is a waist-deep sea of grass. Follow the L edge straight across the meadow for 0.1 mi to the small beginning of the Kunjamuk River at 7.8 mi. It drains both Rock and Long Ponds. In dry weather, wading this river is easy if you don't stand still long enough to sink into the muddy bottom. (For continuation of this trail S, refer to the Cisco Creek to Kunjamuk River Trail, p. 91)

❄ Trail in winter: This trail is not suitable as a point-to-point for skiers because of the blowdown on Petes Hill. However, a round-trip on the N section would be very pleasant.

🐾 Distances: To state land, 1.6 mi; to Round Lake, 2.1 mi; to S end of Round Lake, 2.8 mi; to Kunjamuk Mt. Trail jct., 3.8 mi; to Wakely Brook, 5.6 mi; to height of land, 6.2 mi; to East Brook, 7.6 mi; to Kunjamuk River, 7.8 mi (12.5 km).

Round Pond from Kunjamuk Trail (unmaintained)

Trails Illustrated Map 744: O18

This trail provides an easy route to the E side of Round Pond and an attractive vista.

▶Trailhead: The trailhead is found 1.3 mi along the Kunjamuk Trail (trail 30) from Big Brook Rd. After climbing a curving grade and passing a cabin at R, the trail reaches a T intersection at 1.2 mi and turns L. Another road fork is reached after 0.1 mi, as the main route curves R to the W. The trail to Round Pond is the unmarked, wide, grassy woods road that cuts sharply back L on this curve. ◀

From the trail jct. (0.0 mi), follow the woods road E, bearing 100°. The trail is flat and clear to a jct. at 0.3 mi. The trail to Round Pond turns R and heads S. (The woods road continues E across posted land to the dam at Kings Flow. The owner's permission is needed to cross.)

The path reaches another jct. at 0.7 mi. (The path back to the L crosses the posted land mentioned above.) Bear R. After crossing the outlet of Round Pond at 1.4 mi, the trail reaches an open campsite and fire ring on the E shore of the pond at 1.5 mi.

Crotched Pond Mt. lies due W across the pond and the more peaked Kunjamuk Mt. is to the SW. The old Kunjamuk Trail passes along the opposite shore, well out of sight. (The trail continuing S is the old Wakely Brook trail. It has been abandoned and should not be attempted.)

❋ Trail in winter: For cross-country skiers with good route-finding skills, this trail offers a nice outing. The return trip can be varied by crossing the pond and skiing back to Big Brook Rd. on the Kunjamuk Trail (trail 30).

🚶 Distances: To trailhead from Big Brook Rd., 1.3 mi; to first jct. from trailhead, 0.3 mi; to second jct., 0.7 mi; to Round Pond shore, 1.5 mi (2.4 km).

Kunjamuk Mt. *(unmaintained)*

Trails Illustrated Map 744: N18

The Kunjamuk Mt. Trail is what remains of the old road that led off the Kunjamuk Trail around the E side of Crotched Pond, to join the N road from Big Brook Rd.

▶Trailhead: The trail begins at a jct. on the W side of the Kunjamuk Trail (trail 30) 3.8 mi S of the Big Brook trailhead and 1 mi from the S end of Round Lake.◀

The route heads W as a good woods road up a long, gradual grade and then swings N. A gradual descent at 0.2 mi leads to a low spot, flooded by beaver. This is easily bypassed on the L at 0.4 mi. Gradual climbing leads to a second beaver flow, which again is easily passed on the L. More climbing leads to an open meadow at 0.6 mi where the remains of an old lumber camp can be seen.

Moderate grades head NW to height of land at 0.9 mi. This is an ideal place to begin a bushwhack up Kunjamuk Mt. Height of land is at 2180 ft. Another 769 ft of ascent up the N side of the mountain takes you to the 2949 ft (899 m) summit.

The old road can be followed for another 0.2 mi. It rapidly dissipates to a confusing bushwhack.

❋ Trail in winter: Too far in the woods for day trips, this mountain could make a winter climb for overnight campers.

🚶 Distances: To open meadow, 0.6 mi; to height of land, 0.9 mi; to terminus of clear trail, 1.1 mi (1.8 km). Total distance from trailhead, 4.9 mi (7.8 km).

31 John Pond

Trails Illustrated Map 744: P19

John Pond is a beautiful sheet of water with a lean-to providing views of handsome cliffs in the distance across the pond. The route still retains some of the ruts dug out prior to the closing of the woods road to motorized vehicles. However, the forest en route makes for an attractive trip. A bushwhack to Clear Pond over the ridge and across the lake from the lean-to makes a nice loop trip.

▶Trailhead: Access is from the intersection of NY 30 and NY 28 in the village of Indian Lake. Head 0.6 mi S on NY 30. Turn L onto Big Brook Rd. and drive 3.3 mi to Starbuck Rd. Turn L and follow Starbuck Rd. 0.4 mi to the entrance of the Wilderness Lodge. Immediately past the entrance, take the L fork, which is Lake View Dr. Go 0.5 mi to a T intersection. Turn R and drive 0.2 mi to its end. From the snowplow turnaround at the end, drive 0.1 mi S on a single-lane woods road to the trailhead parking lot. There is room for four or five vehicles. ◀

From the trail register (0.0 mi), blue markers lead S along the woods road. The level route continues to a fork at 0.6 mi, where the route makes a sharp turn L to the E. (Informal campsites are found straight ahead, a short distance into the woods and by a stream.)

The trail continues SE on nearly level ground, generally paralleling John Pond Brook. At 1.2 mi, the forest opens on the R. Bullhead Mt. to the SE overlooks John Pond Brook flowing through a meadow.

The route turns NE, just as it crosses the Hamilton County line into Warren County, at 1.3 mi. A side trail L, at 1.6 mi, leads up a small grade to the grave sites of Peter Savary and Eliza Emilia King, children who died of diphtheria in 1897.

At 1.7 mi, the trail crosses the outlet to John Pond. The John Pond Crossover Trail (trail 32), leading to the Puffer Pond Trail from Kings Flow (trail 27), enters from the R at 1.8 mi. A good open campsite is found just across a brook, 0.2 mi along this side trail.

The terrain becomes rolling as elevation increases in the last 0.4 mi to John Pond. A side path to the L at 2.1 mi leads 100 ft to a fish barrier dam.

The lean-to at John Pond is at 2.2 mi. Beaver have dammed the pond outlet, deepening this 0.3 mi long pond. The cliffs across the water rise nearly 500 ft, forming an open rock ridge from which views of the High Peaks can be found.

(The easiest way to reach the ridge is to return 0.1 mi back to the fish barrier dam. Cross the outlet at the dam base, bushwhack W up to the ridge, and walk it N. Hikers who are proficient with a map and compass may wish to extend the bushwhack to Clear Pond. Continue N along the ridge, then descend through open woods until intersecting the Clear Pond Trail. To complete a loop to the John Pond trailhead, continue to the Clear Pond trailhead at the T intersection, turn L, and L again at the snowplow turnaround.)

❄ Trail in winter: This trail is an excellent ski route in winter.

🦌 Distances: To E turn in trail, 0.6 mi; to county line, 1.3 mi; to burial site side trail, 1.6 mi; to John Pond Crossover Trail jct., 1.8 mi; to John Pond, 2.2 mi (3.5 km).

32 John Pond Crossover

Trails Illustrated Map 744: O19

This trail connects the John Pond Trail (trail 31) with the Puffer Pond from Kings Flow Trail (trail 27), providing the hiker with several options for extended backpacking trips. It is an excellent wilderness trail, perhaps better reflecting what many believe to be the true essence of wilderness than do some of the older, more developed trails. It has gentle, long grades and crosses several brooks.

▶Trailhead: The trail begins at the 1.3 mi point on the Puffer Pond from Kings Flow Trail (trail 27).◀

From the start of this trail (0.0 mi), 1.3 mi along the Puffer Pond from Kings Flow Trail, follow blue trail markers N. The route tends to be wet from 0.2 to 0.4 mi, but this is not a problem except in wet weather. Conditions for the rest of the route are good.

At 1.5 mi a rock shelf resides on the L for 100 yd. Just past this point the trail swings slightly L and begins a long descent. From 2 to 2.1 mi, thick undergrowth and occasional blowdowns require care. After crossing a brook at 2.2 mi, the trail levels and opens up considerably.

At a jct. at 2.7 mi, turn W and head downslope. (The path straight ahead continues N for about a mile before terminating.)

The trail enters a tree plantation at 2.9 mi, crossing a brook twice and then a meadow. The trail then becomes a grassy road. The jct. with the John Pond Trail (trail 31) is at 3.2 mi. John Pond is 0.4 mi N along the John Pond Trail.

❄ Trail in winter: This trail can be used to join the Puffer Pond to Kings Flow Trail (trail 27) to the John Pond Trail (trail 31). This is a true backwoods trip, requiring adequate skills and forest knowledge.

🚶 Distances: Puffer Pond Trail to rock shelf, 1.5 mi; to jct., 2.7 mi; to John Pond Trail, 3.2 mi (5.1 km). Total distance from Kings Flow to John Pond, 4.9 mi (7.8 km).

33 Clear Pond

Trails Illustrated Map 744: P19

The trail to Clear Pond makes a nice short walk to a pretty body of water. The route passes through mature deciduous forest. The trip can be extended by a short bushwhack over the ridge to the John Pond Trail (trail 31).

David Hough

▶Trailhead: To reach the trailhead, follow the same access directions as for the John Pond Trail (see p. 84) to the T intersection. The trailhead has been re-located from its prior position up the road L. It now is located on the S side of the road at the T intersection. Although it can be a bit difficult to see in the foliage, a DEC sign on a tree identifies the trail.◀

After climbing the road bank, the trail follows red markers SE up a gradual grade. At 0.1 mi, it turns R, still heading SE. At 0.2 mi, it turns E, beginning a 0.3 mi curve around to the NE. The old trail enters sharply from the L (W) at 0.5 mi. (Remember to turn L at this jct. on the return trip.) Bearing R, the trail stays on contour to 0.6 mi, where it ascends a moderate slope to 0.8 mi and then levels.

At 0.9 mi, the trail begins a moderate descent to the pond. It crosses the pond outlet L at 1 mi, follows the shore of the pond, and ends at an informal campsite on the N shore at 1.1 mi. The shoreline has been enlarged by beaver activity. Consequently, the informal paths around the pond have been flooded in places, especially on the S side.

❄ Trail in winter: This is an intermediate backwoods trail with skiing possible on Clear Pond if conditions permit. Locating the trailhead may be difficult in winter.

❀ Distances: To trail jct., 0.5 mi; to pond outlet, 1 mi; to Clear Pond, 1.1 mi (1.8 km).

Center Pond

Trails Illustrated Map 744: P19

Center Pond is a small, marsh-edged body of water. The very short walk to its shore takes only a few minutes.

▶Trailhead: Follow the trail access directions for the John Pond trailhead (p. 84) to the fork in the road at the entrance of Wilderness Lodge. Take the L fork, which is Lake View Drive. Turn onto the third side road to the L, 0.3 mi along Lake View Drive. (If you miss it, turn around at the T intersection and drive back 0.2 mi to the side road.) A gray house is kitty-corner to the side road.

Although it might appear to be a driveway for a house on its R, the side road continues past the house, turns L, and dead-ends at a brown building. A small grassy turnout is on the R, 0.1 mi along the road, within sight of the brown building.◀

An unmarked path leads N from this grassy turnout to the pond. The path is a little over 0.1 mi long. It ends at the marshy shore of the pond near a large rock on which one can stand to view the water. A short channel extends out to the deeper part of the pond, and water lilies blanket its S end.

❄ Trail in winter: This is a very short trail, but is suitable for snowshoeing.

❀ Distances: To Center Pond, 0.1 mi (0.2 km).

Kunjamuk River. Mark Bowie

Siamese Ponds Wilderness Area

FROM THE WEST *(Kunjamuk Section)*

The Kunjamuk River enters the Sacandaga River just below Speculator. Its valley runs N to Elm Lake and on to its sources in the Siamese Ponds Wilderness Area. In the early days, the almost level "Cungemunck" valley was a principal stagecoach route to Indian Lake and was even considered for a railroad route. Its fabled cave, supposed silver mines, and logging history have all created an aura of mystique about the valley.

The S part of the valley was purchased by Lyme Timber Company from International Paper in 2006. The people of the State of New York acquired a conservation easement on lands for recreational purposes on 36,000 acres, and the DEC is presently developing a permanent Recreational Management Plan (2013). In the meantime hiking and camping is limited to designated trails and campsites. Hikers should remember that the land is privately owned, and actively timbered, and public recreation is allowed with restrictions. Do not trespass on private lands or near privately leased camps.

Principal access roads are East Rd., Fly Creek Rd., and Robbs Creek Rd. East Rd. is a town road in good condition that can be traveled by ordinary vehicles to within 0.3 mi of the Cisco Creek trailhead. Travel at your own risk during spring breakup, very rainy weather, or icy periods. Yield to logging trucks and steer clear of logging operations.

Recommended hikes in this section include:

SHORT HIKES

Kunjamuk Cave: 1.4 mi (2.2 km) round trip. Shrouded with mystery, this is a fascinating cave to visit.

Lower Pine Lakes: 0.8 mi (1.3 km) round trip. A pleasant walk to a pair of pretty lakes.

MODERATE HIKES

Hayes Flow: 6.2 mi (9.9 km) round trip. A seldom-visited but exquisite body of water.

Rock Pond and Long Pond: 5.4 mi (8.6 km) round trip. Beautiful ponds and excellent hiking are among the rewards of this delightful woodland walk.

Trail Described	Total Miles (one way)		Page
Kunjamuk Cave	0.7	(1.1 km)	90
Lower Pine Lakes:			
North Pine Lake	0.2	(0.3 km)	91
South Pine Lake	0.4	(0.6 km)	91
34 Cisco Creek to the Kunjamuk River	1.2	(1.9 km)	91
35 Rock Pond and Long Pond	2.7	(4.3 km)	92
Hayes Flow	3.1	(5.0 km)	93

Kunjamuk Cave (unmaintained)

Trails Illustrated Map 744: K17

Kunjamuk Cave has been a curiosity for almost a century. The nature of its structure almost certainly indicates it was a small mine of some sort. Who made it and what, if anything, was mined there are unknown.

At one time, it was necessary to bushwhack from an upriver bridge to reach the Kunjamuk River trailhead for the cave. In 1997, a logging bridge was built across from that trailhead. Logging operations also obliterated most of the trail from the river to the cave. The trailhead has since been moved back to Pine Lakes Rd.

▶Trailhead: Access to the trailhead begins in Speculator, at the intersection of NY 30 and NY 8. Drive NE from the intersection on East Rd. Pavement ends at 1.5 mi. Continue another 0.2 mi on a dirt road to a jct. Turn R onto Pine Lakes Rd. Proceed to a logging road on the R at 0.7 mi. A red pine plantation is on the R side of Pine Lakes Rd. just beyond the logging road. Park well off the road at the intersection, taking care not to interfere with logging operations.◀

Avoiding a road 50 yd on the L, follow the logging road 0.3 mi to the logging bridge over the Kunjamuk River at the site of the old trailhead. (If you are a paddler, it is possible to put in at Duck Bay on NY 30 and paddle via the Sacandaga River to the mouth of the Kunjamuk and then on to this point. (See *Adirondack Mountain Club Canoe and Kayak Guide: East-Central New York State*.)

From the bridge, the road continues over a rise to a log collection yard. A logging road leaves the upper L corner of the yard, meeting the old trail on the crest of the second hill. Descending the far side of the hill, it curves R where a side trail goes L. This is 0.4 mi from the river.

Take the side trail to the L and walk 100 ft to Kunjamuk Cave. The 4 ft by 4.5 ft cave entrance cuts directly into the face of Cliff Hill. A ceiling hole has been cut for sunlight. The ceiling increases from the opening to a height of 15 ft at the back of the 20 ft cave. Its walls are smooth. The many possibilities for its history are fascinating to consider.

❄ Trail in winter: Although this is not a good winter trip, to do in winter, there are several ski trails in the Speculator Tree Farm nearby. This is private land owned by IP. Maps can be obtained where use permits are purchased.

🏃 Distances: To bridge, 0.3 mi; to Kunjamuk Cave side trail, 0.7 mi (1.1 km).

Lower Pine Lakes *(unmaintained)*

Trails Illustrated Map 744: K17

The two Lower Pine Lakes are beautiful small lakes ringed by conifers and water plants. This trip can be combined with the Kunjamuk Cave visit for a very nice day's outing.

▶Trailhead: Trail access is identical to that for the Kunjamuk Cave (see above) up to the 0.7 mi point on Pine Lakes Rd. There, instead of taking the R fork as for Kunjamuk Cave, take the L fork. Travel 0.1 mi to the end of the red pine plantation and turn R at the road jct. The road crosses the Kunjamuk River on a wooden bridge 0.2 mi from the jct. Continue to the base of Pine Mt. where the road makes a 90° turn L (N), 1.4 mi from the jct. Park off the road at the bend.◀

From the bend, the road continues 0.2 mi N to a camp on the R side of the road. Opposite it, a side trail L drops down to North Pine Lake. During the 150 ft walk to the lake, one's interest is aroused as the water is observed through the trees. The almost circular shoreline is edged with black spruce, tamarack, and other conifers.

At the base of a knoll opposite the bend, a washed-out road heads S into the woods. After a level stretch, a moderate upgrade begins at 0.3 mi. The road bends L and continues uphill. A bushwhack of approximately 200 yd downslope (W) from the road, after it bends L, leads to the shore of South Pine Lake at 0.4 mi. This is a pleasant place to have lunch. As in the other lake, early signs of eutrophic decline are evident. White pond lilies float on the water.

🏃 Distances: To North Pine Lake, 0.2 mi (0.3 km); to South Pine Lake, 0.4 mi (0.6 km).

34 Cisco Creek to the Kunjamuk River

Trails Illustrated Map 744: M18

The Cisco Creek Trail is an excellent route to the Kunjamuk River from the N end of the Speculator Tree Farm. The first 0.8 mi is used to reach the Rock Pond and Long Pond Trail (trail 35), and is marked with red DEC trail markers.

▶Trailhead: The trailhead is accessed via East Rd. From the NY 30 and NY 8 intersection in Speculator, drive NE on East Rd. Continue straight to a crossroads at 7.9 mi, ignoring a road that bears R at 5.1 mi. Vehicles with high road clearance can continue on to the Cisco Creek trailhead at 8.2 mi, but other vehicles should park well off the road at the intersection.◀

There are parking spaces and an open campsite and fire ring at the Cisco Creek trailhead. A trail register and the remains of an old barrier cable are found 100 ft farther along the road.

From the trail register (0.0 mi), the trail drops down the bank, crosses Cisco Creek, and heads N. Huge white pines are seen along the trail at 0.1 mi. There is a gradual grade over a knoll and then a benchmark is embedded in a boulder, R, at 0.6 mi.

The Rock Pond and Long Pond Trail (trail 35) branches L at a jct. at 0.9 mi. Although USGS topographic maps indicate a state lean-to at this jct., the lean-to no longer exists.

The trail is marked with blue DEC trail markers from this point and is easy to follow, although not well maintained. Expect blowdown. It continues straight to the Kunjamuk River at 1.2 mi. The wide, marshy valley is very attractive. In dry seasons, the Kunjamuk is easily forded here by wading. (For the continuation of this trail, see Kunjamuk Trail, trail 30, p. 81).

❄ Trail in winter: This area is frequently skied in winter. Do not expect the access road to be plowed.

⚄ Distances: To white pines, 0.1 mi; to Rock Pond and Long Pond Trail, 0.9 mi; to Kunjamuk River, 1.2 mi (1.9 km).

35 Rock Pond and Long Pond

Trails Illustrated Map 744: M18

Rock Pond and Long Pond are difficult places to reach from the S. Thus, they have retained a pristine quality, having suffered little abuse from humans. It is hoped that those fortunate enough to visit the ponds will do their best to preserve the natural qualities of this region. The outflows of these two ponds are source waters of the Kunjamuk River.

▶Trailhead: Access is the same as for the Cisco Creek Trail (trail 34 above). The trailhead is at a jct. 0.8 mi along the Cisco Creek Trail. A DEC sign identifies the trail, which is marked with red DEC trail markers to the S end of Long Pond. Turn L and head N.◀

There is corduroy at 0.2 mi. The forest changes from mixed to open deciduous as the trail gradually gains and loses minor elevations.

The trail runs along the top of a low esker-like ridge at 0.8 mi, and at 0.9 mi begins a series of undulating grade changes as it nears Rock Pond. Just after the pond comes into view ahead to the L, the trail crosses its outlet at 1.2 mi and leads uphill. A campsite is found by a large boulder beside the pond. A side trail enters from the main trail, 250 ft beyond the outlet. This large, exquisite pond has boulders along its entire E side. Deep water is found close to shore.

A gradual uphill grade levels at 1.6 mi. After a minor depression, the route drops toward Long Pond. Rock cliffs L indicate Long Pond Ridge at 1.9 mi.

The trail arrives at the S end of Long Pond at 2 mi. Its S shoreline is quite rocky. The trail follows the W shore closely. Several open campsites are located back from the water. The two-tiered cliffs on the opposite shore dominate the scene. Hemlock trees along the shore lend an atmosphere somewhat reminiscent of Lake George on a much smaller scale. A point affectionately named The Whaleback offers fantastic views and invites a swim off its slanted rock plane. The trail breaks up into numerous diverging paths from the third open campsite, located at 2.3 mi, at about the midpoint of the shoreline. Take the trail closest to the water. It soon leads to a wet, brushy area.

The remaining 0.4 mi of this trail is unmarked and unmaintained and in very poor condition. To remain dry, hikers must make a wide circle to the L, crossing a stream where it is smaller. (The careful observer may find a well-maintained spring uphill from this crossing place.) Continue to circle around to the shoreline, where a faint trail heads N. Blowdown confuses the problem as do numerous herd paths leading to the lake. The short distance to the N end of the pond contains many nice views of the ledge and frequent sign of beavers. The terminus of this trail is at 2.7 mi. Here, a DEC sign on a tree indicates the John Mack Pond–Long Pond Cross Trail, which receives little use (see p. 104).

❄ Trail in winter: This is a rugged, isolated area, seldom visited in winter. Only experienced cold-weather campers should travel here in winter.

🚶 Distances: To corduroy, 0.2 mi; to esker-like ridge, 0.8 mi; to Rock Pond, 1.2 mi; to Long Pond, 2 mi; to jct. with cross trail at N end of lake, 2.7 mi (4.3 km). Total distance from Cisco Creek trailhead, 3.5 mi (5.6 km).

Hayes Flow *(unmaintained)*

Trails Illustrated Map 744: K18–19

Hayes Flow is a beautiful drainage sink that collects water from a large surrounding territory. The outlet of the flow has been dammed by beavers to deepen the sink further. The result is an unusually attractive body of water, seldom visited by humans.

▶Trailhead: Access is on Robbs Creek Rd., off Old NY 8. The bridge at the S end of Old NY 8 is closed. To reach Old NY 8, drive 3.1 mi S from the NY 8-NY 30 intersection in Speculator. This is 6.5 mi N from the NY 8-NY 30 intersection N of Wells. Turn E off NY 8/ NY 30, cross the Sacandaga River bridge, and drive 1.8 mi on Old NY 8 to Robbs Creek Rd. Drive N on the hard-packed dirt Robbs Creek Rd., which crosses Robbs Creek at 1 mi on a heavy-duty wood bridge. The Hayes Flow trailhead is on the R, 0.1 mi past the bridge.◀

From the trailhead (0.0 mi), walk 0.1 mi E to a point where the grassy woods road veers away from Hayes Creek. Turn R onto a path that continues along the N bank of the creek. The path is the remains of an old woods road that parallels the rocky creek; it reaches Forest Preserve land at 0.4 mi.

The trail leaves the old woods road and crosses to the S side of Hayes Creek at 1 mi. It then continues E along the creek. An alternate route, to the R, climbs a small hill at 1.2 mi at what appears to be a dry brook bed. This route can be used in wet weather.

At 1.6 mi, the trail angles uphill away from the creek to avoid marshy ground

View from Indian Lake. Mark Bowie

farther up Hayes Creek. It crosses a small brook, then the faint alternate route rejoins the trail from the SW. The trail crosses another brook before passing a very large hunters' camp at 2.4 mi.

The trail heads E, soon forking R. Easy to follow until 2.7 mi, it is then much less distinct, but continues due E. The forest floor drops off sharply to the L at 2.9 mi, as the path continues to follow contours.

Hayes Flow is soon visible ahead to the L through the trees. The path drops down a slope, crosses a stream, and terminates at an open campsite near the flow at 3.1 mi. One can look NE up the beautiful flow, beyond a large beaver dam. To the NW is deep water, with a high bank across the flow.

❄ Trail in winter: This trail is difficult to follow in places. It is seldom used in winter.

Distances: To trail jct., 0.1 mi; to Hayes Creek crossing, 1 mi; to alternate route, 1.2 mi; to turn away from Hayes Creek, 1.6 mi; to hunters' camp, 2.4 mi; to Hayes Flow, 3.1 mi (5 km).

Indian Lake Section

 When the Penobscot Indian Sabael Benedict discovered Indian Lake during the Revolutionary War period, it was actually a series of three small lakes. The mouth of Squaw Brook is the burial place of Benedict's wife, and nearby Snowy Mt. was then called Squaw Bonnet Mt.

Lumber interests first built a dam at the foot of Indian Lake in 1845, building a larger, second dam in the 1860s. This deepened the waters some 33 ft and created the present lake.

The S end of Indian Lake, almost all of the E shoreline, and all of the lake's islands are state land. Distributed at intervals along the shore and on islands are 55 designated campsites. Each has a fireplace, table, and privy. Six open picnic sites at various locations around the lake are also available for day use. Public access to the lake is from the state boat launch near the Lewey Lake Public Campground and from a few privately owned marinas at Sabael.

In season, all campsites must be reserved. This can be done at the Indian Lake Islands Campground headquarters, across the road from Lewey Lake Public Campground on NY 30. Each site is numbered. A free map locating them is available at the headquarters. A charge for each night of camping is levied.

Almost unbounded opportunities for hiking and canoeing are available. The state land to the E of Indian Lake is true wilderness. Trails lead to John Mack Pond and other parts of the Siamese Ponds Wilderness Area. Snowy Mt. and Baldface Mt. have DEC trails. The 14 miles of Indian Lake, Lewey Lake, and the Jessup River offer significant opportunities for paddling. Whitewater paddlers and rafters flock to the Hudson River Gorge to the north of Indian Lake. Several high-quality hiking trails to seldom-visited lakes exist here.

Recommended hikes in the Indian Lake area include:

SHORT HIKES
Baldface Mt.: 2.2 mi (3.5 km) round trip. Seldom can such a magnificent view be gained from such a short climb.

MODERATE HIKES
John Mack Pond: 3.2 mi (5.1 km) round trip. A nice woods walk to a lovely pond.

HARDER HIKES
Snowy Mt.: 7.8 mi (12.5 km) round trip. Almost a 4000 ft peak, this is a challenging trip with a fire tower on top.

	Trail Described	Total Miles (one way)		Page
36	Bullhead Pond	0.6	(1.0 km)	96
37	Whortleberry Pond	3.3	(5.3 km)	96
38	Big Bad Luck Pond	0.7	(1.1 km)	98
39	Ross Pond	0.3	(0.5 km)	98
40	Dug Mt. Brook Falls	0.4	(0.6 km)	99
41	Watch Hill from NY 30	1.2	(1.9 km)	100
	Watch Hill from Indian Lake	0.5	(0.8 km)	101
42	Snowy Mt.	3.9	(6.2 km)	103
43	John Mack Pond	1.6	(2.6 km)	103
	John Mack Pond–Long Pond Cross	2.2	(3.5 km)	104
	Crotched Pond	1.5	(2.4 km)	105
44	Baldface Mt	1.1	(1.8 km)	106

36 Bullhead Pond

Trails Illustrated Map 744: R19

From a contemporary perspective, the name of this pond is curious. However it was first named, DEC began stocking the pond with trout in 1951, and now it is prized more for its trout than its bullheads. The trail is more likely to be used by anglers than hikers. Nevertheless, it offers an easy and pleasant walk to a nice pond.

▶Trailhead: Access is off Chain Lakes Rd. near Indian Lake. Chain Lakes Rd. leaves NY 28 1.3 mi E of the NY 28-NY 30 intersection in Indian Lake. Traveling W on NY 28, Chain Lakes Rd. is on the R immediately past Lake Abanakee. Head N on Chain Lakes Rd. to a large parking lot on the L at 1.4 mi (0.3 mi beyond the Lake Abanakee dam). The trailhead is at the back of the parking lot.◀

Climbing the bank of the parking lot, the red-marked trail continues up a moderate slope and levels after 100 yd. Heading NNW, it follows an old woods road through a pine forest. The grades are easy. At 0.5 mi an intersection with a yellow side trail is reached. The yellow side trail leads 0.1 mi to a fish barrier dam at the pond's outlet, and 0.2 mi to an open campsite with picturesque views of Bullhead Pond. The trail drops down a moderate slope, bears R, and reaches the S shore of the pond at 0.6 mi. DEC signs detailing fishing restrictions are prominent.

❄ Trail in winter: This trail would be suitable for a short snowshoe trip.

🐾 Distances: To jct., 0.5 mi; to pond, 0.6 mi (1 km).

37 Whortleberry Pond

Trails Illustrated Map 744: Q20

Whortleberry Pond is the northernmost of three ponds sharing the same trailhead on NY 28, the others being Ross and Big Bad Luck Ponds. The three ponds are close enough to be visited in one day.

▶Trailhead: Access is off the N side of NY 28, 7.2 mi E of the NY 28-NY 30 intersection in Indian Lake and 4.9 mi W of the Thirteenth Lake Rd.-NY 28 intersection in North River. A macadam parking lot for the trailhead is 0.2 mi farther E on the S side of NY 28. Large DEC signs identify the trailhead and parking lot.◀

The red-marked trail drops down a steep road bank to a DEC trail register (0.0 mi). Heading N, the trail immediately passes through a short muddy stretch. At 0.1 mi, it turns R at a trail sign and crosses a small stream on two hewn logs.

After a few minor ups and downs, at 0.4 mi the trail bears R up a moderate grade and swings around to the NE. Topping at 0.5 mi, it then begins a long gradual descent to Bell Mt. Brook, which it crosses on several logs thrown across the stream at 1.1 mi.

From the brook, the trail heads up a moderate grade and swings around to the W. It reaches a col on the NE shoulder of Bell Mt. at 1.6 mi, having gained 260 ft. Several rock faces are on the R as the trail passes through the col.

Although several knolls are encountered along the way, the trail gradually loses elevation in the next mile-plus. The first sighting of a marsh on the R is at 1.8 mi. The trail levels briefly at 1.9 mi as it passes the marsh R and blowdown L. At 2 mi, just before more blowdown, it turns N. After a few more ups and downs, the trail heads up a small knoll to the jct. with the yellow-marked Ross Pond Trail (trail 39) at 2.3 mi. Continue straight.

Passing over several more small humps, at 2.7 mi the trail reaches the jct. with the blue-marked Big Bad Luck Pond Trail (trail 38). Continuing straight, the Whortleberry Pond trail gradually descends to 2.8 mi, where it makes a brief turn W to another jct. Turning R (N) here, the trail levels. (The trail L is a 0.1 mi shortcut to the Big Bad Luck Pond Trail. Marked with red tape, it heads SW through a glen before climbing a moderate grade to a point 0.1 mi along the Big Bad Luck Pond Trail.)

The trail comes to a rocky clearing at 3 mi, where red markings end. A fishing spot on the tree-lined S shore of Whortleberry Pond can be reached by turning L (NW) and following an angler's trail 0.1 mi as it drops down a short, moderate stretch to the pond. A nicer pond vista and delightful camping area can be found by proceeding straight along a path marked with red surveying tape. A large boulder is reached at 3.2 mi where the trail reaches an unofficial blue spray-painted trail. Avoid the R turn as it leads to private property. Instead turn L following unofficial trail signs, blue spray paint and red surveying tape. A marsh is visible to your R. Soon three large trees are reached, with the middle tree bearing an unofficial sign with an arrow pointing the way to "Big Bad Luck Pond and Snowmobile Clearing." Following the arrow will lead 0.2 mi back to the rocky clearing, including 300 ft on an overgrown trail. For now take the faint path marked with blue spray paint directly behind the three trees. This trail immediately crosses a log bridge at the outlet of Whortleberry Pond. A sharp L turn leads to the water's edge at 3.3 mi at an attractive campsite overlooking a spectacular view of the pond.

❋ Trail in winter: This trail is suitable for intermediate skiers or snowshoers.

🐾 Distances: To height of land, 0.5 mi; to Bell Mt. Brook, 1.1 mi; to col, 1.6 mi; to Ross Pond Trail jct., 2.3 mi; to Big Bad Luck Pond jct., 2.7 mi; to jct. with shortcut, 2.8 mi; to rocky clearing, 3 mi; to Whortleberry Pond camping area, 3.3 mi (5.3 km).

38 Big Bad Luck Pond

Trails Illustrated Map 744: Q20

Bad fishing? Bad hunting? An accident? Not knowing what led to the naming of the pond, one's mind conjures up all kinds of possibilities on the trail to Big Bad Luck Pond.

▶Trailhead: The blue-marked trail begins at a jct. 2.7 mi along the Whortleberry Pond Trail (trail 36).◀

From the Whortleberry Pond Trail, the trail to Big Bad Luck Pond heads W up and over a small knoll. Once over the knoll, the trail is level to the pond. Much of the way is through a pine forest. The trail comes to a jct. at 0.1 mi. Continue straight. (The trail marked with red tape to the R is a shortcut to trail 37, the Whortleberry Pond Trail.) At 0.4 mi, it crosses a small inlet stream. The pond can be seen R. The trail reaches the shoreline at 0.5 mi and turns L (S) briefly, then W as it follows the S shore of the pond.

The trail ends at a small cove on the narrow eastern arm of the pond at 0.7 mi. Although there is a view W along the pond, fuller views can be had by bushwhacking farther W along the shoreline.

❋ Trail in winter: Although this trail is level, skiers must take into account the grades on the Whortleberry Pond Trail.

🐾 Distances: To shortcut jct., 0.1 mi; to stream, 0.4 mi; to shoreline, 0.5 mi; to cove, 0.7 mi (1.1 km). Total distance from NY 28, 3.4 mi (5.4 km).

39 Ross Pond

Trails Illustrated Map 744: Q20

The attractiveness of Ross Pond is enhanced by two small islands and a rocky shelf at the shore that invites a swim.

▶Trailhead: The yellow-marked trail begins at a jct. 2.3 mi along the Whortleberry Pond trail (trail 37). Ross Pond can be glimpsed through the trees from the jct.◀

Heading E on a gentle downgrade, the trail soon drops down a short, moderate pitch, turns R, and contours a knoll on the S shore of the pond. Dropping down another short, moderate slope, at 0.1 mi it crosses an inlet stream. Climbing up a moderate grade from the stream, the trail then gradually ascends as it skirts

Dug Mt. Brook Falls near the brook's intersection with Jessup River. Mark Bowie

the shoreline.

At 0.2 mi, the trail drops down to the SE corner of the pond, turns L, and crosses a brook. It then climbs R up a small bluff to a camping area at 0.3 mi. From the camping area, a path leads down to a rocky shelf at the shoreline. One of the two islands is directly ahead.

✳ Trail in winter: The pond is a nice destination for a winter outing, but the trail from the jct. is more suitable for snowshoeing than skiing.

🐾 Distances: To inlet stream, 0.1 mi; to SE corner, 0.2 mi; to camping area, 0.3 mi (0.5 km). Total distance from NY 28, 2.6 mi (4.2 km).

40 Dug Mt. Brook Falls

Trails Illustrated Map 744: M16

There is a pretty little waterfall at the mouth of Dug Mt. Brook, where it enters the Jessup River. Beside it is a picnic area with a fireplace. Although this is an attractive spot for lunch after a paddle up the Jessup from Indian Lake, many people don't realize there is a much higher waterfall upstream.

▶Trailhead: Access is via watercraft on the Jessup River. The boat access at the Indian Lake Islands Campground headquarters near Lewey Lake is one good put-in point. ◀

From the picnic area (0.0 mi), follow the unmarked path upstream along the N bank of Dug Mt. Brook. The path soon leads to higher ground a short distance back from the waterway. At 0.2 mi it again nears the brook at a point where it bends sharply to the S.

The trail drops down a grade to the water's edge, crosses a small tributary, and climbs to the top of a low, elongated ridge covered with small spruce. Below, the sounds of rapidly moving water may be heard. At 0.4 mi, the path descends to a pool at the base of a 40 ft high waterfall. The trail then ascends to the top of the cataract, where it terminates.

✳ Trail in winter: This is a destination only the adventurous would select in winter. The Panther Pond–Jessup River Trail and an ice crossing could be an access route if the ice were thick enough. Much caution is required whenever on ice.

𝝒 Distances: To S brook bend, 0.2 mi; to Dug Mt. Brook Falls, 0.4 mi (0.6 km).

41 Watch Hill from NY 30

Trails Illustrated Map 744: O17

Watch Hill is a small mountain that makes an excellent beginner's climb. It offers a variety of trail conditions, ending with a magnificent view of Snowy Mt. and the S end of Indian Lake.

▶Trailhead: Access to the trailhead is off the E side of NY 30, 1.1 mi S of the Snowy Mt. parking area. This is 8 mi S of the NY 28-NY 30 intersection at Indian Lake and 3.4 mi N of the Lewey Lake outlet bridge. The unmarked trailhead is a well-defined, grassy woods road that angles into the forest. Care must be taken in locating the trailhead.◀

From the trailhead (0.0 mi), the open woods road heads E, crossing Griffin Brook near the remains of an old log bridge at 0.1 mi. The route becomes more of a path for a short way, as it climbs a small grade. A level section leads to another grade. Near height of land, at 0.7 mi, an orange-painted metal stake is driven into the ground and a trail sign points the way up the hill; the route leaves the woods road to the R (SE) here. It is not marked, but is easy to follow. Avoid a side trail L at 0.8 m. (This alternate 0.4 mi route rejoins the hiking trail farther up the mountain. Horseback riders use it in the summer because of its easy grades. It is the recommended snowshoe route in winter.)

Continuing straight ahead, the hiking trail abruptly becomes steep and angles up the W side of Watch Hill. The trail soon levels. After a few more ups and downs, it reaches a T intersection at 0.9 mi, where the alternate route rejoins the trail from the L. (Note this spot; it is easy to walk past it on the return trip.)

The route turns R at this intersection and heads SW. Soon, it bears R at a fork. The deep valley drops off sharply to the R, as easy climbing continues. At 1 mi, the top of a large rock outcrop provides an excellent view of Snowy Mt. to the W.

The trail soon reaches the base of a knob and circles it to the R. The summit rock outcrop is achieved at 1.2 mi. Bare rock slopes upward slightly and then drops off sharply several hundred feet to the valley floor. Be careful.

The view is outstanding. Snowy Mt. dominates to the W. Lewey and Cellar Mts. are L. The three tongues of the S end of Indian Lake are to the S. The broad bay leading to Lewey Lake is at the R. The narrow neck of Indian Lake, which receives the Jessup River, is in the middle. The beginning of John Mack Bay can be seen to the L front. An informally marked 0.5 mi trail runs E from the summit and then S to Watch Point on Indian Lake (see description below).

Returning to the woods road jct. at 0.7 mi, one can extend the outing by walking farther N along this grassy road. It continues as a wide lane for another 0.6 mi. The last short section swings W and descends slightly. As it begins to enter a wet area, an informal path bears L, crosses a small brook, and climbs up to the bank of NY 30 approximately 75 yd S of the S end of the Snowy Mt. parking area.

✻ Trail in winter: This is a nice little climb for snowshoers. It would be an excellent beginner's ski-shoe or snowshoe trip. It would be wise to carefully locate the trailhead in summer to be sure it can be found in winter.

𝆚 Distances: To Griffin Brook, 0.1 mi; to R turnoff into woods from road, 0.7 mi; to alternate trail, 0.8 mi; to T intersection, 0.9 mi; to first lookout, 1 mi; to summit, 1.2 mi (1.9 km). Ascent, 357 ft (109 m). Summit elevation, 2125 ft (648 m).

Watch Hill from Indian Lake *(unmaintained)*

Trails Illustrated Map 744: O17

Watch Hill has a magnificent view of Snowy Mt. and the S end of Indian Lake. The climb is short. Some care is necessary in locating the trailhead, but after that the trail is easy to follow.

▶Trailhead: Access to the trailhead is on the W shore of Indian Lake. The unmarked trailhead is located at the N end of a small sandy cove near Watch Point. There is a large island 0.1 mi N of Moose Island; the sandy cove, where the trailhead is located, is in a direct line with the northern third of this island and the summit of Kunjamuk Mt. Refer to your topographic map.◀

The trail climbs up a bank from the beach. There is a 10 ft high stone fireplace chimney 30 ft in the woods, not visible from the lake in summer. The trail heads N parallel to the shoreline, but well back in the woods. Blue blazes mark the route.

At 0.1 mi, the path crosses a rocky brook. It continues straight for 50 ft and then turns sharply L. The trail climbs very gradually. Some care is necessary in crossing rocky brook beds, but the path is generally easy to follow.

The slope becomes moderate at 0.3 mi and steep at 0.4 mi. One last steep pitch brings you to the open rock cliff summit at 0.5 mi. Snowy Mt. stands out in the W, with Lewey and Cellar Mts. to its S. The three tongues of the S end of Indian

Snowy Mt. from Indian Lake. Michael N. Kelsey

Lake are seen to the S. A trail leads N, 1.2 mi to NY 30 (trail 41).

❄ Trail in winter: Not recommended for winter use owing to difficult access.

🚶 Distances: To brook, 0.1 mi; to steep section, 0.4 mi; to summit, 0.5 mi (0.8 km). Ascent, 475 ft (145 m). Summit elevation, 2125 ft (648 m).

42 Snowy Mt.

Trails Illustrated Map 744: O17

Snowy Mt. is an imposing giant W of NY 30 near Indian Lake. It lacks being a 4000 ft peak by only 101 ft. The climbing ascent is 2106 ft, which is greater than that of many of the High Peaks. It ranks 51 on the list of Adirondack Hundred Highest. The summit has excellent views.

▶Trailhead: Access to the trailhead is off the W side of NY 30, 6.9 mi S of Indian Lake village and 4.5 mi N of Lewey Lake outlet. A well-marked parking area is found on the E side of the road, opposite the trailhead.◀

The trail is marked with red DEC trail markers. It heads W up Beaver Brook valley on a fairly level track, gaining only 267 ft elevation before crossing Beaver Brook at 1.2 mi. A steep section, followed by a more gradual section, precedes another Beaver Brook crossing at 1.9 mi, another 180 ft higher. The trail has opened up.

The stream and several tributaries are crossed as steady climbing begins. Severe erosion is evident as the route steepens. At 3.2 mi, the trail turns R and ascends an extremely steep slope to a cliff near the summit.

The cliff offers a panoramic view of Indian Lake and beyond to the Siamese Ponds Wilderness Area. There is a spring at the edge of the woods, near where the trail continues on to the fire tower. A side trail extends 50 yd W of the spring to a lookout toward Squaw and Panther Mts. Even Mt. Morris, near Tupper Lake, can be seen beyond Panther Mt.

From the spring, the summit is 500 ft farther SW up a slight grade, at 3.9 mi. The fire tower was repaired in 2001 by members of the Student Conservation Association, part of the AmeriCorps National Service Network, and the observation cabin is open. Prominent features that can be viewed from the cabin include Indian Lake, the Siamese Ponds Wilderness, and distant mountain ranges to the E; Pillsbury Mt. to the S; Wakely Mt. to the W; Blue Mt. beyond the R shoulder of Panther Mt. to the N; and the High Peaks sweeping across the NE.

❋ Trail in winter: This is a popular snowshoe trail in winter. Its 2106 ft vertical ascent and very steep upper slopes require the same skills and equipment used for winter climbs in the High Peaks.

⚚ Distances: To first crossing of Beaver Brook, 1.2 mi; to second crossing, 1.9 mi; to R turn, 3.2 mi; to summit, 3.9 mi (6.2 km). Ascent, 2106 ft (642 m). Elevation, 3899 ft (1188 m).

43 John Mack Pond

Trails Illustrated Map 744: N17

A boat is necessary to reach the John Mack Pond Trail, which begins at John Mack Bay on Indian Lake. From the trailhead, 175 ft elevation will be gained and partially lost before the pond is reached.

▶Trailhead: Access for most hikers begins at the state boat launch near Lewey

Lake Public Campground and includes a paddle to the trailhead. A small island near campsite 26 on the E shore of John Mack Bay indicates you are close to the trailhead. Paddle into the small cove just beyond campsite 26 and continue to the landing at the end of the cove. A DEC signpost marks the shoreline trailhead.◀

From the trailhead (0.0 mi), the red-marked trail heads E, crosses a brook, and begins a gradual upgrade. It levels at 0.3 mi and comes along the L side of a wet zone at 0.5 mi. The trail parallels it on higher dry ground. It crosses a second brook at 0.9 mi and turns SE. Crossing two more brooks at 1.1 mi, the trail then ascends a gentle slope before the final gradual downgrade to John Mack Pond. The John Mack Pond–Long Pond Cross Trail jct. is reached at 1.4 mi. The Long Pond Cross Trail branches R, up a knoll to the S.

Continuing straight ahead, the trail reaches John Mack Pond at 1.6 mi. From the shore, the bulk of Kunjamuk Mt. stands out across the pond to the E. Moose Mt. is to the NW. Lily pads dot the pond and its outlet to the R. An open campsite and fire ring are found 40 ft R of the trail.

✤ Trail in winter: Not recommendeded for winter use owing to its trailhead location.

🐾 Distances: To first level ground, 0.3 mi; to wet zone, 0.5 mi; to Cross Trail, 1.4 mi; to John Mack Pond, 1.6 mi (2.6 km).

John Mack Pond–Long Pond Cross

Trails Illustrated Map 744: N18

The John Mack Pond–Long Pond Cross trail is a true wilderness trail. It is sporadically marked with red DEC trail markers, and is more a path than a trail. It climbs through a gentle drainage area dotted with beaver dams.

▶Trailhead: The trail begins at a jct. at the 1.4 mi point of the John Mack Pond trail (trail 43).◀

The trail climbs S over a knoll and reaches the John Mack Pond outlet at 0.1 mi. Thanks to beaver activity, the trail appears to lead right into the water. A dry crossing is possible, however. Walk back on the trail 50 ft and bushwhack downstream (SW). Stay in open woods, but hug the edge of the thick spruce bordering the outlet. After a very short distance, a beaver dam can easily be crossed to the opposite shore. Walk upstream along the opposite shore until the red trail markers are again found.

The trail turns SE and then W, as it passes over several minor grades. At 1.1 mi, the trail is high above a large beaver-affected drainage flow. At 1.2 mi, the trail descends to water level and soon approaches a large beaver lodge. At that point, the trail again climbs the slope and contours the valley at a higher elevation. The trail descends again when it reaches the inlet brook at the head of the beaver flow.

A gradual climb along the inlet crosses the brook three times before the trail reaches a small, unnamed, but very attractive, beaver pond at 1.8 mi. The trail again leads right into the water, but a small beaver dam across the pond outlet provides an easy way across, where trail markers can once again be located.

The gradual climb over Long Pond Ridge begins from this pond. The trail gradually curves to the S. As it nears the ridge line, cliffs are seen L. Height of land is reached at 2 mi. The trail then descends a moderate grade to the NE end of Long Pond. Here, a DEC signpost on a tree indicates the terminus of the trail at 2.2 mi. The faint Rock Pond–Long Pond Trail leads from this jct. down the W shore of Long Pond. (See trail 35, p. 92.)

❋ Trail in winter: Not recommended for winter use.

𝄞 Distances: To John Mack Pond outlet, 0.1 mi; to beaver flow, 1.1 mi; to beaver pond, 1.8 mi; to height of land, 2 mi; to Long Pond, 2.2 mi (3.5 km). Total distance from John Mack Pond trailhead, 3.6 mi (5.8 km).

Crotched Pond *(unmaintained)*

Trails Illustrated Map 744: O18

The N shore of Crotched Pond, including the peninsula, belongs to the Crotched Pond Club, and is not open to the public. To the E, a dirt road leading up a hill from Big Brook Road crosses the club's land, and should not be used to access the pond. However, the remainder of the shoreline, as well as the first 1.2 mi of the jeep road from Indian Lake, is owned by the state. With some perseverance, the state-owned shoreline can be reached via a short bushwhack from the jeep road.

▶Trailhead: The trailhead is at the rear of campsite 14, on the E shore of Indian Lake near Crotched Pond Island. A good boat landing is found between campsites 13 and 14. A picnic site down the lake to the N, a short distance from campsite 13, makes a good place for lunch and a swim.◀

The unmarked but clear trail heads NE along the W bank of Crotched Pond Brook. It bears L and climbs up a small hill at 0.1 mi, but continues to parallel the brook. The trail drops down off the hill and meets the brook again at 0.3 mi. Both the brook and the trail then swing SE.

The valley closes in at 0.5 mi, but soon widens where a beaver dam has created a backwater. A hunter's cabin is on the L at 0.8 mi, and the trail soon begins a bend to the E, away from the brook. A beaver meadow is seen R and the trail gradually ascends.

Red paint blazes on trees on the R side of the trail at 1.2 mi mark the boundary of state lands. The remaining 0.8 mi of jeep roads leading down the peninsula to the Crotched Pond Club camp should not be traveled without permission of the owners. However, by staying on the R (W) side of the red-marked survey line, the hiker can make a 0.3 mi bushwhack on state land through the woods to the state-owned portion of shoreline. This section is not particularly good for camping because the shore is lined with marsh grasses, but it does offer a nice view of Kunjamuk Mt. to the SE and of Crotched Pond Mt. to the E.

❊ Trail in winter: Not recommended for winter use.

🦌 Distances: To L turn up hill, 0.1 mi; to beaver dam, 0.5 mi; to cabin, 0.8 mi; to survey blazes, 1.2 mi; to state-owned shoreline, 1.5 mi (2.4 km).

44 Baldface Mt.

Trails Illustrated Map 744: P18

This little mountain on the NE shore of Indian Lake provides a marvelous view of the lake. It must be approached by water. A canoe trip, mountain climb, picnic, and swim can all be part of this day trip. For those utilizing the Indian Lake Islands Public Campground, this is an excellent day activity. Vertical ascent is only 580 ft (177 m).

▶Trailhead: The closest access is from Lakeside Cottages, on Lake Shore Drive on the W shore of Indian Lake. Lake Shore Drive is off NY 30, 4.5 mi S of the intersection of NY 30 and NY 28 in the village of Indian Lake. The other end of Lake Shore Drive is off NY 30, 1.7 mi N of the Snowy Mt. parking area. There is a large sign and marina at Lakeside Cottages. There is a small dock charge for day use of the marina. It is a paddle of approximately one mile across the lake to Normans Cove where the trailhead is located. This is 0.2 mi N of Kirpens Island, the northernmost large island in Indian Lake.◀

The entrance to Normans Cove is a narrow neck. A small peninsula extends from the N side of the neck. There is a public picnicking area with several tables and a fireplace.

The cove quickly widens. The trailhead is at the L rear of the cove at a large boulder and DEC sign. It is a good landing area for canoes.

The marked trail climbs a small rise through a predominantly birch forest. Red DEC trail markers guide the way. The route runs up a gradual to moderate grade in a generally SE direction. At 0.7 mi the steep wall of Baldface Mt. becomes evident. The grade becomes moderately steep as the trail begins a large horseshoe turn back to the N through red and white pines. The trail ascends steeply to open ledges on the summit at 1.1 mi.

A few blueberries can be found

Mark Bowie

Normans Cove from Indian Lake. Michael N. Kelsey

in season, but the panorama will keep your attention for several minutes. From R to L across the lake a sequence of mountains beckons. In the distant NW is huge, flat-topped Blue Mt. Little Porter Mt. is overshadowed by Squaw Mt. directly ahead. Panther Mt. is behind the R shoulder of Squaw, and Buell Mt. is to the rear of the L side of Squaw Mt. Farther S is the square summit of 3899 ft Snowy Mt., followed by Lewey and Cellar Mts. Finally, the Blue Ridge stretches far to the S. Floodwood Mt. is seen behind the islands and to the L of the peninsula at the W end of the lake. Below, Normans Cove sits like a jewel. A swim in the sandy-bottomed cove before the return trip is great on a hot day.

✤ Trail in winter: If the ice is thick enough, this can be a very interesting winter trip.

⚤ Distances: To trailhead via canoe, 1 mi; to rock wall, 0.7 mi; to summit, 1.1 mi (1.8 km). Ascent, 580 ft (177 m). Summit elevation, 2230 ft (680 m).

Pillsbury Lake. Michael N. Kelsey

Lewey Lake and West Canada Lakes Section

 N of Speculator, the Lewey Lake section is out of the confining valley, and trails are more expansive, leading through generally flat areas. There are a few small mountains. The Panther Pond Trail extends until stopped by the broad Jessup River. The Miami River Trail ends at a network of beaver dams. In recent years, moose tracks and sightings have been on the rise here.

Other trails lead into the West Canada Lakes Wilderness Area, where hikers need to be a bit more self-reliant, with a sense of direction and expectation for close forest scenery rather than sweeping views. This is the country of Adirondack French Louie, Nat Foster, Jock Wright, Atwell Martin, and a host of other ragged lumberjacks, trappers, and hermits. It is the home of several of the oldest sports clubs in New York State. The region is traversed by the Northville–Placid Trail. Cellar, Lewey, and Blue Ridge Mts. are reasonable bushwhacks from the Sucker Brook Trail. Also included in this section are trails off the Cedar River Rd., Wakely Mt., Wakely Dam, and Pillsbury Mt., and an introduction to the Moose River Recreation Area.

Recommended hikes in this section include:

SHORT HIKES
Sprague Pond: 0.8 mi (1.3 km) round trip. An easy walk to a pretty pond.

MODERATE HIKES
Wakely Mt.: 6 mi (9.6 km) round trip. The first part is easy, but once climbing begins, it is very steep. The trail concludes at a scenic fire tower.

Pillsbury Mt.: 3.2 mi (5.1 km) round trip. The summit affords good views of Lake Pleasant.

HARDER HIKES
Sucker Brook: 15.4 mi (24.6 km) round trip. This connector trail to the Northville–Placid Trail is a real wilderness hike.

Cedar Lakes: 8.6 mi (13.8 km) round trip. A walk into wilderness through rolling terrain and vleis.

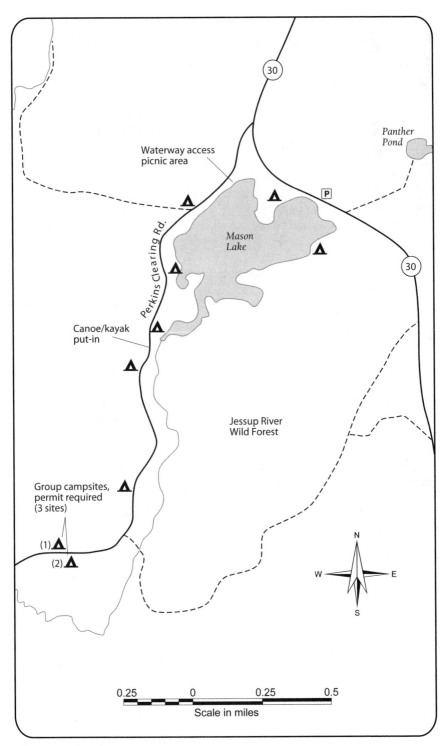

30

Panther
Pond

Waterway access
picnic area

P

Mason
Lake

Perkins Clearing Rd.

30

Canoe/kayak
put-in

Jessup River
Wild Forest

Group campsites,
permit required
(3 sites)

(1)

(2)

N

W   E

S

0.25   0   0.25   0.5

Scale in miles

Trails Described	Total Miles (one way)		Page
Panther Pond and Jessup River	1.3	(2.1 km)	111
Mason Lake Campsites			112
Callahan Brook	1.5	(2.4 km)	112
45 Pillsbury Mt.	1.6	(2.6 km)	113
46 Cedar Lakes Trail: Pillsbury Mt. to First Cedar Lake	4.3	(6.9 km)	114
47 Pillsbury Lake	3.4	(5.4 km)	115
48 Pillsbury Lake to West Canada Creek	5.2	(8.3 km)	116
49 Northville–Placid Trail: Piseco to Wakely Dam	32.6	(52.2 km)	118
50 West Canada Lakes via Brooktrout Lake	8.2	(13.1 km)	125
51 Otter Brook Road to Cedar Lakes	8.4	(13.4 km)	128
52 Sucker Brook	7.7	(12.3 km)	129
Sprague Pond	0.4	(0.6 km)	130
53 Wakely Mt.	3.0	(4.8 km)	131
54 Northville–Placid Trail: Wakely Dam to NY 28/30 at Lake Durant	13.1	(21.0 km)	131

Panther Pond and Jessup River *(unmaintained)*

Trails Illustrated Map 744: M16

This route to the Jessup River follows an abandoned snowmobile trail on easy grades. It offers a pleasant woods walk with the added enticement of a swim in the deep river.

▶Trailhead: Access to the trailhead is from a scenic vista parking area at Mason Lake. This is on the W side of NY 30, 7.7 mi N of Speculator. The trailhead is on the E side of NY 30, 0.1 mi S of the parking area. The trail starts at the base of a road bank and is somewhat difficult to spot. Nearby is a short wooden post which sits back 20 ft from the road.◀

From the trailhead (0.0 mi), the trail follows red tape markers SE on level terrain. Old snowmobile markers and yellow tree blazes occasionally can be spotted. The trail encounters a muddy area with deteriorated corduroy at 0.1 mi and offers a glimpse of Panther Pond N through the open woods at 0.3 mi. With some luck, red tape markers may be found leading to its shore. If not, the pond can be reached with an easy bushwhack of less than 0.1 mi on a compass heading of 30°–40°. Though an attractive pond, its marshy shoreline prevents one from getting close to the water.

Continuing on nearly level ground, the trail passes a large boulder R at 0.4 mi. At 0.6 mi the trail turns S down a gradual grade. It swings E again and climbs a short muddy section on corduroy to a height of land at 0.7 mi.

The route crosses a red-marked snowmobile trail at 0.9 mi. (To the R, the snowmobile trail leads 1.3 mi to NY 30, at a point 0.4 mi N of the Jessup River bridge.) The trail heads SE, but soon resumes its course to the E. A short, moderate downgrade ends on the level valley floor and the trail reaches the Jessup River at 1.3 mi. The river is deep here and approximately 100 yd wide. The mouth of Dug Mt. Brook is located at a small waterfall directly across the river. A picnic area is found here.

❄ Trail in winter: With snowdrifts, this trail might be hard to find, and still more difficult to follow if snowmobiles haven't recently broken trail. For those with map and compass skills, however, it could be a nice woods ramble.

🐾 Distances: To large boulder, 0.4 mi; to red-marked snowmobile trail, 0.9 mi; to Jessup River, 1.3 mi (2.1 km).

Mason Lake Campsites

Trails Illustrated Map 744: M16 / P. 110

Mason Lake is a small but attractive lake visible from NY 30, 8.1 mi N of Speculator and 4 mi S of Lewey Lake outlet. It is on state land, with a picnic area and boat launch located on Perkins Clearing Rd. Several primitive campsites can be found around the lake and along Perkins Clearing Rd. In keeping with the Jessup River unit management plan, many of these campsites have closed (2013). Plan accordingly. A pullout along NY 30 permits viewing of the lake.

Callahan Brook (unmaintained)

Trails Illustrated Map 744: M16

At one time, this trail crossed the Miami River and climbed the shoulder of Blue Ridge along Callahan Brook. Today, Callahan Brook is a very difficult bushwhack owing to beaver activity on the Miami River. At its mouth, where it enters Lewey Lake, the Miami River has always been a marsh. Over the years, the upper valley has been dammed and flooded by beavers. Because this trail description relies on red tapings which may not survive the passing of time, it should only be attempted by those confident of their navigation skills.

▶Trailhead: The trailhead is off the N side of Perkins Clearing Rd. at Mason Lake. Turn W onto Perkins Clearing Rd. just N of Mason Lake, 8.1 mi N of Speculator on NY 30. Turn R into a campsite area at the top of a small hill 0.4 mi along Perkins Clearing Rd. A trail leads W from the L rear of the campsite. A red trail marker is high on an old beech tree 50 ft along the trail. Parts of the trail are marked with red tape.◀

Long stretches of this informal path are clear; where it isn't clear, red tape markers should be kept in sight. Avoid red tape markers heading L (S) at a muddy spot at 0.1 mi. (They head back to the road.) The trail soon begins a gradual downgrade. It levels briefly at 0.4 mi before continuing to descend.

At 0.9 mi, the route turns NE. A jct., visible only because of red tape, is reached at 1.1 mi. The red tapes L head down a boggy streambed to the bank of the Miami River, where the path continues R to a beaver dam 150 yd from the jct. Beyond, beaver activity makes it very difficult to reach Callahan Brook.

The red tapes continuing straight from the jct. at 1.1 mi parallel the R bank of the Miami River N for another 0.4 mi before terminating at a bog area at 1.5 mi.

❄ Trail in winter: Not recommended for winter use.

🏃 Distances: To jct. at Miami River, 1.1 mi; to terminus of trail along river, 1.5 mi (2.4 km).

45 Pillsbury Mt.

Trails Illustrated Map 744: M15

Pillsbury Mt. is a moderately difficult climb that makes a good day trip. Its elevation is 3597 ft, and it ranks 82 on the list of Adirondack Hundred Highest. There is a fire tower at the summit, but it is closed. Limited views can be seen from the ground.

▶Trailhead: Access to the mountain trail is off NY 30 at Mason Lake. This is 8.1 mi N of Speculator and 4 mi S of the bridge over Lewey Lake outlet. Although closed from December 1 to May 1, the dirt road L (Perkins Clearing Rd.) is excellent during the remainder of the year. Follow it SW 3.3 mi to the road jct. at Perkins Clearing. The condition of the road from this point varies considerably with the season and the status of lumbering operations. The careful driver should be able to travel this route in summer without too much trouble.

Turn R from the Perkins Clearing DEC trail sign. The road passes a metal gate at 3.4 mi, and crosses a bridge over the Miami River at 4.6 mi. Sled Harbor is reached at 5.1 mi. At one time, wagons were replaced at this point and oxen were used to pull sleds up the grades ahead. Today, the area is used as a collecting point for storing logs, and considerable activity with hauling trucks periodically takes place here.

The route beyond this point is still more difficult and requires good driving skills. Past Sled Harbor, one drives up a short grade and immediately reaches a road jct. Bear R and ascend a moderate grade. This short section may vary in difficulty depending on recent rainfall and maintenance. Be sure your vehicle is in good operating condition with high road clearance. If not, it is customary to park one's car at the road jct. and hike the final stretch of road to the trailhead. The grade and road soon improve, but are not of the quality found from Perkins Clearing. Grades steepen moderately again at 6.2 mi and the trailhead parking area and road barrier are reached at 6.3 mi. The parking area can hold 10 to 15 vehicles.

It is important to note that the network of roads leading to the trailhead belong to Lyme Timber and the public is given access through a conservation easement acquired by the State of New York in 2005. Respect private property and give logging trucks the right of way. ◀

The Pillsbury trailhead (0.0 mi) is immediately L of the trail register at the rear of the parking area.

Turning L (W), the trail descends promptly 0.1 mi to cross the Miami River, which is a small brook at this point. Once across the stream, climbing begins in earnest. The grade varies from moderate to steep for the next 1 mi. After passing through some minor blowdown, the trail finally levels somewhat at 1.1 mi.

At 1.3 mi, an indistinct trail jct. is found at the base of the last steep rock area before the summit. A side trail R leads 200 yd to a spring, which hasn't been used much since the fire tower ceased to be staffed. Consequently, it is in poor condition. Once past the last steep section, the nearly level trail leads to the fire tower and cabin at 1.6 mi.

Views from the fire tower steps are striking. Snowy Mt. can be seen to the N, dominating Indian Lake to its E and Cedar River Flow to its W. To the W is the West Canada Lakes Wilderness Area. Pillsbury Lake and Whitney Lake are in the foreground, while Cedar Lakes can be seen in the distance beyond Pillsbury Lake. Lake Pleasant and Sacandaga Lake stand out to the S. Mountains dominate the distant horizon to the E.

❄ Trail in winter: Pillsbury Mt. is an excellent snowshoeing mountain, however, the access road is closed in winter, and the round-trip distance from Mason Lake is 15.8 mi.

🐾 Distances: To Miami River, 0.1 mi; to top of first ridge, 1.1 mi; to spring jct., 1.3 mi; to summit, 1.6 mi (2.6 km). Ascent, 1337 ft (408 m). Summit elevation, 3597 ft (1097 m).

46 Cedar Lakes Trail: Pillsbury Mt. to First Cedar Lake
Trails Illustrated Map 744: M15

The Cedar Lakes Trail provides quick entry into the West Canada Lakes Wilderness Area. The first part of the trail is up a very pleasant woods road that becomes a footpath for the remainder of the way to First Cedar Lake.

A small sign near the trailhead identifies this as the French Louie Trail, in honor of the colorful French Canadian trapper and guide whose main camp was at West Lake circa 1880–1915. From here to Pillsbury Lake, the French Louie Trail traces a segment of the route Louie took from West Lake to Newton Corners (now Speculator) to trade furs, stock up on supplies, and binge drink before returning to West Lake.

▶Trailhead: For trail access, follow the same trailhead directions given for Pillsbury Mt. (trail 45, p. 113).◀

The Cedar Lakes Trail heads N up the woods road beyond the road barrier (0.0 mi) at the trail register and DEC signpost. Trailhead elevation is 2260 ft. A series of gradual grades alternating with short level sections parallels the Miami River far below to the W, between the trail and the lower slopes of Pillsbury Mt. Red trail markers are occasionally spotted. A minor dip and washed-out culvert mark a brook crossing at 0.7 mi. The way is generally easy, but a grade at 1.2 mi can challenge those with a heavy pack. At the top of the grade, a welcome level section leads to the Pillsbury Lake jct. at 1.6 mi. Elevation is 2560 ft, 300 ft above the trailhead. (The trail L leads to Pillsbury, Whitney, and Sampson Lakes. See opening of trail 47.)

The Cedar Lakes Trail continues straight ahead N and soon descends to Stony Brook. Here, at 1.9 mi, a skiable bridge crosses the brook and a considerable boardwalk leads to a clearing that is gradually growing in with spruce and berry bushes. The route has now become a footpath, with little sign of the woods road width that must have existed in the past. The enjoyable route continues over almost level terrain. Grassy Brook is at 2.2 mi, where a 75 ft bridge (skiable) traverses an attractive wetland bordered by black spruces. A short, moderate upgrade at 2.4 mi crosses the end of a small ridge, before the trail gradually descends again to more boardwalk. The route begins to parallel the N side of Noisey Ridge, though the grade change is negligible.

This section is excellent in dry weather, but can become wet very quickly if it rains. The very gradual upgrade at 2.8 mi soon levels and the trail returns to lower ground. A minor increase in elevation occurs again at 3 mi and the trail then becomes almost level for a while. Minor changes in grade bring the trail to a brook crossing at 4.2 mi. There is a very brief upgrade before the concrete dam at the outlet of First Cedar Lake at 4.2 mi.

The trail formerly crossed the dam, but the crossway has washed out. The trail now turns R at the dam, drops down a slope, and crosses the Cedar River on a bridge 50 yd downstream from the dam. It then climbs up the opposite bank to the N–P Trail. A trail register is found at a jct. near the dam at 4.3 mi.

❉ Trail in winter: The winter hiker should expect to begin walking from NY 30 at Mason Lake, because the roads are not plowed unless lumbering is taking place. It is 10.6 mi from Mason Lake to First Cedar Lake. This is not a region for the inexperienced in winter. For the experienced winter enthusiast, however, it provides a rugged but exciting area to explore by ski or snowshoe.

🐾 Distances: To Pillsbury Lake jct., 1.6 mi; to Stony Brook, 1.9 mi; to Grassy Brook, 2.2 mi; to Cedar Lakes dam, 4.2 mi; to N–P Trail jct., 4.3 mi (6.9 km).

47 Pillsbury Lake

Trails Illustrated Map 744: M14

Pillsbury Lake is a small, attractive lake on the first leg of a trip into the West Canada Lakes Wilderness Area. Both Whitney Lake and Sampson Lake are within day-trip range of Pillsbury Lake.

▶Trailhead: Access is off NY 30 at Mason Lake. See Pillsbury Mt. Trail (trail 45) and Cedar Lakes Trail (trail 46) for access to the Pillsbury Lake trailhead. This trailhead is at a jct. 1.6 mi along the Cedar Lakes Trail from the parking area at the base of Pillsbury Mt.◀

From the DEC signpost at the trailhead jct. (0.0 mi), the trail follows red trail markers W down a woods road a short distance to a dip. It then climbs a long gradual grade that finally levels at 0.8 mi. The route soon descends gradually to a clearing that once had a lumber camp. There is a small informal campsite on the L at the entrance to the clearing at 0.9 mi.

The trail narrows beyond the clearing. Corduroy and boardwalks are frequent in the low, often wet area ahead. A long boardwalk crosses a wetland at 1.3 mi. After another boardwalk at 1.4 mi, what appears to be a small pond is seen through the trees to the R of the trail. It actually is the E end of Pillsbury Lake. More of the lake can be seen through the trees as the trail gradually ascends to higher ground.

Nearly level trail continues to a lean-to sign and jct. at 1.7 mi. The side trail drops a gradual 100 yd to the lean-to, which sits close to Pillsbury Lake.

❀ Trail in winter: The grades make this trail very skiable, however, the winter trailhead is generally at Mason Lake, unless late-season lumbering keeps the roads open longer than usual. Consequently, one must think in terms of a 20 mi round-trip. For winter camping, this is an excellent but isolated area.

🐾 Distances: To top of first low ridge, 0.8 mi; to E end of Pillsbury Lake, 1.4 mi; to lean-to jct., 1.7 mi; to lean-to, 1.8 mi (2.9 km). From Pillsbury Mt. parking area, 3.4 mi (5.4 km).

48 Pillsbury Lake to West Canada Creek
Trails Illustrated Map 744: M14

This trail is a continuation of the Pillsbury Lake Trail (trail 47) into the West Canada Lakes region. Two lakes, Whitney and Sampson, can be reached from this trail, which connects to the Northville–Placid Trail (N–P Trail). Combining this trail with the N-P Trail offers several loop routes for backpackers.

▶Trailhead: The trailhead is at the Pillsbury Lake lean-to jct. of the Pillsbury Lake Trail (trail 47). This is 3.4 mi from the Pillsbury Mt. parking area and 9.9 mi from NY 30 at Mason Lake.◀

From the lean-to jct. (0.0 mi), the trail continues generally W. The woods road loses elevation very slowly and the W end of Pillsbury Lake can be seen intermittently through the trees. At 0.1 mi, extensive boardwalk passes over wetland. Again at 0.2 mi boardwalk crosses a wetland. There is a large brook here and an abandoned beaver dam. The route passes over a small ridge and down the opposite side to a small wet clearing on the R on 0.5 mi. The trail continues up a rocky grade to a larger clearing on the R at 0.6 mi. This clearing is on an upslope where a building once stood. Now, various objects are found throughout the area. (An informal path once led out of the upper L corner of the clearing to Whitney Lake. It is no longer visible beyond 0.3 mi.)

The woods trail remains a gradual upgrade as it heads W. It nearly levels at 0.8 mi, reaching height of land at 0.9 mi. Then a gradual descent leads to an arrow sign at 1 mi, where the trail leaves the road for a short traverse through the woods to avoid a wet section. Another rise is crossed at 1.2 mi.

The hiker must be careful not to miss the arrow sign at 1.5 mi on the next descent. Here, the trail turns L, off the woods road, and enters the forest. A short, moderate-to-steep downgrade ends at a brook before the trail rejoins the woods road. (At this point there is another arrow sign for hikers traveling the opposite direction.)

A very pleasant forest is found in this region. Easy rolling terrain provides enjoyable walking. Whitney Lake is seen eventually through the trees at R. (At 2.1 and 2.2 mi informal paths once led R approximately 0.3 mi

Along the trail to Pillsbury Lake. Michael N.Kelsey

downslope to a former camp on Whitney Lake. The paths are no longer visible, but this section of the trail parallels the lake, and a bushwhack to the lake should not be difficult.)

The descending trail soon levels, swings R, and then winds back and forth before beginning another downgrade at 2.6 mi. There is a spring on the L at 2.7 mi. Sampson Lake is seen through the trees. A lean-to sign on a large tree once marked a jct at 2.8 mi, but the sign was no longer apparent in 2013. (This side trail leads 0.1 mi to the Sampson Lake lean-to, passing another spring on the way)

From the lean-to jct. the trail has long gradual ups and downs before the last view of Sampson Lake at 3.1 mi. The route then levels and becomes less open. Trail signs are plentiful, but brush is slowly invading the pathway. A short wet section is crossed at 3.3 mi. Soon after, the trail has a long, gradual ascent up a ridge. The path levels for a while before beginning a descent at 3.6 mi.

Crossing very gradually rolling terrain through attractive forest, the trail passes two small wet sections. The trail turns R at 4.8 mi. (There was once a cutoff trail here connecting the N–P Trail, but it has been officially abandoned and is now difficult to find.)

The easy rolling terrain continues to the end of Mud Lake and West Canada Creek. The trail immediately meets the N–P Trail at a jct. at 5.2 mi. Formerly a tricky intersection to spot if traveling in reverse from the N–P Trail, new signs were erected in 2012. (Turning R and walking N, it is 75 ft to the trail crossing over West Canada Creek. A sturdy bridge was built here in 2012 to replace the bridge that washed out in Hurricane Irene the year before. The West Canada Creek lean-to is up the bank on the opposite side of the bridge.)

❄ Trail in winter: This is excellent snowshoe country and good skiing for experts, but far from civilization. Only highly experienced campers should venture into this wild area in winter.

⚹ Distances: To the first arrow sign, 1 mi; to second arrow signs, 1.5 mi; to Sampson Lake lean-to jct.; 2.8 mi, to top of ridge, 3.5 mi; to N–P Trail jct., 5.2 mi (8.3 km). This is 8.5 mi (13.6 km) from Pillsbury Mt. parking area and 14.8 mi (23.7 km) from NY 30 at Mason Lake.

49 Northville–Placid Trail: Piseco to Wakely Dam

Trails Illustrated Map 744: J14

This is one of the most scenic segments of the N-P Trail. The terrain varies from serene lakes to swamp flats to rolling hills, from dense, dark spruce thickets to the awesome vista from the bridge over the outlet of South Lake.

For more information about the N–P Trail, see the *Adirondack Mountain Club Northville–Placid Trail.*

▶Southern trailhead: From the S, leaving the post office in Piseco, drive 0.2 mi W on CR 24 and turn R onto Haskells Rd. Park in the parking area on the R just before the Cold Stream bridge, 0.7 mi from CR 24.◀

▶Northern trailhead: Wakely Dam is at the outlet of Cedar River Flow, 12 mi along Cedar River Rd. Cedar River Rd. is 2.2 mi W of Indian Lake village on NY 28. The N–P Trail passes through the Moose River Recreation Area at Wakely Dam.

From the caretaker cabin at Wakely Dam, pass through the entrance gate to the Moose River Recreation Area. A dirt road leads 1.3 mi W to a jct., where the N–P Trail turns S. Here there is a barrier cable. Blue trail markers guide the hiker along the dirt woods road S. Vehicles can be parked in this area.◀

South to north. From the parking area on Haskells Rd. (0.0 mi), the trail crosses the Cold Stream bridge and private land to a pipe barrier and covered DEC trailhead register at 0.1 mi. The familiar blue markers now guide the hiker onto state land and into the forest. This section follows an old tote road through a stand of mixed hardwoods and is a very enjoyable walk. The long, flat stretch is about a mile long, crossing just one stream at 0.9 mi. (If the water is high in spring, there's a bridge 25 yd off to the R, on a cross-country ski trail.)

The trail eventually curves L and begins a gradual ascent. After steeply pitching downward, it crosses a stream at 2.6 mi. The trail swings NW and the upward climb resumes along rock shoulders. After gaining some 180 ft in elevation the trail levels off. The easily-followed trail crosses several streams and passes a PBM (1962 ft) at 4.3 mi. Just ahead is Fall Stream at 4.4 mi. At one time this was a very heavily used camping spot with numerous clearings. A lean-to is slated for

TRAIL TO ← MILES
W. CANADA LAKE Lean-to 6.5
SPRUCE LAKE 10.3
PISECO 22.0
NYSDEC

FOLLOW MARKERS

TRAIL TO → MILES
CEDAR RIVER Lean-to 4.7
CEDAR RIVER Hdqts. 9.0
BLUE MT. LAKE 22.8
NYSDEC

FOLLOW MARKERS

CAMP ONLY AT DESIGNATED SITES OR 150′ FROM SHORELINE — Thank You —

Michael N. Kelsey

construction at this location. Fall Stream is usually crossed on stones, except in times of high water.

After the crossing, the trail follows the bank for about 150 yd. Then it swings W, away from the stream, and ascends a long, steady grade through some beautiful hardwood forest. It levels off at about 5.5 mi and enters a private property landholding at about 5.8 mi. The trail soon descends to a narrow clearing at 6 mi. The remains of an old camp can be seen to the R, along with barrels and other detritus from past logging operations farther on.

The route crosses a small brook, then pitches up to the end of a clearing at 6.2 mi. Soon after, it descends fairly steeply to the edge of a vlei at 6.6 mi. The hill on the opposite side of the pond once was home to a substantial lumber camp, as evidenced by numerous bed springs, bottles, and other remnants.

The N–P Trail descends to an intersection at 6.7 mi. The route R leads back to the pond and lumber camp area. The N–P Trail continues to the L, as the arrows indicate, to a moderately steep drop, then a brief steep ascent followed by another drop.

A stand of conifers signals the appearance of the Jessup River at 6.8 mi. This crossing can be tricky during snowmelt or after rains. After the crossing, the trail passes two clearings; the second, high above the river, has a fire ring.

The trail now follows an old lumber road that swings R. Partway up a moderate grade, the trail makes a L turn away from the road at 7 mi. (The road R, or E, is the recommended evacuation route to Sled Harbor, Perkins Clearing, and NY 30.) It pitches up a steep grade, and then rejoins the logging road.

The trail swings L and reenters Forest Preserve land. After another ascent, it reaches height of land at 7.5 mi. A slight descent leads to another jct. with an arrow sign. If you're traveling S–N there should be no problem following the trail; if you're heading N–S, be sure to follow the blue markers and arrow signs.

The trail now follows a level woods road for some time. The wet route is made easier by the addition of wooden walkways, some of which are decades old. Watch for the trail to drop down to the R and cross Bloodgood Brook at 8 mi; this can easily be missed.

The trail ascends gradually along a grassy lumber road to another brook at about 8.3 mi. A short steep pitch leads to a gradual descent. An arrow sign at 8.9 mi directs the hiker to the R. Another wet stretch, with some boardwalk, leads to a brook crossing at 9.1 mi. An extensive hand-cut log walkway carries the trail through conifer woods to Spruce Lake.

The first of three lean-tos is visible off a spur to the L at 9.5 mi. The spur continues past the lean-to some 200 ft to the shore of Spruce Lake (elev. 2378 ft). This lean-to was built to replace an old one on the lake shore. Although nicely constructed, it sits directly on the trail, can be a little muddy in front, and is shaded by the forest. From the lean-to it is a short walk to the shoreline of Spruce Lake.

The trail climbs past the lean-to and navigates some steep ascents and descents along the lake before coming to an unmarked jct. for lean-to number two at 10.3 mi. This jct. is easily missed. Look for a big rock with a tree growing on top in the middle of the trail. The side trail climbs over a small rise and descends, leading several hundred yards to the shore and the small clearing containing the lean-to. (Lean-to relocation efforts are underway as this guidebook goes to press. The DEC plans to move the lean-to away from the shoreline to the height of land near the N-P Trail.)

A little farther, the trail dips and then crosses the rocky outlet of Balsam Lake. This crossing can be tricky in high water, requiring navigation of logs and ledges. Balsam Lake is about one-half mile upstream and makes a nice side trip if time permits.

At about 10.5 mi a third jct. is marked by a sign indicating the lean-to. (The side trail, marked with yellow disks, winds its way to the R, eventually reaching a small clearing and then the lean-to.) The clearing before the lean-to is a nice grassy site.

Past the jct. for the third lean-to, the N–P Trail continues to parallel the shoreline of Spruce Lake before leaving it behind at 10.8 mi. A brook crossing at 11.6 mi leads to an increase in elevation of about 100 ft. The trail passes a PBM (2464 ft) at 11.9 mi, with a spring-fed brook to the L. It follows this brook for a time, and crosses another at 12.4 mi.

At 12.7 mi the trail pitches down a steep grade, levels off in a wonderfully fragrant patch of balsam fir, and drops sharply down to beautiful Sampson Bog (elev. 2350 ft). The outlet of this pretty little body of water is crossed on a log bridge.

From the bank of the bog, the trail pitches up through trees before descending to the outlet. It then swings up and away. A steep pitch at 13.8 mi follows a brook crossing. After the end of a vlei at 13.9 mi, another steep pitch follows. The trail crosses two vlei outlets; several stretches of boardwalk can be found here.

At 14.9 mi, distance signs indicate what was once a cross-over route to the Pillsbury Lake trails (trails 47 and 48). This route is no longer maintained and is not useable. The actual jct. with the red-marked Pillsbury Lake trails is at 15.2 mi. This trail, from the Pillsbury Mt. trailhead parking area 8.5 mi E, joins the N–P Trail at this jct. and continues on the N–P Trail to West Lake at West Canada Lakes, one-time home of French Louie. The combination is now known as the French Louie Trail.

The N–P Trail continues from this jct. through some sloppy areas. Finally, at 15.3 mi, it reaches West Canada Creek. A nice new bridge has been constructed here (2012). Previous bridges washed out in storms in 2011 and before than in 2001. The trail continues up the steep bank on the opposite side to the West Canada Creek Lean-to, where it abruptly turns L at the lean-to and goes down a small slope before ascending a grade R toward South Lake.

The trail gently curves around a knoll and then descends toward South Lake in the distance. At the bottom of the grade, look for a side trail L at 15.7 mi that leads to the lean-to on the shore of the lake. The lean-to sits just back from a sandy beach jutting out into the lake. Along with snow-white birches and dark green balsam firs, it makes for quite an idyllic setting.

The N–P Trail continues through a stand of white birches, passing a nice camping spot on the R. It passes some stunted spruces just before coming to an extensive wooden bridge that crosses the outlet of the lake at 15.8 mi. The panoramic view here is magnificent.

Beyond the bridge the trail ascends the divide between South Lake and West Lake. The trail bears L and heads back down. Near the bottom, at 16.3 mi, watch for a rock cairn and trail that leads L to the shore of West Lake and a lean-to remarkably close to the water.

The N–P Trail leads straight ahead from this jct. to a grassy clearing at 16.4 mi. This is the site of the ranger cabin that was removed by burning in the winter of 1987. All that remains are the stones of the fireplace and foundation. The remains of another fireplace off to the side are those of French Louie's. There was to be a new, larger cabin for his paying guests; building the fireplace was as far as he got. In the middle of the clearing is a signpost and DEC register. The red-marked trail from this jct. leads about 2.5 mi to the lean-to on Brooktrout Lake (trail 50).

From the DEC register, the trail heads due E along an old tote road toward Mud Lake. Along the trail are remnants of the old telephone line that linked the West Canada Lakes station with the Cedar Lakes station: creosote-soaked poles, coiled telephone wire, and numerous holes in the ground where the poles once stood.

At 16.5 mi the trail abruptly leaves the old tote road and enters the woods. (This rerouting was necessitated by beaver activity flooding the dilapidated old log bridge ahead.) Carefully follow the markers and blue tape across a woody area of difficult footing, with large rocks and downed trees.

The trail crosses a stream at 16.6 mi and another at 16.7 mi. At 16.8 mi it rejoins the tote road coming from the water that was bypassed to the S.

At 18.4 mi, the trail crosses Mud Creek on a log bridge. The remnants of several other bridges at this site testify to the meandering water's potential. After an old lumbered area with tall grass along the tote road, the trail enters a more forested spot at about 18.6 mi, followed by an ascent up a steep pitch. Thereafter, it continues to climb on an easy grade until another pitch ends at a height of land at 17.2 mi.

The trail descends past a small vlei on the L at 19.4 mi. Shortly thereafter, Kings Pond becomes visible on the R. The trail crosses its outlet and parallels the pond's shore for a time, then leaves it to climb NE through a col. It descends steadily to an unmarked jct. at 20.1 mi. (A tree with an easily-missed lean-to carving marks the start of a trail that eventually sports some yellow markers and goes straight ahead to the E. After some wet spots, the trail travels 0.5 mi to a lean-to on the shore of Third Cedar Lake, elevation 2442 ft.)

From the jct. the N–P Trail turns sharply L, drops down a slight grade, and crosses a brook on walkways. The trail then heads away from the lake and swings NW. At 20.9 mi it begins the long, steady ascent up what is known as Cobble Hill. The route gains about 200 ft elevation before reaching height of land at 21 mi. The trail is fairly level for a good distance before descending an easy grade

West Lake. Michael N. Kelsey

to the NE. Beaver Pond comes into view through the trees to the L, and shortly thereafter, First Cedar Lake to the R.

At 22.1 mi an unmarked trail joins from the L. It leads about 0.2 mi to a lovely spring. At the bottom of the grade, at 22.2 mi, an unmarked trail ascends the R bank of an old tote road and leads to a lean-to on First Cedar Lake, known as the Beaver Pond Lean-to. This lean-to is very nicely situated above the lake, with several overgrown old tote roads leading away from the site.

The N–P Trail continues past this jct. The landscape opens up as the trail crosses a bridge over the outlet between Beaver Pond on the L and First Cedar Lake on the R at 22.3 mi. Just past this spot, a trail L goes to some camping sites on a knoll in the trees.

The trail then climbs over a low shoulder of land and swings away from the lake before reaching a trail jct. at 22.4 mi. This can be easily missed by the north-bound hiker, because the side trail descends L at a sharp angle. The yellow-marked trail looks seldom used and is correspondingly rough, although it is a very pleasant woods walk. It leads first to Lost Pond at 2.2 mi, then 10 mi to Otter Brook bridge (trail 51).

The N–P Trail continues a short distance downhill to the site of the former interior caretaker's cabin at First Cedar Lake. In this grassy clearing, at 22.9 mi, sits First Cedar Lake Lean-to. It is surrounded by a variety of rusted artifacts and the remains of what was evidently a food-storage cellar.

The trail continues to another clearing with large birches at 23 mi. This area was once the location of a lean-to, but now provides a very picturesque tent site. Just beyond, at 23.1 mi, the trail arrives at a DEC trail register and Cedar Lakes Dam. At one time there was a walkway across the top of the dam. Signs warn against trying to cross the dam now, because it is extremely dangerous; instead, look for the trail on the R that crosses on a very nice treated lumber bridge about 50 yd beyond the dam. There are several attractive camping spots on the opposite side. The yellow-marked trail there leads 10.6 mi to Perkins Clearing Rd., then Mason Rd., and eventually NY 30 (trail 46).

The N–P Trail continues past the dam, following the familiar blue markers. This segment of the trail is pleasant, with the Cedar River visible below through the trees. The trail ascends several steep grades before resuming a gentle downhill path that leads to Lamphere Ridge.

The trail crosses a small brook and soon begins to ascend. At 25.9 mi, a steep pitch gains 200 ft elevation. The trail parallels some rock cliffs to the L along the top of the ridge.

After this level stretch the trail descends gradually to a marked trail jct. at 27.1 mi. The red-marked trail that enters from the R, Sucker Brook Trail (trail 52), leads 1 mi to the Colvin Brook lean-to, and 7.9 mi E to the Lewey Lake Public Campground on NY 30.

Past this jct. the trail continues to descend the ridge on a pleasant route through rolling hills and an emerging hardwood forest. At 27.5 mi it crosses a brook on a bridge.

At 28.3 mi the trail comes to a jct., with another in view just beyond. They both lead 0.1 mi to the Cedar River Lean-to, also known as Carry (as in canoe carry) Lean-to. This lean-to sits on an open grassy knoll above the twisting, turning Cedar River. From the front of the lean-to is a postcard Adirondack view downstream.

Past the two lean-to jcts., the trail quickly becomes an old two-rut tote road that sometimes sports recent tire tracks, signifying that the trail is no longer on Forest Preserve land. The road crosses a truck-grade log bridge at 28.6 mi.

At 29 mi the route joins a two-lane dirt road and follows it until it merges with a larger one at 29.2 mi. The land shows all the evidence of lumbering, such as grassy clearings and numerous tote roads, in the not-too-distant past. The blue-marked N–P Trail is easy to follow. It crosses Wilson Brook on a bridge at 29.3 mi. A sign on a beech tree indicates the presence nearby of a PBM signaling 2150 ft elevation.

At 30.1 mi the road passes closer to the Cedar River Flow and turns a bend to the L. This dirt road leads around Sturges Hills, heading NW before turning NE and crossing Payne Brook at 31.1 mi. Another dirt road joins this one from the L with a pipe barrier at 31.3 mi. There is a small parking area and register here; be sure to sign the register.

This dirt road, part of the Moose River Plains Wild Forest (MRPWF), now follows a gentle descent, arriving at Wakely Dam and the buildings of the Cedar River Caretaker Station and public campground at 32.4 mi.

❄ Trail in winter: Because most of the access roads are either not totally plowed in winter or are snowmobile trails, there is little use by skiers or snowshoers of this section in winter. It is extremely desolate and should be entered in winter only by a party of adequate numbers and winter camping skills to be completely self-sufficient. Temperatures regularly plunge well below zero, with persistent winds. This is not a setting for winter camping by the unskilled. There is a vehicle parking area several miles before Wakely Dam off the dirt road. This is to accommodate the numerous snowmobile trailers and vehicles in the winter months.

🐾 Distance: South to north: to Fall Stream, 4.4 mi; to Jessup River, 6.8 mi; to First lean-to at Spruce Lake, 9.5 mi; to Second lean-to at Spruce Lake, 10.3 mi; to Third lean-to at Spruce Lake, 10.8 mi; to Sampson Bog outlet, 12.7 mi; to Sampson Lake and Perkins Clearing Trail jct., 15.2 mi; to West Canada Creek Lean-to, 15.3 mi; to South Lake Lean-to, 15.7 mi; to West Lake Lean-to, 16.3 mi; to former caretaker clearing, West Lake, 16.4 mi; to Beaver Pond Lean-to,24.2 mi; to First Cedar Lake Lean-to, 24.9 mi; to Cedar Lakes Dam (access route to Perkins Clearing), 23.1 mi; to Sucker Brook Trail, 27.1 mi; to Cedar River Lean-to jct., 28.3 mi; to Wakely Dam Cedar River Caretaker Station, 32.6 mi (52.2 km).

50 West Canada Lakes via Brooktrout Lake
Trails Illustrated Map 744: M12

This trail offers visits to several bodies of water, including Falls Pond, Brooktrout Lake, and West Lake, that are beautiful and remote. The trail lies wholly in the West Canada Lake Wilderness Area. It starts from Indian River Rd. as a yellow trail and goes SE 5.6 mi to the lean-to at the E end of Brooktrout Lake. Then, as a red-marked trail, it continues E to the lean-to at the NE end of West Lake at 8 mi and goes S a short distance to end at 8.2 mi at the N–P Trail by the foundation of a former caretaker's lodge on the E shore of the lake. (Another lean-to is located 0.2 mi S on the lake.) The trail provides the closest access to West Lake from a drivable road.

Along the first 2.2 mi of the trail there are side trails leading to three ponds: Falls Pond, Deep Lake, and Wolf Lake. The first is especially worth a visit. There are various ascents and descents along the trail, the principal change in elevation being a 500 ft ascent along easy or moderate grades in the first 1.5 mi.

▶Trailhead: Start at the jct. of Moose River Rd. and Otter Brook Rd. in the MRPWF (8.3 mi from the W entrance and 12.9 mi from the E entrance). Drive S on Otter Brook Rd. for 3.3 mi to the crossing of Otter Brook. Continue past the Otter Brook Rd. to the Cedar Lakes Trail (trail 51) road on the L just after the bridge. After another 1 mi (4.3 mi from road jct.), park on the L in an area with a trailhead sign where the road bends R. There are yellow DEC markers to Brooktrout Lake, then red DEC markers to the N–P Trail.◀

Heading SE (0.0 mi), the old logging road gradually ascends through small tree growth. At 1.5 mi, a yellow side trail goes R (W) to Falls Pond. (The yellow-marked Falls Pond trail goes W. At 0.3 mi from the main trail, where conifers begin to prevail, the trail crosses a wet area and the pond's outlet and then traverses a stand of spruce-fir. The trail reaches the pond next to its outlet and continues another 70 yd, going R in a muddy section along the water's edge and ending at an informal campsite at a N corner of the pond. By following a narrow path R, W, near the rock-lined water's edge, you will arrive at a point of land with an informal campsite and a better view of the pond. Small, rocky islands—including one rock split by freeze-thaw cycles over the years—lie off the shore here. The pond is an attractive, conifer-lined body of water at an elevation of 2500 ft.)

The West Canada Lakes Trail, after further ascent and a descent, spans Wolf Creek on a bridge at 2.2 mi, where an open area has the remains of a logging operation. Some 140 yd beyond, in an open area of bedrock, a yellow side trail goes L and soon forks into two trails leading to Deep Lake and Wolf Lake. These bodies of water are at high elevation and devoid of fish owing to acid rain.

The combined yellow-marked trail goes E as a woods road with mudholes, splitting at 0.1 with Wolf Lake L and Deep Lake R. The Deep Lake trail ascends over 200 ft to an elevation of 2800 ft. The trail narrows and descends approximately SE the rest of the way. It enters a spruce-fir forest and ends at an informal campsite at the N end of Deep Lake, 1 mi from the West Canada Lakes Trail. Typical of the region, the pond is conifer-lined and partly boggy on the shoreline. Despite its name, it is shallow from the inlet stream next to the end of the trail out to a large rock R.

[The Wolf Lake trail is for wetland devotees who don't mind getting their feet wet. From the fork with the Deep Lake trail, it goes N and E at first as a grassy avenue through a new growth of trees. It reaches the wetland of Wolf Creek on the L with nice views of a beaver pond at 0.3 mi from the West Canada Lakes Trail jct. (0.2 mi from the Deep Lake split). This is a good turnaround point. The trail is flooded—not because of beavers, as it is higher than the beaver pond—and it goes through wet, marshy sections interspersed with areas of bedrock. The route narrows, and at 1 mi from the West Canada Lakes Trail one has to wade through a flooded marsh to reach an adequate view of Wolf Lake. It is 2600 ft in elevation, lined by wetlands and conifers.]

Beyond the Deep-Wolf side trail at 2.2 mi, the main trail continues as a wide route, much of it stony, with some bedrock. It reaches its highest elevation of about 2650 ft and after 2.5 mi becomes narrower, often stony or grassy, with many wet places. At 3 mi there is a beaver pond and a long curving beaver dam with an old moss-encrusted beaver lodge in view. Larger tree specimens begin to appear. At 3.4 mi, the formerly logged-over area ends and the trail becomes a footpath in a mature forest.

The trail crosses the outlet of Twin Lakes and Deep Lake at 3.8 mi. It descends moderately steeply past stately yellow birches to parallel the NE side of Brooktrout Lake, visible through the trees. After some ups and downs, it passes an informal campsite on the R at 5.5 mi, and at 5.6 mi a spur trail leads 25 yd R to the Brooktrout Lake Lean-to.

The lean-to faces a rock wall that serves as backing for the fireplace. A few yards by trail through dense spruce brings one to the E corner of this attractive lake, 2369 ft in elevation. It has a rocky shoreline fringed with conifers; a bluff rises from the far end. Walk L along the rocks at the edge of the lake for a more open view.

The West Canada Lakes Trail continues SE with the yellow markers replaced by red ones. Between Brooktrout Lake and West Lake, the trail crosses the inconspicuous divide between the St. Lawrence and Hudson River drainage basins. At 6.3 mi, 40 yd beyond a great boulder on the R, a spur trail goes R 30 yd to an informal campsite on the westernmost corner of beautiful West Lake. Beyond the far end of the lake one sees Pillsbury Mt., 3597 ft elevation.

After a short steep climb, the trail parallels the N side of the lake. This is an especially attractive section with some large yellow birch and several open glimpses of the lake. There is a short stretch of open wetland with a view L of a steep ridge (Twin Lakes Mt.).

At 7.9 mi, West Canada Lake Lean-to 2 is located in the woods, with the nearby lake visible through the trees on the R. Just beyond, the trail passes the edge of the lake's NE corner. A shallow sandy bottom, a nearby island, and a view of South Lake Mt. rising from the far side of the lake are attractive features of this location, just off the N–P Trail and so possibly not used as much as the next lean-to 0.5 mi S.

The trail goes S on the E side of the lake, passing through a stand of spruce-fir and crossing the lake's broad outlet. There is an informal campsite nearby. At 8.2 mi (13.2 km) the trail ends in a field at a jct. with the N–P Trail (trail 49), which makes a sharp turn here. On the R is the site of the former caretaker's lodge and French Louie's fireplace, with a fine view overlooking the lake.

Going straight ahead (S) on the broad, blue-marked N–P Trail, one reaches a side trail leading to West Canada Lake Lean-to 1 at 0.2 mi from the jct. This nice shelter on the E shore has a good view of the lake with its clean-cut, conifer-lined shores fringed by highlands. There are rocks along the edge here and a small island nearby to complete the idyllic scene.

From the end of the West Canada Lakes Trail, and turning L (E) on the N–P Trail, one reaches an informal campsite L in 115 yd. To make a circuit hike rather than a round-trip, continue E and NE for 6.3 mi on the N–P Trail, passing Mud Lake and two separate lean-tos located off to the R on Cedar Lakes. Turn L on the yellow-marked Otter Brook Rd. to Cedar Lakes Trail (trail 51) and follow it 8.4 mi NW and W to Otter Brook Rd., from where it is 1.5 mi W and S along Otter Brook and Indian River Rds. back to the West Canada Lakes trailhead at Indian River Rd. This makes a total of 24.4 mi for the circuit hike, briefly described in the reverse direction in the description for Cedar Lakes Trail (trail 51).

❃ Trail in winter: This trail is very remote. It is 20 mi from the nearest winter trailhead, the end of snowplowing on Cedar River Rd. A more practical access for winter backpackers is via the N–P Trail.

🏃 Distances: Indian River Rd. trailhead to Falls Pond, 1.5 mi; to Deep Lake and Wolf Lake, 3.2 mi; to Brooktrout Lake Lean-to, 5.6 mi; to West Canada Lake Lean-to 2, 7.9 mi; to N–P Trail, 8.2 mi (13.1 km). To West Canada Lake Lean-to 1, 8.4 mi; to Cedar Lake Trail, 14.5 mi; to trailhead via Cedar Lakes Trail (trail 51) and roads, 24.4 mi (39 km).

51 Otter Brook Road to Cedar Lakes

Trails Illustrated Map 744: N13

▶Trailhead: Start at the jct. of Moose River Rd. and Otter Brook Rd. in the MRPWF (8.3 mi from the W entrance and 12.9 mi from the E entrance). Drive S on Otter Brook Rd. for 3.3 mi to the crossing of Otter Brook, turning L immediately after crossing the bridge. This L branch is the continuation of Otter Brook Rd. (The main road R continues as Indian River Rd.) Go 0.6 mi above and parallel to the brook until you reach a barrier and trailhead.◀

From the barrier (0.0 mi), the yellow-marked trail heads E on a logging road on the N boundary of the West Canada Lakes Wilderness, crossing a number of streams, then turns R into the wilderness area on a logging road and goes generally SE. It crosses Jimmy Creek on a bridge at 1.7 mi. The trail descends sharply at 3.3 mi (offering views not available earlier) and crosses a stream at 3.4 mi via wading, rocks, or fallen trees to an informal campsite on the other side. Avoid the trail E from a clearing with a large machine, apparently a piece of old logging equipment, L at 5.8 mi. In another 0.2 mi a spur trail coming in from the S, also yellow marked, but unmaintained, leads L (E) 0.5 mi to Lost Pond.

The route changes to a footpath, ascends 300 ft, and crosses the divide between the St. Lawrence and Hudson River basins. The trail then descends, passes around the NE end of Beaver Pond, and ends at the blue-marked Northville–Placid (N–P) Trail near the N end of Cedar Lakes at 8.4 mi. See *Adirondack Mountain Club Northville–Placid Trail* (trail 49 in this volume).

To the L (E) on the N–P Trail it is 0.7 mi to a lean-to at the N end of First Cedar Lake. A little beyond it is the dam in the outlet of Cedar Lakes, which is the beginning of the Cedar River. The beautiful Cedar Lakes are a single body of water 2 mi long, divided into three segments. At 2442 ft, it is one of the highest large Adirondack lakes.

Going R (SW) on the N–P Trail from the end of the Cedar Lakes Trail, at 0.3 mi there is a lean-to 100 yd to the L of the trail by the Beaver Pond outlet and First Cedar Lake.

If you wish to make a circuit backpacking hike rather than a round-trip, continue SW on the N–P Trail, passing a side trail on the L at 2.3 mi leading 0.5 mi to a lean-to on Third Cedar Lake. Later the trail goes W, passing Mud Lake and reaching a jct. with the red-marked West Canada Lakes Trail via Brooktrout Lake (trail 50) at 6.3 mi. This is near the site of the former caretaker's cabin on the E shore of beautiful West Lake, one of the West Canada Lakes. From there it is 8.2 mi NW on the West Canada Lakes via Brooktrout Lake Trail, and another 1.5 mi on the Indian River and Otter Brook Rds. back to the Cedar Lakes trailhead. Total distance is 24.4 mi (39.4 km), not including any side trails taken.

❄ Trail in winter: This trail is very remote. It is 20 mi from the nearest winter trailhead, the end of snowplowing on Cedar River Rd. Access to the West Canada Lakes is more reasonably done via the N–P Trail.

⚙ Distances: To Jimmy Creek bridge, 1.7 mi; to stream ford, 3.4 mi; to Lost Pond spur, 6 mi; to N–P Trail jct., 8.4 mi (13.4 km). To first Cedar Lake lean-to N of jct., 9.1 mi; to Beaver Pond Outlet lean-to S of jct., 8.7 mi; to West Canada Lakes Trail (trail 50), 14.7 mi; to loop back to Indian River Rd. by West Canada Lakes Trail, 22.1 mi; to loop back to trailhead, 24.4 mi (39 km).

52 Sucker Brook

Trails Illustrated Map 744: N16

The Sucker Brook trail is a connector trail to the Northville–Placid (N–P) Trail (trail 49). It is not heavily used because considerable climbing is required to reach the col between 3742 ft Lewey and 3447 ft Cellar Mts. However, it is a true wilderness trail with much to offer the hiker, especially the backpacker on a weekend trip. Those pursuing the Adirondack Hundred Highest list frequent this trail in order to climb Lewey, Cellar, and 3860 ft Blue Ridge Mts., which rank 69, 96, and 56 highest, respectively.

▶Trailhead: The trailhead is reached off the W side of NY 30, N of Lewey Lake. Just N of the bridge over the Lewey Lake outlet, a macadam road heads W into the state campground. A sign marks the trailhead a short distance down the road on the R. Please do not obstruct the campground road. Parking is available at a large pullout on the L, 0.3 mi N of the Lewey Lake outlet bridge.◀

The trail heads W through a hardwood forest. Wide and well-marked with red DEC trail markers, it climbs very gradually. It turns R on a woods road at 0.4 mi and then, within a few yards, L off the road at a DEC trail register. Sucker Brook can be heard, but not seen, to the L. A large tributary stream is crossed at 1.5 mi. A steady grade proceeds upward to 2.7 mi, where the grade levels. Then, at 3.1 mi, the route markedly steepens to the col between Lewey and Cellar Mts. at 3.5 mi and an elevation of 2870 ft (1210 ft higher than the trailhead). (This col is often used as the jump-off point for the relatively easy, open-woods bushwhack up Lewey Mt. and for the more difficult bushwhack through blowdown up Cellar Mt.) The col is level and has ferns and red spruce.

As the trail begins its descent beyond the col, a significant difference is evident. The trail is now much more a path. It is easy to follow, however, and is well marked. It is a real wilderness trail from this point forward.

The trail crosses Colvin Brook, reached at 4.4 mi, ten times before diverging

Lewey Lake view. Mark Bowie

from it. The trail passes through a swampy area shortly after the tenth crossing, but the remainder of the way to the lean-to is level and dry.

The trail reaches the lean-to beside Cedar River at 6.6 mi. The river can usually be rock-hopped, although it is quite wide. The trail heads NW another 1.1 mi, intersecting the N–P Trail (trail 49) at 7.7 mi. (From this point, it is 3.5 mi S over Lamphere Ridge to the dam at First Cedar Lake and 6 mi N to Wakely Dam.)

❄ Trail in winter: The trail to the col is a good access route for winter bushwhacks of Cellar and Lewey Mts. Not recommended for winter use beyond the col.

🏃 Distances: To tributary crossing, 1.5 mi; to col, 3.5 mi; to Colvin Brook, 4.4 mi; to lean-to on Cedar River, 6.6 mi; to N–P Trail, 7.7 mi (12.3 km). Ascent to col, 1210 ft (369 m).

Sprague Pond

Trails Illustrated Map 744: Q16

Sprague Pond is a large, attractive body of water on state land. The trail follows a firm woods road and is readily conducive to portaging a canoe.

▶ Trailhead: Access is off the N side of Cedar River Rd., 2.2 mi W of Indian Lake village. Turn off NY 28/30 and drive 4.3 mi W on Cedar River Rd. A large parking pullout is on the S side of the road and a yellow barrier gate indicates the trailhead across the road. There is no sign. Coming from Wakely Dam, the trailhead is 1.1 mi E of the land formerly known as McCanes Resort. ◀

The trail heads N on a nearly level, wide woods road. At 0.4 mi, Sprague Pond can be seen through the trees. The trail curves down a gentle grade to the shore.

This is an ideal picnic spot.

❋ Trail in winter: This can be an interesting little trail for an afternoon outing.

🚶 Distance: To Sprague Pond, 0.4 mi (0.6 km).

53 Wakely Mt.

Trails Illustrated Map 744: P15

Wakely Mt. is only 256 ft short of being a 4000 ft peak. It ranks 67 on the Adirondack Hundred Highest list. The trail ascends 1194 ft in the last 1.1 mi, and a fire tower is found on the summit.

▶Trailhead: Access is via Cedar River Rd. This road is off the W side of NY 28/30 on a sharp curve, 2.2 mi W of Indian Lake village. Drive along Cedar River Rd. 11.6 mi to the trailhead sign. A large parking area is on the R off the road.◀

From the trailhead (0.0 mi), walk NW along a gravel road. The red DEC trail markers are infrequent. A brief glimpse of the summit can be had at 0.3 mi. The remains of an old lumber camp are found over a bank L at 0.7 mi. The trail passes by a side road at R and then crosses a stream on a bridge at 1.1 mi. The route parallels the stream for a short time before veering away.

The trail crosses two more streams before the Wakely Mt. tower sign comes into view R at 1.9 mi. The clearing, visible from the jct., is the site of an old beaver pond and worth a brief visit.

The trail turns R and climbs steeply to the summit. Yellow and red markers are intermixed on the ascent, and unmarked trails branch off the main trail at several points. A side trail to the R leads to a helipad site 240 ft from the fire tower clearing.

The summit fire tower, from which views are plentiful, is at 3 mi. Ground views are only to the SE toward Cedar River Flow.

❋ Trail in winter: Wakely Mt. is a short but rugged little climb in winter. However, from December to April, Cedar River Rd. is plowed only to a point 4.6 mi from the trailhead. Beyond, the road is a winter snowmobile trail.

🚶 Distances: To first view of summit, 0.3 mi; to logging camp, 0.7 mi; to first stream crossing, 1.1 mi; to fire tower sign, 1.9 mi; to summit, 3 mi (4.8 km). Ascent, 1635 ft (498 m). Elevation, 3744 ft (1141 m).

54 Northville–Placid Trail: Wakely Dam to NY 28/30 at Lake Durant

Trails Illustrated Map 744: P15

A reroute of the N–P Trail off Cedar River Rd. was completed in 2009. The old section of Northville–Placid (N–P) Trail from Cedar River Rd. N of Wakely Dam through the former McCanes Resort land, N to just S of Stephens Pond Lean-to, is privately owned and has been permanently closed to the public.

Wakely Mountain fire tower. Michael N. Kelsey

The new trail begins about 0.7 mi N of Wakely Dam. The first section follows an old logging road (at L, W) known as Gould Rd. before it heads into the woods on the newly constructed foot trail. (Careful observers will note the remnants of old tote roads along the way.) The forest changes from birch to maple, including some very large old specimens, before blending into balsam fir and mixed hardwoods. The trail crosses numerous small streams. Midway through, Stephens Pond is a pretty little pond with a lean-to. It is visited principally by backpackers on the N–P Trail, but also makes a nice day trip from the N. The pond has a variety of birds and water life. Beavers have dammed up its S end and built a large lodge along the shore. To the N, a 3000 ft ridge is prominent. Be sure to store food properly when camping here; bear sightings have been on the rise.

▶Northern trailhead: Access is from NY 28/30 at Lake Durant state campground, 2.6 mi SE of the NY 30/28/28N intersection in Blue Mt. Lake village. A large DEC sign marks the point where the N–P Trail crosses the highway; ample parking space is provided on each side of the road. By parking here, rather than driving into the campsite, one is not required to pay a day-use fee.◀

North to south: Leaving the highway (0.0 mi), the route climbs the bank from the parking zone on the S side of NY 28/30, following blue trail markers. It crosses Rock River on a bridge, then turns R and crosses the parking area near the bathing area.

Follow the paved road S from the parking area. Passing over the Stephens Pond outlet bridge, the route turns L at 0.4 mi onto the campground truck road at campsite number 3. A gradual upgrade leads to a jct. at 0.8 mi. The road turns L up a hill. Continue straight ahead.

Another jct. with a DEC trail register is reached at 0.9 mi. The unmarked trail R heads back to the campground road. The route passes through an open grassy area at 1 mi.

The trail continues SW at a gradual incline to a jct. at 2.7 mi. The red-marked trail R leads 0.9 mi to Cascade Pond (trail 55). The N–P Trail goes down an incline to the L, descending 150 ft before reaching Stephens Pond. A side trail L at 3.3 mi leads 85 ft to the Stephens Pond lean-to. Continue straight ahead. At 3.8 mi the 2009 reroute of the N–P Trail is reached. The trail passes through a forest of mature hemlocks before crossing a plank bridge at 6.9 mi. The first of two log bridges is crossed at 8.6 mi and then at 8.9 mi after a slight ascent. At 9.9 mi the trail leaves the Forest Preserve. It joins Gould Rd. at 11.4 mi. An arrow sign is found here. Turn L and follow the gravel road for 1 mi. The N–P Trail turns R onto Cedar River Road at 12.4 mi. The Wakely Mt. Trail (trail 53) comes in from the R at 12.8 mi. A Wakely Dam DEC signpost is reached at 13.1 mi.

❄ Trail in Winter: During snowmobile season, Cedar River Rd. is maintained only as far as Brown's farm, 4.4 mi NE of the intersection with the new trail and Wakely Dam. Beyond Brown's farm, the road is a busy snowmobile trail.

Ski and snowshoe day trippers should plan an out and back, starting at the N–P trailhead parking on NY 28/30, 2 mi E of Blue Mt. Lake hamlet near Lake Durant. One can also stage a car at either Brown's farm or the N–P trailhead parking on NY 28/30 near Lake Durant, and plan on a 15 mi hike with 4.4 mi on busy snowmobile trails. Mrs. Brown charges for parking.

🏃 Distances: To campground road, 0.4 mi; to DEC trail register, 0.9 mi; to Cascade Pond Trail, 2.7 mi; to Stephen's Pond Trail, 3.3 mi; to N–P Trail reroute, 3.8 mi; to Gould Rd., 11.4 mi; to Cedar River Rd., 12.4 mi; to Wakely Mt. Trail, 12.8 mi; to Wakely Dam, 13.1 mi (21 km).

Upper Sargent Pond campsite. Michael N. Kelsey

Blue Mountain Lake and Sargent Ponds Section

 Summer campers and hikers have been coming to the Blue Mt. Lake region ever since Henry Eckford surveyed the Eckford Chain (Blue Mt. Lake, Eagle Lake, Utowana Lake) in 1811. It cost $10.00 for a stagecoach ticket from North Creek to Blue Mt. Lake in the 1870s. A traveler could reach Blue Mt. Lake from New York City in 26 hours after being conveyed by boat, train, and stagecoach. The first hotel in the world to have electric lights in every room was Prospect House at Blue Mt. Lake. Today, the nationally recognized Adirondack Museum is found here, and the village has become a center for Adirondack artists and craftspeople.

More famed for its waterways than its hiking trails, the Blue Mt. Lake region nevertheless has several fine trails. Blue Mt. and Castle Rock provide places for exquisite vistas. Many ponds offer destinations for pleasant day trips. The Northville–Placid (N–P) Trail passes E of Blue Mt. on its way to Long Lake.

Recommended hikes in this section include:

SHORT HIKES
Rock Lake: 1.4 mi (2.2 km) round trip. A level walk to a pretty lake.

Cascade Pond: 5.6 mi (9 km) round trip. An attractive combination of forest and ponds.

MODERATE HIKES
Castle Rock: 3 or 4 mi (4.8 or 6.4 km) round trip. Some climbing, but not too difficult. A beautiful view of Blue Mt. Lake is your reward.

Tirrell Pond from Blue Mt. trailhead: 6.6 mi (10.6 km) round trip. A woods walk to a sandy beach and a very attractive pond.

HARDER HIKES
Blue Mt.: 4 mi (6.4 km) round trip. A short climb with a 1550 ft ascent to the summit at 3759 ft (1146 m)

Tioga Point: 12.2 mi (19.5 km). On the E side of Raquette Lake. A beautiful and popular destination, accessed from the Long Lake area.

Michael N. Kelsey

	Trail Described	Total Miles (one way)		Page
55	Cascade Pond	2.8	(4.5 km)	136
56	Wilson Pond–Cascade Pond Connector	1.4	(2.2 km)	137
57	Wilson Pond	2.9	(4.6 km)	138
58	Rock Lake	0.7	(1.1 km)	139
59	Rock River	3.0	(4.8 km)	140
60	Sawyer Mt.	1.1	(1.8 km)	140
61	N–P Trail to Tirrell Pond	4.7	(7.5 km)	141
62	Tirrell Pond from Blue Mt. Trailhead	3.3	(5.3 km)	143
63	Blue Mt.	2.0	(3.2 km)	143
64	Upper Sargent Pond	4.7	(7.5 km)	144
65	South Castle Rock Trail	1.5	(2.4 km)	146
66	North Castle Rock Trail	2.0	(3.2 km)	146
	Blue Mountain Lake from South Castle Rock Trail	0.3	(0.5 km)	147
67	Sargent Ponds Loop	3.3	(5.3 km)	148
68	Tioga Point	6.1	(9.8 km)	149

55 Cascade Pond

Trails Illustrated Map 744: R15

The Cascade Pond Trail has an unusual variety of water and forest settings of great beauty. It can be combined with the Northville–Placid Trail (trail 54) as it skirts Stephens Pond towards Lake Durant or combined with the Wilson Pond Connector Trail (trail 56) and the Wilson Pond trail (trail 57) for a delightful loop. The latter requires a car at each trailhead.

▶Trailhead: The trailhead is reached by driving E on NY 28/30 from the NY 30/28/28N intersection in Blue Mt. Lake village. Turn R onto Durant Rd. 0.9 mi from the intersection, then travel 0.2 mi to the small trailhead sign on the L at a narrow dirt road just before a cemetery. Parking is at the edge of the road.◀

From the trailhead (0.0 mi), red DEC trail markers lead to a DEC sign at 0.1 mi identifying a R turn. A small brook is crossed as the path heads W.

At 0.6 mi, a small decline leads to a 200 ft bridge across Rock Pond. This is a very attractive body of water. Across the bridge, a short, steep section heads S to the top of a minor ridge. The trail then descends steeply to a valley floor, crossing a stream at 1.1 mi.

Traveling W again, the route winds its way up a beautiful wooded valley. There is a brief incline at 1.8 mi as the trail climbs up to level ground. At 2.3 mi, the trail turns L at a DEC sign and heads E. The yellow-blazed trail to the R is the Wilson Pond–Cascade Pond Connector Trail (trail 56). The tree type is now mostly spruce. The trail narrows as it approaches Cascade Pond. There is a nice clearing at the pond's outlet where the Cascade Pond lean-to was once located

Cascade Pond lean-to. Michael N. Kelsey

at 2.8 mi. The clearing offers a commanding view of the pond. Cross the outlet and climb E, away from the lake, to find the new lean-to secluded in the woods. Although within sight of the lake and in earshot of the outlet stream, the views are not as expansive as that of the old lean-to site, now marked as a noncamping site. (The trail continues around the E side of the lake another 0.9 mi to the jct. with the N–P Trail, 0.6 mi N of Stephens Pond.)

✵ Trail in winter: This is an excellent ski route when combined with the Northville–Placid Trail by Stephens Pond to Lake Durant (trail 53).

🐾 Distances: To Rock Pond, 0.6 mi; to stream crossing, 1.1 mi; to end of valley, 1.8 mi; to jct., 2.3 mi; to Cascade Pond, 2.8 mi (4.5 km).

56 Wilson Pond–Cascade Pond Connector
Trails Illustrated Map 744: R15

The Wilson Pond–Cascade Pond Connector Trail is a short but scenic route by a pretty lake on a wide trail. It allows hikers to visit both ponds in a single day or extend the trip farther to Stephens Pond.

▶Trailhead: Access is the same as for Cascade Pond Trail (trail 55). The yellow blazed trail begins 2.3 miles from the Cascade Pond trailhead.◀

Turn R at an unmarked jct. 2.3 mi into the Cascade Pond Trail. A sign indicates that the Cascade Pond Trail continues 0.5 to the L. A yellow surveyor's tape (2012) marks the start of the Wilson Pond–Cascade Pond Connector Trail on the R (0.0 mi). Although the trail is well marked with yellow DEC discs starting at 0.1 mi and continuing the whole way, the start of the trail is unmarked (2012). The trail is wide and easy to follow, as it descends and crosses a log bridge at 0.2 mi. Soon an unnamed pond becomes visible through the trees on the R. A second bridge is crossed at 0.5 mi as the trail parallels the pond's shore. At 1mi the trail begins its long descent, crossing a small stream at 1.2 mi. The trail veers R here, descends farther, and then turns sharply L at 1.3 mi. A tree with yellow and pink flagging wrapped around it is located here (2012). A herd path goes R and drops to a bend in the red-blazed Wilson Pond Trail (trail 57) just after it crosses the Long Pond outlet. Turn L at the flagging-wrapped tree and follow yellow discs along a less discernible trail. Following a ridge, the yellow-blazed trail ends abruptly at 1.4 mi. The red-blazed footpath for Wilson Pond Trail leads in either direction. Go L for Wilson Pond or R to reach NY 28.

❄ Trail in Winter: This trail is excellent for skiers when joined with trails 55 and 57.

🐾 Distance: to first log bridge, 0.2 mi; to second log bridge, 0.5 mi; to start of descent, 1 mi; to Wilson Pond Trail, 1.4 mi (2.2 km).

57 Wilson Pond

Trails Illustrated Map 744: R15

Wilson Pond is an attractive body of water in the Blue Ridge Wilderness Area. The trail exhibits considerable variety in both conditions and flora. There is a lean-to at the pond. The trail can be joined with the Wilson Pond–Cascade Pond Connector (trail 56) and the Cascade Pond Trail (trail 55) for a nice loop. Those pursuing the Adirondack Hundred Highest list sometimes use Wilson Pond as a starting point to ascend nearby Blue Ridge Mt.

▶Trailhead: The trailhead is off the SE side of NY 28, opposite Eagle Lake. At a point 2.8 mi W of the jct. of NY 28, NY 28N, and NY 30 in Blue Mt. Lake village, there is a small parking area. The trailhead sign (0.0 mi) is located a few feet into the trees.◀

Red DEC trail markers indicate the route SE through balsam fir and other conifers. The way is muddy in spots. A path cuts across the trail at 0.3 mi. The trail crosses Grass Pond outlet at 0.5 mi. The small pond, on the L, has many tamaracks around its shore.

At 0.7 mi, the route crosses the outlet stream of Long Pond, which flows through a wetland with open water lying to the R. After passing through a field of ferns, the trail then crosses another wetland zone as it negotiates the Slim Pond outlet. Corduroy and a bridge ease the difficulty of travel. At the far end of the wet area a side trail to the L leads to a spring. In times of heavy rain, this area may flood, making passage impossible.

The trail makes an abrupt R turn following arrow signs. As it begins to ascend, watch for inconspicuous yellow blazes entering from the L. These announce the Wilson Pond–Cascade Pond Connector (trail 56). Here the path looks seldom-used, but the trail is actually in great shape past the first 0.1 mi. It leads 1.4 mi to an intersection with the Cascade Pond Trail (trail 55), and 1.9 mi to the shoreline of Cascade Pond.

The Wilson Pond Trail gains elevation to drier ground gradually over the next 0.4 mi, and enters an open hardwood forest. It crosses Wilson Pond outlet at 1.8 mi. The pond is to the L past a marshy area, but the trail circles around it on higher dry ground. Vegetation is again coniferous.

The route turns L at 2.5 mi, heading NE. It again crosses Wilson Pond outlet at 2.7 mi. The trail then enters a stand of spruce trees and comes to Wilson Pond lean-to at 2.9 mi.

The pond has boggy growth and is surrounded by conifers. An island is not far from the lean-to. There is a rocky ledge at the water's edge, and Blue Ridge is across the water to the S.

❋ Trail in winter: This trail is little used in winter, but can be excellent if conditions are good.

❀ Distances: To Grass Pond, 0.5 mi; to Long Pond, 0.7 mi; to first crossing of Wilson Pond outlet, 1.8 mi; to second crossing of Wilson Pond outlet, 2.7 mi; to Wilson Pond lean-to, 2.9 mi (4.6 km).

58 Rock Lake

Trails Illustrated Map 744: R17

This is the easiest hike in the Blue Mt. region. It offers a short walk to an attractive lake, with nice mountains in the distance.

▶Trailhead: Access is from a well-marked parking area on the N side of NY 30/28. This is 5.1 mi E from the intersection of NY30, NY28, and NY28N at Blue Mt. Lake village, and 1.6 mi W of the Sawyer Mt. trailhead (trail 60).◀

From the parking area (0.0 mi), the red-marked trail passes through a forest of red and white pines. It draws near the L bank of Johnny Mack Brook at 0.3 mi and follows it to Rock Lake. At 0.5 mi, the trail intersects a snowmobile trail with large red markers. This multi-use snowmobile trail connects Indian Lake with Blue Mt. Lake village. The foot trail turns R, crossing Johnny Mack Brook on a snowmobile bridge. It then bears L off the snowmobile trail at 0.6 mi, but returns to it shortly thereafter.

At 0.7 mi, the foot trail turns L, reaching a small campsite on the shore of the lake in less than 50 yd. Views of Blue Mt. (NW) and Dun Brook Mt. (N) are interesting. A second campsite with a sandy beach and fire ring can be found by following the snowmobile trail an additional 450 ft. Hikers planning a circuitroute using the snowmobile trail to connect to Rock River Trail (trail 59) should be warned that the bridge over the outlet of Rock Lake may be washed out.

❋ Trail in winter: A short trail, it provides access to Rock Lake, which could be traveled on in winter. Snowmobilers use this area.

ᏰᏰ Distances: To Johnny Mack Brook, 0.3 mi; to snowmobile trail, 0.5 mi; to Rock Lake, 0.7 mi (1.1 km).

59 Rock River

Trails Illustrated Map 744: R17

In its first 2 mi, the trail to Rock River was once part of the stagecoach route from North Creek to Blue Mt. Lake. Today the route is mostly an angler's path and winter snowmobile trail. It passes through a good growth of maple and hemlock.

▶Trailhead: Access is off NY 28/30, 6.6 mi SE of the jct. of NY 30, NY 28, and NY 28N at Blue Mt. Lake village. This is 0.1 mi W of the Sawyer Mt. trailhead. There is a well-marked parking area on the N side of the highway.◀

From the parking area (0.0 mi), the red-marked trail heads N. The trail begins a moderate descent at 0.4 mi, reaching a jct. with a red-marked snowmobile trail at the base of the slope at 0.9 mi. Crossing a small inlet of Rock Lake on a snowmobile bridge, the trail reaches a second jct. in 75 yd. It continues straight ahead and crosses a muddy stretch of lowland.

One of the bays of Rock Lake is visible through the trees, L, at 1.2 mi. More wetland is found at 1.4 mi. The trail climbs from the wet area and curves R at 1.5 mi.

Rock Lake can again be seen to the L at 1.6 mi. A short bushwhack will bring you to the sandy beach on its shoreline. This sandy-bottomed lake makes a fine destination if a short trip is desired. There is an excellent campsite on the N end of the lake, just E of the outlet.

The remaining distance to Rock River contours the W edge of Stark Hill on relatively level dry ground. Follow red snowmobile markers on this stretch of the trail. The trail descends a moderate slope at 2.9 mi and reaches the S bank of Rock River at 3 mi.

❋ Trail in winter: This little trail is not used much in winter but does have potential. Snowmobile trails intersect it in places.

ᏰᏰ Distances: To descent, 0.4 mi; to first view of lake, 1.2 mi; to start of bushwhack to lake, 1.6 mi; to Rock River, 3 mi (4.8 km).

60 Sawyer Mt.

Trails Illustrated Map 744: R17

Sawyer Mt. is an easy climb and an excellent beginner's hike for adults or children. It has a nice view and will whet the appetite for greater challenges.

▶Trailhead: Access is off NY 28/30 between Indian Lake and Blue Mt. Lake. A well-marked parking area is on the W side of the road 6.7 mi E of Blue Mt. Lake village.◀

The yellow-marked trail climbs S from the parking area (0.0 mi). Rolling grades soon level off for a short time, before moderate climbing begins in a deciduous forest. After crossing an open stretch of rock, at 1 mi the trail turns R across sloping rock and reenters the forest. A side trail to the L, 200 ft beyond the turn, provides a lookout to the E.

The wooded summit is reached at 1.1 mi. However, the trail descends slightly to a good lookout 270 ft beyond the summit. The pond on the Wakely Lodge Golf Course is below; Sprague Pond can be seen in the distance. Beyond (from L to R) are distant Snowy Mt., nearby Burgess Mt., Panther Mt., Wakely Mt., Metcalf Mt., rocky Sugarloaf Mt., the long Blue Ridge, and, finally, flat-topped Blue Mt. A herd path heads L (S) from the lookout toward another knob, but disappears in the woods.

❋ Trail in winter: The trail is easily reached in winter, and could be a rewarding, short snowshoe outing.

⋈ Distances: To first lookout, 1 mi; to summit, 1.1 mi (1.8 km). Ascent, 630 ft (192 m). Elevation, 2610 ft (796 m).

61 N–P Trail to Tirrell Pond

Trails Illustrated Map 744: S17

Tirrell Pond is a beautiful body of water with an enormous sandy beach at its NW end. There is a lean-to at each end of the pond. This waterway is somewhat overused because of its beauty and proximity to the highway. Recreationists are encouraged to carry out a little more than they carry in to help keep this area attractive. Those wishing a longer trip may continue along the N–P Trail as far as Long Lake (see *Adirondack Mountain Club Northville–Placid Trail*).

▶Trailhead: The trailhead for this section is located along NY 28/30 just W of the entrance to the DEC Lake Durant Public Campground, which is about 3 mi E of Blue Mountain Lake village. ◀

From the parking area along the shoulder of the road (0.0 mi), the N-P Trail proceeds diagonally up the bank, leading to the DEC register and sign at the top of the hill. From the sign, the trail follows a gradual downhill grade before swinging uphill along an old tote road that passes some fine old hemlocks. At 0.6 mi the trail veers L from the road and follows the forest as a nice footpath. From 0.8 mi to 0.1 mi the trail descends some. Two marshy areas are then crossed on walkways.

At 1.4 mi the trail enters Finch, Pruyn and Company land, as indicated by signs. Respect their property rights and follow their instructions as posted. This grassy stretch is marked by creosote-soaked corduroy that is extremely slippery when wet, and akward to walk on with a full pack in any condition. Shortly afterwards, O'Neil Flow and assorted buildings can be seen to the R through the trees.

A grassy area is reached at about 1.7 mi. The trail then climbs a bit and reaches

O'Ñeil Lean-to at Tirrell Pond. Michael N. Kelsey

another grassy area. A brook that flows off of Blue Mt. is reached at 1.9 mi. The remnants of a bridge indicate that the crossing was easier at one time. Just past this brook the trail makes a sharp L turn and follows the L bank of the brook. At 2.1 mi a PBM (1883 ft.) is passed.

The N-P crosses the brook twice before climbing away from it. At 2.5 mi a lumber road is crossed. Here the grade rounds off as a clearing is reached. The trail leaves the clearing and reenters the woods. A brook is crossed, and another clearing is reached at 2.8 mi. Just beyond the clearing the trail turns R and passes a lumbered area before entering the woods again at 3.1 mi.

At 3.4 mi the end of Finch Pruyn land is reached, as indicated by signs. The trail enters Forest Preserve land once again. Soon after, it crosses a boardwalk in a stand of firs. This leads downward through some wet spots and spills out into a clearing and the O'Neil Flow Lean-to. This sits some distance back from the shore of Tirrell Pond along the bank of the outlet.

The trail continues past the lean-to along the W shore of Tirrell Pond. It sometimes follows the shore closely, at other times it moves away from it. It has been improved several times with walkways and stone work, but various storms and accompanying blowdown have affected the ease of travel some. At about 4.5 mi the N end of Tirrell Pond comes into view. At 4.6 mi a small sandy beach and campsite are reached. The trail then bears L and leads back 0.1 mi to the Tirrell Pond lean-to. This lean-to receives very heavy use. Be sure to hang your food here as there are porcupines and bears. A hundred feet or so in front of the lean-to, a footpath leads L through the trees, across a footbridge and through a swampy area to the large crescent-shaped sandy beach that is the S shore of Tirrell Pond. It is truly a magnificent spot with a commanding view of Tirrell Mt. and the whole pond. Note that camping is not allowed on the beach.

❋ Trail in winter: Offers an excellent ski trip to the pond, perhaps as part of a trip through to NY 30 near the Adirondack Museum via the Tirrell Pond from Blue Mt. trailhead (trail 62).

🐾 Distances: To O'Neil Flow Lean-to, 3.5 mi; to Tirrell Pond lean-to, 4.7 mi (7.5 km).

62 Tirrell Pond from Blue Mt. Trailhead

Trails Illustrated Map 744: S16

The trail to Tirrell Pond from the Blue Mt. trailhead passes through private woods and circles the base of Blue Mt. from the N. The forest was lumbered a few years ago, but is recovering. Young growth sometimes closes in on the trail, but generally the way is open and quite pleasant.

▶Trailhead: Access is off the E side of NY 30/28N, 1.4 mi N of the intersection of NY30, NY28, and NY28N in Blue Mt. Lake village. This trailhead is at the top of the hill, 0.1 mi N of the Adirondack Museum. There is ample parking available at this dual trailhead.◀

The yellow-marked trail leaves the highway (0.0 mi) and heads N. The route is almost level as it gradually swings to the E. A break in the deciduous growth occurs at 0.5 mi, when the trail passes through a power line right-of-way. NY 30/28N can be seen far downhill to the L. Half grown-in old lumber roads frequently cross the trail, but offer no confusion. A large flat boulder sits on the L at 1.2 mi. A well-maintained dirt road crosses the trail at 1.6 mi.

At the low col between Blue Mt. and Buck Mt., it is possible to glimpse each peak occasionally. The 470 ft vertical descent to Tirrell Pond begins at 2.1 mi. The trail crosses two sets of grassy logging roads at 2.4 mi. The descent steepens somewhat, and the eroded path has many loose cobblestones at 3.1 mi. Then, the route levels before coming along the L bank of a brook.

The trail crosses a branch of the brook 60 yd before reaching the jct. of the N–P Trail at 3 mi. Several DEC signs are found on trees. Turn R for Tirrell Pond. (The N–P Trail L goes N 9.9 mi to Long Lake.) Avoid an unmarked side trail to the R a short distance farther along the trail.

The trail crosses a large brook at 3.1 mi and reaches Tirrell Pond lean-to at 3.3 mi. The N end of the pond is several hundred feet in front of the lean-to. Its crescent beach and attractive Tirrell Mt. view to the E make the pond an oft-visited area. Please be careful to carry out everything you carried in to this beach, so future hikers will be able to enjoy its environment.

❄ Trail in winter: This trail is best skied heading E. It is often combined with the N–P Trail out to Lake Durant (trail 61).

🐾 Distances: To power line right-of-way, 0.5 mi; to dirt road, 1.4 mi; to downgrade, 2.1 mi; to N–P Trail jct., 3 mi; to Tirrell Pond lean-to, 3.3 mi (5.3 km).

63 Blue Mt.

Trails Illustrated Map 744: S16

First named To-war-loon-da, the Hill of Storms, by the Iroquois, this mountain was then named Mt. Clinch, after a state assemblyman who supported the Eckford survey of 1811. (The lake was named Lake Janet, after Eckford's daughter.) Fortunately, the many thousands of annual visitors to this area don't have to climb Mt. Clinch from Lake Janet. Instead, beautiful Blue Mt. is the name of the summit from which Verplanck Colvin's men set off their bright explosions at night to permit Adirondack Survey crews to zero in their triangulation points. Perhaps because it is so accessible from a major highway, and earlier was near a hub of hotels, Blue Mt. has been one of the most frequently climbed Adirondack peaks for over a century. At 3760 ft, Blue Mountain ranks 66 on the Adirondack Hundred Highest list of mountains. A popular fire tower extends views in every direction.

▶Trailhead: Access coexists with the Tirrell Pond trailhead on NY 30/28N, 1.4 mi N of the NY 30/28/28N intersection in Blue Mt. Lake village. This is 0.1 mi up the hill past the Adirondack Museum on the E side of the road. There is ample parking at the trailhead on private property.◀

The trail heads E from the parking area following red trail markers that begin SE from a barrier cable blocking vehicular use to a flat logging road. There is a DEC register located at the trailhead. (Avoid the yellow-marked DEC trail heading N to Tirrell Pond; see trail 62.) The red Blue Mt. trail runs N before quickly joining the logging road. It then swings SE, and gradually gains elevation. At 0.2 mi, the trail enters woods at the site of an abandoned DEC trail registry now used to store nature trail guides. After crossing the creek, elevation continues to be gained at a comfortable rate.

At 0.9 mi, a moderate grade soon eases. Then, the route steepens until it climbs over bare rock sheets. The grade finally levels at 1.5 mi and heads NE through attractive spruce.

The last half-mile is very enjoyable and ends at the summit at 2 mi. Good views are to be had from the flat-topped summit at ground level, but excellent views are the reward for climbing the fire observer's tower. To the W is Blue Mt. Lake. To its L are Eagle Lake and beyond it Utowana Lake. Beyond the ridges, Raquette Lake is visible. To the N are Minnow Pond, Mud Pond, South Pond, and finally part of Long Lake. In the NE, Tirrell Mt. with beautiful Tirrell Pond below. Just to the L is Tongue Mt. Algonquin Mt. (second highest in the Adirondacks), 25 mi to the NE in the High Peaks, is in line with Tongue Mt. To the R of the gap by Algonquin are Avalanche Pass and then Mt. Colden. Somewhat farther L of Algonquin are Ampersand Mt. and the Seward Range. Much closer is Kempshall Mt. on the E shore of Long Lake.

❄ Trail in winter: Blue Mt. is an excellent winter climb. Instep or full crampons are recommended for this trip.

🐾 Distances: To beginning of steeper grades, 0.9 mi; to level area, 1.5 mi; to summit, 2 mi (3.2 km). Ascent, 1550 ft (473 m). Summit elevation, 3759 ft (1146 m).

64 Upper Sargent Pond

Trails Illustrated Map 744: S15

Upper Sargent Pond has long been used for fishing. Guides had fishing camps there in the heyday of the Adirondack hotels in the 1800s. The trail to Upper

Sargent Pond is relatively level past the initial upgrades, and passes through deciduous forest.

▶Trailhead: Access is off NY 30/28N. Turn L onto Maple Lodge Rd., 0.6 mi N of the NY 30/28/28N intersection in Blue Mt. Lake village. Drive 1.3 mi along a paved and then gravel road to the DEC trailhead sign beside the Minnowbrook Conference Center control station. Minnowbrook has provided a long pullout for trailhead parking on the L just before the control station. If this is full, the closest parking is 1.3 mi back on NY 30/28N.◀

From the trailhead (0.0 mi), head W on a private road. Bear R uphill at a fork at 0.2 mi. There is another DEC trail sign on the R side of the road at 0.3 mi. Here, the trail leaves the road and enters the woods following red DEC trail markers. The road straight ahead enters private land and should be avoided.

The trail reaches a jct. at 0.4 mi. L is the South Castle Rock Trail (trail 65), the first of two trails to Castle Rock. Continue straight.

The trail passes E of Chub Pond at 0.7 mi and then generally swings W. At a jct. at 1.5 mi, the trail L is the North Castle Rock Trail (trail 66). It follows yellow markers 0.5 mi to the summit of Castle Rock.

The trail now parallels the N edge of a wetland on dry ground for nearly a mile. Helms Pond is to the N, but is not visible. At 3.1 mi, the trail descends to the level of another wetland, where it meets the outlet of Helms Pond. The trail hugs the S side of the outlet all the way to Upper Sargent Pond, passing through large stands of yellow birch and sugar maple.

The pond is reached at 4.7 mi. The informal campsite at the trail terminus is surrounded by large conifers.

For other access to Upper Sargent Pond, see trail 67.

❀ Trail in winter: Limited parking at the trailhead in winter makes use of this trail difficult, but the trail itself is excellent.

ᛘ Distances: To turn off road, 0.3 mi; to South Castle Rock Trail, 0.4 mi; to Chub Pond, 0.7 mi; to North Castle Rock Trail, 1.5 mi; to outlet of Helms Pond, 3.1 mi; to Upper Sargent Pond, 4.7 mi (7.5 km).

Upper Sargent Pond. Michael N. Kelsey

65 South Castle Rock Trail

Trails Illustrated Map 744: S15

Castle Rock juts 200 ft above the surrounding forest trees like a medieval castle. It offers a magnificent view of both Blue Mt. and Blue Mt. Lake. There are two trails to its summit, one approaching from the S (trail 65) and the other from the N (trail 66). Both branch off the Upper Sargent Pond Trail (trail 64), making round trips of 3, 3.5, or 4 mi possible.

▶Trailhead: Access is the same as that for Upper Sargent Pond (trail 64). Follow the Upper Sargent Pond route from its trailhead for 0.4 mi to the jct. mentioned in the Upper Sargent Pond Trail description.◀

The yellow-marked trail heads W across a bridge (0.0 mi). It bears R off the woods road at 0.1 mi, continuing on easy grades. Chub Pond can be seen R at 0.3 mi. Shortly thereafter, the trail turns SW, following a stream down a gradual grade to a jct. at 0.4 mi. The blue-marked trail L heads down to Blue Mt. Lake (see below).

The trail continues W from the jct. on the level, but the grade soon increases to moderate and then steep. At 0.6 mi, the trail turns NW on easy to moderate grades. It drops down into a hollow at 0.8 mi and then ascends a short, steep pitch along the S face of Castle Rock to an overhang R at 0.9 mi. (A herd path heads R at the overhang, meeting up with the yellow-marked trail again partway up the W face.)

From the overhang, the trail heads NW on easy to moderate grades to a jct. at 1 mi. The yellow-marked trail L is the North Castle Rock Trail (trail 66). Turning R, the trail heads steeply up the W face of Castle Rock, and reaches the top at 1.1 mi. See the North Castle Rock Trail (trail 66) for a description of the view.

❋ Trail in winter: Exercise caution: The upper part and lookout ledge are quite dangerous in winter.

🚶 Distances: To Blue Mt. Lake Trail jct., 0.4 mi; to overhang, 0.9 mi; to jct. with North Castle Rock Trail, 1 mi; to summit, 1.1 mi (1.8 km). Total distance from Upper Sargent Pond trailhead, 1.5 mi (2.4 km). Ascent from Upper Sargent Pond Trail, 580 ft (177 m). Summit elevation, 2480 ft (756 m).

66 North Castle Rock Trail

Trails Illustrated Map 744: S15

This route to Castle Rock from the Upper Sargent Pond trailhead is longer than the route from the S (trail 65). However, combining the trails in a loop adds variety to the round-trip and only 0.5 mi to the total distance.

▶Trailhead: Access is the same as that for Upper Sargent Pond (trail 64). Follow the Upper Sargent Pond route from its trailhead for 1.5 mi to the jct. mentioned in the Upper Sargent Pond Trail description. ◀

From the jct. (0.0 mi), the yellow-marked trail climbs S and E to a jct. at 0.4 mi.

Autumn dawn from Castle Rock. Chris Murray

The South Castle Rock Trail (trail 65) enters R. Turning L, the trail to the summit climbs steeply up the W face of Castle Rock.

Passing through a corridor with a high rock wall, the trail reaches the summit at 0.5 mi. Here it breaks out onto a large, flat, open rock platform overlooking Blue Mt. Lake. The summit is 700 ft above the water level. Green islands stand out of the blue water below like emeralds in ice. To the E, Blue Mt. dominates. Far on the horizon to the SW is Snowy Mt. near Indian Lake. Lake Durant (SE) and Eagle Lake (SSW) are visible. Helms Pond is to your right rear (WNW).

✸ Trail in winter: Exercise caution: The upper part and lookout ledge are quite dangerous in winter.

𝍔 Distances: Trailhead to jct. with South Castle Rock Trail, 0.4 mi; to summit, 0.5 mi (0.8 km). Total distance from Upper Sargent Pond trailhead, 2 mi (3.2 km). Ascent from Upper Sargent Pond Trail, 380 ft (117 m). Summit elevation, 2480 ft (756 m).

Blue Mountain Lake from South Castle Rock Trail
Trails Illustrated Map 744: S15

This short trail can be used as a pleasant side trip on the way to or from Castle Rock, or to climb Castle Rock from the lake.

▶Trailhead: Access is the same as for the South Castle Rock Trail (trail 65). The trailhead is at a jct. 0.4 mi along the South Castle Rock Trail. If approached from the lake, the trail can be accessed by circling around the W side of Bluff Point. The W tip of Long Island is directly S of the landing. A DEC trail sign is posted on a tree at the shore. ◀

Blue Mountain Lake and Sargent Ponds Section **147**

The blue-marked trail heads S down a gradual grade beside a stream, passing by the ruins of a stone structure in the middle of the stream before reaching Blue Mt. Lake at 0.3 mi. A small clearing and sandy beach mark the terminus. Long Island and other small islands are straight ahead.

❋ Trail in winter: Unlikely to be a destination in and of itself in the winter, the trail could be used as part of a ski trip across the lake and a snowshoe climb of Castle Rock. *Caution:* As noted elsewhere, care is advised at the top of Castle Rock, where the upper part and lookout ledge are precipitous.

🐾 Distances: To Blue Mt. Lake, 0.3 mi (0.5 km). Total distance from Upper Sargent Pond trailhead, 1.1 mi (1.8 km).

67 Sargent Ponds Loop

Trails Illustrated Map 744: S14

This trail gives access to Upper and Lower Sargent Ponds. Both are very scenic. Side trails to both ponds lead to beautifully located campsites. The Lower Pond campsite has a lean-to.

▶Trailhead: From NY 30 at Deerland, on the S end of Long Lake, take North Point Rd. W to the DEC trailhead at 6.3 mi.◀

From North Point Rd. (0.0 mi), the trail (with DEC red and snowmobile markers) heads S on easy ground above a creek. After passing over a slight hill at 1 mi, the path descends somewhat steeply to a jct. at 1.2 mi. To the L, the red trail goes to a campsite amid evergreens on the shore of Upper Sargent Pond at 1.4 mi. Nearby, an island in the lake adds great beauty to the scenery.

From the jct., the snowmobile trail turns R and continues along the edge of a hill N of the outlet creek. After some weaving along the contour, the trail reaches a jct. at 2.7 mi with the Tioga Point Trail (trail 68).

Continuing ahead, the Tioga Point Trail soon crosses the outlet stream from Upper and Middle Ponds. In another 0.1 mi, there is another jct. as the trail approaches a fish barrier dam on the outlet of Lower Sargent Pond. To the L, a DEC yellow-marked side trail leads 0.4 mi to Sargent Pond lean-to. This lean-to is very well located on a point of land with some tenting space nearby. The scenery is fine, and the fishing is good. Near the start of this side trail, a trail branch to the R leads quickly to the shore of the pond.

❋ Trail in winter: Easy skiing most of the way, suitable for intermediate skiers familiar with wilderness travel. The trail down to Upper Sargent Pond is somewhat steep. Shared with snowmobiles.

🐾 Distances: North Point Rd. to Upper Sargent Pond, 1.4 mi; to Tioga Point Trail (trail 68), 2.7 mi; to Sargent Pond Lean-to via Tioga Point Trail (trail 68), 3.3 mi (5.3 km).

68 Tioga Point

Tioga Point is located at about the center region of Raquette Lake, and contains many lean-tos intended for canoe camping. This trail gives access to the point through a region of mature forests, but has not been maintained in some time and is likely to be overgrown. The site receives heavy use during the summer from boat campers from the community of Raquette Lake and the surrounding area. In general, lean-tos must be reserved ahead of time. Call 800-456-2267, days, for credit card reservations. There are 15 lean-tos and 10 campsites administered by a caretaker at Tioga Point.

▶Trailhead: From NY 30 at Deerland, on the S end of Long Lake, take North Point Rd. W to the second DEC trailhead at 7.8 mi (the first DEC trailhead at 6.3 mi is for trail 67).◀

From North Point Rd. (0.0 mi), the trail (with DEC red and snowmobile markers) heads S along the hillside W of Grass Pond outlet, with mild ups and downs in an older hardwood forest. Grass Pond, more or less living up to its name, is visible to the L at 1 mi. Beaver activity here has made the trail wet in several places.

The trail continues on easy ground to a jct. L with the Sargent Ponds Loop Trail (trail 67) at 2 mi. Continuing R (SW), the Tioga Point Trail soon crosses the outlet stream from Upper and Middle Ponds. At 2.2 mi, there is another jct. as the trail approaches a fish barrier dam on the outlet of Lower Sargent Pond. To the L, a DEC yellow-marked spur trail leads four-tenths of a mi to Sargent Pond lean-to (see trail 64). Near the start of this spur trail, a branch to the R leads quickly to the shore of the pond.

At the trail jct. by the fish barrier dam, the trail goes R, crossing the outlet stream on a snowmobile bridge. There is a freshwater spring on the R just after this bridge. The trail climbs a ridge above the pond's W side and stays on the ridge until reaching a jct. at 2.4 mi. The unmarked route L leads down 300 ft to the shore of Lower Sargent Pond at an unofficial camping area and boat landing. From the jct., the trail turns R and heads W. There is a boggy stream crossing at 3.2 mi and another wet spot at 4.6 mi. The trail curves W and parallels the inlet bog of Eldon Lake as it approaches Raquette Lake. From there on, the route is on the pleasant high ground of Tioga Point peninsula. The water can be seen on the R for some distance before the trail reaches the Tioga Point lean-tos at 6.1 mi. The abundant lean-tos and manicured grassy areas here are in sharp contrast to the silent majestic forest passed through in reaching the point.

❄ Trail in winter: Easy skiing most of the way, suitable for intermediate skiers familiar with wilderness travel. Shared with snowmobiles.

🚶 Distances: North Point Rd. to Grass Pond, 1 mi; to Lower Sargent Pond, 2.2 mi; to Sargent Pond lean-to, 2.6 mi; to Tioga Point, 6.1 mi (9.8 km).

Along the Browns Tract. Mark Bowie

The Great Camps, Pigeon Lake Wilderness Area, and Moose River Recreation Area

 This region once attracted the rich and powerful, including railroad executives and prominent bankers. Today it lures vacationers in summer and winter alike.

The trails north of NY 28 provide instant rewards for short climbs. Popular with trout fishermen as well as hikers, the Pigeon Lake Wilderness Area borders Raquette Lake on the W. Trails meander through mature forests of soft- and hardwoods including old growth white pine. West Mt., at 2902 ft in the far NE corner, hovers high above several clear lakes in a terrain known for its rolling hills. For an extensive description of the complete network of trails in the Pigeon Lake Wilderness Area, see *Adirondack Mountain Club Western Trails*, volume four in the Forest Preserve Series.

The trails S of NY 28 and in the N of the Moose River Plains were developed from old roads built in 1895–96 for the "Great Camps": Sagamore, Uncas, and Kamp Kill Kare. For a good introduction to these camps, see Craig Gilborn's book, *Durant*. Sagamore Lodge and Conference Center gives public tours daily during the summer, has a varied summer program of one-week educational programs, and is open for recreational skiing weekends during the winter. Uncas and Kill Kare are private and not open to the public.

The Moose River Recreation Area is 50,000 acres of state-owned land stretching across the northern boundary of the West Canada Lakes Wilderness Area. Its E entrance is at Wakely Dam; its W entrance is at Limekiln Lake. Although the land has been part of the Forest Preserve since 1963 (when it was purchased from the Gould Paper Co.), the 41.3 mi of roads that run throughout it are not. Through a complex conservation law, the roads were acquired as a gift for the purposes of fish and wildlife management. This has permitted development of many primitive campsites and opened them to vehicular access.

No daily use fees have been levied in recent years in the Moose River Plains, but a free permit is required if the same campsite is used for more than three consecutive days. Current information can be obtained from the forest ranger at Limekiln Lake, 315-357-4401, or DEC regional office at Northville, 518-863-4176.

▶Trailhead: Wakely Dam is reached via Cedar River Rd., which is off NY 28/30, 2.2 mi W of Indian Lake village. Follow Cedar River Rd. 12 mi to its end at Wakely Dam and Cedar River Flow.◀

Campsites and access to Cedar River Flow are available at Wakely Dam, outside the gate to the Moose River Recreation Area. There are 27.4 mi of hiking trails in the Moose River Recreation Area, the gate to which normally opens for vehicular traffic on Memorial Day and closes at the end of deer season. Entry into the area on foot is permitted year round, though from December to April the Cedar River Rd. is plowed only to a point 4.9 mi from Wakely Dam. This is a heavily used snowmobile area in winter.

Recommended hikes in this section include:

SHORT HIKES
Ferds Bog: 0.6 mi (1 km) round trip. A wonderland for bird watching and seeing bog plants between Eagle Bay and Raquette Lake.

Cathedral Pines: 0.1 mi loop (0.2 km) round trip. A very short route to see a small grove of beautiful large white pines.

Death Falls: 0.6 mi(1 km) round trip. A short trip to view a nice waterfall.

MODERATE HIKES
Shallow Lake: 3.2 mi (5.1 km) round trip. Near the village of Raquette Lake. A beautiful lake, with the appearance of great remoteness.

Rocky Mt.: 1.2 mi (1.9 km) round trip. Climbs to a great view of Fourth Lake, Eagle Bay, and Inlet. The trail is short, but the climb is vigorous.

Uncus Rd. to Black Bear Mt.: 4.6 mi (7.4 km) round trip. A very scenic trail to the open summit of Black Bear Mt.

Seventh Lake: 4.4 mi (7 km) round trip. A pleasant trail leads to a picturesque location on the lake's edge that is ideal for camping.

Beaver Lake: 4.2 mi (6.7 km) round trip. A pleasant walk to an attractive lake steeped in history. Magnificent white pines line the trail.

HARDER HIKES
Raquette Lake–West Mt.: 10 mi (16 km) round trip. A steep climb to a view over much of Raquette Lake.

Indian River (Horn Lake) Trail: 12.6 mi (20.2 km) round trip. Wading rivers; narrow, tree-lined paths; bushwhacking options; backcountry ponds; and primitive campsites provide numerous opportunities for a wilderness experience.

Sly Pond: 15.4 mi (24.7 km) round trip. One of the highest water bodies in the Adirondacks, this remote pond is generally a good choice for solitude.

Trail Described	Miles (one way)		Page
Ferds Bog	0.3	(0.5 km)	153
69 Shallow Lake	1.6	(2.6 km)	154
70 Sucker Brook Bay	3.1	(5.0 km)	155
71 Raquette Lake–West Mt.	5.0	(8.0 km)	156
72 Constable Pond–West Mt.	8.1	(13.0 km)	158
73 Rocky Mt.	0.5	(0.8 km)	160
74 Fourth Lake–Black Bear Mt.	3.1	(5.0 km)	161
75 Uncas Rd.–Black Bear Mt.	2.3	(3.7 km)	163
76 Black Bear Mt. Ski Trail	3.0	(4.8 km)	164
77 Old Black Bear Mt. Trail	1.4	(2.2 km)	165
78 Seventh Lake	2.2	(3.5 km)	166
79 Uncas Trail	2.7	(4.3 km)	167
80 Cathedral Pines	0.1	(0.2 km)	169
81 Death Falls	0.3	(0.5 km)	169
82 Sagamore Cascades	3.3	(5.3 km)	170
83 Sagamore Lake	3.9	(6.3 km)	172
84 Uncas Rd.–Mohegan Lake	5.3	(8.5 km)	173
85 East Shore Path and Snowmobile Trail	2.7	(4.3 km)	175
Bear Pond	2.5	(4.0 km)	176
Benedict Creek			176
86 Mitchell Ponds	2.8	(4.5 km)	177
87 Helldiver Pond	0.2	(0.3 km)	178
88 Ice House Pond	0.4	(0.6 km)	178
89 Beaver Lake	2.1	(3.4 km)	179
90 Lost Ponds	0.7	(1.1 km)	179
91 Sly Pond	7.7	(12.3 km)	180
Short Trails on Indian River Rd.			182
92 Squaw Lake	0.3	(0.5 km)	182
93 Muskrat Pond	0.1	(0.2 km)	182
94 Indian Lake	0.1	(0.2 km)	182
95 Indian River (Horn Lake)	7.4	(11.8 km)	182

Ferds Bog

Trails Illustrated Map 744: Q11

Tamaracks, pitcher plants, and other bog plants abound, along with many boreal (northern) birds, all visible from a plastic boardwalk floating on the bog at the end of a short walk on a state nature trail in the Pigeon Lake Wilderness Area. (This kind of boardwalk requires less maintenance and won't leak toxins as treated lumber might.) The bog is named for Ferdinand LaFrance, "who owned a cabin nearby and who discovered the good variety of resident boreal birds," according to the New York State *Conservationist* magazine (February 2004).

▶Trailhead: From NY 28 at Eagle Bay, take Uncas Rd., which starts out paved, 3.2 mi E to a small parking area sufficient for three or four vehicles. (Be careful not to block the adjacent driveway.) This parking area, on the L (N) side of the dirt road, bears a state marker. This point is also 5.3 mi from the E end of Uncas Rd. starting from NY 28 and driving 0.7 mi N through Raquette Lake. For those staying at Browns Tract Pond State Campground, it's 3.5 mi W of the campground.◀

Starting from a register (0.0 mi), the trail angles R from the corner of the parking lot, passing some side trails R that lead to private property and should be avoided on the return trip. There may be state nature trail or blue markers.

After about 100 yd, the trail turns L and starts downhill, then turns R, passing along the base of a small ridge. It bends L onto a boardwalk at 0.3 mi. The boardwalk keeps visitors above the open bog mat but allows a view straight down into pitcher plants and a close-up look at tamaracks and numerous other bog flora growing next to, and sometimes trying to grow up through, the walkway. The trail ends at a viewing platform at just over 0.3 mi.

❈ Trail in winter: Suitable for backwoods skiing or snowshoeing.

🚶 Distance: 0.3 mi (0.5 km).

69 Shallow Lake

Trails Illustrated Map 744: R11

Shallow Lake is notable for its wilderness quality and its relative ease of access. It's an easily followed yellow-marked trail.

▶Trailhead: The trail starts within Brown Tract Pond State Campground. To reach the state campground, go N through the community of Raquette Lake for 0.7 mi from NY 28. Take Uncas Rd. L (W) for 1.8 mi and turn R (N) into the campground. Or, from Old Forge, take Uncas Rd. 6.7 mi from Eagle Bay, turning L at the campground. A day-use fee is charged when the campground is open.

Drive 0.6 mi through the campground to the parking for campsites 68–70 just down the hill from the end of the loop road. There is some parking for the trailhead. Park with care to avoid blocking a campsite.

An alternate trailhead is 0.9 mi farther W on the Uncas Rd., at the Sucker Brook Bay Trail (trail 70). The route is 0.7 mi longer, but there is no parking fee.◀

Starting E (uphill) of campsite 68 (0.0 mi), the yellow-marked footpath goes W within view of Lower Brown Tract Pond. The pond is very attractive, with a rocky island opposite the trail. At 0.2 mi, the route meets an old road that is now the Sucker Brook Bay Trail (trail 70).

Turning L for 10 yd, the Shallow Lake route then turns R uphill and leaves the old road. Again, there are yellow markers and the footpath is quite obvious. This upland route follows the contour. Then at 0.5 mi it plunges into a level, marshy area with pitcher and similar bog-loving plants and crosses the wide and deep Beaver Brook at 0.6 mi on a bridge of 6- to 8-inch logs. The trail continues NW in marshy terrain, passing tamaracks and gradually larger evergreens.

David Hough

At 0.7 mi the route climbs slightly to provide a comfortable footpath on the gentle hillside. This continues with small ups and downs until a turn at 1.3 mi takes the route NW over a slight rise, then down to the shore of Shallow Lake at a boat landing site at 1.6 mi. The lake does not seem particularly shallow. The view is one of untouched Adirondack beauty, with a sense of extreme remoteness. There are boulders along the shore R, from which one can get a better view.

❊ Trail in winter: Suitable for backcountry skiing or snowshoeing. The campground is closed in winter, so going through the campground would add 0.6 mi to the trip. One could also use the Sucker Brook trailhead.

⚐ Distances: Campsite 68 to Sucker Brook Bay Trail (trail 70), 0.2 mi; to Beaver Brook, 0.6 mi; to Shallow Lake, 1.6 mi (2.6 km).

70 Sucker Brook Bay

Trails Illustrated Map 744: R11

The Sucker Brook Bay Rd., also called West Mt. Rd., is a mostly broad, smooth woods road going from the gravel of Uncas Rd. N and NE to private camps on the NW shore of Raquette Lake's Sucker Brook Bay. According to Harold Hochschild's book *Township 34*, most of this route is the final section of a wagon road privately built in 1897–98 from Eagle Bay to Sucker Brook Bay.

▶Trailhead: Go 5.8 mi E from Eagle Bay on Uncas Rd. To reach this point from NY 28 near Raquette Lake village, drive 0.7 mi N on a paved road through the hamlet and beyond (Antlers Rd). Turn L on unpaved Uncas Rd. and drive 2.7 mi. Park on the R (N) near the barricade across the old road. Upper Brown Tract Pond is just to the W of the trail. ◀

The blue-marked trail starts beside Upper Brown Tract Pond (0.0 mi), with good views along the pond, bends R away from the pond past a trail register, and crosses the upper pond's outlet on a bridge. The route turns N and passes W of the lower pond. At 0.5 mi, an unmarked truck trail to the L should be avoided. An unofficial spur trail R at 0.6 mi leads to a large swimming rock with a good view at the edge of the pond.

The wide, easy old road continues N past a jct. at 0.9 mi. On the L (W) is the Shallow Lake Trail (trail 69) going W around the base of a hill. A sign says "trail" and there are yellow markers. The two trails share the path for another 10 yd before trail 69 heads R toward its trailhead at the Brown Tract Pond State Campground, also with a jct. marked "trail."

Beyond this jct., Sucker Brook Bay Rd. climbs a minor hillside and continues N on easy grades. The Raquette Lake–West Mt. Trail (trail 71) joins on the R (SE) at 2.3 mi, just before the road crosses Beaver Brook. The combined trails turn NW to cross the brook, then curve back NE over a broad hilltop to a road jct. at 3.1 mi. To continue L to West Mt., see trail 71. Trail 70 continues straight ahead (NE) 130 yd to the shore of Raquette Lake at the head of Sucker Brook Bay. This was the end of the original Sucker Brook Bay Rd. There is a narrow beach with a shallow sandy lake bottom and a view of the N part of this very large and handsome lake.

❄ Trail in winter: Easy on skis or snowshoes. If continuing on to West Mt., skiing the steep slopes is for experts only.

🐾 Distances: Uncas Rd. to Shallow Lake Trail (trail 69), 0.9 mi; to Raquette Lake–West Mt. Trail (trail 71), 2.3 mi; to Sucker Brook Bay, 3.1 mi (5 km).

71 Raquette Lake–West Mt.

Trails Illustrated Map 744: R12

This route extends along the W side of Raquette Lake from Uncas Rd., going roughly N and finally W to the summit of West Mt., 2902 ft elevation. The round-trip hike is 10 mi and the ascent is nearly 1100 ft from the road, of which 950 ft is a steady, moderately steep climb. With the fire tower gone, the view from West Mt. is limited to Raquette Lake. A handsome forest clothes most of the trail route, the northern part of which is in the Pigeon Lake Wilderness Area.

The first section of the route is a 1.4 mi path through the woods. The second section, 0.8 mi long, follows the Sucker Brook Bay Trail (trail 70) to a point 130 yd from Raquette Lake, where trail 70 diverges to the lake. Here a boat could be beached, shortening the hike to West Mt. (see below). The third section, 2.8 mi long, is a trail going N from the Sucker Brook Bay Trail, then turning W 2 mi up the mountain. There are blue markers in this section because the route is a continuation of the blue-marked Constable Pond–West Mt. Trail (trail 72).

▶ Trailhead: From NY 28 by the community of Raquette Lake, drive 0.7 mi N on a paved road through the village and beyond (Antlers Rd.). Turn L on unpaved Uncas Rd. and drive W. The trailhead is at 0.6 mi, but a small area suitable for parking is 100 yd before it on the L. There is a sign.

An alternative is to start the trip on the Sucker Brook Bay Trail (trail 70). A shorter route on that trail can be had by using the Shallow Lake Trail (trail 69) and paying a day-use fee at the Brown Tract Pond State Campground when it is open. This variation crosses the Sucker Brook Bay Trail. ◀

After dropping to a register (0.0 mi), the blue-marked trail crosses an open grassy area. It then goes over the edge of Wadsworth Mt. and down and up, over the shoulder of a smaller hill, bending L (nearly W) along Beaver Brook. At 1.4 mi, the trail joins the old road that is the Sucker Brook Bay Trail (trail 70). The route follows the road R across Beaver Brook. At 2.2 mi there is a jct. where the trail goes L and the old road/trail 70 goes straight ahead 130 yd to the shore of Raquette Lake at the head (SW end) of large Sucker Brook Bay. There is a narrow beach with a shallow sandy lake bottom and a view of the N part of this very large and handsome lake.

(Arriving at this point by boat would reduce the hike up West Mt. from 5 to 3.6 mi one way. Canoes and motor boats may be rented in the community of Raquette Lake or nearby on NY 28 on the S shore of the lake. The distance by water is long but may be shortened, if canoeing or kayaking, by carrying 0.2 mi across the base of 1.5 mile-long Indian Point. The two-pronged end of Indian Pt. is private. When heading for the landing place at the end of Sucker Brook Bay, aim to the R of the wetland and its brook flowing into the lake.)

Continuing from the jct., the route passes a stand of tall white pines, and at 2.4 mi a side woods road leads R to a private camp. After a section of stately hardwoods and conifers, the route crosses Sucker Brook at 3 mi.

After an unmarked trail R, at 3.1 mi there is a roadway L and then at 3.2 mi an arrow indicates that the trail leaves the roadway, turning L onto a footpath. The trail heads NE over a slight hill and crosses Stillman Brook at 3.6 mi.

At 4 mi, the ascent of West Mt. begins. The steady, moderately steep ascent is largely along straight stretches of broad trail. With the footpath increasingly on bedrock, the trail reaches a clearing near the summit at 4.9 mi, with the foundation of the former observer's cabin. There follows a short steep pitch through spruce to the summit. Partway up, the blue- or red-marked Constable Pond–West Mt. Trail (trail 72) joins on the R. (This 8 mi trail from Higby Rd. near Big Moose Lake travels through a remote section of the Pigeon Lake Wilderness Area. A more extensive trip can include this trail, but the trailheads are widely separated and there are no other trails looping back to Uncas Rd.)

The trail ends at the summit clearing at 5 mi, where there is a good, if narrow view SF of most of Raquette Lake. A few yards farther W along the crest is the site of the former fire tower. There are two U.S. Geological Survey benchmarks here. The divide between the Raquette River watershed on the E and that of the Moose–Black River on the W passes over the summit.

❄ Trail in winter: Suitable for backwoods skiing or snowshoeing. Owing to the steep slope, West Mt. requires good skiing ability. Only groups with winter experience should attempt the full distance on an unbroken trail to West Mt.

🐾 Distances: Uncas Rd. to Sucker Brook Bay Trail (trail 70), 1.4 mi; to Sucker Brook Bay, 2.1 mi; to split from roadway, 3.2 mi; to summit of West Mt., 5 mi (8 km). To trailhead on Higby Rd. (via trail 72), 13 mi (21 km). Using the Shallow Lake trailhead in the Browns Tract Pond Campground, the distances are 0.2 mi more. Using the Sucker Brook trail adds 0.9 mi more each way. Ascent, 1100 ft (335 m). Summit elevation, 2902 ft (885 m).

72 Constable Pond–West Mt.

Trails Illustrated Map 744: S10-11 / Trails Illustrated Map 745: R10 / P. 162

This long wilderness trail extends from Higby Rd. just S of Big Moose Lake NE past Constable Pond, Pigeon Lake, and Otter Pond to the summit of West Mt., W of the northern part of Raquette Lake. There it meets the end of the Raquette Lake–West Mt. Trail (trail 71). The part of the trail beyond Constable Pond is remote. It has wet areas, blowdowns, and wet stream crossings, passes several magnificent specimens of white pine between Constable Pond and the end of Pigeon Lake, and makes an 800 ft ascent of West Mt., the last 600 ft of which are steep or moderately steep. Once a fire tower peak, today's view from the summit is mostly over Raquette Lake. Although most of this trail is depicted on the map cited above, its western reaches are found on Trails Illustrated Map 745 (S–R10).

Branching SE off the trail are the Hermitage Trail, the Mays Pond Trail, and the Queer Lake Trail (trails described in full in *Adirondack Mountain Club Western Trails*), permitting various circuit and through hikes. A round-trip hike of the network involves backpacking, but the lack of lean-tos or informal campsites along the way is a limiting factor. Because this trail is in a designated Wilderness Area (Pigeon Lake), bicycles are not allowed.

▶Trailhead: From NY 28 in Eagle Bay, drive 3.7 mi on Big Moose Rd. Turn R on Higby Rd. for 1.3 mi to Judson Rd. (R), and park along the road (without blocking Judson Rd.). If necessary, park along the boat landing road on the R, a little farther down Higby Rd. The trail starts on Judson Rd., a private unpaved road with a barrier (on the E). There are state symbols on a sign, but it may not be evident that that is the trail, and there are no markers along Judson Rd. The rest of the trail is marked with DEC blue markers, with additional red markers near West Mt.◀

From Higby Rd. (0.0 mi), the route follows Judson Rd. for the first 0.2 mi, then turns R just before the road turns L to cross Constable Brook. After about 20 yd there is a vehicle barrier, a large map sign, and a trail register. The blue trail follows an old road along the S side of broad, rocky Constable Brook.

At 0.5 mi the red-marked Hermitage Trail (*Western Trails*, trail 22) goes R (SSE) toward Queer Lake. Some 25 yd beyond this jct. the path turns L, crosses Constable Brook on a bridge, and goes E, now on a footpath, on the N side of the brook, reentering private land.

The trail meets another old road at 0.9 mi and follows it R. In 100 yd, the trail re-crosses Constable Brook on a logging bridge, and within 20 yd turns L on the other side, leaving the old road. This footpath soon enters the state Forest Preserve and the Pigeon Lake Wilderness Area. Another jct. on the R at 1.3 mi is for the yellow-marked Mays Pond Trail (*Western Trails*, trail 23), which goes to that pond and on to the Queer Lake area.

The trail parallels Constable Brook and its open wetland L. At 2.2 mi the path nears Constable Pond, visible through tall spruce and hemlock, and parallels its

S shore. At just before 2.6 mi, a spur path goes L a few yards to the edge of the pond. Fifty-five yd beyond, the yellow-marked Queer Lake Trail (*Western Trails*, trail 24) goes R (SE) 0.6 mi to Chub Lake and the Queer Lake region. Seventy yd beyond the jct., with a brook on the L, an informal campsite is on the R, the only one to be found along this trail.

Some streams and wet spots alternate with sections of nice woodland path. Pigeon Lake's outlet stream crosses the trail at 3.9 mi. The trail then turns R, going through messy undergrowth and across a bog. The water of Pigeon Lake becomes visible through the trees on the R by a sign at 4.9 mi. In less than 100 yd, the trail comes closer to the lake at its narrow N section and another sign.

Pigeon Lake. James Appleyard

This lake is about the size of Constable Pond, 0.7 mi long, with a boggy shoreline fringed by white pine and spruce. Some red markers start to appear near the lake. Both blue and red markers are found on the rest of the trail.

At 5.4 mi, about opposite the end of the lake, the trail passes a magnificent white pine on the L as Pigeon Lake passes from the scene. At 5.6 and 5.8 mi, in a spruce forest, there are two crossings of the outlet of Otter Pond, which includes another pond well out of sight to the R. For the rest of the way the trail is on higher, drier ground in a forest of hardwoods and scattered spruce and fir.

After paralleling Otter Pond's outlet for a considerable distance, the route crosses it a third time and then a small pond appears on the R just below Otter Pond. Otter Pond may be detected through the trees R after the trail passes the small pond, at 6.7 mi.

At 7.6 mi, having already gradually ascended 1280 ft, the trail begins the final, steeper 620 ft ascent of West Mt. At 8 mi the trail levels near the summit, crosses a saddle between the N peak and summit, and then turns R (S) to climb slightly before reaching a jct. with the Raquette Lake–West Mt. Trail (trail 71) at 8.1 mi. Turn R on that trail and reach the open summit of West Mt. in 50 yd. A fair section of Raquette Lake can be seen, but trees fringing the top limit views in other directions.

One may continue the trip down the Raquette Lake–West Mt. Trail to Brown's Tract Rd., but the two trailheads are far apart and there are no trails to complete a loop. Thus two cars are required.

❄ Trail in winter: Suitable for snowshoeing. West Mt. would require excellent skiing ability. Only groups with strong winter experience should attempt the full distance on unbroken trail.

🐾 Distances: Higby Rd. to Hermitage Trail (*Western Trails*, trail 22), 0.5 mi; to Mays Pond Trail (*Western Trails*, trail 23), 1.3 mi; to Constable Pond and Queer Lake Trail (*Western Trails*, trail 24), 2.6 mi; to Pigeon Lake outlet crossing, 3.9 mi; to Pigeon Lake, 4.9 mi; to Otter Pond, 6.7 mi; to summit of West Mt., 8.1 mi (13 km). Continuation to Brown's Tract Rd., via trail 71, 13 mi (20.8 km). West Mt. ascent (from Higby Rd.), 1073 ft (327 m). Summit elevation, 2902 ft (885 m).

73 Rocky Mt.

Trails Illustrated Map 745: Q10

This short, popular trail ascends 445 ft from NY 28 to the ledges atop Rocky Mt. near the head of Fourth Lake, offering a splendid view of the lake. It is a round-trip hike of 1.2 mi.

▶Trailhead: From the jct. of NY 28 and Big Moose Rd. in Eagle Bay, drive 1.2 mi E on NY 28. Turn L onto the old road, now a parking area off the highway. From the opposite direction drive 0.9 mi toward Eagle Bay on NY 28 from the public parking area in the center of Inlet. Turn R into the trailhead parking area.◀

Near the center of the parking area, the yellow-marked trail (markers are sparse) starts (0.0 mi) in a NNE direction, then soon turns L. It is wide, eroded from much use, and steep in several places.

Ascending through a hardwood forest, the trail turns NW and finally W along bedrock to the summit (elevation 2225 ft) at 0.5 mi. In another 60 yd along the open cliff top with a SW drop off, there is a wide open view over most of Fourth Lake lying 500 ft below. To the L on the wide E end of this large lake, one can see the village of Inlet.

❄ Trail in winter: Suitable only for snowshoes. The route is steep. Care must be taken at the cliffs, where the rock can be windswept and icy.

🐾 Distances: To summit, 0.5 mi (0.8 km). Ascent, 445 ft (136 m). Summit elevation, 222 ft (68 m).

74 Fourth Lake–Black Bear Mt.

Trails Illustrated Map 744 and 745: Q10

Scenic Black Bear Mt., at 2448 ft elevation, stands 1.7 mi E of Fourth Lake and over 1 mi N of the W part of Seventh Lake. One has excellent views from this mountain, especially from the long expanse of open rock at the SE side of the crest. The mountain may be ascended from Fourth Lake on the W (trail 74) or from Uncas Rd. on the N (trail 75). The more traditional and popular route is from Fourth Lake, although the top part is steeper than the Uncas Rd. approach. The trails lend themselves to round-trip, circuit, and through hikes. Parts of the mountain hold beautiful stands of larger trees, with open woods beneath.

The Fourth Lake–Black Bear Mt. Trail route has yellow ski trail markers and occasional yellow hiking trail markers. At the base of Black Bear Mt., the trail divides into two routes: the skiable yellow route L and the steep but shorter blue route R. In winter the last part of the yellow trail to the summit (part of the Uncas Rd.–Black Bear Mt. Trail) should be undertaken by advanced skiers only. In springtime and in wet weather, the blue route can be difficult, and hikers' boots can cause a lot of erosion damage. Both routes are described below.

▶Trailhead: From the jct. of NY 28 and Big Moose Rd. in Eagle Bay, drive 1.2 mi E on NY 28 and turn L into an extensive parking area (part of the old highway) off the highway. From the opposite direction, drive 0.9 mi toward Eagle Bay on NY 28 from the public parking area in the center of Inlet and turn R into the trailhead parking area. ◀

From the end of the pavement at the SE end of the parking area (toward Inlet) (0.0 mi), walk 50 yd to the trail sign. The trail is marked with DEC yellow markers, with blue markers on an alternate route.

Turn L onto the beginning of a woods road, and pass a barrier across it in another 30 yd. The yellow-marked route proceeds E on the woods road in a pleasant hardwood forest with a stream on the L. It ascends a rather wet grassy section.

At 0.7 mi, in a clearing, the route forks. Uphill R, first with yellow markers and later with blue, is the Old Black Bear Mt. Trail (trail 77). Continuing on the level straight across the clearing, the yellow trail follows a grassy old woods road through a partly wet area for 0.3 mi. In wet season, a pleasant 10 ft cascade can be heard on the L, just below the trail.

Beyond 1.2 mi, the trail becomes a narrow footpath with tall hardwoods and spruce trees along the way. The route passes on the N side of Black Bear Mt., and at 2.3 mi ends at the Uncas Rd.–Black Bear Mt. Trail (trail 75), from Uncas Rd. This jct. does not have a sign and could easily be missed. Users should take a good look at the trail if they plan to return this way. Follow trail 75 R the rest of the way to the top for a total distance of 3.1 mi.

The most direct route from the summit back to the starting point is to follow the mostly blue-blazed trail W over the summit, and to the jct. with the Old Black Bear Mt. Trail (trail 77), turning R and following trail 77 NW back to the jct. with the Fourth Lake–Black Bear Mt. Trail, making a 5.2 mi round-trip.

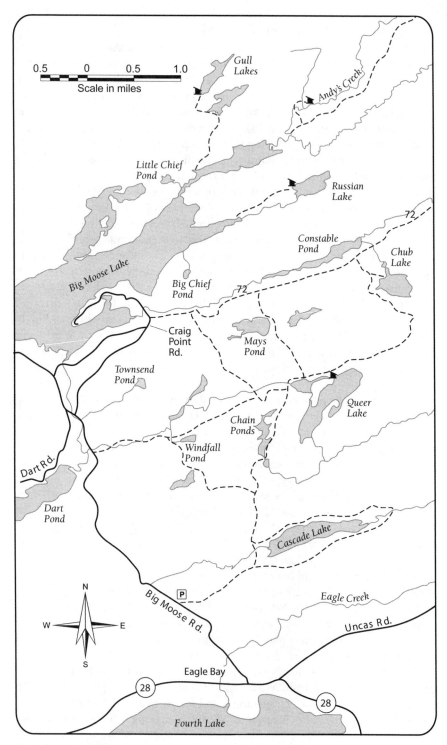

0.5   0   0.5   1.0
Scale in miles

Gull Lakes

Andy's Creek

Little Chief Pond

Russian Lake

72

Constable Pond

Chub Lake

Big Moose Lake

Big Chief Pond

72

Mays Pond

Craig Point Rd.

Townsend Pond

Queer Lake

Chain Ponds

Dart Rd.

Windfall Pond

Dart Pond

Cascade Lake

N
W   E
S

Big Moose Rd.

P

Eagle Creek

Uncas Rd.

Eagle Bay

28

28

Fourth Lake

Retracing your steps on the return trip will avoid the steep and slippery descent on trail 77, for a round-trip of 6.2 mi.

The cross-country skier, whether ascending Black Bear Mt. or not, may return to NY 28 either over the same route, or by the Black Bear Mt. Ski Trail (trail 76). To reach this latter trail, not open in hiking season, from the end of trail 74, turn L (NE) down the Uncas Rd.–Black Bear Mt. Trail (trail 75) for 0.3 mi. The yellow-marked ski trail (trail 76) goes R (S) then W for about 3 mi to reach NY 28 on the N edge of Inlet, just N of the telephone building (about 0.6 mi S of the Fourth Lake–Black Bear Mt. trailhead).

❋ Trail in winter: Suitable for snowshoes. Also skiable, but those who continue on trail 75 to the top would probably need to be expert skiers owing to steeper slopes.

❧ Distances: NY 28 to jct. with Old Black Bear Mt. Trail (trail 77), 0.7 mi; to jct. with Uncas Rd.–Black Bear Mt. Trail (trail 75), 2.3 mi (3.7 km). To summit via trail 75, 3.1 mi (5 km). Ascent, 728 ft (222 m). Summit elevation, 2448 ft (746 m).

75 Uncas Rd.–Black Bear Mt.

Trails Illustrated Map 744: Q10

The original Uncas Rd. began at Eagle Bay, went past Uncas Station on the Raquette Lake Railroad, then turned R and went SE and E to luxurious Uncas Camp on Mohegan Lake. At the R turn onto what is now trail 75, the Brown Tract Rd. (not to be confused with the original Brown's Tract Rd. from Moose River Settlement to Old Forge) continued N to Raquette Lake. It was built as a public road in 1914.

Starting from the corner of Uncas Rd., its route as far as the Brown Tract Ponds ran next to the Raquette Lake Railroad (built in 1899), and more or less followed a previous road privately built in 1897–98 to Sucker Brook Bay on Raquette Lake. After years of confusion with people leaving the Eagle Bay end on Uncas and mysteriously coming out the other end on Brown Tract Road (as there were no signs where the road switched names next to the trailhead), the entire public highway is now called Uncas. Trail 75 follows the course of the old Uncas Rd. over the shoulder of Black Bear Mt.

▶Trailhead: In Eagle Bay at the jct. of Big Moose Rd., drive E on NY 28 for about 0.3 mi, then turn L onto Uncas Rd., paved for the first 1.7 mi. At 2.7 mi, trailhead parking is on a slight uphill route to the R. This is 5.8 mi from the E end of the road off Antlers Rd. in Raquette Lake, 4 mi W of Browns Tract Campground, and 0.5 mi W of Ferds Bog, which could be hiked the same day.◀

From the road (0.0 mi), the yellow-marked route crosses a stream and heads up a gentle hill on the old road. Soon the stately forest environment is interrupted by two grassy areas fringed by small conifers. At 0.8 mi the route turns R at a jct. onto a footpath. (Straight ahead leads down to NY 28 at Eighth Lake campground between Seventh and Eighth Lakes. See trails 76 and 79.

After the R turn, the trail heads down (S) to the base of the hill, then climbs again, turning gradually more W. At 1.2 mi, the Black Bear Mt. Ski Trail (trail 76) goes L. This trail is not open in hiking season.

At 1.5 mi, the yellow Fourth Lake–Black Bear Mt. Trail (trail 74) comes in from the R. Continuing ahead, yellow markers lead uphill toward Black Bear Mt. Along moderate grades on an attractive route, the forest changes from hardwood to spruce-fir. On the L are open areas along cliffs to which one may divert to observe the view.

At about 1.7 mi, open rock becomes more prevalent and paint blazes are used. The route arrives near the edge of the cliffs and then ascends SW along the open ledges near the drop-off. This is a highly scenic route with fine views of Seventh Lake and its forested surroundings on the L (SE). Behind to the NE one sees the extensive open wetland of No Luck Brook with Raquette Lake and Blue Mt. in the distance. The route up is easy enough to follow, but can be difficult to find going down. If you plan to return by this route, take careful note of landmarks along the way.

At 2.3 mi, the open summit has mostly the same views. On very clear days, some of the High Peaks can be seen on the far horizon above Raquette Lake, with Mt. Marcy appearing to the L of prominent Blue Mt. Other mountains are seen on the E and SE.

✵ Trail in winter: Snowmobile trail at the start. Suitable for backcountry skiing and snowshoeing, but the last part at the top is for expert skiers only. The exposed summit can be windblown with arctic conditions.

🐾 Distances: Uncas Rd. trailhead to Uncas Trail, 0.8 mi; to Black Bear Mt. Ski Trail to Inlet, 1.2 mi; to Fourth Lake–Black Bear Mt. yellow trail, 1.5 mi; to summit of Black Bear Mt., 2.3 mi (3.7 km). Ascent, 592 ft (180 m). Summit elevation, 2448 ft (746 m).

76 Black Bear Mt. Ski Trail

Trails Illustrated Map 744 and 745: Q10

This route is open only in winter, owing to wet trail conditions.

▶Trailhead: The trailhead is on NY 28 on the N side of Inlet, just N of a telephone building near Black Bear Trading Post, a quilt shop, and across the street from Stiefvaters Motel. Look carefully in the trees about 20 ft up the road from the building for the trailhead. Parking depends on snow conditions. For a loop trip, one may return to NY 28 via the Fourth Lake–Black Bear Mt. Trail (trail 74) without having to go over the summit of Black Bear Mt.◀

Passing through the trees at the road's edge (0.0 mi), this yellow-marked trail has a nondescript start. It follows nearly level terrain through an area that is very wet in summer.

At 0.2 mi, the route meets a woods road and turns L on the road. In another

David Hough

500 ft, the route curves R and continues on easy ground until crossing Cedar Creek at 1 mi. The climbing leads to a jct. with the abandoned and impassable Seventh Lake–Black Bear Mt. trail at 2.3 mi with the ski trail terminating at another jct. with the Uncas Rd.–Black Bear Mt. Trail (trail 75), at 3 mi.

To continue to the summit of Black Bear Mt., turn L and go up more steeply. This route to the summit, totaling 3.7 mi, is suitable for expert skiers only.

To continue on a loop of Black Bear Mt., turn L and follow the Uncas Rd.–Black Bear Mt. Trail (trail 75) up (SW) for 0.3 mi and turn R onto the Fourth Lake–Black Bear Mt. Trail (trail 74). This jct. is not well marked. Keep a careful watch for the yellow ski trail markers. It is an additional 2.3 mi of easy skiing down to the highway.

❋ Trail in winter: For cross-country skiers only. It is a generally easy trail, except for the summit of Black Bear Mt; that part is for expert skiers only.

🐾 Distances: Telephone building to Cedar Creek, 1 mi; to Uncas Rd.–Black Bear Mt. Trail, 3 mi (4.8 km); to summit, 3.7 mi (5.9 km). Loop to NY 28 via Fourth Lake–Black Bear Mt. Trail, 5.3 mi (8.5 km). Ascent to highest point on ski loop, 335 ft (102 m).

77 Old Black Bear Mt. Trail

Trails Illustrated Map 744: Q10

This older, steeper section of trail, combined with the first part of the Fourth Lake–Black Bear Mt. Trail (trail 74), is the shortest route up Black Bear Mt.

▶Locator: Interior trail starting at 0.7 mi from the NY 28 trailhead on trail 74. ◀

From the clearing (0.0 mi) at 0.7 mi on the Fourth Lake–Black Bear Mt. Trail (trail 74), the Old Black Bear Mt. trail heads R, uphill, following yellow and then blue markers. The trail climbs E on an old logging road to a nearly level clearing at 0.2 mi. Beyond the clearing, the old road curves L and continues on level ground as an open, grassy, but often wet route to about 0.4 mi.

After a gradual ascent on an eroding, rocky, and root-filled trail to the base of the final slope—where a careful watch must be kept for markers—a steep ascent starts at 1 mi with the forest partly changing from hardwoods to conifers. The rest of the ascent is mostly on rock, with several pitches requiring some scrambling. Ledges provide fine S outlooks over Sixth and Seventh Lakes, and at 1.3 mi one has a beautiful view W and SW of Fourth Lake, the only view of that lake to be had from the trails on this mountain. The summit is reached at 1.4 mi, or 2.1 mi from NY 28.

❆ Trail in winter: Too steep to ski; also not suitable for snowshoers owing to some steep sections.

🏃 Distances: Trail 74 to clearing, 0.2 mi; to steep ascent, 1 mi; to summit, 1.4 mi (2.2 km). Summit distance from trailhead, 2.1 mi (3.4 km). Ascent, 728 ft (222 m). Summit elevation, 2448 ft (746 m).

78 Seventh Lake

Trails Illustrated Map 744: P11

This is a nice trail, although difficult to get to. The W end has no parking and the E end is an unmarked path.

▶Trailheads: At 1.5 mi SE of the public parking lot at Inlet, a paved town road —Seventh Lake Rd. or Drive—turns L (NE) to go to the back side of Seventh Lake. The road turns to dirt and from there on is a private road with no parking available. Payne's Boat Livery has parking only for its boat/canoe rental customers. The trail is at the end of the road, but there is no parking there, so users would have to park before the end of the town road if a spot could be found on public property. The E end of the trail is an unmarked path.◀

After parking (0.0 mi), hikers can walk down the private road to the end, a private camp at a turn-around at 1.4 mi. The trail continues past the garage for that camp and enters state land. The route becomes especially attractive here, going through a grove of paper birch and then, for most of the rest of the way, through stands of stately white pine that provide a footpath covered with needles. Informal campsites by the lake's clean-cut shoreline lie along the route.

The main attraction of the trail is at 2.8 mi from the start of the road: a point of land with a large rock (Arnolds Rock) rising from the lake, a lean-to, and a cleared area under the pines ideal for camping. The trail goes in front of the lean-to and continues along the lake shore past more informal campsites. At 3.2 mi it enters a 225 yd stretch of cleared forest floor looking like a long, continuous campground, at the end of which is a second, unusually large, lean-to.

The trail ends at 3.6 mi at a small beach opposite the W side of an island in Seventh Lake, with some stumps standing in the near part of the lake. The edge of the lake here has a shallow, sandy bottom. It is less than a half mile on unmarked path from here to the Uncas Trail (trail 79).

❄ Trail in winter: Parking may be difficult from either end. Suitable for skiing or snowshoeing.

🐾 Distances: Payne's Boat Livery to beginning of trail, 1.1 mi; to Arnolds Rock, 1.4 mi; to clearing before second lean-to, 1.8 mi; to end, 2.2 mi (3.5 km).

79 Uncas Trail

Trails Illustrated Map 744: Q11

The Uncas Trail, a broad, smooth trail with easy or moderate grades, goes through a majestic forest. It extends from the Eighth Lake Public Campground W and NW to Uncas Rd., passing the W side of Bug Lake, which is popular for fishing. It has a side loop trail to Eagles Nest Lake and the SE end of Bug Lake, and provides access to the top of Black Bear Mt. This trail is designated as a hiking, mountain biking, and snowmobile trail.

The Uncas Trail is part of the original Uncas Rd., built by W.W. Durant in 1896 from Eagle Bay to Mohegan Lake as an access to Uncas Camp on that lake and to other luxurious camps he had built on Sagamore Lake and Lake Kora. (Until then, the camps had been reached only by roads from the head of navigation of Raquette Lake's South Inlet.) After the Raquette Lake Railroad started operating in 1900, visitors to these camps could get off the train at Uncas Station and continue on the Uncas Rd. The present-day hiker on Uncas Trail can imagine the New York financial tycoon J.P. Morgan riding along this route with his elegant carriage and team of horses to Uncas Camp, which he purchased from Durant in 1896.

▶Trailheads: To reach the S trailhead, start from the public parking area in the center of Inlet. Drive 6.1 mi E and NE on NY 28 to the entrance of the Eighth Lake Public Campground on the L. Tell the registration booth attendant that you are going to hike the Uncas Trail (you will not have to pay the day-use fee). Sign in and out at the trail register near the booth. Go straight ahead (W) into the

campground on the paved road, continuing into the woods on an unimproved vehicle track for 0.2 mi, and park on either side.

The N trailhead is at 0.8 mi on trail 75. ◀

From the S trailhead (0.0 mi), the old road, marked with yellow DEC trail markers, goes W for 100 yd and crosses a bridge over the inlet of Seventh Lake, the northernmost arm of that lake lying on the L. (This is a takeout point for the canoe carry from Seventh to Eighth Lake.) The route starts uphill.

At 0.6 mi, just before crossing the outlet of Bug and Eagles Nest Lakes, the trail forks L, the R fork being the side trail to Eagles Nest Lake, also with yellow trail markers. There is no trail sign here. The loop trip recommended below starts at this point.

Continuing L, the trail crosses the stream and goes SW, then NW. The end of the side loop comes in on the R at 0.9 mi. The route goes along the W side of Bug Lake, passing an anglers' launch site.

After climbing above the lake, the trail turns NW and crosses the divide between the Moose–Black River and Raquette River watersheds.

At 2.3 mi a snowmobile trail goes L (SW) toward NY 28 near Inlet, and at 2.4 mi the trail crosses No Luck Brook, the inlet to the Browns Tract Ponds, on a long bridge. At 2.7 mi, the trail ends at Black Bear Mt. Ski Trail (trail 76) leading toward Uncas Rd.–Black Bear Mt. Trail (trail 75). L is the Black Bear Mt. summit, R is the Uncas Rd. trailhead.

The side trail mentioned above (0.6 and 0.9 mi) can be accessed from either end, although the one going from Bug Lake at 0.9 mi takes you down a steep bank to Eagles Nest, while coming the other way you climb the steep bank.

From 0.6 mi the trail goes N through splendid hemlocks, though not without a couple of muddy places. At 0.1 mi on the side trail, keep R at the fork, arriving in 30 yd at the edge of Eagles Nest Lake with its impressive stand of hemlocks on the R. This is, in reality, a modest pond, with dead wood lining the shore and an 80 ft cliff on the opposite side.

A narrow trail L along the pond's outlet leads in 40 yd to a point where an alternate stretch of the yellow side trail comes in on the L. Cross the wood-clogged outlet on the R and climb steeply NW for a short distance to a beautiful area at the SE end of Bug Lake at 0.3 on the side trail. Here on a forest floor carpeted with needles are tall hemlocks and a few great white pines. Tall pines grace part of the lake's shoreline.

To retrace your steps from here would make a round-trip hike of 1.8 mi. To return to the Uncas Trail so as to go farther N on it by Bug Lake, or return by it, go L (S) a short distance, cross the lake's outlet on the R, and follow a footpath that initially winds its way through a thick stand of spruce and then goes SW and S past majestic trees to reach the Uncas Trail at 1.1 mi. (There is no trail sign at this jct.) This completes a 0.4 mi side loop off the Uncas Trail. From here, it is 0.9 mi back to the trailhead.

❄ Trail in winter: Easy skiing or snowshoeing, but trail must be shared with snowmobiles. The steep bank between Bug and Eagles Nest Lakes is best avoided. The campground is not open.

🏃 Distances: S trailhead to Eagles Nest Lake, 0.7 mi; to Bug Lake, 1.1 mi; to Uncas Rd.–Black Bear Mt. Trail (trail 75), 2.7 mi (4.3 km). To N trailhead via trail 75, 3.5 mi (5.6 km).

80 Cathedral Pines

Trails Illustrated Map 744: P11

This is one of the shortest circuit trails in the Adirondacks and one of the most rewarding for its length. Only 210 yd long, it visits a stand of great white pines lying between NY 28 and the upper, narrow section of Seventh Lake.

▶Trailhead: The trail starts on the W side of the highway at a point 0.9 mi SW of the entrance to the Eighth Lake Public Campground and 1 mi NE of the Fishing Access Site on Seventh Lake. Park along the highway, cross a ditch by a DEC signpost (sometimes without a sign), and take the path marked with blue painted blazes.◀

Most of these great pines are along the first, upper part of the trail, including a spur a few yards long. On the lower part, a stone pillar holds a plaque commemorating a young U.S. Air Force officer, the son of a local district ranger, killed in action in World War II. The plaque, dedicated by Governor Thomas Dewey in September 1946, was secured to a great white pine that snapped about 20 ft above the ground in 1989. The pillar in front of that tree was erected in 1992. The circuit ends at the highway a few yards from where it started.

❄ Trail in winter: Suitable for snowshoes. One steep bank would make it difficult for skiers, unless they descend by sidestepping.

🏃 Distance: 0.1 mi loop (0.2 km).

81 Death Falls

Trails Illustrated Map 744: R13

The falls are close to but not visible from NY 28 near Raquette Lake. They are situated on a broad headwall about 100 ft high, on a tributary creek of Death Brook.

▶Trailhead: From the jct. with Raquette Lake village road, go E on NY 28. Pass the bridge over South Inlet at 2.5 mi. The trailhead is on the R at 3.3 mi near the top of a hill. There is a yellow barrier gate, but no sign. There are no trail markers.◀

From the gate (0.0 mi), a dirt road goes 0.2 mi across level ground to a jct. at the base of a hill. The L fork leads 100 ft to an open view near the foot of the falls. The R fork leads around the hill with a gentle climb to the shelf of land above the falls. This "wide route" (R fork) to the top is recommended. Those who scramble up next to the falls are creating erosion, or "wrecking it," in the words of one DEC official; this steeper route is also potentially dangerous. Turn L at the creek crossing and follow the water to the falls at 0.3 mi. Exercise caution, and remember the name of the falls.

❋ Trail in winter: Easy for skis or snowshoes to the foot of the falls, though short. Easy for snowshoes to the top of the falls. Access to the view at the top of the falls is dangerous in winter.

🏃 Distances: NY 28 to base of falls, 0.2 mi; to top, 0.3 mi (0.5 km).

82 Sagamore Cascades

Trails Illustrated Map 744: Q12

This route leads to the Cascades, formerly known as South Inlet Falls, a minor waterfall on Raquette Lake's South Inlet. Below the falls, the quiet water seems suitable for swimming, but the water appears nutrient-laden and the bottom is slick. A loop trip can be made by wading the inlet stream and returning on the trail along the E bank, although that section is wet in many places. Canoeists paddle to the falls from NY 28 at the edge of Raquette Lake's South Bay.

▶Trailhead: From NY 28 across from the turnoff to Raquette Lake village, head S on Sagamore Rd. Go 2.9 mi to an old dirt road L, blocked by large boulders. There is space for several cars in front of the boulders. There is a DEC foot trail notice on a tree. The trail is an old road, marked occasionally by red ribbons. The second trailhead is 280 yd down the road at another old road L, just after the road crosses South Inlet stream.◀

From the parking area (0.0 mi), the old road is nearly level, wide, and smooth for 0.2 mi. The remaining trail heads very gently down, with a level section at a clearing at 0.5 mi. The trail approaches the creek, then curves to the W, following the contour above the water.

After a curve N again, another clearing has two roads leaving its N end. The trail follows the R one, proceeding along the high bank of the stream. At 1.3 mi, there is an S curve leading down to the stream and the first of several landings with views. A short section N along the stream leads to the Cascades at 1.4 mi, and the trail ends at a canoe launch at 1.5 mi.

There was once a bridge across the Cascades, but hikers must now wade the stream above if they wish to cross. There is a shallow but slippery spot near an island above the cascades. A Sagamore trail guide leaflet notes that skiers, accompanied by a guide, could cross the inlet about 100 yd below the falls, but extreme caution is advised. The water is deep and the ice may be thin.

After crossing the stream, the trail follows a very wet old road (built by Durant in 1895) generally S along the stream bank to the second trailhead at 3.1 mi. The footpath is adequate and marked well enough with red ribbons, but in at least one spot leaves the soggy road for higher ground. There is a trail jct. on the L at 2.5 mi (1 mi from the Cascades). That unmarked trail is the Powerhouse Loop,

Raquette Lake. Mark Bowie

on public land but mostly used by skiers from Sagamore. Farther along the creek, at 2.7 mi (1.2 mi from the Cascades), there is an old dam and brick powerhouse, once used for power at Sagamore.

The remaining route is a pleasant old road along quiet water, passing through a parking clearing and ending at the gravel Sagamore Rd. at 3.1 mi. Another 280 yd of road walking to the R will close the loop back to the first trailhead.

❄ Trail in winter: Easy skiing or snowshoeing, except the crossing of South Inlet, which can be dangerous if the ice is not thick enough.

🚶 Distances: First trailhead to end of trail below Cascades, 1.5 mi; to second trailhead, 3.1 mi. A complete loop is 3.3 mi (5.3 km).

83 Sagamore Lake

Trails Illustrated Map 744: Q13

This trail is mostly used by guests at the Sagamore Lodge and Conference Center. Except for a minor section at the end, it is all on public land. Hikers and skiers not staying at Sagamore should follow the route described here and not enter private land. For those wishing to see the camp, public tours are given daily during the summer. For the tour, follow the signs at the entrance just across the road from the DEC parking lot. (See www.sagamore.org.) There are no state markers, but there is orange flagging at intersections and other spots. This pleasant, mostly shaded trail winds clockwise around the lake, forking R at trail jcts., except to avoid Sagamore property at the start and near the end, where L turns are necessary.

▶Trailhead: From NY 28 across from the turnoff to Raquette Lake village, head S on Sagamore Rd. Go 3.3 mi to a jct., then turn R and cross a creek. At 3.4 mi, with some Sagamore buildings on the L, turn R into a DEC parking lot by a sign that says, "Tour parking, 300 ft."◀

From the parking lot (0.0 mi), return to the road and turn L. Go downhill and across the outlet bridge you just drove over and to the road jct. 0.2 mi from the parking lot. Turn R and go toward the lake, reaching another jct. at 0.3 mi. A gated bridge R allows registered guests into Sagamore. Turn L onto an old road blocked at about 50 yd by boulders with a side path leading 20 yd to the lake.

Continue ahead on the old road as it follows along the W shore of Sagamore Lake. At 0.4 mi, there is a small trail R to the shore of the lake with a nice view. At 0.6 mi, there is another trail R, just steps to an overlook with a very nice view near the NW corner of the lake. Use caution taking in the view from the top of the cliff.

At 0.8 mi, the trail turns R (straight ahead N leads to South Inlet). Almost immediately (in 30–40 yd), there is another jct. The trail follows the R fork, marked with orange ribbon, whereas the other trail has yellow and blue flagging. The old carriage road passes near an open hilltop L and continues in pleasant woods. At 1.3 mi, there is an iron cross planted 10 ft off the trail L. This is a monument to John Hoy. If you take the Sagamore tour, ask about this tragic tale.

Soon there are again glimpses of the lake R. There is another jct. with a yellow- and blue-flagged trail (L) in a clearing at 1.4 mi. The old carriage road continues straight through the clearing with orange flagging and soon starts gently downhill.

After leveling out, the trail crosses the inlet on a wide plank bridge at 2 mi. The trail turns R and follows the contour, keeping R at two old road jcts.

After 2.4 mi, there are again glimpses of the lake as the trail goes through mixed woods. At 2.7 mi, the trail heads toward the water. At the turn L, there is a path about 50 yd to a rocky edge of the lake. The trail then generally parallels the shore, close and then farther away, with another easy access (about 10 yd) to the lake at 3 mi.

Just before 3.5 mi, cars and buildings can be seen through the trees R. The trail makes a slight climb and reaches a clearing with a two-track road R, which goes onto the Sagamore Institute property and should be used only by guests staying there. "Lake Trail" signs point the way, L, on a footpath S, which reaches the gravel road jct. a few yd away from the Mohegan Rd. gate before 3.7 mi. Turn R on the road and proceed another 0.2 mi to the parking lot entrance L, reaching the parking lot at 3.9 mi (6.3 km).

❋ Trail in winter: Suitable for cross-country skiing, although lot may not be plowed.

🚶 Distance: Parking lot to start of old road next to lake, 0.3 mi; to clearing and R turn at South Inlet Trail, 0.8 mi; to bridge over inlet, 2 mi; to edge of lake, 3 mi; to clearing next to Sagamore, nearly 3.5; to road, 3.7; back to parking lot, 3.9 mi (6.2 km).

84 Uncas Rd.–Mohegan Lake

Trails Illustrated Map 744: P11

Originally, Uncas Rd., built in 1896, began at Eagle Bay, went past Uncas Station on the Raquette Lake Railroad, then turned R (E) and went SE and E to luxurious Uncas Camp on Mohegan Lake. It then continued E to another great camp at Sagamore Lake. These were the summer homes of J. P. Morgan and Alfred G. Vanderbilt.

Today, the route is named Uncas Rd. all the way through, rather than changing to Browns Tract Rd. This section of Uncas Rd. is used by hikers to reach the road at Mohegan Lake. There is a private Camp Uncas on the NE peninsula. Coming from the Sagamore Lake (E) end, access is shorter, but not as woodsy.

▶ Trailheads: To reach the W trailhead, go 4.6 mi S from the turnoff to the community of Raquette Lake (or 5 mi N from Inlet, about 0.8 mi N of the Seventh Lake Boat Launch) on NY 28. The trailhead is on the E side about 300 ft S of the entrance to Eighth Lake Campground. Park in the open area near the road. Two trails leave the open spot. The Uncas Road Trail is on level ground to the R (SE).

The E trailhead is the same as for the Sagamore Lake Trail (trail 83). ◀

From the W trailhead on NY 28 (0.0 mi), the old road, with only an occasional snowmobile marker, rises gently and crosses Seventh Lake Inlet at 0.2 mi, then bends L and starts to ascend. The next 1.5 mi is a gentle climb, with occasional flat spots on the grassy roadway. At 1.8 mi, an unnamed pond can be seen through the trees to the L for several yards. The trail tops out at 2 mi, turns S, and starts gently down.

There is a jct. at 2.6 mi with the old snowmobile trail heading uphill to the R. Uncas Rd. continues ahead, now with blue markers, passing another grassy road going uphill R and reaching an old cable barrier across the road at 2.8. Shortly beyond the barrier, the rotten stringers of a collapsed bridge dangle across a steep-banked stream. About 30 yd before the chasm, however, the trail leaves

Uncas Rd., becoming a blue-marked footpath R going upstream to avoid the steep banks. It soon reaches another road which takes a southerly route that comes close to the W side of Mohegan Lake.

(A side trip R of up to 0.9 mi one way provides views of the W side of the lake with the road coming within 60 ft of the lake before bending away. That side road goes about 3 mi to a private camp of the Bear Pond Sportsmen's Club. The club's land extends for about 1000 ft around the clubhouse. The remainder is state land, including old unmarked routes to Bear Pond, which is on state land. The overgrown, mostly unmarked trail from Moose River Rd. can be used to reach Bear Pond from the S.)

From the point where the footpath along the outlet stream reaches the extension road, the blue-marked trail turns L, goes downhill, and uses the extension road's bridge to cross the outlet. Uphill, there is a bend to the R and a small clearing, then before 3.2 mi another bend R and a larger clearing. At this point the trail is back on Uncas Rd. At 3.5 mi, just yards E of small clearings on both sides of the road, there is an unmarked but well-used trail R (S).

(This path, with a slight bend R, leads through a pine grove to water's edge in a little over 0.1 mi. There are some benches, a fire ring, and a sandy beach at the foot of the white pine grove, with views of the Great Camp from the point above.)

From the pine grove side trail, Uncas Rd. continues past the N side of the lake to a jct. at 3.8 mi. The road R leads to Camp Uncas on Mohegan Lake and the road ahead leads to Camp Sagamore and Sagamore Lake in another 1.5 mi. That route, along maintained road with no markers, heads NE, follows the contours of a hill, goes NE along a hilltop, goes N down a hill, and turns NE for 0.2 mi, reaching the gate at 5.1 mi. (The R fork at the gate goes to private land at Kamp Kill Kare.) It's another 0.2 mi to the DEC parking lot next to Sagamore on the L (N) side of the road.

Except for the footpath cutover from Uncas Rd. to the extension road and the pine grove path to the lake, both less than 0.2 mi, mountain biking would be an option. A sign at the Sagamore Lake end notes that hiking and biking are permitted.

❋ Trail in winter: Snowmobile trail, except for the last section near Mohegan Lake. If snowmobile traffic is light, this could be a nice trip for strong skiers. The return trip is a long glide down.

🦌 Distances: NY 28 trailhead to view of pond, 1.8 mi; to jct. with old snowmobile trail, 2.6 mi; to footpath off Uncas Rd., 2.8 mi; to jct. with extension road to Bear Pond Club, 3 mi; to pine grove campsite, 3.5 mi; to E trailhead at DEC parking lot by Sagamore Lake, 5.3 mi (8.5 km).

Ann Hough

85 East Shore Path and Snowmobile Trail

Trails Illustrated Map 744: O10

The East Shore Path gives access to the shores of Limekiln Lake below Fawn Lake Mt. Public access to this beautiful shoreline is via a snowmobile trail from Moose River Rd. The other end of the trail connects with Limekiln Rd. on the N, but as a private path going right through the front yards of many cottages along the E bay. Hikers who have not obtained permission should not use that route.

▶Trailhead: From the W entrance to MRPWF, go E on Moose River Rd. for 3 mi. As the road takes a sharp turn to the L, an almost unnoticed snowmobile trail goes straight off the road, headed downhill. There is a slight clear spot for parking one or two cars 30 ft down the road at the bend.◀

The trail passes across the lower rear of the small clearing (0.0 mi), headed downhill L. This is a very pleasant old road, somewhat overgrown, with a green, soft-carpeted surface. It passes a wetland on the L, then goes over a slight hill before descending to cross Limekiln Lake inlet at 0.6 mi. From here on, the almost level trail follows the side of the inlet, which bubbles along rock ledges and under large boulders, until it reaches quiet meadowlands.

Continuing W, the width of the meadows grows, while the trail keeps on solid ground at its edge. The forest on the uphill side is of well-established open hardwoods. Soon after first glimpses of the lake appear, the wide old road ends abruptly at the lake's edge at 1.8 mi. There is heavy brush on either side of the trail, seeming to block all further travel. The view over Limekiln Lake is quite nice, with the prominent W peninsula dominating the scene.

About 30 ft back from the end of the snowmobile trail, there is an unmarked but maintained path on the R (N) side of the trail which continues on around the lake. This is the East Shore Path. Continuing on this path, there is an unofficial campsite above the lake shore at 1.9 mi. The path continues near the shore until it turns abruptly R at 2.1 mi and passes behind a slight hill at the tip of the E shore peninsula. This inland passage doesn't last long, and the lake shore is soon close on the L. Thereafter, the route stays close to the shore and its beautiful views.

State land ends at 2.7 mi, where a house is visible uphill R. From this point on, the path crosses right through the tiny front yards of side-by-side private cottages and

Moose River Plains. Richard Nowicki

is clearly not a public trail. The hiker should return by the snowmobile trail.

❄ Trail in winter: Easy snowshoeing; easy and pleasant skiing, although the beginner may find the first half mile a bit steep. Parking is no closer than the W entrance, 3 mi from the trailhead. Note that much of this route is a snowmobile trail.

🐾 Distances: Moose River Rd. to level ground at creek crossing, 0.6 mi; to end of snowmobile trail, 1.8 mi; to informal campsite, 1.9 mi; to end of state land, 2.7 mi (4.3 km).

Bear Pond

Trails Illustrated Map 744: O11

A remote pond with boggy edges and a so-called trail best left to experienced bushwhackers.

▶Trailhead: Drive E for about 300 ft from the jct. of Moose River Rd. and Rock Dam Rd. (4.6 mi from the W entrance and 16.6 mi from the E entrance to the MRPWF), starting up a slight hill. The first road L goes to a gravel pit. Some 100 ft farther on, at the top of the slight rise, turn L onto a two-track dirt road. Go 0.7 mi along this side road to an overgrown parking area on the L with a barricaded road beyond. The two-track road continues E past this trailhead to rejoin Moose River Rd. in another 0.5 mi.◀

Beyond the barricade (0.0 mi), the trail follows an overgrown old road to a wetland at the SW tip of Bear Pond at 2.5 mi. It climbs a little at first, then contours along the flank of Mt. Tom before descending to the pond. It is not marked.

❄ Trail in winter: Far from a plowed road, very thick undergrowth.

🐾 Distances: To SW end of Bear Pond, 2.5 mi (4 km).

Benedict Creek

Trails Illustrated Map 744: O11

This is not a marked or maintained trail, even though it continues to appear as a snowmobile trail on the maps handed out at the entrance gates. It could serve as a wet nature walk into a celebration of old-growth forest with magnificent white pines and birch trees.

▶Trailhead: From the jct. of Moose River Rd. and Rock Dam Rd., drive E for 2.6 mi. Or, from the jct. of Moose River Rd. and Otter Brook Rd., go N uphill toward Inlet for 1.1 mi to a sharp L turn in the road. Turn E to a campsite on the sharp turn on a steep hill.◀

From the barricade at the campsite (0.0 mi), the trail, going NE, heads gently downhill on an old road, passes along the lower edge of a small clearing L at 0.2 mi, and continues downhill straight ahead. It soon reaches the creek level and continues along the L edge of the marshy bottom. There is no particular end to the trail; it just becomes fainter and fainter.

❄ Trail in winter: Listed as a snowmobile trail, but no longer useable as such. Fine skiing and snowshoeing, but it is far from drivable roads.

🏃 Distance: Your choice.

86 Mitchell Ponds

Trails Illustrated Map 744: O11

The Mitchell Ponds are beautiful remote waters, easy to reach on a pleasant path and offering some opportunities for camping. Robert West, a WWI veteran, set up camp here some years after the war, having been advised to spend time in the open air. He lived quite alone, fishing, guiding sportsmen, and trapping in the area until WWII.

▶Trailheads: To reach the E (main) trailhead, from the W entrance to the MRPWF near Limekiln Lake, go E for 7.9 mi. Turn R onto an old two-track road and park in the grassy space about 50 ft ahead. From the E (Cedar River) gate, the trail is 10.3 mi from the entrance and 0.3 mi past the Otter Brook Rd. jct.

The W trailhead, unmarked, is 0.3 mi E of the Rock Dam Rd. jct. (which is 4.6 mi E of the W entrance to MRPWF). Park near the entrance to a camping area where a snowmobile trailhead continues through the back (S) of the camp-site.◀

From the barrier and parking area at the E trailhead (0.0 mi), the route follows an old road, in good condition, with views of lowlands L and a steep bank R. There are occasional yellow markers, but the road is obvious. At 1.3 mi, the valley narrows and the road comes close to a stream.

As the trail comes into the open in a grassy area at 1.8 mi, a slight but marked trail joins on the R. This is the continuation of the route. Straight ahead is a trail leading to the end of Upper Mitchell Pond, the higher of the two ponds.

(Continuing ahead on the side trail past the jct., the road almost disappears at the edge of the clearing, and a foot trail continues with yellow DEC markers. In another 100 yd this trail ends at a scenic picnic site near the edge of the water, which is not inviting, but views of a rock face R make it worth the trip.)

Back at the jct., next to an 8 ft rock at the side of the clearing, the main trail continues on a lesser-noticed woods road going R, with yellow markers, across a small creek. The road soon reaches another trail jct. just as it turns uphill on a steady climb. The yellow trail turns L at the base of the hill. (The road up the hill is a snowmobile trail leading in 1.7 mi to the N trailhead on Moose River Rd. This snowmobile trail is a generally pleasant and easy route up and over a hill, except for a crossing of a beaver dam, marked with yellow and snowmobile markers.)

Continuing L (W) from the jct. at the base of the hill, the yellow trail follows the contour near Upper Mitchell Pond on a footpath. Coming even with Lower Mitchell Pond at 2.2 mi, the trail gets bumpier along the hillside but with views of the lower pond. It passes rock formations R, rounds the end of Lower Mitchell Pond, turns L, and ends at 2.8 mi at the outlet stream. To reach an informal campsite, cross the stream on rocks or logs and go up the hillside for 50 ft onto a point, which has a nice small picnic or swimming beach on the other side.

❋ Trail in winter: The MRPWF gates are closed to cars in winter. Snowmobiling area.

🚶 Distances: To Upper Mitchell Pond, 1.9 mi; to far end of Lower Mitchell Pond, 2.8 mi (4.5 km). To alternate trailhead via snowmobile trail, 3.5 mi (5.6 km).

87 Helldiver Pond

Trails Illustrated Map 744: O11

Leads to a small pond that can be explored with a canoe or kayak after a brief carry.

▶Trailhead: A small dirt road goes S from the Moose River Rd. at 8.1 mi from the W entrance, or 13.1 mi from the E entrance, to the MRPWF (0.8 mi E of the jct. with Otter Brook Rd.). Drive 0.2 mi down this road to a camping and parking area.◀

From the trailhead (0.0 mi), the trail goes briefly through open forest, then twists through dense forest on corduroy to the shore of the pond. The pond is pretty, but the only effective access beyond the trail is by boat. Its most likely use is for fishing or camping and lazily paddling about. It's held back by a beaver dam at the NW corner.

❋ Trail in winter: Far from drivable roads.

🚶 Distance: To Helldiver Pond, 0.2 mi (0.3 km).

88 Ice House Pond

Trails Illustrated Map 744: N11

Early market hunters had an ice house here, in which they stored venison destined for the market in Saratoga. The plains here are notably open, and deer were no doubt easy to find.

▶Trailhead: Start at the jct. of Moose River Rd. and Otter Brook Rd., 8.3 mi from the W entrance or 12.9 mi from the E entrance to the MRPWF. Drive S on Otter Brook Rd. for 0.8 mi. Trailhead is on the L (E), parking on the shoulder on the R (W). This point is 0.4 mi N of the Moose River.◀

A gate on an old road is the trailhead (0.0 mi). The route goes through a large field of bushes, re-enters the forest, and ends at a campsite by the edge of the pond. Generally wide, the trail is an easy canoe carry. The pond has nice scenery and appears to be popular with anglers.

❋ Trail in winter: Snowmobile trail.

🚶 Distance: To Ice House Pond, 0.4 mi (0.6 km).

89 Beaver Lake

This was once the Chapin estate, established about 1904. The lodge had seven buildings, now all gone. Chapin had stayed with the Kenwells before that, and apparently liked the area. Wellington Alexander Kenwell had a hotel on the Moose River near the trailhead from 1891 to 1901. This is presumed to be the Sportsmen's Lodge at Indian Clearing listed in S.R. Stoddard's 1894 tourist guide, *The Adirondacks Illustrated.* Stoddard warned that, "The way is rough, and the accommodations primitive...." Things in this area haven't changed much since then. Gerald Kenwell established another public lodge later about 3 mi up Otter Brook from the trailhead at a spot labeled "Kenwells" on older maps. The lodge was still in business in 1947, but is now gone. A state brochure on the area says the lake "is named for its odd shape which resembles a beaver."

▶Trailhead: From the jct. of Moose River Rd. and Otter Brook Rd. (8.3 mi from the W entrance, or 12.9 mi from the E entrance to the MRPWF), drive S on Otter Brook Rd. for 1.2 mi to the bridge across the South Branch of the Moose River. The trailhead road is on the right (W) just S of the bridge. Drive 0.2 mi on the access road and park near the barricade, without blocking it.◀

The trail starts at a bridge with a double sluice designed to handle a large flow (0.0 mi). It passes along the South Branch of the Moose River for a short ways, then swings inland through a dark forest of large trees. Starting at 1.2 mi, a stand of white pines pokes majestically above the forest. Their limbs start where the other trees leave off.

Beyond the white pines, the trail tops out at the cleared site of an old sawmill at 1.9 mi. From there, a short road plunges diagonally downhill to the shore of the lake and another clearing at the site of a long-departed cabin at 2.1 mi. Informal campsites here and at another spot nearby give excellent lake scenery, although they are close to the water.

❋ Trail in winter: Snowmobile trail. Very far from drivable roads.

🚶 Distance: To Beaver Lake, 2.1 mi (3.4 km).

90 Lost Ponds

This trail passes a stillwater on Sumner Stream and then continues to another pond visited by anglers and picnickers.

▶Trailhead: From the jct. of Moose River Rd. and Otter Brook Rd. (8.3 mi from the W entrance, or 12.9 mi from the E entrance to the MRPWF), drive E on Moose River Rd. for 1.9 mi. Turn L (N) onto a dirt road, leading to a parking spot after 0.4 mi.◀

Starting at the barrier just beyond the parking area with two campsites (0.0 mi), the trail takes a jeep road N, passing a camping site on the R (E) just before bridging Sumner Stream. There is a path next to the campsite leading a short way R to the remains of a dam in the stream. The dam has backed up the picturesque stillwater, which has handsome conifers around it.

Beyond the bridge, the route L (W) leads to a picnic spot above the S shore of the eastern pond at 0.7 mi. The route beyond is an old logging road, now overgrown and choked off, although sporadic flagging may continue. The alternate route straight ahead from the jct. at the bridge leads around the N side of the pond to a fish barrier dam on the outlet stream. The rock ledge on the N shore of the pond is covered with poison ivy, the only place with that plant in the MRPWF. Plant researchers Brian and Eileen Keelan say there are several outcroppings of marble there, which is uncommon in the Adirondacks and usually has a distinct plant community. Because poison ivy is not a true calciphile—a species that grows exclusively on calcium carbonate substrates such as limestone, marble, and even artificial cement or mortar—its growth only there may be partly coincidental. Growing with it, also found nowhere else in the MRPWF, are early saxifrage, purple clematis, and slender wheatgrass.

❄ Trail in winter: Snowmobile trail. Far from accessible roads, but otherwise suitable for skis or snowshoes.

🐾 Distance: To picnic spot on E Lost Pond, 0.7 mi (1.1 km); to outlet stream, 1.3 mi (2.1 km).

91 Sly Pond

Trails Illustrated Map 744: O13

A real wilderness experience is the climb through a col and down to Sly Pond at 2872 ft. Primitive camping might be possible a suitable distance (150 ft from stream and trail is the legal minimum) from where streams cross the trail for water access.

▶Trailheads: From the jct. of the Moose River and Otter Brook Rds. (8.3 mi from the W entrance, or 12.9 mi from the E entrance to the MRPWF), go S on Otter Brook Rd. 2.3 mi to a truck road on the L (NE), 1.1 mi beyond the Moose River. Parking is along the start of the trail off Otter Brook Rd., with spots for as many as five vehicles on the R and a couple of spots for a vehicle on the L (make sure not to block the roadway). A flat spot opposite the trail on Otter Brook Rd. is not suitable; it collects water.

A second summer trailhead requires wading the Moose River. From the jct. of Moose River Rd. and Otter Brook Rd. in the MRPWF, go E on Moose River Rd. for 3.8 mi. Take the side road R (S) for 0.1 mi to parking by a campsite.◀

From the barrier above Otter Brook Rd (0.0 mi), the trail starts uphill on a red-marked truck road with a gate. Soon a rock wall several feet high extending some 40 yd is seen L. At 0.3 mi a more impressive rock formation, maybe 20 ft high, is seen on the R. After rising about 140 ft from the road to about 2100 ft, the trail drops to about the 2000 ft line and continues with slight grade changes,

Moose River. Mark Bowie

crossing a bridge at 2.6 mi and reaching a jct. at 2.7 mi.

(Ahead is a 0.6 mi access trail that requires crossing the Moose River. The river is within sight L soon after the jct. and parallels it to the site of a former bridge, but now fording, possibly 30 ft downstream, is required, unless one can find enough rocks.)

From the jct., the main trail turns R on a gradual uphill with mostly red markers and a roaring stream R. The trail crosses a small side stream before it bends around a hill, turning nearly E. Sand banks are crossed at 4.3 mi and 4.6 mi. At 5.1 mi there is a Y in the trail at which hikers need to be sure to keep L. The trail bends R (SE) around another hill and at 6.2 mi reaches a beaver dam and flooding. At 6.3 mi, the trail avoids some former beaver ponds, bending L and starting uphill, with far fewer markers and more blowdowns. The climb is moderate, with some views L, and then becomes steeper, reaching height of land (elevation 2940 ft) on the Little Moose Mt. range at 7.3 mi. From there the roadway becomes obscure, but in 20 yd (or more when there are more leaves) there are glimpses of water downhill as the route descends slightly. The trail goes through a wet area of spruce-fir to the edge of Sly Pond at 7.7 mi and about 1000 ft above the Otter Brook Rd. trailhead. This lofty pond, at 2872 ft elevation, is lined by conifers and has boggy edges. It is doubtless devoid of fish. From the pond's far end, the crest of Little Moose Mt. rises to a summit of 3620 ft.

❄ Trail in winter: Snowmobile trail. Far from accessible roads, but otherwise could be skied or snowshoed.

🐾 Distances: To trail jct., 2.7 mi; to first sand bank, 4.3 mi; to height of land, 7.3 mi; to Sly Pond, 7.7 mi (12.3 km). Ascent from Otter Brook Rd, 1000 ft (305 m). Elevation (height of land), 2940 ft (896 m).

Short Trails on Indian River Rd.

▶Trailhead: Start at the jct. of Moose River Rd. and Otter Brook Rd. in the MRPWF (8.3 mi from the W entrance and 12.9 mi from the E entrance). Drive S on Otter Brook Rd. for 1.3 mi to the crossing of Otter Brook. Take the R fork just after the brook. The road continues past several ponds and trails and ends at a barrier and trailhead next to Indian Lake, 5.2 mi from Otter Brook.◀

92 Squaw Lake

Trails Illustrated Map 744: N11

Three and two-tenths mi from Otter Brook on the R side of the road. It is 0.3 mi downhill all the way on yellow markers to the E end of Squaw Lake, about 100 ft below, where an informal campsite lies. Three other campsites, accessible by boat, are on the SE shore of the lake. Reaching them, boaters will pass on the L a towering rock wall, visible only from watercraft.

🚶 Distances: Squaw Lake Trail, 0.3 mi (0.5 km).

93 Muskrat Pond

Trails Illustrated Map 744: M11

Four and four-tenths mi from Otter Brook, on the L. This 0.1 mi trail goes from the SE side of Indian River Rd. to narrow, boggy Muskrat Pond.

🚶 Distances: Muskrat Pond trail, 0.1 mi (0.2 km).

94 Indian Lake

Trails Illustrated Map 744: M11

Five and two-tenths mi from Otter Brook, at the end-of-road trailhead. This is a minor piece of trail going R (N) 0.1 mi to the SW corner of Indian Lake. Two informal campsites on the W shore are reachable by boat. The outlet is at the far NW end of the lake. At the SW end, near a beaver lodge, there are pitcher plants and other wetland varieties of plants. The Indian River (Horn Lake) Trail (trail 95) begins at the same trailhead.

❄ Trails in winter: Snowmobile trails, far from drivable roads.

🚶 Distances: Indian Lake trail, 0.1 mi (0.2 km).

95 Indian River (Horn Lake)

Trails Illustrated Map 744: M10

Indian River Rd. formerly continued past Indian Lake as a private road extending to Canachagala Brook near the Moose River (now on private land). The old road is now an access route into a remote section of the West Canada Lakes Wilderness Area. After it crosses the Indian River, marked trails lead to Balsam, Stink, and Horn Lakes.

►Trailhead: Start at the jct. of Moose River Rd. and Otter Brook Rd. in the MRPWF (8.3 mi from the W entrance and 12.9 mi from the E entrance). Drive S on Otter Brook Rd. for 3.3 mi to the crossing of Otter Brook. Turn R at the next jct. Continue past several ponds and trails and park at a barrier and trailhead next to Indian Lake, 5.2 mi from Otter Brook. ◄

Starting at the barrier at the Indian Lake trailhead (0.0 mi), the route goes SW through a gentle notch below Indian Lake Mt., passing beaver meadows, first L and then R. At 1.9 mi, the road reaches the Indian River and turns R to follow along it. To the L at the turn, a clearing leads down to the banks of the river. This is a possible crossover spot for wilderness travel by experienced bushwhackers to the group of lakes near Mountain Lake; however, if the water is high, this can be quite dangerous.

Continuing on around the tip of Indian Lake Mt., the route turns N across a swampy low ground, and at 2.6 mi enters the first of several "hallways" along this route—a trail with conifers packed tightly along each side and sharply limited visibility. The trail climbs slightly along a shoulder of the mountain and descends again to the Indian River at 3.8 mi. An old bridge is long gone, and the river must be waded. The hiker can choose water that is ankle deep over slippery rocks, or nearly waist-deep water with firmer footing under a cable upstream. It can be dangerously high in wet times. A rock for changing back into boots about 50 yd beyond the river has a benchmark showing an elevation of 1899 ft. From here on, the main route is generally W.

Horn Lake provides the first side trail at 4.4 mi. Turn L (S) onto an old road. The yellow-marked trail, with little maples trying to impinge on the roadway, climbs continuously, but not too steeply, to a jct. at 1.9 mi. The Horn Lake Trail goes L while another road goes R. After turning L at the jct., the trail crosses a creek and climbs again to reach an informal campsite on Horn Lake at 3 mi (7.4 mi from the trailhead). There is a jct. in the old road not far from Horn Lake. When going up, the branch to the R is an old logging road which leads W along the lower edge of Ice Cave Mt. This would give experienced bushwhackers a path to continue on to North Lake in the J.P. Lewis Tract. (See *Adirondack Mountain Club Western Trails.* That route has been suggested for the North Country Trail from North Dakota to Lake Champlain.

Continuing on the main trail past the Horn Lake turnoff, it is a short way to the Balsam Lake trail R (N) at 4.6 mi. This trail goes N on yellow markers to the shore of boggy, pond-size Balsam Lake (4.7 mi from the trailhead) with a round-trip distance from the main trail of less than a quarter mile.

Past the Balsam Lake turnoff, the main trail parallels the Balsam Lake outlet R, now a beaver pond nearly 0.3 mi long. It then crosses the end of another beaver pond L, making travel wet, and reaching a clearing with a trail jct. at 5.9 mi. The 0.4 mi side trail goes N on level ground to the SW end of pond-sized Stink Lake (6.3 mi from the trailhead). The old road continues but eventually crosses into posted private land of the Adirondack League Club, and is not

Indian River rapids. Richard Nowicki

recommended past the Stink Lake spur.

❄ Trail in winter: Extremely remote, accessible only by snowmobiles, which can legally go as far as the wilderness boundary at the trailhead. Otherwise, it is suitable for backcountry skiing and snowshoeing, taking into consideration the river crossing. Any group attempting this trip should be well prepared for winter wilderness conditions.

🚶 Distances: Indian Lake trailhead to Indian River crossing, 3.8 mi; to Horn Lake via spur, 7.4 mi (11.8 km); to Balsam Lake via spur, 4.7 mi (7.5 km); to Stink Lake via spur, 6.3 mi (10.1 km).

Piseco–Powley Road Vicinity

The road between Piseco and Stratford, known both as Piseco Rd. and Powley Rd., provides motorized access to some of the most remote trailheads. The largely unpaved road splits the 147,454 acre Ferris Lake Wild Forest down the middle. The road, which runs N–S, was constructed in the 1850s in preparation for a railway between Little Falls and Raquette Lake that never came to pass. Twenty miles long, this seasonal dirt road stretches between NY 10 and NY 29A from Piseco to Stratford, New York, and at times has old growth spruce stands visible from the roadside. The road is very popular with sportsmen, birders, and campers for the free primitive campsites that line it. The road is seldom traveled, so be sure to have a full tank of gas before setting out. Popular roadside campsites include the "Oregon" area along East Canada Creek. Most of the trails described as beginning along this road are snowmobile trails. Although fine for skiing, the road is not plowed in winter.

Northwest of the Piseco–Powley Road is the southern section of the West Canada Wilderness Area that offers several trails to scenic ponds with possibilities for deep exploration in the seldom visited wilderness interior.

Recommended hikes in this section include:

EASY HIKES
G Lake: 1.0 mi (1.6 km) round trip. A short hike leads to a picnic area and primitive campsites sheltered in the pines on a beautiful lake.

Echo Cliff Trail: 1.2 mi (1.9 km) round trip. A short but steep climb to an overlook of Piseco Lake.

MODERATE HIKES
T Lake: 7 mi (11.2 km) round trip. A scenic lake with a nearby lean-to is reached after a lovely ascent of a ravine.

Big Alderbed: 6.2 mi (9.9 km) round trip. An easy walk through beautiful hardwoods to a challenging stream crossing and finally a pretty little lake.

HARDER HIKES
Goldmine Falls: 2.3 mi (3.7 km) round trip. While not a far distance, the path leading to Goldmine Falls is not marked and may not be maintained. Good map and compass skills are recommended.

Michael N. Kelsey

Trail Described	Miles (one way)		Page
96 Alder Brook Trail	3.4 or 4.9	(5.4 or 7.8 km)	186
Morehouseville Wilderness Access			187
97 South Branch Trail			187
Low Trail	2.7	(4.3 km)	188
High Trail	4.7	(7.5 km)	188
G Lake	0.4	(0.6 km)	189
Big Marsh Mt.	2.3	(3.7 km)	190
98 T Lake	3.5	(5.6 km)	191
99 Echo Cliff	0.6	(1.0 km)	191
100 Bearpath Inn	1.5	(2.4 km)	192
101 Sheriff Lake via Bearpath Inn			192
102 Sand Lake	0.5	(0.8 km)	192
103 Meco Lake	2.0	(3.2 km)	193
104 Goldmine Stream Falls	1.2	(1.9 km)	194
105 Big Alderbed Lake	3.1	(5.0 km)	196
106 Clockmill Pond	1.7	(2.7 km)	198
107 Rock Lake and Kennels Pond from Clockmill Corners	4.0	(6.4 km)	199
Black Cat Lake	3.0	(4.8 km)	201

96 Alder Brook

Trails Illustrated Map 744: H12

This snowmobile trail extends into a pleasant region of open hardwood forest along Alder Brook. It is a piece of a trail network extending from Ohio to Speculator, but parts of the network are on private land, which may not be open to hikers. There are three other trailheads in this region, all shown on the map, but the one on G Lake Rd. is the only usable one on public land. (The trailhead on NY 8 near Alder Brook Rd. is on state land, but very boggy, and would be severely damaged by foot traffic.)

▶Trailhead: Found on G Lake Rd., which is easy to miss. Measure highway distances carefully. From the jct. of NY 8 and West Shore Rd. on Piseco Lake, go W on NY 8 for 2.5 mi. Turn R and go downhill steeply from the highway shoulder. From Hoffmeister, go 3.8 mi E on NY 8 and turn L (N) onto G Lake Rd. Go 1.1 mi on this rocky seasonal road to a slight parking area and snowmobile trail signs on the L.◀

The trail begins on level ground at the rim of the marsh just W of Evergreen Lake (0.0 mi). The path is easy, but can be somewhat wet. At 0.5 mi, it turns S and crosses a brook on a small bridge. After climbing out of the bottomland, the trail turns W again and continues along the rim through easy, open, hardwood forest.

At 1 mi, the old trail continues straight ahead (W) while the new route turns

R and descends the hillside. At the bottom, the trail turns L and follows Alder Brook for a short distance before meeting the former trail route at a bridge across the brook. This is a very pleasant region, with opportunities for camping along the brook just a little downstream.

From the bridge, the trail continues W along the gentle hillside to a jct. with the Alder Brook Rd. Trail at 1.5 mi. This side trail is not difficult to follow, but is rougher underfoot and passes through extensive boggy sections. These bogs do not have bridges or corduroy, and will become dreadful hogwallows if used by hikers when the ground is not frozen.

The main trail continues along Alder Brook and passes above the S shore of The Floe; however, state land ends just as the trail reaches The Floe (3.4 mi). The remainder of the trail down to NY 8 (4.9 mi) at Hoffmeister is on private land. Another side trail down to NY 8 at 2.4 mi also passes through private land on its way to the road.

❊ Trail in winter: Snowmobile trail.

🏃 Distances: G Lake Rd. to Alder Brook Rd. Trail, 1.5 mi; to second side trail, 2.4 mi; to end of state land at The Floe, 3.4 mi (5.4 km). (Through private land to end of trail, 4.9 mi or 7.8 km.)

Morehouseville Wilderness Access

Trails Illustrated Map 744: I10

There are no trails in this region, but the road crossing the South Branch of West Canada Creek at Morehouseville provides access to the trailless interior of the West Canada Lakes Wilderness Area.

▶Locator: From the center of Morehouseville on NY 8, turn N on Fayle Rd., a gravel road heading downhill across a bridge and uphill again for about 0.5 mi. Fayle Rd. turns W upon reaching level ground and soon enters private land. Park along the road just after it reaches the high ground. Note that past the bridge, Fayle Rd. is seasonal and unplowed in winter, and may not be passable until after spring thaw.◀

97 South Branch Trail

Trails Illustrated Map 744: I12

This trail along the South Branch of West Canada Creek gives access to the S part of the West Canada Lakes Wilderness Area. There is a trail register at the start, and the path is cleared for a considerable distance, but this is not a marked trail. It is intended for experienced sportsmen and wilderness hikers.

▶Trailhead: From Piseco Lake, go W on NY 8 through Hoffmeister to a jct. with Mountain Home Rd., 1.6 mi W of Hoffmeister. From Nobleboro, go E on NY 8 for 4.8 mi to a road jct. on the L. Turn onto Mountain Home Rd. Go past Wilmurt Lake Rd. at about 1.3 mi. At 2.1 mi there is a wide turnaround. Note that road conditions are poor. If your car has a low center, or it's winter, park as close as you can to the turnaround and proceed on foot. Be respectful of "No parking" signs at the turnaround. Vehicles with high clearance can proceed beyond the gate (in season) through a section of private land to an old road on the L at 3.3 mi. Park out of the way on the L. If you go too far on the main road, it is only 0.1 mi farther to a ford across West Canada Creek. The road on the other side leads to private land at Pine Lake. This is a DEC trail, but it is not marked. ◀

The trail L leads 200 ft to the trail register (0.0 mi) at the crossing of a small creek, Mad Tom Brook. The trail climbs gently for the first 0.8 mi, then levels out and parallels West Canada Creek. Some minor downhill travel leads to Roaring Brook at 1 mi and a minor creek at 1.3 mi. The Roaring Brook crossing is 20 ft wide, but in midsummer is typically very small.

The path continues on easy ground to the crossing of Wagoner Brook at 1.8 mi. The trail goes modestly uphill after Wagoner Brook, then levels out. Shortly after, at 1.9 mi, an obscure trail goes L on an old road. This is the High Trail. The Low Trail continues straight ahead.

LOW TRAIL

The route straight ahead from the trail jct. leads mostly downhill for another 0.8 mi to West Canada Creek at 2.7 mi. The old road crossed the creek on a long-gone bridge and headed uphill along Twin Lakes Outlet. The route is still discernible, but requires some expertise to follow. Several branches of the old logging road lead to slopes and hilltops in the region of L–D Pond. This access to the L–D Pond area is not a marked hiking trail, but is intended to give hunters a route to the interior.

Bushwhackers intending to walk upstream on West Canada Creek are in for a tough time. The lowland is choked with viburnum (witch hobble) and heavy bushes and is a nightmare to navigate. If you are determined to use this route instead of the High Trail, the best travel is somewhat up the hillside on the W.

HIGH TRAIL

This route turns L at the obscure jct. at 1.9 mi and starts gently uphill. The route is mostly a very old road, but only the most experienced hikers would believe it when they see the trail. The footpath is used just enough to make the route easy to follow in most places. In others, the hiker must be careful not to lose the known trail while searching for the continuation on the other side of old blowdowns. (The trail is maintained, and blowdowns are cut away, but occasional massive trees are simply bypassed.)

The route goes N up the slope, then turns NE to follow along the contour for another half mile. At 2.8 mi, the trail turns NW uphill and climbs to the summit of a hill. The route along the hilltop is open and easy, but still not used enough to let the hiker daydream without watching the footpath. After a gentle downhill slope, the trail reaches Beaudry Brook at 3.6 mi. The hiker is right to wonder how a brook can go sideways along the top of a hill. In fact, the hill is just the

Piseco Lake. Michael N. Kelsey

shoulder of a somewhat level area of Buck Pond Mt.

The trail crosses Beaudry Brook. There is no obvious footpath at this point, but one can see a former lumber clearing just above on the far side. The trail continues its N course from the far corner on the N side of the clearing. It is not very obvious for the first 100 ft, but does go through the most open part of the evergreen thicket. After that, it again becomes a noticeable footpath on an old logging road. After traversing easy open summit forest, it comes to Jones Brook at 4.7 mi. This brook was mislocated on the old quad maps. The location was corrected on the new quad, but the name was dropped.

On the other side, another old logging camp includes pipe frames, debris, and a logging camp barrel stove. This seems to be used by present-day sportsmen in season. The trail and old road continue NE past the lumber camp, becoming too difficult to follow within the next half mile, but the forest is quite open.

❄ Trail in winter: Suitable for skiing or snowshoeing. The High Ttrail may be too difficult to follow in winter, but the Low Trail makes a fine day's outing.

🐾 Distances: Trailhead to jct. of High and Low Trails, 1.9 mi; to West Canada Creek by Low Trail, 2.7 mi; to lumber camp on Beaudry Brook, 3.6 mi; to lumber camp on unnamed creek, 4.7 mi (7.5 km).

G Lake

Trails Illustrated Map 744: I12

G Lake is a pretty little lake, used by anglers and paddlers. There are various spots suitable for picnicking and primitive camping. Other than the main trail down to the near shore of G Lake and an old road around the N shore, this lake is essentially trailless. The main trail to the lake is very suitable as a canoe/kayak access trail, as it would be for families with small children.

▶Trailhead: G Lake Rd. is marked by a small street sign on the N side of NY 8. From the jct. of NY 8 and West Shore Rd. for Piseco Lake (marked by the sign, "Piseco 6"), go W on NY 8 for 2.4 mi. Turn R and go downhill steeply from the highway shoulder. This turnoff is also 0.7 mi E on NY 8 from Alderbrook Rd. Turn L (N) onto G Lake Rd. Drive 2.1 mi on this good seasonal road to a parking spot at a barrier. This road, although a little bumpy in spots, is suitable for regular-clearance vehicles.◀

The main trail from the parking lot is smooth, fairly wide, and well traveled. The first 0.3 mi is flat before curving L slightly down for the final 0.1 mi to the shore of G Lake. A picnic site and possible camping spot can be found here on the shore of the lake.

At 0.3 mi, a faint path goes R 0.5 mi to the NE side of the lake, where a house once sat. This trail is not maintained and requires rock-hopping across an 8 ft wide inflow stream for G Lake.

An angler's path leaves the picnic area and heads around the S shore of the lake.

🦌 Distances: NY 8 to trailhead, 2.1 mi; trailhead to picnic/put in, 0.4 mi (0.6 km).

Big Marsh Mt.

Trails Illustrated Map 744: I13

This side route on an unmaintained old road passes through some small clearings and a large clearing at 1 mi. Just after the large clearing, the old road crosses a small stream and curves L to go along the hillside parallel to the stream. At 1.2 mi the route forks. The L branch goes down through soggy terrain to the pond N of Big Marsh Mt. The R branch continues on drier ground above the pond and reaches another large clearing at 1.4 mi.

The former route up Big Marsh Mt. starts from the high point of this clearing on an older woods road. The old road is reasonably easy to follow, but is nonetheless not suitable for hikers who are inexperienced with map and compass. To reach the summit, follow the old road N for 0.1 mi and take the R branch, which starts more steeply uphill. The old route is obvious until the long hilltop at 1.9 mi, where it suddenly ends. From here it is fairly easy walking on open ground, but the forest has regrown nicely, with scant views.

❋ Trail in winter: A remote trail at the end of a seasonal-use road; would add more than 4 mi to a round-trip in winter. Otherwise, suitable for snowshoeing.

🦌 Distances: Trailhead to peninsula tip, 0.5 mi. Trailhead to homesite on E side, 0.6 mi; to end of either trail around lake, 1.3 mi (2.1 km); to summit of Big Marsh Mt., 2.3 mi (3.7 km).

98 T Lake

Trails Illustrated Map 744: I14

T Lake is a readily accessible and quite scenic lake in the West Canada Lakes Wilderness Area. It has a genuine T shape, although the T section is not readily recognizable from the S shore. A lean-to is up the hill, with the lake barely visible through foliage.

▶Trailhead: From NY 8 at the S end of Piseco Lake, go N on West Shore Rd. for 4 mi. The trailhead is on the L (W), just before the Poplar Point Campground. Park at the trailhead, or if necessary at the campground, where a day-use fee is charged. ◀

Leaving the highway (0.0 mi), the blue-marked trail follows up the L bank of a ravine. The first mile of the trail continues in this manner, often steeply up. After 1.3 mi, the path heads down, sometimes steeply, to cross Mill Stream before ascending again.

At 2.6 mi, the trail turns L onto the route of an older trail. The trail R leads to posted private land. Going L, the trail goes up fairly steeply, then levels out and goes above the long arm of T Lake, finally reaching the T Lake Lean-to at 3.5 mi. The lake is quite scenic from the lean-to, and even better if you go a short distance W along the shore.

Note: The former trail to T Lake Falls has been closed by the DEC. The area around T Lake Falls is deceptively dangerous, and several people have been killed in falls from the steep slopes.

❋ Trail in winter: Campground parking is not available and the parking lot may not be plowed. Suitable for snowshoes. The initial climb is too steep for all but expert skiers.

🐾 Distances: West Shore Rd. to first height of land, 1.2 mi; to T Lake Lean-to, 3.5 mi (5.6 km).

99 Echo Cliff

Trails Illustrated Map 744: I14

This is a short but steep climb to a nice view over Piseco Lake.

Trailhead: From NY 8 at the S end of Piseco Lake, go N on West Shore Rd. for 2.6 mi. The trailhead is on the L (W). Park along the side of the road.

Leaving the road (0.0 mi), the trail goes up somewhat steeply on the L slope of a ravine. It levels out in a col at 0.5 mi, then turns R and goes uphill with a small creek on the L. The route soon turns R and ascends a steep slope, staying more or less on the ridge until leveling out on a narrow hilltop. The extensive view from the cliff includes Piseco Lake in the foreground, with Higgins Bay on the L and Spy Lake in the background.

❋ Trail in winter: Short and steep, a possibility for accomplished snowshoers.

🐾 Distance: To hilltop and Echo Cliff, 0.6 mi (1 km).

100 Bearpath Inn

Trails Illustrated Map 744: H12

This is a short, relatively flat walk through open hardwoods that follows a marked snowmobile trail. The trail includes some marshy sections and several small stream crossings.

▶Trailhead: The trail begins about 150 yd E of Alderbrook Rd. on the S side of NY 8. It is a snowmobile crossing point on Route 8.◀

Marked as a snowmobile trail, the path proceeds through open woods with prolific fern growth. At 0.2 mi the trail passes through a brief marshy area and then crosses a plank snowmobile bridge. A second swampy area is reached shortly after the bridge. At 0.3 mi the trail bends L to head SE.

For the next three-quarters of a mile the trail traverses flat open woodlands, in a generally E direction. It crosses several nice streams on snowmobile bridges and begins a barely perceptible descent at 1 mi. At 1.2 mi the trail begins to descend moderately. The woods are pleasant, predominantly hardwoods with few conifers. At 1.5 mi the boundary between state land and private land is reached. Turn back here. It is possible to continue 0.1 mi to a jct. with an old road. The private land beyond this point is no longer open to hikers owing to the construction of private summer homes on Sheriff Lake.

❄ Trail in winter: Suitable for the intermediate cross-country skier, but proceed with caution: The trail is shared with snowmobiles.

🐾 Distances: To state land boundary, 1.5 mi; to old road jct., 1.6 mi (2.6 km).

101 Sheriff Lake via Bearpath Inn

Trails Illustrated Map 744: H12

A short, relatively flat walk through open hardwoods with some marshy sections to negotiate, this is, nevertheless, a pleasant walk.

Trailhead: The trail begins one-quarter mile E of Alderbrook Rd. on the S side of NY 8.

Please note that this trail is currently under review owing to recent development of private land around Sheriff Lake. The viability of this trail (as well as the future status of trail 100) will be reviewed prior to reprinting.

102 Sand Lake

Trails Illustrated Map 744: H13

A trail to a deep, wild, and remote lake, this is a very short trip, passing through several wet areas. At the end of the trail on the shore is a pleasant clearing with pretty views across one end of the lake. Bring a canoe for further explorations.

▶Trailhead: This large trailhead is located off the Piseco-Powley Rd., a wide gravel road in generally good condition. This road is located 0.1 mi S of the Piseco Outlet flowing under NY 10, or 3.8 mi beyond the Shaker Place parking lot along

NY 10 if traveling from the S. The trailhead is 2 mi from the intersection with NY 10 on the L (E) of the road. It is in the form of a large, U-shaped pullout. ◀

As the trail commences, it immediately passes through two clearings and begins to descend. Owing to erosion, the upper portion seems almost to be a streambed. Watch for the trail to turn L as trail drainage is diverted to the R. At 0.3 mi it traverses a large wet, mucky section. This boggy area cannot easily be avoided, and the hiker must pick a way through and over, using grass tufts, skinny branches, and roots as stepping areas, sometimes getting a wet and muddy boot. After this swampy area, the trail crosses a small stream on a makeshift log bridge and begins to climb a small grade. Sand Lake can be seen through the trees at the top of the knoll. Near the end of the trail, a smaller giant mud puddle can be avoided by swinging L. At 0.5 mi, the path ends in a grassy clearing on the N shore of Sand Lake.

The lake outlet, where evidence of sporadic beaver activity exists in the form of washed-out dams and debris, is L of the clearing. Sand Lake, long rather than wide, curves out of sight. Big, beautiful rocks come down to the shore. An irregular shoreline with many little bays makes this an interesting lake to explore by canoe. Much of the shoreline is impenetrable spruce and tangled underbrush, making exploration by foot difficult. Loons may be seen or heard.

❄ Trail in winter: Skiing is restricted owing to the distances required on unplowed Piseco-Powley Rd. Although the skiing along Piseco-Powley Rd. is enjoyable, skiers must share the road with, snowmobiles. Skiers might do best to come in from the N for 2 mi. and then proceed to Sand Lake.

🏃 Distances: To unavoidable boggy area, 0.3 mi; to Sand Lake, 0.5 mi (0.8 km).

103 Meco Lake

Trails Illustrated Map 744: H13

This is a walk on the wild side, recommended for anyone curious to see what lumbering does to a forest. In the right season, numerous wild berries can be picked enroute.

▶ Trailhead: The trail begins off the Piseco-Powley Rd. across from Mud Pond, 4.5 mi from the iron bridge over East Canada Creek. A snowmobile trail, it has no sign other than the prominent disks marking the path. The trail begins traveling due N on the W side of the Piseco-Powley Rd. ◀

For the first 0.1 mi, the trail climbs a small incline. There are numerous large hardwood trees, especially large yellow birches. Although the trail is discernible and adequately marked with disks and old blazes, it is not well defined or recently improved. The top of a ridge is reached at 0.2 mi. The forest is open and attractive.

Still heading N, at 0.3 mi the trail crosses a small brook that has no bridge, and continues up a gentle grade. After a quick jog to the R, the trail reveals the remains of old logs underfoot. Someone has strategically placed wooden pallets across wet sections of the trail. The trail traverses a swampy area at 0.4 mi, and crosses a stream at 0.5 mi. Again, there is no bridge.

Continuing up a gentle grade, the trail passes a huge maple tree at 0.6 mi. The crest of this ridge is reached at 0.7 mi. The trail then descends slightly and bends a bit to the R. Mature beech and birch trees, but no evergreens, are encountered along this section.

The trail passes through a rough, rocky area at 1 mi. The undergrowth becomes lush with ferns and nettles. Crossing a soggy, swampy area, the trail becomes difficult to follow. On the other side of this bog the trail is easily found again, after which it begins a gentle descent. (This trail is flat for most of its length.)

A small stream with a rustic makeshift bridge is crossed at 1.2 mi At 1.3 mi a tree bears a sign indicating that motorized vehicles are prohibited beyond this point; this is the boundary line between private and state land. Within 50 ft. the trail jogs L, then continues down a gentle descent. Past a logging road at 1.4 mi, berry bushes begin. This is a seemingly endless blackberry and raspberry patch with treacherous footing—depressions and rocks one cannot see while walking through vines and leaves.

The trail crosses a small stream at 1.5 mi; the prickly berry bushes continue as far as the eye can see. The direction of travel is NW. There is a big log culvert at 1.7 mi on the R. There are no snowmobile disks or trail markers in this area. At 1.8 mi another stream is difficult to cross, owing to deep pits filled with water and slippery old logs.

At 1.9 mi Meco Lake can be seen through trees on the L. To reach the lakeshore, the hiker must leave the old logging road and descend about 150 yd through brush to the boggy shore. Meco Lake is small and picturesque, but it has a swampy shoreline and the water is out of reach for the hiker.

Although the old logging trail continues W, it is very difficult to walk owing to berry bushes and numerous huge ruts, and is filled with water and debris left by logging operations in the late 1970s. It will be years before the forest returns and heals the scars.

❄ Trail in winter: Distances required for the skier or snowshoer to access the trailhead along the unplowed Piseco-Powley Rd. make this trail a "no go."

🐾 Distances: To state land boundary, 1.3 mi; to Meco Lake, 2 mi (3.2 km).

104 Goldmine Stream Falls

Trails Illustrated Map 744: G12

The series of small waterfalls at the end of this trail are lovely, with several outcroppings of rock that can be used as viewpoints and picnic areas. At the top of the cascades is an interesting gold-colored granite section of rounded bedrock over which the Goldmine Stream rushes.

▶Trailhead: Access is 12.2 mi from the beginning of the Piseco-Powley Rd. coming from the S and NY 29A. Watch for a small camping area at 12.1 mi to the E (or R), and in less than a tenth of a mile a tiny open swamp, also on the E (R). There is parking along the rather wide shoulders of the road. The path is marked by three faint old blazes on a hemlock tree a bit S on the W (L if coming from NY 29A). The tree is not quite opposite the meadow, but a few yards S of it. Look carefully for a path leading into the woods beside the tree. ◀

Although not an official DEC marked trail, the path to Goldmine Stream Falls has been in use for decades and is very well defined, except at the falls themselves. At various times in the past, some individual or group has kept the path well cleared and built several corduroys over wet areas, and at least one substantial footbridge. It appears such attention has waned, but the trail/path is still used frequently and thereby kept well defined by hikers and anglers. Throughout the trip there are no markers of any kind, however.

Entering the forest at the blazed hemlock, the path opens up almost immediately, and is very easy to follow, much used, and soft underfoot. At a wet area at 0.1 mi, cut rounds of trees might assist in crossing, but they are old, mossy, and very slippery. A few yards farther a small stream is crossed on a rugged plank and log footbridge. The trail continues and, although flat for the most part, has brief up and down sections. At 0.2 mi there are more lumber rounds, then the trail jogs R and L through mixed hardwoods. At 0.3 mi the trail enters an open stand of mature yellow birch.

At 0.5 mi a brook is crossed on small stepping stones. Shortly thereafter, the trail jogs L to avoid a blowdown tree on the R. Traveling due S, the trail leads through dense witch-hobble. A huge old hemlock to the L is a beautiful tree that escaped the loggers. At 0.6 mi the trail descends to the bottom of a draw and becomes a little more overgrown. Here a path enters from the S (L). In another 200 ft or so this leads to an old hunting camp, which at one time appears to have been quite substantial. There are numerous pieces of rope, plastic, plywood, and other debris scattered about.

The main trail now runs briefly parallel to the stream, and is open and quite lovely with large mature trees. At 0.7 mi it crosses, on slippery logs, a small but deeper stream that runs through a vlei. This is the outlet of Christian Lake. Evidence of a once-substantial bridge is visible, but it has deteriorated to only two ancient logs.

At 0.8 mi the trail follows a higher section along the edge of the vlei (to the L) through a hemlock grove. The trail is still relatively flat, easy walking, and easy to see. The direction is now more N. The trail tops a knoll and leads on to a steep but short descent at 1 mi. At this point Goldmine Stream can be heard on the L, but not seen, as the hemlocks and brush are quite dense.

At a tiny, wet clearing at 1.1 mi one can either continue along the faint path, or bear L and bushwhack to the creek banks below the first falls. The draw through which Goldmine Stream flows is overgrown and rough going, but by keeping the water within sight or sound one can explore and enjoy this area without becoming completely confused. Map and compass should be consulted to orient oneself, however. (The greatest difficulty may be in finding the trail on the return. After leaving the draw, stay on the high ground along the N edge of the vlei, and travel E. You will encounter the outlet of Christian Lake and must cross on the logs there, as it is the only obvious crossing point. This will put you back on the main path.)

The main trail continues to the top of a waterfall, although in the past it was in wretched condition, with blowdown and small hemlocks restricting one at almost every step. Nevertheless, it is discernible, and at 1.2 mi the top of a series of step falls is reached. Here one will see the red- and gold-colored bedrock that obviously contributed to the stream's name. Continuing on the faint path for another tenth of a mile along the stream, one encounters a twisted pile of large dead trees, marking the end of any path. Climbing on the trees provides a good view of Big Alderbed Mt. to the W (L), across another large vlei.

❉ Trail in winter: Not recommended. It is unmarked (not a snowmobile trail) and distances are too great for skiers to efficiently access the trailhead on unplowed Piseco-Powley Rd.

𝕄 Distances: To rugged footbridge, 0.1 mi; to hunter's camp fork, 0.5 mi; to Christian Lake outlet log crossing, 0.7 mi; to top of falls, 1.2 mi (1.9 km).

105 Big Alderbed Lake

Trails Illustrated Map 744: G12

Big Alderbed is an attractive small lake that was made much larger at one time by the addition of a dam to accommodate the needs of the logging industry in the early 1900s. Since then most of the dam has eroded and flooded away, although periodically it is partially rebuilt by beavers. The old road, now a marked snowmobile trail, is a pleasant day's round-trip walk for the average hiker. The area's history dates back to the 1870s when John Powely attempted to build a farm near the headwaters of East Canada Creek. A clearing now referred to as Powely Place is all that remains.

▶Trailhead: To reach the start of the trail, take Piseco Rd. (also known as the Powley Rd.) N for approximately 11.1 mi to a bridge with iron railings that resemble old bed headboards. The bridge spans the West Branch of East Canada Creek. Park on the S side of the bridge where there is plenty of room on both road shoulders. Piseco Rd. is a seasonal road, unmaintained from November 1 to May 1, starting at 6.1 mi. Plan accordingly and remember that in long or very cold winters, thawing and melting can render the roads inaccessible until mid-May or later.◀

The trail begins on the L (W) side of the road, a bit S of the iron-rail bridge (0.0 mi). This former logging road is generally flat and passes through an attractive forest of hardwoods mixed with scattered stands of evergreens.

There is a camping area just off the road through which the trail passes to enter a small thicket of hemlocks. A series of railroad ties has been laid over a

wet area at 0.1 mi with a slight jog L at 0.2 mi. Walking is pleasant owing to the absence of boulders and blowdown; the terrain is flat for the most part. The trail reaches a clearing at 0.3 mi and soon crosses a brook.

A short uphill section traverses the side of a ridge, still following the old roadbed, and at 0.4 mi the trail reaches the crest of the ridge. A tiny stream flowing in from the L is crossed at 0.7 mi.

Still traveling W, the trail crosses a small brook at 0.9 mi and then begins a moderate climb out of its gully. A larger stream can be rock-hopped at 1 mi. The forest is open; several very large trees obviously escaped the axes of the lumberjacks, perhaps because they shaded their road. At 1.3 mi the trail passes through a boggy area strewn with big rocks and crosses yet another small stream at 1.4 mi. Snowmobile signs point the way through a grove of birch and beech trees.

At 1.7 mi just after a quick jog L the trail begins climbing moderately, reaching the crest of the ridge at 1.9 mi. Continuing downhill, it crosses a wet area at 2.1 mi, arriving at a larger stream at 2.2 mi which can be crossed to the L near a huge moss-covered boulder.

Once across, the path leads up a ridge to the R. In the vicinity of 2.3 mi the trail becomes wildly overgrown in midsummer although it is still faintly discernible. At 2.4 mi a swing R occurs, then a slight descent. At 2.6 mi another brook is crossed, followed by a steeper descent.

At 2.7 mi the trail reaches the swift-flowing outlet of Big Alderbed. This is an exciting watercourse whose crossing can be dicey during periods of high water. The hiker should scout carefully for a safe crossing. Boulders (or perhaps a log) can almost always be found downstream, unless the water is very high. There is also an old rusted cable about 50 yd downstream that has been used in the past for crossing. Its safety is questionable, however. Hikers may want to bushwhack upstream to the dam across the outlet of Big Alderbed, approximately 0.3 mi, and attempt to cross there. One of the exciting aspects of this hike is solving the dilemma of crossing the stream, although in midsummer and dry times it is not a big problem.

After crossing the stream, the trail follows the creek due W to a feeder stream at 2.9 mi. Here the trail swings away from the water and up a knoll through a rocky area marked sporadically by snowmobile signs. The path again becomes indistinct, but with care it can still be followed.

At 3.1 mi the trail reaches Big Alderbed Lake. A small, grass-covered camping area graces the shore at the end of the trail and is very pleasant. Note the remains of the wood and rock dam to the L, about 50 yd from the camping area where the outlet begins. Proceed R, following the anglers' path around the NE shore. Boulders offer attractive places to eat lunch and meditate on the quiet loveliness of this wild little lake, parts of which are all too quickly changing into swampland. The entire N end is now a marsh, and the relative absence of trees along the shore attests to the recent loss of several feet of water when the old dam eroded. Mountains in the near distance contribute to this small lake's overall scenic attractiveness.

❋ Trail in winter: Not accessible to the backcountry skier owing to the long distances involved in getting to the trailhead. Piseco Rd. is unplowed in winter and is used extensively by snowmobilers.

🏃 Distances: To large stream to rock-hop, 1 mi; to stream with large mossy boulder, 2.1 mi; to outlet crossing, 2.7 mi; to Big Alderbed Lake, 3.1 mi (5 km).

106 Clockmill Pond

Trails Illustrated Map 744: G13

An attractive old logging road has become a marked hiking and snowmobile trail leading into several ponds, including picturesque Clockmill Pond. This pretty pond once boasted a large dam at its W end, the remnants of which can be found with a bit of effort.

▶Trailhead: The start of the trail is on the E (R, if coming from the S) side of Piseco-Powley Rd. (also known as Powley Rd.). After about 6.1 mi, the road becomes a seasonal road, closed from November 1 to May 1. Follow Piseco Rd. 14.7 mi from its S end on NY 29A outside of Stratford. A brown and yellow DEC sign at the trailhead says "Clockmill Pond [no mileage listed]; Kennel Pond, 5 mi; Avery's Place, 6 mi. Snowmobile Trail—No Motorized Vehicles Except Snowmobiles." ◀

The beginning of the trail traverses a small wet area, after which the path begins a slight ascent. It is relatively flat and travels through mixed hardwood forest. At 0.1 mi the trail bends L. On the L is a lush and pretty grassy vlei. A rough snowmobile bridge spans part of this swampy section at 0.2 mi.

A small stream is crossed, and at 0.3 mi the path leads over another wooden-plank snowmobile bridge that cuts across the vlei in a SE direction. The trail still bears occasional resemblances to the old road, offering relatively flat and pleasant walking through maple, beech, and other hardwoods. On a ridge at 0.4 mi, the trail continues through a stand of very mature trees, then descends to cross another bridge at 0.5 mi. This is a wood bridge in good condition over a fast-flowing stream. After a swing L, another tiny feeder stream is channeled by an aluminum culvert across the trail at 0.6 mi. At 0.7 mi the trail cuts to the R, and up a gentle grade. At 0.9 mi a brief descent leads to a crossing on a snowmobile bridge at the bottom of a gully.

The trail crosses another stream before entering a large clearing filled with tall grasses at 1.1 mi. It crosses this open meadow and forks L (E) to continue to Clockmill Pond on an unmarked but well-defined path. To the R is the marked snowmobile trail to Rock Lake and Kennels Pond (see trail 107).

Continuing to Clockmill Pond, proceed through a grove of hemlocks, then downhill at 1.2 mi until at 1.3 mi a jct. offers a choice of L or R. The L (E) fork has several blowdowns on the trail, which is part of the old road to the dam, and this fork soon takes the hiker to a view of a small back bay at 1.5 mi. Continue along the R shore approximately 0.2 mi through wild brush and small trees to reach the remains of the dam. This was probably a logging camp or sawmill operation in the late 1800s, but its brief history is now lost.

An easier path to the shore of Clockmill Pond may be the R fork, which continues another 0.2 mi. The path, in some places, is very faint and difficult to follow in midsummer. Keep bearing L along and then over a small ridge; the S shore of the pond is soon accessible at 1.6 mi. There is a grassy campsite with room for at least one tent. Looking across this lovely little pond, it appears that there are additional camping spots, although there are no trails around the pond. This means the determined camper will have to bushwhack to discover a suitable camping area on the opposite shore.

❄ Trail in winter: Not recommended for skiers owing to the distances needed to access the trailhead on unplowed Piseco-Powley Rd. Find a friend with a snowmobile or plan to winter camp.

🐾 Distances: To clearing and jct., 1.1 mi; to Clockmill Pond, 1.5 mi; to old dam, 1.7 mi (2.7 km).

107 Rock Lake and Kennels Pond from Clockmill Corners
Trails Illustrated Map 744: G13

Rock Lake and Kennels Pond are connected by snowmobile trails, but while the hike to Rock Lake is surely a treat, the push through to Kennels Pond is something of a challenge and not terribly interesting, except as an exercise to see what the interior looks like. Moreover, Kennels Pond is private, and while snowmobilers may use the surrounding land in winter, hikers must ask permission to return to a parked car on the NY 10 exit, or hike only to the private land boundaries and then return on the same trail for a round-trip of 8 mi. Forest Preserve land does go up to the NW tip of Kennels Pond, but traversing the shore path around it puts one on private land.

▶Trailhead: Take the Clockmill Pond Trail (trail 106) to the meadow and jct. at 1.1 mi. The hiker who wishes to proceed to Rock Lake, Black Cat Lake, and/or Kennels Pond should take the marked snowmobile trail to the R.◀

Proceed downhill and across a large area of blowdown at 1.1 mi. At 1.2 mi cross a creek on a wooden snowmobile bridge. The trail follows the contours of a ridge for a short distance until at 1.4 mi it passes on the L an unnamed pond surrounded by an impenetrable swamp. A little creek flows into the pond, and then another small stream comes from the R to gurgle across the trail. After a short but steep uphill section, the trail swings away from the lake. At 1.5 mi a wooden bridge with beautiful side rails spans a large brook.

Rock Lake comes into view between the trees and at 1.8 mi can be seen clearly on the L. The trail does not go near the shore but rather keeps to the higher ground of a ridge.

[A faint trace of the old path to Black Cat Lake is 10 to 15 ft up a small ridge after a stream is crossed directly opposite Rock Pond. Look for a blaze on a tree. Go R if you are coming from Clockmill Corners. This bushwhack proceeds WSW. See Black Cat Lake Bushwhack below.]

At 2 mi an enormous hemlock has been cleared from the trail. Notice the exceptionally mature specimens of large paper birch on both sides of the trail. At 2.3 mi the trail continues S, descending sharply to a lower section of the ridge. At 2.6 mi another snowmobile bridge is laid across another boggy area. At this point the trail becomes indistinct and most difficult to discern. It appears that a new trail was once partially cleared along the side of the ridge, probably to avoid the lower wet areas. At 2.8 mi another stream is crossed. The trail is rocky and wildly overgrown here, the result of erosion during periods of heavy rain.

A jct. at 3 mi marks the NW end of Teeter Creek Vlei and a snowmobile trail to the L (N) known as Wagnor's Loop. Do not try to hike this trail as it is so overgrown it is impossible to find after the first half-mile. The determined hiker will need a map and compass and must be prepared to walk 6 mi through swamps to NY 10 and Piseco-Powley Rd.

The main trail continues R and across another wooden snowmobile bridge, heading SE. It crosses another creek at 3.9 mi and has left the vlei on the L. Kennels Pond comes into view at 4 mi. The hiker is now on private property. The trail continues along the lake, then across a short ridge, to reach a jct. at 4.5 mi with an old road that appears to be infrequently walked. Continue along the private road for approximately one mile to NY 10, where hikers could spot a car, if permission is sought and received. Otherwise, the trek to return to Piseco-Powley Rd. is in excess of 8 mi round-trip.

❋ Trail in winter: This would be a lovely area to explore on skis, but access for skiers must begin at Kennels Pond on NY 10 as the distances to ski unplowed

Piseco-Powley Rd. and then the trail from the W are too great. Trails will be shared with snowmobiles.

🚶 Distances:Piseco-Powley Rd. to view of Rock Lake, 1.8 mi; to jct. and Teeter Creek Vlei, 3 mi; to Kennels Pond, 4 mi (6.4 km).

Black Cat Lake *(bushwhack)*

Trails Illustrated Map 744: G13

Black Cat Lake—an intriguing name belonging to a pretty little body of water that is slowly degenerating into a swamp. Although there is said to have been, years ago, a primitive road to this picturesque body of water, all outward signs have been obliterated by the regrowth of the forest. Using a map and compass, however, the intrepid hiker can, with careful observation, bushwhack to this lake. The trip is challenging, although not long, and the hiker must pay close attention to landmarks as well as the map and compass.

▶Trailhead: See trail 107, Rock Lake and Kennels Pond from Clockmill Corners, for trail description to Rock Lake.◀

To find the cut-off point, follow the Clockmill Pond trail 1.9 mi to where it crosses a medium-sized stream opposite Rock Lake, then continues up a hill to the top of a ridge. A small beech tree on the L has a blaze cut into its trunk at eye level. Here a careful perusal to the R of the trail will disclose a faint path heading WSW. This very faint path peters out rather quickly, but the determined hiker should continue W through the draw and then jog a bit to the R. Occasional old blazes will be found on trees. Continue on this W compass bearing and a small marshy area will appear on the L.

Proceed through the draw, bearing somewhat R and up to get to the top of a ridge. Then descend the ridge through the col until a dry stream bed is encountered. Follow this rock-strewn, washed-out streambed until the lake comes into sight. No trail is evident in midsummer; thus the old wagon road has, for all practical purposes, reverted back to the forest. Witch hobble and other shrubs and large ferns are found in abundance.

Black Cat Lake should be sighted after 40 to 45 minutes of tedious bushwhacking. The lake is lovely but swampy and boggy around its entire shoreline. The hiker can, however, carefully walk to the edge of the water on exposed mud flats and grass tufts. It is approximately 3 miles (one way) to Black Cat Lake from the Piseco Road trailhead at Clockmill Corners.

❋ Trail in winter: Not recommended owing to the distances involved from the W (Piseco-Powley Rd.) end. Determined skiers will need to ask permission at Avery's to cross private land and utilize the snowmobile trails along Kennels Pond from NY 10.

🚶 Distances: To cutoff from Clockmill Corners Trail, 1.9 mi; to Black Cat Lake, (approx.) 3 mi (4.8 km). 🐾

Nine Corners Lake. Michael N. Kelsey

New York 10 Corridor

Numerous trails stem from the NY 10 corridor leading hikers into the Ferris Lake and Shaker Mountain Wild Forests. The area is blessed with several attractive lakes with easy access from the road, most connected by snowmobile trails that follow old logging and wagon roads. The area also has some long trails, difficult to walk owing to lowlands, swamps, and lush plant growth in summer. Hiking here can be an adventure precisely because it is so wild.

The larger lakes are often encircled by private land, and the lakes in the Forest Preserve are often surrounded by swamps. They are lovely and isolated, nevertheless. Exploration will generally reveal one or two campsites on high ground.

Recommended hikes in this section include:

EASY HIKES

Kane Mt. via S: 1.8 mi (2.9 km) round-trip. A short but fairly vigorous hike up this popular mountain rewards one with views if the hiker also climbs the unstaffed firetower.

Nine Corner Lake: 1.8 mi (2.9 km) round-trip. Trek to a very pretty and popular blue-green lake with boulders along its shore that facilitate access to the shore for swimming. Nearby erratics are popular with rock climbers for bouldering.

MODERATE HIKES

Stewart and Indian Lakes: 4.6 mi (7.4 km) round-trip. An easy trek to two charming lakes.

Good Luck Lake and Cliffs: mileage varies depending upon route. One of few lakes in the region with a sandy beach, a trip to Good Luck Lake is not complete without also visiting its namesake cliffs.

HARDER HIKES

Hillibrandt Lake and Vlei from Stewart Landing: 6.2 mi (9.9 km) round-trip. A longer hike using wild, seldom walked snowmobile trails to an interesting dam and small attractive lake. Can be lengthened by adding a second car.

Michael N. Kelsey

Trail Described		Miles (one way)		Page
108	Jockeybush Lake	1.0	(1.6 km)	204
109	Dry and Dexter Lakes (bushwhack to Spectacle Lake)	2.9 or 4.6	(4.6 or 7.4 km)	205
110	Good Luck Lake from NY 10	1.8	(2.9 km)	208
111	Good Luck Mt. Cliffs	2.5	(4.0 km)	210
112	Good Luck Lake Short Path	0.4	(0.6 km)	211
113	Spectacle Lake from NY 10	2.6	(4.2 km)	212
114	Good Luck Lake from West Stoner Lake	1.7	(2.7 km)	213
115	Third and Fourth Lakes	3.4	(5.4 km)	215
116	Spectacle Lake from NY 29A	4.8	(7.7 km)	217
117	Nine Corner Lake	0.9	(1.4 km)	219
118	Broomstick Lake	0.7	(1.1 km)	220
119	Kane Mt. South and North Trails	0.7	(1.1 km)	222
120	Kane Mt. East Trail	0.9	(1.4 km)	223
121	Stewart and Indian Lakes	2.3	(3.7 km)	224
122	Glasgow Mills and Hillbrandt Lake and Vlei	3.3	(5.3 km)	226
123	Mud Lake from Stewart Landing	1.5	(2.4 km)	227
124	Hillabrandt Lake and Vlei from Trail 123	3.1	(5 km)	229
125	Irving Pond and Bellows Lake to Peters Corners	9.5	(15.2 km)	230
126	Chase Lake	2.5	(4.0 km)	232

108 Jockeybush Lake

Trails Illustrated Map 744: F13

Jockeybush Lake is sparkling clear, deep, and cold—unlike most of the shallow, bog-rimmed lakes in the area. It has large accessible boulders for trail picnics, one superb swimming spot, and is surrounded by stately pines. Its short distance from NY 10 makes it a popular destination for hikers and anglers.

▶Trailhead: The trail begins at the parking area on NY 10 directly across from Lake Alma, 0.3 mi N of Avery's Hotel. A brown and yellow DEC sign says "Jockeybush Lake 1.1 mi." This parking area is large enough for 8-plus vehicles and is well used.◀

The trail begins with a moderate uphill grade, heading W through mixed hardwood and evergreen forest. It is very well-defined, although poorly marked. When markers are located they are the orange or yellow snowmobile disks, although they are low enough to be seen easily by the hiker. (On many snowmobile trails, the disks, having been tacked up in winter, are so high they are hidden from the summer hiker by leaves.) At 0.1 mi a slight jog R occurs, after which the trail squiggles a bit L and R. At 0.2 mi it flattens out briefly. Here many hikers have turned L, creating a faint path down to a stream, but stay R on the ridge trail and shortly bear L around an uprooted tree, after which a descent begins. There is a wet area at 0.3 mi and the outlet stream is now seen on the L. Cross this outlet stream at 0.4 mi by rock-hopping, as it is usually quite shallow, although on at least one occasion this writer has had to wade. It is also usually possible to continue upstream a few hundred feet and find a log to cross.

The direction of travel is still W and the trail follows the outlet stream, which is now on the R. In spring look for numerous yellow trout lilies, purple and white violets, painted trilliums, and red trilliums.

As the outlet veers R, note a series of small waterfalls at 0.5 mi. The trail enters a small ravine and swings L. At 0.6 mi it traverses a rocky area, continuing to climb moderately. Passing two large boulders on the R, the trail now becomes quite rocky and rough, traversing the upper part of the ravine. After passing two wet areas, which in midsummer may be dry, the trail becomes a bit difficult to find as it goes over rocks. The stream again appears on the R. After negotiating more rocky sections, at 0.9 mi the trail begins climbing out of the draw and up more steeply, reaching the top of this small ridge. The E end of Jockeybush Lake is sighted at 1 mi and after a jog R is reached at 1.1 mi. Cross the outlet using an old beaver dam to reach the rock ledges on the N shore. Look for water snakes; they love to sun themselves on the high areas of the dam.

The large, granite rock ledges provide ample fishing and picnic spots with views up the lake. Jockeybush is narrow, but quite attractive and one of the few natural deep-water lakes of the southern Adirondacks.

To reach a favorite swimming area along the N shore, after crossing the beaver dam, follow an anglers' path to the L (W) along the shore for about 0.2 mi. There you will see two large rock extrusions jutting into the deeper waters, perfect for swimming, or just sitting to meditate and enjoy the scenery.

❋ Trail in winter: An excellent snowshoe trip. Can be skied only by the more skilled backcountry skiers as there are two fairly steep grades. Good snow cover is necessary, as well as adequate cold to freeze the outlet stream, allowing skiers to cross without difficulty. As on most southern trails, snowmobiles will most likely be encountered.

🐾 Distances: To stream crossing, 0.4 mi; to waterfalls, 0.5 mi; to Jockeybush Lake, 1 mi (1.6 km).

109 Dry and Dexter Lakes (bushwhack to Spectacle Lake)

Trails Illustrated Map 744: E13

The hike to Dry and Dexter Lakes is an easy and attractive walk along an old road through open forests. The terrain is relatively flat, with moderate ups and downs that make the area most agreeable for cross-country skiing as well as hiking. Dexter and Dry Lakes are small and relatively isolated, but accessible to the hiker who wants an easy day's walk. For the more adventurous, this walk can be combined with a bushwhack to Spectacle Lake for a circular return. Although the trail as far as Dexter Lake is well defined and marked as a snowmobile route, a topographic map and compass are imperative for the bushwhack to Spectacle Lake. (See trail 116.)

▶Trailhead: The trail begins opposite the parking turnout on NY 10, which is located on the R (E) immediately after the second bridge over the West Branch of the Sacandaga River. It is well marked with brown and yellow DEC signboards that indicate trails to Spectacle, Dry, and Dexter Lakes (trail 113), as well as Good Luck Lake. For additional routes to Good Luck Lake, see also trail 110.◀

The trail enters the forest after passing an iron barrier prohibiting motorized access during all seasons except winter when these trails become snowmobile trails. Climbing moderately, the trail is rocky in places, and heads in a general NW direction. At 0.2 mi it jogs L and then R, leveling off at 0.3 mi. Continuing through tall open hardwoods, it descends into a boggy area before reaching a three-pronged trail fork at 0.5 mi. Take the middle fork to Dry and Dexter Lakes. A brown and yellow DEC trail sign also identifies them and points that way. The L fork goes to Good Luck Lake (see trail 110). The far R fork is almost hidden in the underbrush, overgrown and seldom, if ever, used by hikers, as it merely parallels NY 10 for the convenience of snowmobilers.

The trail to Dry and Dexter Lakes immediately curves L and is smooth and dry, passing through well-spaced mature birch, ash, maple, and beech, among other hardwoods. The general direction is due W, continuing over some blow-down and then up a slight rise.

At 0.7 mi the trail makes a gentle curve R and then a slight descent. It is now going in a WNW direction. This is a very attractive section of the old road, wide and softly cushioned by layers of leaves underfoot, with very few rocks.

At 0.8 mi a sturdy wooden plank bridge crosses a tiny stream. At 1 mi the walking is still through level terrain, easy and pleasant. A brief descent begins at 1.1 mi and the path continues through an overgrown section, although it is still discernible.

At 1.2 mi the trail descends to an extensive, wildly overgrown wet stretch, and turns R to avoid some of the muckiest areas. There is approximately 0.1 mi of this lush wetland. The heavy shrubbery along both sides provides little or no easy way to traverse this area, indicating that perhaps this wet section is either newly created or temporary.

At 1.3 mi, yet another wet section is encountered. This one, however, is rocky rather than mucky as the water runs downhill, creating a small stream in the trail. The woods, open and lovely, consist of large maple, birch, and beech, with scattered boulders adding interest. The trail crosses a stream at 1.4 mi and the hiker must balance on a slippery, old log bridge. After a brief ascent, a bend R occurs, as the trail follows a small stream.

Leaving the stream, the trail climbs a gentle ridge and enters a rocky ravine. The general direction is still due W. At 1.5 mi a large hemlock obstructs the trail, which is now descending. A heavy growth of witch hobble makes it difficult to go around this obstacle. Now crossing a level section, the trail begins a gentle upward grade and at 1.6 mi cuts across another wet area, then bends R and exits the ravine.

The old road now goes across the top of the ridge, and at 1.7 mi there is another muddy, sloppy area, after which the path jogs R and down a tiny incline. At 1.8 mi the trail bends L to hug the contours of the ridge and descends briefly at 1.9 mi. After it enters a hemlock grove at 2 mi it bends R, and Dry Lake comes into view at 2.1 mi. This is a tiny, attractive lake with rocky shores, cradled in dark green hemlocks.

The trail traverses the N side of the lake and then moves away from the shore and crosses an inlet brook, bending R and going up a draw and over a steep, rocky rib of land that juts into the lake. At 2.3 mi it descends into a smooth grassy area near the shore of the lake. Here the path is very difficult to follow in midsummer owing to abundantly overgrown vegetation. Follow the shore and pick up the trail again in about 50 yd.

Leaving Dry Lake and heading generally W, at 2.4 mi the trail bends slightly R and at 2.6 mi jogs L. It enters a ravine shaded by hardwoods mixed with hemlocks. At 2.7 mi the trail begins to descend through an extremely rocky ravine that is quite steep.

After a considerable drop of nearly 100 ft from the top of the ridge, the trail reaches the shore of Dexter Lake at 2.9 mi. The trail turns L and crosses the inlet by traversing an old beaver dam and then a large grassy wet area, heading WSW along the shore of Dexter Lake. Snowmobile markers are tacked to trees on the far side of the wet area, although the area itself is without evidence of the trail. There is much evidence of deer browsing. In midsummer and fall ostrich ferns grow 4 and 5 ft tall.

At 3 mi there is a great quantity of beaver-cut trees and shrubs, leaving large sections of cleared shoreline. For the most part the shoreline is dry, with a preponderance of hemlocks. A dip occurs at 3.1 mi through a wet area, and the trail continues past a camping area with two or three huge boulders jutting into the water. The water appears to be deep enough for swimming, but it is cluttered with downed tree trunks just below the surface. The S end of the lake is reached at 3.6 mi.

The marked snowmobile trail continues across the end of the lake. The hiker who wishes to explore farther should seek the trail to the L, which is so overgrown and unused that a continuation to Spectacle Lake must be considered a bushwhack. The hiker who decides to continue should proceed in a SW direction through a wooded area and, with luck, locate an old logging road, also much overgrown. All paths are barely discernible. Bear WSW from the S end of Dexter Lake. Spectacle Lake will be encountered in approximately 1 mi.

Beaver have raised the level of Spectacle Lake at least 3 ft in recent years. Notice at the W end the concrete foundations and other evidence of buildings that once graced its shores. Much of the section marked as swamp on the topographic map is currently under water, thanks to the engineering powers of beavers.

There is no easy way to round the lake to pick up one of the trails back to NY 10 or NY 29. The trails are overgrown, the shores are flooded, and the crisscross sections of snowmobile trails are often lost to hikers as the trails traverse swamps. There is only sporadic evidence of an old road, and it is impossible to follow it for any length of time, so the hiker must repeatedly return to higher ground to stay out of the swamps. (See trails 113 and 116 for descriptions to Spectacle Lake from NY 10 and NY 29A.)

❄ Trail in winter: Very good backcountry skiing for the intermediate group. The descent to Dexter Lake is rather steep, but with prudence and good snow cover there should be no major problems. As on all trails marked for snowmobiles, skiers should be alert to avoid them.

🚶 Distances: To trail jct., 0.5 mi; to stream crossing on log bridge, 1.4 mi; to Dry Lake, 2.1 mi; to Dexter Lake, 2.9 mi (4.6 km); to Spectacle Lake (approx.) 4.6 mi (7.4 km).

110 Good Luck Lake from NY 10

Trails Illustrated Map 744: E14

This charming, shallow lake is an easy walk through attractive, relatively level terrain. Its tiny, rocky, but sandy beaches provide suitable sites for swimming. The primitive camping areas that ring the shore are extremely popular and overused.

▶Trailhead: The trail begins opposite the parking turnout on NY 10, which is located on the R (E) immediately after the second bridge over the West Branch of the Sacandaga River. Directly across from the parking turnout is the trail entrance. It is well marked with brown and yellow DEC signboards that indicate trails to Spectacle, Dry, and Dexter Lakes (trails 109 and 113), as well as Good Luck Lake. For additional routes to Good Luck Lake, see also trails 109 and 112.◀

The trail enters the forest after passing an iron barrier prohibiting motorized access during all seasons except winter when these trails become snowmobile trails. Climbing moderately, the trail is rocky in places, and heads in a general NW direction. At 0.2 mi it jogs L and then R, leveling off at 0.3 mi. Continuing through tall open hardwoods, it descends into a boggy area before reaching a three-pronged trail fork at 0.5 mi. Take the L fork; the middle one goes to Dry and Dexter Lakes (see trail 109). The far R trail is almost hidden in the underbrush, overgrown and seldom, if ever, used by hikers as it merely parallels NY 10 for the convenience of snowmobilers.

After the L turn a wet area is crossed almost immediately. The trail is level at 0.6 mi and at 0.7 mi begins to descend into a depression with another wet area at 0.9 mi. The woods are composed of mature hardwoods and are open and lovely.

After a short ascent, Good Luck Lake comes into view on the L at 1 mi. A side

Good Luck Lake. Michael N. Kelsey

trail leads to an idyllic campsite. The trail is easy and pleasant. Although the lake continues to be glimpsed through the trees, the trail remains on the ridge. At 1.1 mi a small snowmobile bridge spans a wet area, and another, larger bridge crosses a larger stream at 1.2 mi. The trail rises out of a small ravine after first crossing yet another snowmobile bridge. At 1.2 mi a big board bridge traverses a section of swamp. (Note a path just before crossing this second plank bridge. This is the blue-blazed path to Gook Luck Mt. Cliffs. See trail 111.)

The trail jogs L after crossing the swamp on a large wooden snowmobile bridge and continues up a small hill. At 1.3 mi another wet area is crossed, and after a short rise a jct. is reached. Good Luck Lake is out of sight. A side trail leading R to Spectacle Lake is marked by a sign at 1.4 mi. Continue straight ahead. In less than a tenth of a mile the trail is intersected again. A R turn will lead to Spectacle Lake (trail 113). Straight ahead is trail 114.

To reach the shores of Good Luck Lake, seek the unmarked path to the L. It goes down the side of the ridge to the lake and then along the shore for about 0.4 mi (or 1.8 mi from the trailhead). There are two waterfront campsites located on the trail including a large, well-used campsite with a lovely sandy beach along the S shore. Enormous old white pines shade the area.

Additional camping areas along the shore are favorites of canoeists and small boaters but these are difficult for the hiker to reach, owing to the swamps that comprise much of the shoreline. The E and W ends of Good Luck Lake are exclusively swamplands.

❄ Trail in winter: Good backcountry skiing under proper snow conditions. There are enough ups and downs to provide nice runs. Note that snowmobiles share this and almost all other trails in the area.

🏃 Distances: To first trail jct. from NY 10, 0.5 mi; to Good Luck–Spectacle Lake jct., 1.3 mi; to Good Luck Lake, 1.8 mi (2.9 km).

111 Good Luck Mt. Cliffs

Trails Illustrated Map 744: E14

A visit to the cliffs of Good Luck Mt. requires the hiker to take a well-defined path, although without markers, up a small mountainside and over the top to a wonderful lookout ledge. In recent years this route has been used enough to qualify as a path, and is no longer a bushwhack.

▶Trailhead: The trailhead is the same used for trips into Good Luck, Dexter, Dry, and Spectacle Lakes, and is located on NY 10 at the parking turnout just after the second northern bridge over the West Branch of the Sacandaga River. (See trail 109.)◀

Follow the Good Luck Lake from NY 10 Trail (trail 110) to the trail jct. with the Good Luck Mt Cliffs. Take this unmarked footpath, which leads NW to Good Luck Mt. and the cliffs.

The path bends R, away from the stream in a WNW direction on a well-defined track that is easy to follow even in midsummer. At 1.5 mi the stream is encountered again; this time it can be crossed easily by rock-hopping. Once on the other (W) side, the trail proceeds up a draw, clogged here with large, picturesque boulders.

The path starts to climb steeply now, beginning the 600 ft ascent to the top of the cliffs, which can be partially seen in dramatic splendor, at 1.9 mi on the other side of the draw. Here, next to the path, several enormous boulders are jumbled together to create tiny caves, which are most interesting to explore.

Proceeding around the boulders, the path crosses the floor of the gorge, then the stream again at 2 mi, and continues up the opposite side, heading due N. A small clearing is crossed at 2.1 mi where a fork can be discerned. The main footpath goes a bit L, although a jog R will simply take one through a scrubby grove of hemlocks to rejoin the other fork in 0.2 mi.

The path climbs rather steeply now, then levels off through the saddle. It bends L at 2.4 mi to begin a traverse of the ridge. It soon turns sharply R to reach the top of the cliffs at 2.5 mi.

There is a spectacular view of the valley below and hills to the W. On a clear day one can see part of Spectacle Lake to the SW. There are boulders to rest on, and the ledge is a good size, shaded by beautiful, twisted white pines—a goal well worth the effort expended.

❄ Trail in winter: A nice ski/snowshoe climb, skiing at least to the second bridge where the R (NW) turn is made. Stash the skis here or at the stream crossing right below the cliffs at 1.5 mi. On a clear winter day, no other short, local climb will match the incredible scenery both enroute and at the top. Snowmobiles will pack the trail until you turn off it just before the second bridge and begin the climb. Although map and compass are important to carry winter or summer, the mountain is the only one in the immediate area, so winter climbers are unlikely to miss it, despite a lack of trail markers.

🏃 Distances: To jct., 0.5 mi; to cutoff and herd path, 1.5 mi; to top of cliffs, 2.5 mi (4 km).

112 Good Luck Lake Short Path

Trails Illustrated Map 744: E14

Good Luck Lake is a wonderful little lake with many access paths, this one being by far the shortest, although not necessarily the clearest. It appears to have been used for many years, however, as the trail in a few places is actually worn several inches into the soft ground. (See also trails 110 and 114.)

▶Trailhead: This path begins directly opposite the large parking area on the E side of NY 10 immediately after the second, northerly bridge over the West Branch of the Sacandaga. The path is unmarked, but can be located a few yd S (directly across the road from the parking area) from the officially marked DEC trail to Good Luck, Spectacle, Dry, and Dexter Lakes. Look for an opening through the trees that appears to be a rocky gully.◀

The path begins as an uphill in a SW direction. Although a bit difficult to see from the road, once located it is well-defined and easy to follow, if brushy in spots. It travels through open hardwoods with a scattering of hemlocks here and there. At 0.1 mi the path goes uphill very gently, and can be followed easily as a well-worn depression in the soft ground. At 0.2 mi, look on both sides for huge tree stumps that give one a good indication of the size of trees in the virgin forests felled in the 1800s.

The path flattens out and swings a bit R as it crosses the top of the ridge at 0.3 mi after climbing steadily on a moderate uphill. Now begins a somewhat steeper downhill section to the bottom of the ridge. The lake comes into view at 0.4 mi after a swing to the SSW. There are several primitive camping sites along the shore of Good Luck Lake, most officially too close to the lake. Good Luck Lake is a favorite of anglers and campers as its N and S shores are quite solid and rocky and, occasionally, one will find an attractive sandy stretch of beach. The E and W ends of the lake, however, are typical Adirondack bogs.

❄ Trail in winter: Not recommended for skiers, but a nice snowshoe trip. Too short and rather rugged to ski as it is somewhat overgrown and thus harder to follow in snow. The descent to the lake is steep and difficult for all but the most expert backcountry skiers. Snowshoers with map and compass may wish to use this path to access the entire area for longer trips such as Good Luck Mt. Cliffs. A party can also snowshoe to the lake, cross it, and explore the vlei. Use map and compass to intersect snowmobile trails to points N, W, or S toward West Stoner Lake.

🐾 Distances: To top of ridge, 0.3 mi; to Good Luck Lake shore, 0.4 mi (0.6 km).

113 Spectacle Lake from NY 10

Trails Illustrated Map 744: E14

Spectacle Lake is really three lakes that run into each other, and it was probably so named because on a map its shape looks a bit like a pair of old-fashioned spectacles. Years ago there were several buildings on its W end and at least two old roads leading to and around the lake. The lake water level has been raised in recent years by beaver, and the increased swamplands make walking its shores a difficult and wet proposition. They are, however, lovely, very wild and remote.

Four snowmobile trails lead to the lake and its vicinity, but these trails are often, wet, boggy, and sometimes difficult to find and follow for the summer hiker. In recent years they have been used more frequently and seem to be maintained by snowmobilers. Nevertheless, they provide a challenge and hold promise for adventures in a remote and seldom-visited area.

▶Trailhead: The trail begins opposite the parking turnout on NY 10, which is located on the R (E) immediately after the second bridge over the West Branch of the Sacandaga River. It is well marked with brown and yellow DEC signboards that indicate trails to Spectacle, Dry, and Dexter Lakes (trail 109), as well as Good Luck Lake (trail 110).◀

The trail enters the forest after passing an iron barrier prohibiting motorized access during all seasons except winter, when these trails become snowmobile trails. Climbing moderately, the trail is rocky in places, and heads in a general NW direction. At 0.2 mi it jogs L and then R, leveling off at 0.3 mi. Continuing through tall open hardwoods, it descends into a boggy area before reaching a three-pronged trail fork at 0.5 mi. Take the L fork; the middle one goes to Dry and Dexter Lakes (see trail 109). The far R trail is almost hidden in the underbrush, overgrown and seldom, if ever, used by hikers as it merely parallels NY 10 for the convenience of snowmobilers.

After the L turn a wet area is crossed almost immediately. The trail is level at 0.6 mi and at 0.7 mi begins to descend into a depression with another wet area at 0.9 mi. The woods are composed of mature hardwoods and are open and lovely.

After a short ascent, Good Luck Lake comes into view on the L at 1 mi. The trail is easy and pleasant. Although the lake continues to be glimpsed through the trees, the trail remains on the ridge. At 1.1 mi a small snowmobile bridge spans a wet area, and another, larger bridge crosses a larger stream at 1.2 mi. The trail rises out of a small ravine after first crossing yet another snowmobile bridge. At 1.2 mi a big board bridge traverses a section of swamp. (Note a path just before crossing this second plank bridge. This is the path to Good Luck Mt. Cliffs. See trail 111.)

The trail jogs L after crossing the swamp and continues up a small hill. At 1.3 mi another wet area is crossed, and after a short rise a jct. is reached. Good Luck Lake is out of sight. Two signs, one on each side of a triangle created by the trails from the S and E both turning W, point to Spectacle Lake to the W (R).

At this jct. (1.3 mi from NY 10) turn R and up a little rise. The trail bends R and crosses a section of very old, slippery corduroy at 1.6 mi. The general direction is W heading toward Spectacle Lake. At 1.7 mi, after a few snake-like turns, the trail levels off. Here there are small wet areas to cross before the trail climbs another ridge at 1.8 mi.

The trail continues through a little valley with a stream to the L, and at 2 mi makes an easy curve R. Up another little hill at 2.1 mi, the trail approaches a large wet area with a trail cutoff R around it. The forest is still open, with mature hardwoods predominating. Ascending a small hill, the trail enters a ravine. At 2.4 mi it leaves the ravine and bears R to enter a tiny clearing bordering the shore of Spectacle Lake at 2.6 mi.

Wild pink azalea bushes add color to the little clearing, and although there is limited access to the lake, what one does see is beautiful. It looks as if the trail continues L along the lake shore, but it goes only to two smaller clearings in another 0.1 mi and then disappears.

Hikers will find it difficult to continue to explore the shores, as swamplands and very dense underbrush make this almost impossible, but with a map and compass it is an adventure to cut SW to intersect the snowmobile trail from NY 29A (trail 116). The forest is young second growth but quite open and, for the most part, fairly level and easy going. A tip: Believe your compass—there are no hills to use for landmarks, but it is less than 1 mi and the trail you will intersect is very broad, rutted, and difficult to miss. From this trail hikers can explore the other "spectacle eye" of these interesting, truly wild lakes. This bushwhack, however, should be planned ahead and a car left at the NY 29 trailhead (trail 116) or the West Stoner Lake trailhead (trail 114).

❄ Trail in winter: Good backcountry skiing; nice ups and downs, but nothing too difficult. Trails are shared with snowmobiles, but with good snow cover this could be an advantage as they pack the snow for skiers.

🎿 Distances: To first trail jct. from NY 10, 0.5 mi; to Good Luck–Spectacle Lake jct., 1.3 mi; to Spectacle Lake, 2.6 mi (4.2 km).

114 Good Luck Lake from West Stoner Lake
Trails Illustrated Map 744: E14

A day's hiking commencing at the trailhead at West Stoner Lake will give one a true appreciation for the many varieties of lakes and trails in the Caroga Lake area of the southern Adirondacks. The complex of trails is maintained by local residents and snowmobilers and provides easy access to some very wild, yet historically interesting areas. To appreciate the rapidity of the natural return of forests, consider that this area was largely cleared and settled in the late 1800s with farms, lumbering, tanneries, vacationing tourists, and small-town merchants. The trails we now walk were often rough roads of commerce or lumbering in earlier times.

▶Trailhead: To reach the trailhead, at the jct. of NY 10 and NY 29A, go N on NY 10 for 2.8 mi and turn L onto North Shore West Stoner Lake Rd. Continue 0.6 mi on this rather narrow dirt road to the end where a parking area is on the R (N) side of the road next to the trailhead. There is no signboard, but it is marked with snowmobile trail markers and a Forest Preserve sign. There are several summer camps along the road. Parking is poor, but two or three cars can be accommodated without blocking access to these camps.◀

The trail enters the trees going N on the remnants of an old road, locally referred to as the "Military Road." Its military significance, if any, has been lost, however. A snowmobile bridge over a small stream is crossed at 0.1 mi, and the trail begins a gentle uphill climb. Easy to follow through hardwood forests of beech and yellow birch, the trail is well marked with yellow snowmobile disks. Very shortly, there is yet another distinct path that forks to the R, and back to the road; continue straight ahead.

At 0.2 mi an uphill section begins traversing a shoulder of Rooster Hill. It is evident that the old road was carefully engineered and leveled along this section. The trail is wide and very easy to follow, and the forest is open. The top of the ridge is reached at 0.2 mi. A wet area, wide and very attractive with grasses and many rocks to use as stepping stones, is encountered at 0.3 mi. Now the trail begins a long gentle descent down the ridge. Hay ferns and wildflowers are in abundance.

The trail reaches the Four Corners jct. at 0.5 mi. Here there is a trail register and signs point to the various paths and their destinations. The Four Corners clearing is a well-used crossroads, very pretty at any time of year. Here the hiker can choose from several options. Go straight ahead to Good Luck Lake, R to NY 10 and the Arietta Hotel, or L to Third and Fourth Lakes (trail 115), or Spectacle Lake, from NY 29A (trail 116).

Continuing straight ahead, N, to Good Luck Lake, at 0.6 mi the trail crosses another small brook on a wooden bridge. Very shortly the trail becomes quite wet, and begins to twist and turn in snaky undulations. Wildflowers include wood sorrel and goldthread; look for interesting staghorn clubmosses. The trail passes through several stands of hemlocks scattered throughout a predominantly deciduous landscape. Another small stream is crossed at 1 mi, and then another at 1.1 mi. There is a short and steep ascent up a small knoll, after which a large bog requires rock hopping at 1.3 mi. After a moderate uphill, a jct. is reached at 1.5 mi. Spectacle Lake is to the L (W) (trail 113). To reach Good Luck Lake, turn R here and descend the hill another 0.2 mi to the shore and several well-used camping and fishing areas. You may also wish to take a side trek up Good Lake Mt. Cliffs for stunning views of the area. (See trail 111.)

Fourth Lake. Mark Bowie

Good Luck Lake is one of the few lakes with several lovely stretches of sandy beaches—small, but welcome to campers and swimmers. Their size depends upon the water level in the lake in any given season.

❄ Trail in winter: Sharing with snowmobiles is a fact of life on these as on almost every other trail in the southern Adirondacks. Nevertheless skiing can be enjoyed, with care and under the right snow conditions, throughout this region. In fact the trails are often packed nicely for skiers by the snowmobiles. Prudence suggests that skiers give way, however, as snowmobiles have limited maneuverability among the trees.

🐾 Distances: To Four Corners, 0.5 mi; to Spectacle Lake jct., 1.5 mi; to Good Luck Lake, 1.7 mi (2.7 km).

115 Third and Fourth Lakes

Trails Illustrated Map 744: E14

Third and Fourth lakes are only a quarter mile apart and between them are the ruins of several old buildings. There is an old garbage dump, and with some exploration one may still find it, as well as the foundations of a building or two. The rapidity with which the forest is reclaiming the area is a reminder of Mother Nature's ability to obliterate man's works entirely.

Third Lake has a few high camping spots along its wet shores and is very attractive. Fourth Lake, although not readily accessible, is also very pretty. The trail from NY 10 also provides access to many other old roads and snowmobile trails. It is a pleasant, if sometimes wet, fairly easy walk through varied terrain.

▶Trailhead: Drive N on NY 10 to a quarter mile S of the Arietta Hotel. The brown and yellow DEC trail sign is readily seen from the road on its W (L) side. Park along the shoulder of NY 10.◀

Immediately at the bottom of the embankment of the road, this marked snowmobile trail is very likely to be quite wet and mucky for at least the first 500 yd. At 0.2 mi a second wet area must be crossed. This first 0.3 mi has been established to avoid private land, although the original tote road is intersected at 0.3 mi where the trail makes a sharp L. To the R used to be the road leading back to NY 10. A sign here at R warns not to trespass on this section of private land.

The trail is overgrown (unless recently brushed out by snowmobilers, which occurs infrequently), but a definite path can be discerned heading W. It passes through a mixed forest that includes balsam and apple trees. After a bend L and another wet area at 0.4 mi, the trail curves R to enter a thicket of aromatic balsam trees. Although lush with plant life, this section is easy, pleasant walking in mid-summer.

At 0.5 mi the trail passes through mixed hardwoods. There is a jog R at 0.6 mi, and the trail begins climbing a rise at 0.7 mi. This is the NW shoulder of Rooster Hill. The trail levels again at 0.8 mi and makes a curve to the L, then begins to descend at 0.9 mi. Soon the trail becomes rocky and uneven, and at 1 mi a mucky section must be crossed.

At 1.1 mi a jct. is reached. This is the area locally known as Four Corners. (See trail 114.) There is a DEC trail register and guideboards which point N (R) to Good Luck Lake, Avery's Place, and Piseco; S (L) to West Stoner Lake; and straight ahead, WSW, toward Pleasant Lake and NY 29A. The latter is also the direction to Third and Fourth Lakes, although the sign does not mention them.

Continue straight, or W. At 1.1 mi the trail bends L and goes up a short incline. At 1.2 mi it jogs R and then crests the small ridge at 1.3 mi. Climbing a bit more steeply to top another small ridge on the N face of West Lake Mt. at 1.4 mi, the trail then descends moderately to cross a small stream. It soon bends slightly L at 1.5 mi. The trail goes L or R through a wet spot at 1.7 mi, and at 1.8 mi passes through more open hardwood forest, heading W.

At 1.9 mi a clearing with large, attractive rocks scattered about is traversed. The trail passes through very lovely rocky terrain at 2 mi and then encounters a swampy area. It crosses a major creek at 2.4 mi and several small wet areas until at 2.7 mi Third Lake can be seen through the trees. The lake has a predominantly mucky shore line. The snowmobile trail winds along the SE side, traveling in a SSW direction. A camping area is reached at 2.8 mi on higher ground on the shore of the lake.

Third Lake is attractive, although seldom visited, probably because of limited access to its waters owing to the boggy shoreline.

Continue on the snowmobile trail to a plank bridge over the swift-running outlet stream between Third and Fourth Lakes. An overgrown clearing is entered to the S. One can usually continue through the clearing and a wet area for approximately 0.2 mi to reach the shore of Fourth Lake.

This entire area around Third and Fourth Lakes is lush with wild tangles of vegetation by midsummer, and depending upon use and time of year, the trails can be confusing. Refer to the map and compass frequently.

Continuing along this trail another 0.3 mi brings one to the Spectacle Lake Trail from NY 29A (trail 116).

❈ Trail in winter: Shared with snowmobiles. The backcountry skier will need energy to climb Rooster Hill's knolls and then a long, steeper shoulder of West Lake Mt. A shorter, somewhat easier trail to use to ski into this area is the West Stoner Lake Trail (trail 114).

🐾 Distances: To jct. of snowmobile trail to West Stoner Lake and Good Luck Lake, 1 mi; to clearing, 1.9 mi; to Third Lake, 2.7 mi; to Fourth Lake, 3.4 mi (5.4 km).

116 Spectacle Lake from NY 29A

Trails Illustrated Map 744: D13

This route to Spectacle Lake has improved in recent years owing to maintenance by local snowmobile clubs, but is still a challenge requiring endurance and the ability to read a map and relocate a trail after bog-hopping and skirting beaver swamps. In summer, the insects in this wet area demand their blood sacrifices to excess! The trail sign on NY 29A says "Spectacle Lake, 6.0; Dexter Lake, 6.5." Do not attempt to reach Dexter Lake by this route; the trail is impossible to follow in spring, summer, or fall as it goes through swamps; the easier trail by far is from NY 10. (See trail 109.)

▶Trailhead: Access to the trailhead is off NY 29A, 3 mi from the split of NY 29A and NY 10 in the hamlet of Pine Lake. Parking is provided on the S side of the highway, while the trail begins across the road, heading N.◀

The trail starts with a moderate downhill until at 0.2 mi, after crossing a wet area, it begins a gradual climb. The forest is mixed hardwoods and conifers and is fairly smooth underfoot. A stream spanned by a wood bridge is crossed at 0.3 mi, and a second smaller one with a washed-out bridge is rock-hopped at 0.4 mi. At 0.6 mi a large grassy clearing indicates that this is an old beaver pond going back to meadow.

Soon the trail commences to climb a small rocky ridge curving R. The forest here is very young, as the trees are saplings. A major wet section, created by a small stream filled with black moss, occurs at 0.8 mi.

At a jct. at 0.9 mi a sign pointing L says "Lakes." To the R is the trail to Nine Corner Lake (See trail 117.) Continue L toward "Lakes." Immediately after the jct., the trail bends L. Witch hobble and other shrubs grow in profusion, but the trail is still wide and easy to walk.

James Appleyard

A swamp, Burnt Vlei, becomes visible on the L at 1 mi. At 1.1 mi the trail begins to climb briefly away from the vlei, but skirts its E side for at least the next mile. At 1.2 mi the trail bends away from Burnt Vlei and at 1.3 mi crosses another section of swamp on a log bridge.

At 1.4 mi, to the L is more swampy area, which is still part of Burnt Vlei. After a bend L, the trail enters a cathedral of hemlocks. Here the trail is wide and dry. Heading N, it begins climbing a ridge, and at 1.5 mi, now on top of the ridge, enters young hardwoods again. Descending at 1.6 mi, it makes a slight jog L. A large stream at 1.7 mi is crossed on a snowmobile bridge.

An impressive beaver dam is on the R at 1.8 mi. The trail turns away from the beaver dam through a washed-out rocky area, then jogs R and continues due N. Another wet area at 2.1 mi can be skirted L or R.

The next trail jct. reached is a T. Signs point R to Arietta and NY 10, giving no mileage. (The L fork is a snowmobile trail to Pleasant Lake. This trail is not described in this guide as it is another snowmobile trail traversing numerous wet areas without redeeming points of interest to the summer hiker.) Take the R fork.

After a brief ascent and more small wet areas, the trail becomes wilder at 2.6 mi. Follow this trail to another jct. at 2.9 mi. A sign here says R to the Arietta Hotel and Log Cabin; this is also the trail to Fourth Lake, Four Corners, and points E. (See trail 115). Straight ahead are Spectacle and (after a bushwhack) Dexter Lakes.

Third Lake appears on the R at 3 mi. The trail traverses part of the shore of this lake which has a large beaver lodge at its S end. There is a camping area on the R. Leaving the camping area, the trail passes more wet areas and then descends through a pretty, mature hardwood forest into a small clearing. Another trail goes L; the main one continues straight ahead. A clearing is passed at 3.3 mi. The trail goes through a thicket of attractive hemlocks and yet another mucky area.

Another jct. is reached at 3.4 mi, where a snowmobile bridge crosses a larger stream. Here a sign says "NY 29A via Long Lake to the L and Dexter Lake 3 mi straight ahead." (Dexter can be reached only after Spectacle is passed, and the trail is presently lost to the hiker in the swamps, although snowmobilers will no doubt find it.)

After leaving the stream the trail goes through a large wet area. At 3.5 mi it passes through another stand of evergreens and hemlocks. The trail is wide and shows evidence of wheel ruts indicating recent motorized use.

At 3.6 mi, after climbing a small hill, the trail reaches another jct. (A turn R would lead to the E shore of Spectacle and eventually to Good Luck Lake, but this trail is currently unused and completely overgrown.) A turn L leads through another boggy section, after which Spectacle Lake comes into view at 4 mi. For the next 0.8 mi, however, it is necessary to walk the high ground to the S to avoid the swampy shores. At 4.8 mi the faint trail finally descends to the edge of the water, from which one can see an enormous rock in the middle of the lake.

Spectacle Lake is an interesting place to visit, but who would want to live there! In fall, hikers may wish to bushwhack along the S shore to visit the ruins of a dam and settlement on the W end. Boggy and buggy, it is best visited during cooler times of the year. It has an isolated charm, a pristine quality maintained by its inaccessibility.

✼ Trail in winter: Experienced backcountry skiers would find this area a worthwhile challenge, with much to see that is inaccessible at any other time of year. Distances in and out must be taken into consideration as it is at least a 10 or 11 mi round-trip with explorations of the lake included. The trail is broad and well used by snowmobilers, and thus likely to be packed for skiers. With new snowfall, a (potentially) memorable ski trip!

𝐍 Distances: To first jct., 0.9 mi; to beaver dam, 1.8 mi; to Third Lake, 2.9 mi; to jct. and large stream crossing, 3.4 mi; to view of Spectacle Lake, 4 mi; to Spectacle Lake shore, 4.8 mi (7.7 km).

117 Nine Corner Lake

Trails Illustrated Map 744: D14

An old road forms the trail bed to this extremely attractive little lake, 0.9 mi from NY 29A, which provides numerous campers with an interesting destination without much effort. Heavily used, especially in summer, and again by snowmobilers in winter, Nine Corner Lake is one of the jewels of the southern Adirondacks. It is worth the short hike to savor the visual delights of a blue lake surrounded by enormous boulders and dark green pines. Walk the anglers' paths to access less-used shoreline.

Hikers who wish to extend this trek can take the S path around the lake, which is the Burnt Vlei snowmobile trail, and continue on an unremarkable and sometimes obscure path to an intersection with the Spectacle Lake trail from NY 29A. (See trail 116.)

▶Trailhead: The trail begins at the parking turnoff on NY 29A immediately after it splits from NY 10 in the hamlet of Pine Lake. Parking is available on both sides of the highway, but the trail to Nine Corner Lake begins on the N (R) side at a brown and yellow DEC sign. A barrier is encountered as the trail leaves the parking area, with a trail register immediately thereafter. Motorized vehicles (except snowmobiles in winter) are prohibited, according to a posted sign. ◀

The trail is very well used, broad and smooth. It begins to climb immediately, although moderately, becoming quite rocky at 0.2 mi. At 0.4 mi an attractive stream on the L is seen about 100 yd off the trail. At 0.5 mi the trail flattens out, and at 0.6 mi a sturdy plank snowmobile bridge crosses the swift-flowing outlet stream. To the R is a series of small waterfalls.

The trail continues over the rocks, climbing slightly and reaching a fork at 0.8 mi. Turn R for Nine Corner Lake. Note that this E (R) fork shows signs of being the more used of the two trails. The L fork is a continuation of the snowmobile trail to the Spectacle Lake Trail (see trail 116) and Burnt Vlei.

Nine Corner Lake. Michael N. Kelsey

The lovely blue lake is reached at 0.9 mi. The view from here is limited as one can see only one arm of this interesting lake, which has many pretty bays and tiny islands. A rocky dam is on the E (R) side here at the outlet; a path leads across it and continues along the opposite side of the lake to clear areas that are frequently used for camping. The S end is strewn with large boulders that lead down into the water and create excellent access steps for the swimmer. A well-used camping area is a few yd to the L on the S shore.

Returning to the jct. for Burnt Vlei, hikers can push another 0.6 mi W around the lake by first circling a small hill to access the shore again and gain a better view of the lake as a whole. This snowmobile trail continues another 0.6 mi through unremarkable second growth forests to intersect the Spectacle Lake Trail from NY 29A at Burnt Vlei.

❋ Trail in winter: This trail is heavily used by snowmobiles. The backcountry skier will surely share the trails and should be experienced enough to ski steep snowmobile tracks.

🚶 Distances: To bridge over outlet stream, 0.5 mi; to jct., 0.8 mi; to Nine Corner Lake, 0.9 mi (1.4 km). From jct. (0.0) to Burnt Vlei, 1.2 mi (1.9 km).

118 Broomstick Lake

Trails Illustrated Map 744: D14

Broomstick Lake is a beautiful little lake, made more so by colorful rose quartz found in many of the rocks and boulders at its outlet. There is one small camping area, close to the lake shore, but it and the boulders along the outlet make it also an attractive picnic destination for a short hike. Although most of the shoreline is swampy, there is an attractive stand of large hemlocks on the high ground along its N and E shores.

A local historian has unearthed the fact that this was the site of the 1936 filming of the original *Last of the Mohicans*, one of the popular films of its day, which was revised and released again in 1992. The 1936 movie's stockade was built on the relatively flat E shore among the tall hemlocks.

▶Trailhead: The trail is 1 mi N of the jct. of NY 29A and NY 10 in the hamlet of Pine Lake. The trail sign at the entrance says "Broomstick Lake 0.7 mi."◀

The trail begins an immediate uphill through predominantly hardwoods. Shortly after, it crosses a small brook which joins the larger Broomstick Lake outlet stream on the R. The direction of travel is NW at first and then W. The trail is dotted with occasional orange snowmobile disks, and even rarer yellow cross-country ski disks, but is quite easy to follow.

In spring the wildflowers include wood sorrel, bellwort, dwarf ginseng, and several species of violets. At 0.2 mi the trail passes an old clearing on the R. It is now growing back to blend in with the rest of the forest, but closer investigation will reveal rusted barrels and a bed frame, indicating that a dwelling of some kind had been built here.

After passing the clearing, the trail begins to climb again. At the R, a large chunk of earth appears to have been cut from the side of the ridge. Local rumor has it that the area was used by a film crew to stage an explosion. There seems to be no natural cause for this somewhat square depression, although no one seems sure exactly how it originated, or when.

The trail now runs parallel to the stream again. At 0.3 mi to the R there is a small, clear pool, fed by a swift-running section of the outlet stream that forms a small flume of water cascading into the pool.

The trail enters a washed-out section with many rocks underfoot. Continuing to climb moderately, it reaches the top of the ridge at 0.4 mi and becomes smooth and easy to walk again. A small brook at 0.5 mi is crossed as a second clearing comes into view. One can imagine this as a place where the film crews gathered their equipment and perhaps camped for the duration of the shoot.

A pretty little waterfall that may have been used in the film can be found by walking to the R (W) across a fern-filled clearing. Here the outlet stream cascades down a 15 ft ledge, with large hemlocks providing an attractive backdrop.

The trail swings L and climbs briefly before finally flattening out at 0.6 mi. Very shortly, a boggy area is encountered. This is the beginning of the vlei at the outlet of the lake. Avoid the wetter areas by climbing a few feet to the L to higher ground. At 0.7 mi, after a short curve to the R, the lake comes into view. Traverse the pinkish bedrock that makes up the outlet end of Broomstick Lake, and cross the outlet by rock-hopping to reach the sunny boulders on the NE shore. A primitive campsite on the L shore can be found at 0.8 mi.

❊ Trail in winter: Although marked as a snowmobile trail as well as a ski trail, this trip is so short that cross-country skiers and snowshoers may have it all to themselves. Skiers should be cautious in the area of the unnatural ridge-side depression; the cliff created is difficult to see from the top, and the trail goes rather close to it.

🐾 Distances: To clearing with artifacts and mysterious missing chunk, 0.2 mi; to second clearing and side trip to waterfall, 0.6 mi; to lake shore, 0.7 mi (1.1 km).

119 Kane Mt. South and North Trails

Trails Illustrated Map 744: D14

The hike to the summit of Kane Mt. is a short walk to an unstaffed but well-restored fire tower. Views are available only upon climbing the tower. There is also an observer's cabin and grassy picnic area on the summit. Trails lead down the E side (trail 120) as well as across the ridge and down the N slope, then E back to Green Lake, or to Pine Lake Campground. Note that Pine Lake Campground is private, and the owners do not encourage visiting hikers; in fact they charge a fee to cross the campground in summer.

▶Trailhead: To reach the trailhead on the S side, turn onto Schoolhouse Rd. from NY 10. The road is located on the N (R, if driving W) side, approximately 0.4 mi W of Green Lake Rd., which is also on the R immediately after passing Green Lake. About 150 yd up this dirt road is the start of the marked trail, on the R. A parking area carved into the shoulder of the road is large enough for two or three cars. ◀

The trail begins to climb immediately at a moderately steep grade. At 0.2 mi it is rocky and well used, but wide and clear. The forest is open and composed of a preponderance of sugar maples as well as other hardwoods such as ash, yellow birch, and beech.

At 0.3 mi the climb becomes steeper, with sections of loose earth and stone underfoot. A large tree trunk is lying at the side of the trail, and a maple tree is growing in the center at 0.4 mi. At 0.5 mi a few hemlocks come into view; their sporadic dark green against the background of red and yellow maples makes a pretty scene in the fall.

At 0.6 mi the tower comes into view. As the hiker approaches it, the trail levels and the observer's cabin appears on the R about 150 yd off the trail. The tower, restored in 1995, is no longer used, but is in excellent repair and can be climbed. Views are excellent. On a good day, one can see S as far as the Catskills and N to the High Peaks, while in the near distance Pine Lake (NW) and West Canada Lake (S) are a delight to the eye.

Hikers wishing to make a circle trip and return to their cars via Green Lake and NY 10 may take the trail to the R which begins just past the cabin and through a clearing heading due E (trail 120). The total round-trip distance is 1.5 mi.

A longer trek can also be had by traversing the summit ridge N, returning via the N trail, and then turning E at the foot of the mountain, walking the old road circling around the base, and returning to Green Lake. Although sporadically marked with yellow paint, this route is not as clear and easy as the other two. There's also quite a bit of blowdown in some areas, yet a descent of the mountain using this route takes one through some lovely forest glens to reach the jct. of the old road at 0.9 mi. Turn E (R) and hike another 0.8 mi past Fish Hatchery Pond to exit on Green Lake South Shore Rd.

Michael N. Kelsey

❄ Trail in winter: A short snowshoe trek to the summit, which can be combined with a ski trek around the base of the mountain. Skiers can continue through the campground in winter.

🥾 Distance: To summit of Kane Mt., 0.7 mi (1.1 km). If making a loop, to jct. of old road at base, 1.6 mi; to Green Lake South Shore Rd., 2.4 mi (3.8 km).

120 Kane Mt. East Trail

Trails Illustrated Map 744: D14

Kane Mt. is very popular with the summer residents of the Canada and Green Lakes area, and until 1990 had one of the few staffed fire towers. Now, however, the tower is no longer staffed, although can be climbed for a view—and must be, if a view is to be one's reward, as there are no natural lookouts.

▶Trailhead: One of three trails up Kane Mt. (see trail 119 for the N and S trails), the E trail, marked with DEC trail markers, can be reached by turning N on Green Lake Road and driving 0.6 mi to the end of the lake, where there is a fork L. The lake road continues sharply to the R. Take the L fork, which is a less used dirt road. Within 200 yd there is a parking area on the R, with the marked trail to Kane Mt. on the L. The brown and yellow DEC sign says Kane Mt. Observatory 0.5 mi, although the actual distance is 0.9 mi.◀

The trail begins to climb immediately through a broad avenue of mature hardwoods. At 0.1 mi, it bends R, and at 0.2 mi continues through a series of small jogs L and R until at 0.6 mi it straightens out. The trail is moderately steep and well used, although trail markers seem to be less frequent as the ascent continues. There are a number of twists and turns on this old jeep road. As the summit is approached the trail becomes level and passes through a cleared area where numerous berry bushes appear to be trying to gain a permanent foothold. The last several feet are through a grassy clearing, then past the observer's cabin. The trail turns R to the fire tower, which is reached at 0.9 mi.

A loop trek is possible by returning across the summit ridge and down the old N trail, then walking out on the abandoned road at the foot of the mountain back to the trailhead (trail 119).

✳ Trail in winter: An easy snowshoe trip; recommended for practice in preparation for longer, more difficult treks.

🚶 Distances: To summit of Kane Mt., 0.9 mi (1.4 km).

121 Stewart and Indian Lakes

Trails Illustrated Map 744: D15

This hike is a moderate uphill walk to two interesting and charming destinations. Indian Lake is by far the jewel of the two, yet Stewart has its own mystery and peace.

▶Trailhead: Drive on NY 10 to the Canada Lake–Green Lake area, and if coming from the SE turn N immediately after the bridge over the Green Lake outlet onto Green Lake Road, which follows the W shore of Green Lake. Travel 0.6 mi to a L fork; the shore road continues and makes a sharp R. Take the L onto a little-used dirt road extension and go about 200 yd to a parking turnout on the R. To the L is the E trailhead up Kane Mt. Park here, because the road soon becomes very rough and then, immediately after passing tiny Fish Hatchery Pond, is barred by a chain. It continues to Otter Lake, which is private. However, before Fish Hatchery Pond is reached, the trail can be seen on the R, marked with a DEC trail sign that says "Stewart Lake 1.25 mi; Indian Lake 2 mi" The trail is also marked with yellow and black cross-country ski trail markers.◀

A very short walk, less than 0.1 mi up the road past the trailhead, will bring the hiker to the old concrete dam at the outlet of Fish Hatchery Pond. Here one might cross the dam and continue up the small hill to join the trail at the top, but hikers who prefer to stay on the marked trail should pick up the trail on the R from the road. The trail immediately passes through a hemlock grove and across a sturdy plank bridge spanning the outlet of Fish Hatchery Pond. It then climbs the short ridge that overlooks the tiny pond, reaching the top at 0.1 mi.

The trail traverses the shore on top of the ridge for a short distance. It is well defined, traveling through a mixed hardwood and hemlock forest. Wildflowers—red trilliums, bellworts, Canada lilies, and colorful violets—abound in spring. The general direction is E. At 0.2 mi the trail enters an avenue of hemlocks. It twists and turns until at 0.3 mi it leaves Fish Hatchery Pond behind.

Climbing steadily but moderately through a washed-out rocky area, it enters more open hardwoods, where a blanket of witch hobble grows beneath the young beech and ash trees.

A tiny brook is crossed by rock-hopping at 0.4 mi, and the trail continues uphill at a moderate pitch. At the top of a ridge a large downed beech tree provides a resting place. After a jog R at 0.6 mi, the trail soon passes two huge glacial erratics that are most unusual. They are sedimentary and striped subtle colors of yellow, pink, and gray.

A small wet area is encountered at 0.7 mi, after which the trail begins to climb more steeply. At 0.8 mi the trail makes a slight jog L and then follows the contours of a ridge at 0.9 mi. A steady uphill climb again commences at 1.1 mi in a NE direction to top a ridge at 1.2 mi.

The descent to Stewart Lake, which can now be sighted through the trees, begins at 1.3 mi. Because the shoreline is 90 percent marshland, the trail does not go close to the lake but keeps to higher ground. The trail crosses a large wet section that is an arm of the shoreline bog at 1.5 mi.

Hikers who wish to descend to the lake should watch for a hemlock stand at 1.6 mi on the L and bushwhack through it on the high ground, which here continues to the shore, providing minimal access to the water. Stewart Lake is small but attractive and, owing to its protected shores, pristine.

The trail continues to hug the high ground to the E and shortly turns NE toward Indian Lake, veering away from Stewart. It crosses a wet area with a small brook running through it at 1.8 mi and continues through a level section. The woods are very open, and the trail is smooth and easy underfoot, beginning a downhill section at 2 mi.

After a jog R, at 2.1 mi Indian Lake comes into view. The trail descends and crosses a little brook to reach the lake shore.

A path to the L along the shore leads another 0.2 mi to a huge rock that juts out into the lake. This enormous, attractive rock contains small pockets of garnet interspersed with feldspar, an interesting combination. The rock is a fine observation and/or picnic spot, high and surrounded by hemlock and balsam. The shores of Indian Lake are mostly lined with swampy, tangled, low brush, but there are a few rocks here and there, and behind the marshy areas are attractive maple and hemlock thickets that help create a peaceful and picturesque destination.

✷ Trail in winter: Marked as a ski trail (no snowmobiles!), this is a neat trip to do in winter because one can explore the boggy areas and gain access to the lakes with little difficulty. A bit of a challenge, owing to the relentless climbing, which seems more daunting on skis than on foot. Be sure to control speeds on the downhill coming out!

🎿 Distances: To descent to Stewart Lake, 1.3 mi; to Indian Lake shore, 2.1 mi; to huge garnet rock, 2.3 mi (3.7 km).

122 Glasgow Mills and Hillabrandt Lake and Vlei

Trails Illustrated Map 744: B14

The trip to Glasgow Mills and Hillabrandt Lake and Vlei is a moderate walk along an old woods road to the historic site of an old mill and then on to a picturesque vlei, now dammed by beaver to create a shallow but lovely lake. There are no signs or trail markers other than sporadic snowmobile discs. Good navigation skills are needed.

▶Trailhead: Head N on NY 10, and turn L (W) onto Glasgow Mills Rd., 1 mi N of the jct. of NY 10 and NY 10A. Proceed for 1 mi to where a parking and turn-around area is located at the end of the drivable section. A State Land Forest Preserve sign is the only signage visible here.◀

The trail is a continuation of the road and appears to be frequently used by 4WD vehicles. It passes through a predominantly hardwood forest with a few medium-sized hemlocks. The large creek on the R is Glasgow Creek, which is crossed at 0.2 mi on a new wooden bridge. The first of red snowmobile trail markers is seen here.

The trail continues along the road, which is often rutted and muddy, and begins a moderate climb up the side of a ridge at 0.5 mi. At 0.6 mi a cutoff goes to the R, but the marked snowmobile trail continues straight ahead. Hikers may choose to continue to the E side of Hillabrandt Lake by following the snowmobile trail. The trail description herein pertains to the hiking trail.

At 1 mi the trail descends a small hill and enters an area of hemlock and beech trees. The trail is very wet in sections, but these areas can generally be avoided to the R or L. It curves L, and at 0.7 mi, swift-flowing Glasgow Creek comes into view again. There is another muddy section at 0.8 mi and then the trail continues up a small hill. A small stand of white pines tops the hill at 1.3 mi; the clearing known as Glasgow Mills lies beyond. Descending the knoll, at 1.4 mi the trail passes by what remains of the old dam, which in days past created a small lake to power a mill.

A side trail turns L (S) around the old pond, and crosses an open area that shows frequent use by motorized campers and picnickers. Depending upon the time of year and the local beaver population, the size of this pond varies, but it is a very attractive area. There are abundant field flowers in season, and a careful perusal of the shoreline reveals evidence of deer and coyote. Several clear paths lead to the water. This is a pleasant area to rest and have lunch or a trail snack.

A second trail enters from the R, but the main trail continues straight ahead, circling the R (N) side of the old pond. A big, muddy water hole must be circumvented at 1.5 mi as the sparsely marked trail continues W. At least two cellar holes of former houses are passed at 1.6 mi. The trail turns R and crosses a swampy area, then begins a moderate uphill section, still through a predominantly hardwood forest.

At 2.2 mi a creek running down the trail creates a very wet, if shallow, section, after which the soggy trail continues over another knoll. This begins a series of small undulations. At 2.3 mi hemlocks are more in evidence; at 2.7 mi they are especially attractive. At 2.9 mi the trail passes through a thicket of balsam trees, a fragrant reward for a woods walk.

The trail reaches Hillabrandt Lake and Vlei at 3.3 mi and continues around it to the L, but the hiker may wish to stop to enjoy the picturesque clearing to the R along the shore of the lake. The trail continues along the lakeshore, crossing at 3.6 mi a wooden snowmobile bridge, which is partially twisted out of alignment. Beaver have been busy restoring the water level in the vlei to recreate a lake. Their dam, just above and to the R (N) of the twisted bridge, is approximately 3 ft high and has successfully, at least for the past 10 years or so, maintained the water level in what is naturally a large swamp. Here, too, bordering the water, is a small stand of large, very beautiful white pines.

Explore the remains of the man-made dam, enjoying the wonderful scenery. The dam, a substantial structure built with enormous boulders, probably created the lake to hold logs during a time of massive lumbering in the area. (For those who wish to continue a through trip and access the trails in the Stewart Landing area, see trail 123.)

❋ Trail in winter: Certainly skiable, but snowmobiles need to be contended with, as this is a popular trail offering numerous connecting destinations for them. Skiers need to exercise caution and give way, but it could be an interesting and beautiful winter trek.

𝍂 Distances: To Glasgow Mills clearing and pond, 1.4 mi; to Hillabrandt Lake and Vlei, 3.3 mi (5.3 km).

123   Mud Lake from Stewart Landing

Trails Illustrated Map 744: C13

The complex of snowmobile trails beginning at Stewart Landing leads through wild, desolate country. For the hiker, the trails are long and traverse lush, wet lowlands and unremarkable second-growth forests that were logged extensively in the early part of this century. Nevertheless, there are a few interesting destinations, like Mud Lake and Hillabrandt Lake and Vlei, which can be accessed from this direction. (See trail 122 description, for example.)

▶Trailhead: To reach Stewart Landing, take NY 29 to Lassellsville and turn onto North Rd., which is also CR 119. Drive N on North Rd. to Stewart Landing Rd. Proceed on Stewart Landing Rd. another 3.3 mi to the trailhead found to the R (W) about 300 yd before, and on the same side as, the large parking area next to the dam. The Stewart Landing Rd. eventually turns to dirt and continues to several private camps.◀

A brown and yellow DEC sign marks the trail as a snowmobile trail going to Morey Rd. via Stewart Landing Channel, with the mileage listed as 5.5 mi. The trail begins as a rutted dirt road descending quickly to a jct. at 0.1 mi where a high, wooden snowmobile bridge crossing Sprite Creek is seen to the L. The road that continues straight ahead paralleling Sprite Creek is the old service road for an aqueduct that used to carry water to a power station several miles downstream. The remains of the wooden sluice can still be seen along the L side of the road.

The hiker should turn L and proceed across the attractive bridge. A barrier restricts motor vehicle access. In the past, this trail was much used by ATVs and snowmobiles.

The trail immediately begins to climb after the bridge, traversing mixed forests with several larger hemlocks shading the area. The direction is due S; the trail still resembles a dirt road, although rocky and rough for the next tenth of a mile until the top of the small ridge is reached at 0.2 mi. The trail becomes very smooth and easy to walk, and proceeds up and then down again to reach a hemlock grove and a section with several large boulders underfoot. After another small ridge is negotiated, it descends into a swamp traversed by a curved section of raised planking.

After a flat, attractive section through leafy beech and maples, a jct. is reached at 0.5 mi. Here a DEC sign without mileage indicates that a turn to the R will lead to Glasgow, to the L is Morey Rd. and Caroga Lake. Take the R fork (S), unless you wish to hike 5.2 mi through the forest to Caroga Lake via Morey Rd. (That snowmobile trail is not described in this book as there is no reason for the hiker to take it, except as an exercise trek for another 5 mi through nondescript forests and swamps.) Taking the R fork, look for snowmobile trail markers just to make sure you did not stray onto the old logging road that also takes a R here. It is not as clearly defined, or marked, as the main trail, however.

After several small rolling up and down sections, a small swampy area invades the trail in times of heavy rains at 0.8 mi. A meandering beaver dam allows hikers to cross with minimal wading on an otherwise ankle-deep crossing. The trail climbs briefly, and after a slight jog to the L, reaches the top of this small ridge at 0.9 mi. It climbs a bit again, then a sharp jog R points the hiker S again. At 1.2 mi a sharp S turn occurs, and shortly thereafter a second trail jct. is reached at 1.4 mi. Here the longer trek to Glasgow via Hillabrandt Lake (trail 122) is to the L, and the very short 0.2 mi continuation to Mud Lake is to the R. The hiker will note that this section of trail is more heavily used than the others, partly owing to its long history of use as a logging and tote road from the S.

To proceed to Mud Lake, take the R fork. The trail descends the ridge, heading W. As the bottom of the ridge is reached, a cutoff to the R (N) brings the hiker to an attractive hemlock grove located on a small ridge of granite rock overlooking Mud Lake. This is a small lake, slowly filling in with bog plants, and, as are most of the so-called "Mud" lakes in the Adirondacks, it is aptly, if uncreatively, named. The lake is used occasionally by snowmobilers and picnickers, although there are no flat, clear areas suitable for tents. One can proceed past Mud Lake for another 2 mi on the snowmobile trail/road to exit at CR 119, although this route is not described here as it has limited appeal.

❄ Trail in winter: Skiing will be shared with snowmobiles. This is a relatively level trek intermediate backcountry ski groups may want to try.

🏃 Distances: To first jct., 0.5 mi; to second jct., 1.3 mi; to Mud Lake, 1.5 mi (2.4 km).

124 Hillabrandt Lake and Vlei from Trail 123

Trails Illustrated Map 744: C13

This section describes one of two ways to access the interesting, attractive Hillabrandt Lake and Vlei area. The other trail is via Glasgow Mills beginning at NY 10 (trail 122). Hillabrandt Lake was not always a lake, and in fact, on many older maps is shown only as a vlei. A substantial stone and earth dam was built during the logging era at the turn of the century, but by the early 1900s it had been breached and the lake drained. The lands reverted to a large vlei again for several years. In more recent times the returning beaver have plugged the dam with their own substantial earth and wood structure, and the lake has been maintained now for at least 10 to 15 years.

▶Trailhead: See trail 123 for directions to the trailhead at Stewart Landing and for a description to the second jct. on the Mud Lake Trail, 1.3 mi from Stewart Landing. At this jct. the trail to Hillabrandt Lake begins.◀

The trail continues through open second-growth forests, mostly deciduous, but stands of evergreens now appear more frequently and the trail becomes less used and somewhat more difficult to follow. At 1.7 mi (beginning from Stewart Landing as 0.0 mi) it climbs moderately and enters an open area. At 1.8 mi a turnaround can be seen and a larger ridge is descended. The direction is SE at this point. A stream briefly joins the trail (at least in spring) and a larger clearing is reached at 2.1 mi, after which another small rise over a bedrock section is negotiated. At 2.2 mi a mucky section is the first of several in the next half-mile, many likely to be dry or nonexistent in summer.

After another large wet area at 2.4 mi, a small hunting cabin is seen on the L at 2.8 mi. Very shortly the trail leads through a large swampy section requiring the hiker to negotiate several old logs and grass tufts to either the L or R. Both sides are a challenge. The character of the forest has changed to darker, more solid evergreens, which are very attractive and welcome after the airy hardwoods. The trail ascends a small knoll, and then descends to Hillabrandt Lake at 3.1 mi. Look to the L for campsites and old foundations and at least one well hole. Many of the trees look like they were deliberately left as shade trees, but several of these are now broken and dying, perhaps having completed their life span.

The trail leads across the top of the very substantial old dam, built with numerous boulders to a height, in some places, of 6 and 8 ft. Where it was broken, it is now dammed by the beaver. In spring 1992, the lake was filled by a very wet season, aided by the rather solid beaver dam. Before that it had been lower and weedier. It seems as long as the beaver maintain the dam, the lake, although shallow, is also maintained. There is no overt evidence of beaver still living in the immediate area, but the dam seems to be holding, despite their only sporadic maintenance. (To continue to Glasgow Mills and NY 10, another 3.4 mi, see trail 122.)

❄ Trail in winter: Trails must be shared with snowmobilers, but expert skiers with backcountry experience may enjoy exploring the area. A through trip is possible, but spotting the cars at each end will require planning for substantial driving time because the driving routes are so indirect.

🐾 Distances: To second jct. from Stewart Landing, 1.3 mi; to clearing, 2.1 mi; to hunting cabin, 2.8 mi; to Hillabrandt Lake, 3.1 mi (5 km).

125 Irving Pond and Bellows Lake to Peters Corners
Trails Illustrated Map 744: D15

The marked snowmobile trails to Irving Pond, Bellows Lake, and Little Holmes and Holmes Lakes make an invigorating loop trip, but hikers will need to place a car at each end of the trail. Each lake has its own charm, and hikers are advised to allow time also to explore the ruins of an old mill near Holmes Lake.

▶Trailhead: To reach the W end of the trail, drive 2.5 mi along the Benson–Bleecker Rd. or CR 112 E from NY 10. There is a dirt road to the N (L) (Shutts Rd.) and a brown and yellow DEC sign indicating Irving Pond 1.1 mi; Bellows Lake 3 mi; and Peters Corners 5.1 mi. The distance by trail to Peters Corners is short by 2 mi, and if side trips to Little Holmes and Holmes Lakes are included, the loop trip totals 9.5 mi.◀

Hikers who wish to do a through-trek can spot a car at the E end of this loop trail. To reach the E trailhead, drive an additional 3 mi E along Benson Rd. to the jct. at Peters Corners, where during non-winter months there is ample room to park two or three cars along the shoulder of the road. Park on the shoulder of Benson Rd. at the W trailhead and begin walking on Shutts Rd., a dirt road not marked by a sign. Private property signs are posted periodically along the L side. At 0.1 mi the road begins to climb a moderate grade. It reaches the top of the hill at 0.3 mi and passes a small house and outbuilding on the L. There are two picturesque apple trees close to the road, which continues straight ahead.

Proceed down a small hill and cross a large wet area at 0.4 mi. A second grassy marsh must be crossed at 0.5 mi. A snowmobile bridge at 0.6 mi crosses a small stream, after which the trail jogs L. The trail is marked with red trail markers and occasional yellow snowmobile trail markers. The land on the L is still posted, although the road may be used. At 0.7 mi, ATV users have degraded an extensive wet area, made more muddy and difficult by ruts.

The track becomes less of a road and more like a trail at 0.8 mi when it becomes narrow, rocky, and rough. A downhill section through hardwoods and brushy undergrowth leads to a grassy area at 0.9 mi, then the trail jogs R. The direction of travel is now due N. The land is still posted as private property on the L and R, at 1.1 mi.

The trail now bends R and becomes very rocky. It begins to climb gently, heading NNE. At the top of the grade, at 1.2 mi, the trail turns a bit to the R. A large wet area is reached at 1.3 mi, and then the trail descends through another rough, rocky section.

At a jct. at 1.5 mi, a signed intersection is reached. Continue straight ahead on the trail as it veers R along the shore of Irving Pond. The lake was drained several years back, but depending upon rainfall, the lake often returns. The trail crosses a small inlet stream at 2 mi., followed by a larger inlet at 2.4 mi, which it follows to the top of a small ridge.

At 2.6 mi a very wet area must be negotiated. The general direction is now N. At 3 mi Bellows Lake comes into view; at 3.1 mi its shore is reached. Bellows is an attractive, shallow body of water with a shoreline consisting for the most part of marshlands.

The general direction is now ESE as the trail proceeds past Bellows Lake. At 3.5 mi it crosses another small stream and adjacent wet area. This section passes through an open, lovely forest of mixed hardwoods and conifers. Another small inlet at 3.6 mi flows into the lake, which can still be glimpsed through the trees. The trail turns away from the lake at 3.8 mi and goes R, traveling E.

A working snowmobile bridge is reached at 4 mi. It can be crossed with caution. Ample lumber was stashed here (2013) to build a new bridge in the near future. At 4.1 mi, the trail passes through an open section of woods and then begins to climb a ridge and bend R. The climbing becomes steeper and is sustained until the crest at 4.4 mi. Traversing the top of the ridge, the trail crosses a large pocket of muck at 4.7 mi. At 4.8 mi, heading due E, the trail begins to parallel a stream, and a moderate uphill climb begins again. The top of this hillock is reached at 5 mi. A leveling occurs at 5.2 mi, and at 5.3 mi the trail begins to descend. This moderate downhill leads through rocky and wet areas until, at 5.4 mi, the trail jct. for Little Holmes Lake is reached. The intersection is not marked in any way. A 90 degree turn to the right will lead over a bridge to the trail to Little Holmes Lake. There is a yellow trail marker on the main trail opposite this trail.

[The side trip to Little Holmes Lake will add 1.4 mi to the trip (0.7 mi each way). The trail is not marked, but there is pink surveyor tape on some of the trees, and it is well used and easy to follow. On the Little Holmes Lake spur, at 0.3 mi, another wet area occurs, and then an uphill begins. A small stream runs across the trail at 0.4 mi and then flows down it for a short way. At 0.5 mi the trail enters a large, open grassy area and, after passing through this, reaches Little Holmes Lake at 0.7 mi. A small informal camping spot is on the shore. Little Holmes Lake is clear, blue, and very attractive, often visited by anglers. It and Holmes Lake were named after Russell Holmes, who built a mill and wood carving operation for manufacturing furniture pieces in this vicinity in the late 1800s.]

Leaving this jct., the main trail continues S, mostly level and traveling through attractive woods. The trail descends gently; at 6.3 mi the wide settlement trail to Holmes Lake is reached. If you come to the remains of the Holmes sawmill with three pillars of concrete at its entrance at 6.4 mi, you have gone too far. Turn L at 6.3 mi for a visit to Holmes Lake.

[Turn L and walk 0.5 mi for a side-trip through the abandoned settlement to the shore of Holmes Lake, another very pretty jewel, one of many in the string of lakes in this section of the southern Adirondacks. Just before the trail reaches the lake there is a newer lean-to and small fire pit, but no privy (2013). The lean-to register dates back to 2007. This trail is a marked with NYDEC blue footpath trailmarkers.]

A R turn continues to Peters Corners. Continuing S (R) from the Holmes Lake turnoff, the trail is very wide and becomes road-like again after crossing a stream at 6.4 mi. At 6.6 mi a big beaver pond is seen on the L at the S end of the pond. At 6.8 mi the trail crosses a wet area, and at 6.9 mi, just before a trail on the L to Pinnacle Rd./Chase Lake, there is a new cabin/camp with an outhouse. The road shows evidence of use by motorized vehicles but is not in good condition. At 7 mi the trail ends. Bear R (L is private land) and pass two homes to exit on the highway at 7.1 mi.

❄ Trail in winter: Used extensively by snowmobiles, this complex of trails is also good for backcountry skiing. When skiing, keep alert for the snowmobiles and exit the trails to explore the lakes and marshes, taking care to stay far from the swift-running outlets. A few steep sections on the E end will challenge even the best skiers, so use good judgment.

🐾 Distances: To Irving Pond, 1.4 mi; to Bellows Lake, 3.1 mi; to Little Holmes Lake spur jct., 5.4 mi; to Holmes Lake jct. 6.4 mi; (side trips to Little Holmes Lake, 1.4 mi; Holmes Lake, 1 mi); to Peters Corners; 7.1 mi (11.4 km). Total if both Holmes Lakes explored, 9.5 mi (15.2 km).

126 Chase Lake

Trails Illustrated Map 744: D17

A pretty, popular lake with a lean-to, Chase Lake is visited frequently by ATV riders, and as a result sections of the trail may be wet and muddy. Nevertheless, it is an interesting destination for the hiker who enjoys walking old roads.

▶Trailhead: Take the Benson Road, turning W off NY 30 or E off NY 10 if coming from the W. Turn N on Pinnacle Rd. and drive 2.6 mi to the end of this dirt road where parking for two or three cars is available at the turnaround. The trail begins to the E (R) of the turnaround and is well marked as a snowmobile route. It is also occasionally marked with the smaller bright yellow DEC foot trail disks.◀

A swampy area must be crossed at 0.1 mi. This wet section needs to be crossed carefully on small logs and grass tufts. It is not feasible to go around it, as it extends quite a distance both N and S.

The trail heads E but soon turns N (L) on an old logging road. At 0.2 mi a jog to the R occurs and the trail continues through more muck, then crosses a small stream. The next section is easy walking; the trail meanders through small curves to the L, then R and begins to climb a small knoll. There is a fork at 0.3 mi. Take the R, heading SE. At 0.4 mi the trail begins to climb a small hill, then bends gently to the R. Very soon the hill is topped and a gentle descent commences at 0.5 mi. Here boundary marks are seen and the land to the R has been logged very recently.

Ladyslipper. Joanne Kennedy

Twisting and turning, the trail begins a downhill section at 0.6 mi. It is, however, well marked and easy to follow. After a brief but steep descent, it crosses a larger stream on a twisted and broken snowmobile bridge at 0.7 mi. It then makes a jog L and uphill and passes an extensive carpet of lovely tree club moss. These mosses, which look like miniature shiny evergreen trees, once were much more common, but they have been collected for decades for holiday decorations and now are protected by law.

At 1 mi the general direction is S. The trail passes through another grove of hemlocks where it would be easy to lose, except that someone has tacked bright pink and orange plastic rectangles on several trees.

At 1.1 mi the trail joins another old logging road. The trail turns E (L) on this road. From here to Chase Lake it follows this wide, very attractive, though occasionally muddy road. At 1.3 mi a small creek is crossed on rocks and old boards. Although previous visits were marred by mud and ATV tracks, the area has recovered and provides a delightful walk along a high ridge. A small hemlock-filled valley appears on the R. The woods are mature and open and there are numerous species of wildflowers to be seen, especially in spring.

At 1.7 mi the trail descends the ridge and crosses a creek on another broken snowmobile bridge, after which it jogs R again. Several twists and turns lead to a large mucky area at 2 mi, which looks much harder to cross than it is. The general direction is still E. The waters of Chase Lake are visible at 2.3 mi, and the trail reaches the lean-to at 2.5 mi after a brief downhill jog.

Chase Lake is very pretty, but access to the water is restricted by the swampy shoreline. Even at the lean-to, access to the lake must be made through a large boggy area.

Although a marked side trail leads to the southern part of the lake, a circle trip on trails is not possible

❋ Trail in winter: This is a marked snowmobile trail; thus backcountry skiers can plan on sharing it. With the exception of two steep descents, the trek can be done by intermediate-level skiers and above. Skis provide a good method to explore Chase Lake, which is not very accessible, and thus frustrating to hikers during other seasons.

🏔 Distances: To hemlock grove with pink signs, 1 mi; to jct. of logging road, 1.1 mi; to Chase Lake and lean-to, 2.5 mi (4 km).

View of Silver Lake from Silver Lake Mt. Joanne Kennedy

Silver Lake Wilderness Area

 The Silver lake Wilderness Area provides opportunities for deep backcountry treks amid thick forests and picturesque water bodies. The Sacandaga River runs through it, as does the Northville–Placid Trail, the latter starting at the Northville bridge, where each year hundreds of hikers set out to complete the 132 mi journey. Most through-hikers begin their multiday trek at the parking area at Upper Benson to avoid the dreaded paved walk along Benson Rd. Plans are in the works to build a trail through the woods to eliminate the road portion at the N–P Trail's southern terminus, but a construction date has not been set (spring 2014).

The Silver Lake Wilderness Area comprises 105,270 acres of public land classified as Wilderness. As such, it is designated free of noticeable human intrusions, and access by motorized equipment is strictly prohibited. Since the jeep trails, snowmobile trails, fire tower, and associated facilities were removed, the experience here is a finer one. The terrain is wonderfully varied, with rolling hills, beaver meadows, swamps, and streams.

This wilderness is named for a sparkling lake located in the interior that is accessible to hikers using the N–P Trail. Beautiful Silver Lake is the largest body of water among several sizeable lakes and numerous smaller ponds. The forest is a mix of deciduous hardwoods and various conifers, chiefly hemlock. In addition, two impressive suspension bridges await the hiker.

During the latter part of the last century, this area was settled by hearty, hardworking farmers, mill owners, lumbermen, and tannery workers. The lumberjacks stripped the land of its forests, depleting the resource that supplied their employment, while the farmers were slowly defeated by a harsh climate and stony soil. Chemical tanning processes soon negated the need for hemlock bark, and the lands and tiny towns were gradually abandoned. The forests slowly returned, and the overgrown roads to the farms, mills, and settlements are today's hiking and skiing trails, offering many attractive day trips and extended outings.

Recommended hikes in this section include:

EASY HIKES

Woods Lake: 0.6 mi (1 km) round trip. Attractive, easily accessible, and mostly in the state-owned Forest Preserve, this tiny lake is a coveted destination for campers and anglers.

Auger Falls (East): 2.6 mi (4.2 km) round trip. Described on p. 43, this is a short walk along an old woods road to a charming waterfall.

Auger Falls (West): 2.4 mi (3.8 km) round trip. Described on p. 45, this is a short hemlock-lined gorge with a series of waterfalls.

East Branch Sacandaga Gorge and Square Falls: 2.4 mi (3.8 km) round trip. Described on p. 51, this is an unmarked footpath to a narrow gorge, waterfall, and swimming hole.

MODERATE HIKES
Dunning Pond: mileage can vary. Accessible from either side, Dunning Pond makes for a nice destination in its own right or a stopover as part of a longer trek through the wooded forest.

HARDER HIKES
Big Eddy and West Branch Gorge and Falls: 9 mi (14.4 km) round trip. The payoff is big, but the route to these lovely cascading falls can be strenuous with slippery rocks and bushwhacking among the challenges.

The Northville-Placid Trail: Upper Benson to Piseco: 22.3 mi (35.7 km) one way. An excellent backpacking trail that provides plenty to see on a three-day, two-night trip.

	Trail Described	*Miles* *(one way)*		*Page*
	Cathead Mt.			236
127	Woods Lake	0.3	(0.5 km)	236
128	Northville Placid Trail: Upper Benson to Piseco	22.3	(35.7 km)	237
129	Big Eddy and the West Branch Gorge and Falls (partial bushwhack)	2.0 or 4.5	(3.2 or 7.2 km)	241
130	Dunning Pond from Gilmantown Road	1.2	(1.9 km)	244
131	Dunning Pond from NY 30	4.2	(6.7 km)	245

Cathead Mt.

Trails Illustrated Map 744: F18

The Cathead Mt. Trail has been closed owing to a land dispute and there is presently no public access (2014). Proposed legislation has been introduced in the NYS Legislature to effect a land swap that would allow hikers access to Cathead Mt., but the bill has not received much traction. In the meantime hiking is not permitted, and hikers are asked to respect the landowner's privacy by not trespassing.

127 Woods Lake

Trails Illustrated Map 744: E18

Woods Lake is a very pretty small lake that is close to the road, and thus attracts more than its share of campers, canoers, anglers, and short-trek hikers. Any summer weekend will find campers there in force, as the lake is so attractive, easy to reach, and for all but about 10 percent of its shoreline, state-owned.

▶Trailhead: Take NY 30 to Benson and turn W on Benson Rd. Drive 4.5 mi and look for a wide, sandy shoulder which serves as a parking area to the L (S), just after a curve. The unmarked path begins on the opposite (N) side of the road, about 20 ft W of the parking space. ◀

The path begins as a rocky uphill, which quickly turns into a well-defined, pine-needle-cushioned path, passing through a grove of several very large hemlocks. The path enters a small ravine and passes through a more open hardwood forest. It jogs L to avoid a wet area at 0.2 mi and very shortly forks. A turn L leads in another 200 ft to the first view of Woods Lake at 0.3 mi. The R fork also leads to the lake in another 0.1 mi, as well as to at least three primitive campsites. This section of shoreline is particularly lovely with mossy rock ledges, large boulders, and towering hemlocks. There are informal campsites all along this SW shore. The density of the woods across the lake on the NE shore, and the inlet swamp along the E end, have prohibited campers from easy access there, although there is a least one site accessible by boat. At 0.6 mi the path peters out at the edge of a swamp.

The NW end of the lake is privately owned in part by the popular Lapland Lake Nordic Ski and Vacation Resort. In winter, this area seems to have consistently good snow cover when many other ski centers do not.

❄ Trail in winter: The path is short, and destinations for skiers require crossing the lake to private lands. Therefore an exploration of Woods Lake in winter would indicate a visit to Lapland Lake to ski their trail complex as well. (Lapland Lake: 518-863-4974.)

🚶 Distances: To Woods Lake shore, 0.3 mi (0.5 km).

128 Northville–Placid Trail: Upper Benson to Piseco
Trails Illustrated Map 744:115

The trail in this section enters the Silver Lake Wilderness Area at Upper Benson and travels 22.3 mi to Piseco. The woods are varied, the terrain is rolling, the trail is easy, and there are several lean-tos along the way. There are massive hemlocks, pretty little beaver ponds, and plenty of moss-covered rocky stream crossings. It is possible to drive a car on Algonquin Avenue and West River Road in Wells to Whitehouse to break this section into parts.

▶Trailhead: From the S leaving the jct. of NY 30 and Benson Rd., drive W on Benson Rd., crossing West Stony Creek at 5.9 mi. Turn R onto the dirt road located just

Signs of beaver activity. Mary Coffin

beyond the bridge and bear R almost immediately. Drive 0.6 mi to Godfrey Rd. Turn L and park in the small parking area 0.6 mi on the R. Another 0.2 mi down the road, there is a parking area on the property of the Shepard family. For a small fee, vehicles may be parked here. ◀

From the parking area on Godfrey Rd., proceed 0.1 mi to the DEC register (0.0 mi) and sign in. Avoid Grant Rd. L of the register; instead, turn R and follow the trail along a woods road past a private home and across a brook. A little farther on, a rod and gun club marks the end of the road for all vehicles. The trail enters the woods and follows what will soon become familiar blue markers.

The North Branch of West Stony Creek is reached in a clearing with a privy at 1.3 mi. Here the trail turns abruptly L past a pipe barrier. Be careful not to cross the creek (the trail on the opposite bank dead-ends at an informal campsite), or follow the trail to the R.

The blue-marked trail continues along an old tote road that follows the S bank of the creek. Quite a bit of exposed flat rock is visible just before a well-constructed footbridge that crosses the creek at 1.6 mi. A nice campsite can be found here. The trail heads W away from the stream and assumes a moderate grade.

At 2.5 mi the trail crosses Goldmine Creek. The moderate grade continues as the trail crosses several small streams. A marked jct. with many old signboards is on a hillside at 4.5 mi. The trail to the L leads 0.1 mi to Rock Lake (elevation 1917 ft). Evidently, there was a lean-to here at one time; there are now several slightly sloped clearings to pitch a tent for those desiring to stay near this pretty little body of water.

Continuing straight ahead from the jct., the trail descends gradually to a brook at 5.4 mi. Proceeding through the grassy clearing and on into the woods, the trail crosses the West Branch of the Sacandaga River on stones at 5.6 mi. On the opposite bank is a PBM with an elevation of 1865 ft. The trail turns N and parallels the creek, gaining about 250 ft elevation as it winds its way past interesting pools and cascades into the creek below. In warm weather the pools pose quite an invitation for a refreshing dip.

At 6.4 mi the trail meets the shore of Meco Lake (elevation 2106 ft). The trail along the shore is rough, with many ups and downs. Unfortunately, the steep grades do not lend themselves to campsites.

At 6.5 mi the trail pitches up a bit and then follows a pleasant downward grade toward Silver Lake, which can be seen through the trees before the trail reaches the shoreline at 7.2 mi (elevation 2072 ft). The trail winds around to the N and crosses a wet spot or two before reaching the former site of a lean-to (removed in 1993) at 7.4 mi. Just beyond this the trail turns R and heads up a grade. The current lean-to, a fine one in excellent shape, is at 7.5 mi. A footpath leads to a privy on the other side of the N–P Trail.

From the lean-to the trail continues a gradual and steady climb, with occasional dips. It crosses a large brook at 7.9 mi, and another at 8.1 mi. The route mostly levels off as it crosses a flat, marshy area N of Silver Lake. At 9.3 mi it

crosses a vlei on corduroy that is slippery when wet. A boardwalk of treated lumber crosses another vlei at 9.4 mi. Carefully follow the blue markers as the trail continues toward Canary Pond at 9.5 mi, after a marshy spot. This pond (elevation 2007 ft) provides a very pleasant place to camp, with several attractive sites.

Away from the pond the trail ascends moderately, flanked by large spruce trees. It then dips down to another vlei at 10.2 mi, which it crosses on a boardwalk. Once past this vlei and a long descent, the trail reaches a very large beaver pond. The marked trail to the R skirts the shoreline as it works its way around this formidable obstacle that may or may not be present, depending on the year. (When the pond is not here you can walk right across the grassy meadow to the other side.) The trail crosses the outlet just below the substantial dam at 10.8 mi.

The trail now levels and crosses several small brooks, while the forest changes from deciduous to mixed conifer. The W end of Mud Lake comes into view next. The trail navigates a couple of wet spots and crosses the outlet of a small beaver pond on wet planks. The Mud Lake lean-to is found at 13.2 mi. It was destroyed by a fallen tree in August 2012, but has since been repaired. Scattered tent sites are also available. At 1730 ft elevation, this lake is appropriately named, as a trip to the shoreline soon confirms. The best source of water is back at the beaver pond outlet. Mud Lake is known to be a popular spot for trout fishing.

From the clearing the N–P Trail continues N, gaining about 200 ft in elevation. After reaching the height of land between two knobby hills at 14.2 mi, the trail winds through a few wet spots. It then begins a long, gradual descent of 600 ft toward the Sacandaga River. Most of the way the trail follows an old tote road that slowly winds around the bends.

At 15.5 mi, an unmarked footpath branches L. The marked N–P Trail continues toward the river and turns abruptly L before reaching the bank. Soon the aforementioned footpath rejoins the main trail, which parallels the river and crosses a small brook at 15.8 mi.

The trail comes to the footings of the very impressive suspension bridge at the Whitehouse crossing of the Sacandaga River at 16.2 mi. Caution should be observed when climbing the approach ramp to the bridge; when wet, it can be very slippery. On the far bank the bridge ends in front of a large stone chimney. This was once the site of a summer camp, and the chimney was part of the recreation building.

The trail continues past the chimney and up a small grade to a jct. at 16.3 mi. Be sure to sign the DEC register here.

The N–P Trail turns L and heads toward Piseco. The trail R leads about 0.1 mi to a parking area at the terminus of West River Rd. Beyond this it is 8.6 mi to the village of Wells and NY 30.

From the DEC register at the jct. N of the suspension bridge across the Sacandaga River (16.3 mi), the N–P Trail continues L and follows an old tote road NW, crossing a brook at 16.5 mi. After an enjoyable stroll down the road, watch for a fork at 16.9 mi; the N–P Trail drops down to the R and becomes a woods trail again. (The tote road swings up to the L and to the Big Eddy and Falls side trip; see trail 129.)

The trail provides a pleasant woods walk that generally ascends. There are several steeper grades along the way. At 1.4 mi the trail crosses a brook; there is a PBM here with an elevation of 1501 ft. The trail passes a large rock L at 18.1 mi, again following an old tote road heading NW, and then W as it gets closer to Hamilton Lake Stream. At 18.3 mi, a fine suspension bridge crosses the outlet of Hamilton Lake. This bridge is similar to the one over the Sacandaga at Whitehouse, but about half the length. At one time this was a popular camping spot.

Continuing past the bridge, the trail soon skirts a small marshy area. At 18.6 mi a side trail R leads to Hamilton Lake Stream lean-to, the roof of which can be seen in the distance. The lean-to sits at the top of the grade, high on a bluff overlooking the meandering river below, which has a reputation for good trout fishing.

The trail crosses the outlet of Priests Vly at 19.5 mi. This has been a spot of considerable beaver activity in the past. This is also the location of a PBM at 1665 ft. The trail continues upward for several hundred more feet, crossing several small brooks, before descending.

At 21 mi the trail crosses the outlet of Buckhorn Lake on a wooden bridge. This is a very picturesque spot. The N–P Trail continues through a pleasant variety of woodland settings. At 22 mi the grade bears downhill toward the end of the woods. At 22.1 mi the trail comes to a DEC register; be sure to sign it. The trail continues through an open area that is deeply rutted owing to past lumbering. Follow the posts with markers to end up at the right spot across the open area.

At 22.3 mi the trail reaches the shoulder of NY 8 and a large N–P Trail sign. There is a general store across the street.

✵ Trail in winter: One of the most pleasant cross-country ski trips in the southern Adirondacks is from Benson to Rock Lake. The whole area is ideal for backcountry exploring, since frozen vleis and lakes make excellent routes for winter travel. Beyond Rock Lake there is little human activity in winter, so those on skis and snowshoes must be self-sufficient and expect no immediate help if lost or injured.

🏃 Distance: Godfrey Rd. parking area to DEC register, 0.1 mi; to North Branch of West Stony Creek, 1.3 mi; to Goldmine Creek, 2.5 mi; to West Branch of Sacandaga River, 5.6 mi; to Meco Lake, 6.4 mi; to Silver Lake, 7.2 mi; to lean-to, 7.5 mi; to Canary Pond, 9.5 mi; to Mud Lake lean-to, 13.2 mi; to height of land, 14.2 mi; to Sacandaga River suspension bridge, 16.2 mi; to DEC register, 16.3 mi (26.3 km).

DEC register to Hamilton Lake outlet, 18.3 mi; to spur to lean-to, 18.6 mi; to Priests Vly outlet, 19.5 mi; to Buckhorn Lake outlet, 21 mi; to DEC register, 22.1 mi; to NY 8, 22.3 mi; (35.7 km).

129 Big Eddy and West Branch Gorge and Falls

(partial bushwhack)   **Trails Illustrated Map 744: H16**

Big Eddy is a popular, quiet pool along the West Branch of the Sacandaga River where the waters rest after their violent cascade through the West Branch Gorge. The walk to Big Eddy is easy and filled with scenic woods and streams.

To continue into the gorge to visit the four falls is a worthy challenge indeed, and should be undertaken only by hikers with prudence and perseverance, who also carry, and know how to use, a map and compass.

The Whitehouse area where the trail begins was a large lumber camp, then a private hunting camp with a main "Whitehouse" lodge (named for the Washington Whitehouse) during the 1950s. It is now a large clearing well along in its natural evolution to an overgrown forest. There is plenty of parking space and several popular campsites in addition to the foundations of the old "Whitehouse," now buried among the poplar trees to the L. The chimney of a former building called "Blair House" can be seen on the R. Here the hunting camp proprietor housed his more favored guests.

Also to see in the Whitehouse area are the remains of a children's camp and the still intact, much admired swinging suspension bridge over the West Branch of the Sacandaga.

▶Trailhead: Turn W off NY 30 in the town of Wells, onto Algonquin Drive, which immediately crosses a bridge over the Sacandaga River below Lake Algonquin's dam. Turn L at 0.7 mi onto West River Rd. Follow this road 8.3 mi to Whitehouse and the trailhead. ◀

Michael N. Kelsey

The trail begins as a well-beaten path from the parking area at the end of West River Rd., heading generally W to the DEC trail register at 0.1 mi. This is a jct. of the Northville–Placid (N–P) Trail. The trail to Big Eddy and the gorge is the R fork, but a short walk along the L path brings one to the picturesque White-house suspension footbridge across the West Branch of the Sacandaga. The prominent chimney in the clearing in front of the bridge is the remains of a sum-mer camp recreational building. The camp flourished briefly in the 1940s—as one local said, in every way but financially.

The R fork traverses an old road, still quite wide, smooth, and easy to walk, going NNW. A small stream, formerly known as "Boy's Camp Brook," is crossed on a sturdy wooden footbridge at 0.3 mi. At 0.5 mi the road takes a slight jog R while a well-used path forks L. To remain on the N–P Trail and the road, stay R and continue through pleasant hardwoods interspersed with occasional hem-locks and pines. A choice to turn R, however, takes one over a small ridge and cuts off about 0.2 mi to Big Eddy, but the N–P Trail turns R off the road before this shortcut rejoins it. (For the N–P Trail, see trail 128.)

The hiker who bears R on the road/trail reaches a jct. at 0.7 mi. The N–P Trail continues R (N) toward Piseco, and the old road meanders L (WNW) toward the confluence of Hamilton Lake Stream (a major inlet of the Sacandaga) and the West Branch of the Sacandaga. At 1.1 mi, Hamilton Lake Stream comes into sight on the R, and the trail continues down an incline to a large clearing at 1.2 mi. This clearing is frequently used as a camping area and has several logs and rocks strategically placed by previous campers. The area is clean and attractive, and has been used for 40 or 50 years as a campsite. Until the late 1950s, the old farm road was negotiable by rugged vehicles up to this point. Now, occasional illegal ATVs ply the woods.

To the R of the clearing is a well-beaten path to the shore of Hamilton Lake Stream. Here the hiker can most easily cross, but in the spring, especially, one must be prepared to wade. Although the stream is shallow and gently flowing with numerous round red rocks in its bed, only during a dry midsummer hike is one likely to find sufficient exposed logs or boulders to rock-hop it. Plan on a possibly dicey stroll through icy waters with slippery rocks underfoot.

After crossing the stream, the well-beaten anglers' path turns briefly L in a WSW direction, passing through avenues of mature hardwoods. At 1.3 mi the banks of the West Branch of the Sacandaga come into sight. The path now swings more N and is occasionally obscured by vegetation and fallen trees, but it is merely a matter of following the stream bank to Big Eddy. The West Branch of the Sacandaga is a fast-flowing stream at this point, cavorting over numerous rocks that create sometimes spectacular rapids. Big Eddy, which is reached at ap-proximately 2 mi, in contrast, is a quiet, peaceful section of the stream, occurring immediately after the water's violent cascade through the gorge. There are several campsites along the river, all much too near the water, and all quite popular.

At the W end of Big Eddy, Cold Brook must be crossed by rock hopping. Cliffs begin to close in and the path becomes extremely rugged and increasingly difficult.

Finally, after winding over many large rocks and granite outcroppings, always hugging the N shore, the path enters the West Branch Gorge. The hiker is urged to take great care because the water cascades through the gorge at a tremendous velocity, especially in spring. In fact, it is not recommended that one even enter the gorge then. A glimpse of the powerful flow can be had from two spectacular viewing areas on the top of the cliff to the R. To reach these vantage points, it is suggested that the hiker begin climbing the slopes away from the stream before the actual need forces one to scale the steeper sections.

West Branch of the Sacandaga River. Michael N. Kelsey

Hikers are reminded to use a compass and carry a topographic map should they decide to climb to the top, even though, ideally, keeping the river within sight and sound is all that is needed. Search for a beautiful stand of huge white pines and hemlocks for the areas where the best views will be found.

Hikers who wish to descend to the valley again and at least view one of the spectacular falls can continue E and then S, following the contours of the river along the top, for approximately 1 mi until a relatively gentle descent can be made down into the valley at the W end of the gorge. Here a huge rock protrusion juts out into the river, providing an overlook point from the top of a powerful flow of water, in addition to wild and wonderful scenery in every direction.

✻ Trail in winter: Skiing is possible into Whitehouse on the unplowed portion of West River Rd. (plowing stops at the last year-round residence and may vary from year to year); plan on approximately 3 mi. The road will be shared with snowmobiles. Once in the Whitehouse area, it is a nice ski trip to Hamilton Lake Stream, but unless winter camping (or snowmobiling), distances and the rugged terrain preclude extensive winter activity in the area.

🐾 Distances: To Hamilton Lake Stream crossing, 1.2 mi; to banks of West Branch of the Sacandaga, 1.4 mi; to Big Eddy, 2 mi (3.2 km). Bushwhack to the Fourth Falls, approximately 4.5 mi (7.2 km).

130 Dunning Pond from Gilmantown Road

Trails Illustrated Map 744: J18

This is a short walk to an interesting pond that is in final transition to a swamp. The trail traverses an old road leading to the former site of a mill and dam. The hike can also be made into a 5 mi through trip to NY 30, just above Wells. (See trail 131.) If planning to hike both trails end-to-end, starting at NY 30 and ending at Gilmantown Rd. is the recommended direction.

▶Trailhead: Approaching from the W, turn N on Gilmantown Rd. (which leaves NY 30 0.2 mi W of the Algonquin Lake bridge in Wells). The beginning of the trail is 0.1 mi from the end of the paved road on the R, 3.8 mi from Wells (or 0.5 mi past Charley Lake). In wetter seasons, a small brook runs out of the trail and down an embankment into the ditch at the side of the road. Cross an easily traversed ditch and follow snowmobile trail markers. A brown and yellow DEC trail sign can be found partially hidden by the trees. The trail is difficult to spot from the road in summer. There is ample parking along both shoulders of Gilmantown Rd. ◀

This is the continuation of an old wagon road, with evidence that at one time it was deeply rutted. At 0.4 mi the trail begins a slight descent. The woods are composed predominantly of hardwoods, and many species of ferns and wildflowers, as well as the attractive staghorn moss, can also be found.

At 0.6 mi the trail turns slightly L. Even the most inexperienced hiker will have no trouble following this broad, old road bed, even though it is poorly marked and overgrown in some areas. Heavily eroded, the path is rocky and rough in several places.

A jog R occurs at 1 mi, and Dunning Pond comes into sight through trees to the L. At 1.2 mi watch for a blaze on a tree on the L and then a big orange snowmobile disk on another nearby tree. Cut L, then continue down to the W end of the pond to the outlet where there is a small camping area. Large old hemlocks grace the banks of this small pond, which has been enlarged and temporarily deepened by beaver activity. If beaver are no longer active, look for the remains of the human-built dam and foundations near the outlet. This is the site of a mill operated by the Dunning family in the mid-1800s. The pond is pleasant and attractive, although in the final stages of the gradual transition into a swampy Adirondack bog, a transition delayed by beaver periodically rebuilding the dam.

❋ Trail in winter: This is a designated snowmobile trail, but with enough snow, skiers will find the trek to Dunning Pond easy and interesting. Explore the pond fringes and swamps, then exit using the same trail again, or spot a car on the NY 30 end and ski through. Skiing through requires the backcountry skier to cross Dunning Creek, which has no bridge, and to negotiate several steeper sections along the shoulders of an unnamed 1900 ft mountain to the N, making a descent of approximately 600 ft. in 2 mi.

🐾 Distances: To view of Dunning Pond, 1 mi; to path to pond, 1.2 mi (1.9 km).

131 Dunning Pond from NY 30

Trails Illustrated Map 744: J18

Primarily a snowmobile route to Gilmantown Road over an old road, this walk leads the hiker through some very wild sections within sight and sound of some beautiful cascading waterfalls. The trail seems to be little used by snowmobilers, probably because it isn't very long for motorized travel. In some areas it is overgrown and hidden by blowdown and beaver flooding and thus should be undertaken only by those with some expertise in trail finding.

There are stretches of difficult walking owing to rocks exposed on washed-out sections, yet this area is lovely and worth the effort to explore. An impressive beaver dam and pond are encountered at 3.2 mi and the casual hiker may wish to terminate the trip there.

Note also that Dunning Pond is rapidly becoming "Dunning Swamp." Look for the ruins of an old mill and dam at the outlet of the pond/swamp. Beaver have, in recent years, reestablished the pond by rebuilding a dam at the outlet.

▶Trailhead: To reach this E trailhead take NY 30 N through Wells. At the N end of town, a sharp curve to the R must be executed. At 3.1 mi from this curve, a DEC yellow and brown trail sign on the L is easily observed from the highway. Park on the shoulders of NY 30, either side, as this is a wide, flat section. One may also turn L and drive up the embankment on a dirt track; however, the tiny parking area among the trees will accommodate only two or three cars at the most, before a barrier is reached at 0.1 mi. ◀

The DEC sign reads: "Dunning Pond 3.4 mi and Gilmantown Road 4.3 mi." The distances are actually considerably longer for the hiker owing to the need to circumvent swamps, a beaver dam, and a number of fallen trees.

Past the sturdy steel barrier that bars motor vehicles during all but the winter months, the road begins a gentle climb through a mixed forest of hemlock and several species of hardwoods. On the L is Dunning Creek, but at 0.5 mi the road curves NW and leaves the creek to climb higher on the ridge. For the rest of the first mile, the road is a series of ups and downs but always climbing higher up the shoulder of the unnamed mountain on the R. Finally at 1.2 mi it enters a clearing and then descends briefly to parallel a small stream, which it crosses in another 50 ft. (During low water, rock-hopping in the stream bed will be easy.)

The road climbs up a rocky washout, then turns L to traverse a flat, curved section of another ridge. On the L is a very steep ravine banked by mature hemlocks. The creek far below can be heard but not seen.

At 1.7 mi the top of the ridge is reached and the path becomes smooth and pleasant. After another small uphill grade, it crosses a second small stream at 2.2 mi. Gradually, evidence of the road disappears, but the footpath is still easy to follow, although it is poorly marked at long intervals with snowmobile signs and marked not at all with foot trail signs.

The descent now begins, heading W at 2.5 mi over a series of dips and level areas. An enormous upraised multiple tree root system is seen on the R at 2.9 mi at the bottom of a col. This interesting tangle is the result of the trees' growth in an extremely shallow layer of soil. The underlying rocks are now exposed to create a mossy, rocky, and damp area. Rock-hopping these, the hiker will find that the path descends to the creek at 3.2 mi through a beautiful open section of mature trees.

The creek has been dammed 75 ft upstream on the R by beaver. At this writing (2013) the dam is 3 ft high and in excellent condition, creating a large pond the continuing hiker will have to circumvent. An anglers' path to the R can be used to investigate the beaver dam, but it disappears very quickly.

The marked snowmobile trail crosses the creek and continues SW upstream, disappearing into the pond. The snowmobile bridge has been washed out by spring floods and lies partially on the L bank (looking downstream) across the path. In spring the creek may be impossible to cross, at least here, owing to high water, but the many rocks exposed during summer and fall permit easy access to the opposite bank.

After crossing Dunning Creek, the hiker must keep to the L bank of the pond, pushing through about 50 ft of spruce scrub and generally bushwhacking through brush and blowdown and wet areas, until at 3.5 mi the trail reappears where the creek enters the newly created pond.

The trail continues along the creek, passing a pretty three-tier waterfall approximately 15 ft high at 3.9 mi. Still heading SW along the creek, the trail provides vistas of an older beaver pond now turned into a meadow. The path rises to join again with the vestiges of an old tote road at 4.1 mi, now heading W. Here it is once again easy walking on the smoother roadbed, and here too, down the ridge to the R, lies the swamp that comprises most of what was once Dunning Pond.

In recent years beaver have rebuilt the dam and the pond has been enlarged. Nevertheless, this is not always the case from one year to the next. Turn to the R and seek a small clearing at the outlet. Look for evidence of the old human-built dam and the foundations of a mill that once stood here. It was built and operated by the Dunning family in the mid-1800s.

If hikers have spotted a car at the Gilmantown Rd. end, the trip through will be another 1 mi. (See also trail 130.)

❄ Trail in winter: This trail will be shared by snowmobiles. Skiers should begin from Gilmantown Rd. (see trail 130), as this E end requires a climb of approximately 600 ft over some fairly steep terrain. Unless snowmobiles have traversed it first, the trail will be difficult to follow in some areas as the marker disks are infrequent. Not highly recommended.

🐾 Distances: First stream crossing, 1.2 mi; to beaver dam, 3.2 mi; to waterfall, 3.9 mi; to Dunning Pond, 4.2 mi (6.7 km). 🐾

Glossary of Terms

Azimuth	A clockwise compass bearing swung from north.
Bivouac	Camping in the open with improvised shelter or no shelter.
Bushwhacking	Off-trail hiking, often with compass and map essential for direction.
Col	A pass between high points of a ridgeline.
Corduroy	Logs laid side by side across a trail to assist travel in wet areas.
Fire ring	A rough circle of stones used as a site in which to build small fires.
Lean-to	A three-sided shelter with an overhanging roof and one open side.
Logging road	A road used to haul logs after lumbering; often found in marshy areas that would be frozen in winter.
Summit	The top of a mountain.
Tote road	A woods road used year-round for hauling supplies; found on dry ground slopes.
Vlei	A low marshy area (pronounced "vly")

State Campgrounds
Central Trails Region

Campgrounds have been established by the DEC at many attractive spots throughout the state. Listed below are those campgrounds that might be useful as bases of operations for hiking in the *Central Trails* region of the Adirondacks.

Information on state campgrounds and procedures for making reservations can be found on the Web at www.dec-campgrounds.com and in a booklet titled *New York Camping Guide*. The latter is available at DEC regional offices; by telephoning the DEC Bureau of Recreation at 518-457-2500; or by writing DEC at 625 Broadway, Albany, NY 12233-5253.

Campgrounds in the region

Caroga Lake. NY 29A, 9 mi N of Gloversville

Indian Lake Islands. NY 30, 14 mi N of Speculator. Offers open camping on E shore of Indian Lake and on Indian Lake Islands. Sites have privies and picnic tables and can be reached only by boat.

Lake Durant. NY 28, 3 mi E of Blue Mt. Lake. Beautiful swimming area in full view of Blue Mt.

Lewey Lake. NY 30, 14 mi N of Speculator

Little Sand Point. Off NY 8, 3 mi W of Piseco

Moffit Beach. NY 8, 4 mi W of Speculator

Northampton Beach. NY 30, 1.5 mi S of Northville

Point Comfort. Off NY 8, 4 mi W of Piseco

Poplar Point. Off NY 8, 2 mi W of Piseco

Sacandaga. NY 30, 4 mi S of Wells. A camping area along the West Branch Sacandaga River

Campgrounds near the region

Eagle Point. US 9, 2 mi N of Pottersville. On Schroon Lake, E of region.

Lake Eaton. NY 30, 2.5 mi W of Long Lake. N and slightly W of region.

Lake Harris. Off NY 28N, 3 mi N of Newcomb. This is a good base for many seldom-hiked trails. N of region.

Luzerne. NY 9N, 8 mi SW of Lake George village. E of region.

Acknowledgments

The Adirondack Mountain Club has been helping residents and visitors alike to enjoy the Forest Preserve, owned by the people of New York State, since 1922. ADK's work to educate recreationists about these lands includes the publishing of trail guides, other books, and maps.

The *Central Trails* guidebook, now in its fourth edition, covers an enlarged area that includes parts of the former West-Central and Southern Region guides. For the baseline research that informed earlier editions of those guidebooks, I owe thanks to their respective editors: Norm Landis, Arthur W. Haberl, and Robert J. Redington (West-Central Region) and Jack Freeman and Linda Laing (Southern Region). Sections of this new, fourth edition pertaining to the Northville–Placid Trail are the work of Jeffrey and Donna Case. Similarly the breadth of *Central Trails* is forever indebted to the diligence of my capable predecessors, Laurence T. Cagle and the late Bruce Wadsworth. I extend thanks as well to Neal Burdick, past editor of the Forest Preserve Series.

ADK Publications Editor Andrea Masters provided the direction, coordination, and management for the fourth edition. Andrea was an utmost pleasure to work with and kept the project moving along at every juncture. Likewise, former Publications & Marketing Manager John Kettlewell was always quick to lend a hand and offer assistance in the years between guidebook editions. Freelancer Terry Brosseau provided stellar professional editing for this edition of the guide and for the second edition of *Trails Illustrated Map 742*. David Lambert, of the National Geographic Society, provided outstanding cartographic services for the companion map.

ADK volunteers were ever-ready to contribute trail observations. More than a few stepped forward when a deadline loomed to walk trails, including during cold, snowy conditions. For field checks, I am especially indebted to Tony Goodwin and Bob Goodwin, as well as ADK Foothills Chapter members Scott Hammons, Brenda Hammons, Shawn Neese, Jeremy Preston, Jody Rothmeyer, and Justin Thalheimer. I am grateful to my own hiking companions, who tolerated my surveying wheel and frequent stops to jot down notes during field checks. These include Brendan, Bob, Donna, Leigh-Anne, Richie, Mark, Beth, Ben, Kenny, George, and the Boy Scouts of Troop 95, Fishkill: Dan, Justin, Louis, Jared, and Tommy.

Foresters and rangers from the NYS Department of Environmental Conservation were readily available to answer questions. In particular, this edition benefitted from the insights of Tad Norton, Michael Curley, Tom Kapelewski, and Eric Kasza. Furthermore the area unit management plans generated by DEC staff overflow with research data and information that have been incorporated, where appropriate, into this guide.

Last but not least, the World Wide Web has greatly enhanced information sharing. The online trail reports of hikers posted at sites like www.ADKForum.com have proved another valuable tool in the ongoing effort to stay current on trail conditions and prioritize trail inspections.

—*Michael N. Kelsey*

About the Editor

Michael N. Kelsey's passion for the outdoors was kindled in the central Adirondacks, where he climbed his first mountain at age eight (Blue Mt., in the rain), got lost for more than nine hours on Moxham Mt. at age 12, and completed his first 50 mile backpacking trip with the Boy Scouts, starting at Tirrell Pond, at age 14. He vacations with his family every year in Minerva and has been making weekend trips to the region since graduating college in 2000.

Kelsey lives in New York's Hudson Highlands, where he is a licensed guide and kayak outfitter with his own business, www.AWAYAdventureGuide.com. A three-time end-to-ender on the Northville–Placid Trail, Kelsey is also an Adirondack 46-R and a Northeast 115-R. In 2011, he reached the top of Africa's tallest peak, Mt. Kilimanjaro. His outdoor photography and trip narratives have appeared in Adirondac, Adirondack Life, Backpacker, Berkshire HomeStyle, Canoe & Kayak, Adirondack Journal of Environmental Studies, and New England Peaked Experiences. In addition, he writes an adventure blog at www.MikeKelseyAdventures.com and maintains a Web site of his images at www.KelseyOutdoorPhoto.com.

When not on the trail, Kelsey serves as a Dutchess County legislator representing five municipalities; practices family law and wills and estate planning as an attorney in private practice; teaches philosophy, religion, and law at Marist College; and writes weekly columns on public policy for two local newspapers.

Join us!

30,000 members count on us, and so can you
- We produce the most trusted, comprehensive trail maps and books
- Our outdoor activities take you around the world
- Our advocacy team concentrates on issues that affect the wild lands and waters important to our members and chapters
- Our professional and volunteer crews construct and maintain trails
- Our wilderness lodges and information centers give you shelter and direction

Benefits of membership include:
- Fun outdoor recreation opportunities for all levels
- *Adirondac* magazine (bimonthly)
- Special rates for ADK education and skill-building programs, lodging, parking, publications, and logo merchandise
- Rewarding volunteer opportunities
- Supporting ADK's mission, thereby ensuring protection of the wild lands and waters of New York State

Lodges and campground
- Adirondak Loj, on the shores of Heart Lake, near Lake Placid, offers year-round accommodations in private and family rooms, a coed loft, and cabins. It is accessible by car, and parking is available.
- The Adirondak Loj Wilderness Campground, located on ADK's Heart Lake property, offers thirty-two campsites and sixteen Adirondack lean-tos.
- Johns Brook Lodge (JBL), located near Keene Valley, is a backcountry facility accessible only on foot and open on a seasonal basis. Facilities include coed bunkrooms or small family rooms. Cabins near JBL are available year-round.

Both lodges offer home-cooked meals and trail lunches. Member discounts are available at all lodges and the campground.

Visit us
ADK centers in Lake George and on our Heart Lake property near Lake Placid offer ADK publications and other merchandise for sale, as well as backcountry and general Adirondack information, educational displays, outdoor equipment, and snacks.

Adirondak Loj
James Bullard

ADK Publications

Forest Preserve Series
1 Adirondack Mountain Club High Peaks Trails
2 Adirondack Mountain Club Eastern Trails
3 Adirondack Mountain Club Central Trails
4 Adirondack Mountain Club Western Trails
5 Adirondack Mountain Club Northville–Placid Trail
6 Adirondack Mountain Club Catskill Trails

Other Titles
Adirondack Alpine Summits: An Ecological Field Guide
Adirondack Birding: 60 Great Places to Find Birds
Adirondack Canoe Waters: North Flow
Adirondack Mountain Club Canoe and Kayak Guide: East-Central New York State
Adirondack Mountain Club Canoe Guide to Western & Central New York State
Adirondack Paddling: 60 Great Flatwater Adventures
An Adirondack Sampler I: Day Hikes for All Seasons
Catskill Day Hikes for All Seasons
Forests and Trees of the Adirondack High Peaks Region
Kids on the Trail! Hiking with Children in the Adirondacks
No Place I'd Rather Be: Wit and Wisdom from Adirondack Lean-to Journals
Ski and Snowshoe Trails in the Adirondacks
The Adirondack Reader
The Catskill 67: A Hiker's Guide to the Catskill 100 Highest Peaks under 3500'
Views from on High: Fire Tower Trails in the Adirondacks and Catskills
Winterwise: A Backpacker's Guide

Maps
Trails of the Adirondack High Peaks Region
Northville-Placid Trail
Trails Illustrated Map 742: Lake Placid/High Peaks
Trails Illustrated Map 743: Lake George/Great Sacandaga
Trails Illustrated Map 744: Northville/Raquette Lake
Trails Illustrated Map 745: Old Forge/Oswegatchie
Trails Illustrated Map 746: Saranac/Paul Smiths
Trails Illustrated Map 755: Catskill Park

Adirondack Mountain Club Calendar

Price list available upon request, or see www.adk.org

Contact Us

ADK Member Services Center
(Exit 21 off I-87, the Northway)
814 Goggins Road
Lake George, NY 12845-4117
Website: www. adk.org   Information: 518-668-4447
Membership, donations, publications, and merchandise: 800-395-8080

ADK Heart Lake Program Center
(at Adirondak Loj on Heart Lake)
PO Box 867
1002 Adirondack Loj Road
Lake Placid, NY 12946-0867
Educational programs and facility reservations: 518-523-3441

ADK Public Affairs Office
301 Hamilton Street
Albany, NY 12210-1738
Public Affairs: 518-449-3870

The Adirondack Mountain Club (ADK) is dedicated to the protection and responsible recreational use of the New York State Forest Preserve, and other parks, wild lands, and waters vital to our members and chapters. The Club, founded in 1922, is a member-directed organization committed to public service and stewardship. ADK employs a balanced approach to outdoor recreation, advocacy, environmental education, and natural resource conservation.

ADK encourages the involvement of all people in its mission and activities; its goal is to be a community that is comfortable, inviting, and accessible.

The Adirondack Mountain Club is a charitable organization, 501(c)(3). Contributions are tax deductible to the extent the law allows.

Index

Locations are indexed by proper name, with Camp, Lake, Mount, or Mountain following.

A

Abanakee Lake, 33
Adirondack Hundred Highest, 7, 60, 72, 103, 113, 129, 131, 138, 144
Adirondack League Club, 183–184
Adirondack Mountain Club (ADK)
  contact information, 4, 253
  membership and programs, 251
  publications, 252
  see also Forest Preserve Series guidebooks, of ADK
Adirondack Museum, 135
Adirondack Park Agency, 13
Adirondack region
  ecology of, 12
  exploration, settlement, and resource use in, 12–13
  geology of, 11–12
Adirondack State Park, 13
  map, 6
Adirondacks Illustrated, The (Stoddard), 179
Alder Brook Trail, 186–187
Americans with Disabilities Act, compliant campsite, 59, 62
archery season, 23
Auger Falls Trails
  east side, 41, 42, 43, 235
  map, 44
  west side, 41–42, 45, 235
Austin Falls Walk Trail, 42, 45–46

B

Baldface Mt. Trail, 95, 96, 106–107
Balm of Gilead Mt. Trail, 60, 67–68
Balsam Lake, 121
Barnes, Wesley, 27
Barnes Pond, 29
Bear Pond Sportsmen's Club, 174
Bear Pond Trail, 153, 176
Bearpath Inn Trail, 186, 192
  Sheriff Lake via, 186, 192

bears
  hunting season for, 23
  safety issues and, 19, 23–24
"beaver fever" (giardiasis), 21
Beaver Lake Trail, 152, 153, 179
Bellows Lake, and Irving Pond to Peters Corners Trail, 204, 230–232
Benedict, Sabael, 95
Benedict Creek Trail, 153, 176–177
Big Alderbed Lake Trail, 185, 186, 196–198
Big Bad Luck Pond Trail, 96, 98
Big Eddy and West Branch Gorge and Falls Trail, 236, 241–243
Big Marsh Mt. Trail, 186, 190
big-game seasons, 23
Black Bear Mt.
  Black Bear Mt. Ski Trail, 153, 164–165
  elevation, 161
  Fourth Lake-Black Bear Mt. Trail, 153, 161, 163
  Old Black Bear Mt. Trail, 153, 165–166
  Uncas Rd.–Black Bear Mt. Trail, 152, 153, 163–164
Black Cat Lake Trail, 186, 200, 201
Blue Ledges Trail, 27, 28, 33–34
"blue line," 13
Blue Mountain Lake and Sargent Ponds Section trails, 135–149
  Blue Mountain Lake from South Castle Rock, 136, 147–148
  Blue Mt., 135, 136, 143–144
  Cascade Pond, 135, 136–137
  North Castle Rock, 136, 146–147
  Northville-Placid Trail to Tirrell Pond 136, 141–142
  Rock Lake, 135, 136, 139–140
  Rock River, 136, 140
  Sargent Ponds Loop, 136, 148
  Sawyer Mt., 136, 140–141
  South Castle Rock, 136, 146
  Tioga Point, 135, 136, 149

Tirrell Pond from Blue Mt. Trailhead, 135, 136, 143
Upper Sargent Pond, 136, 144–145
Wilson Pond, 136, 138–139
Wilson Pond–Cascade Pond Connector, 136, 137–138
Blue Mt.
  Blue Mt. Trail, 135, 136, 143–144
  previous names of, 143
boating and canoeing
  Baldface Mt. Trail, 106
  Bug Lake, 168
  Crotched Pond Trail, 105
  Helldiver Pond Trail, 178
  Indian Lake Section, 95
  John Mack Pond Trail, 103–104
  Kunjamuk Cave Trail, 90
  Mason Lake Campsites, 112
  near Auger Falls, 45
  Peaked Mt. Pond and Peaked Mt. Trail, 62
  Raquette Lake–West Mt. Trail, 156, 157
  rentals, 157, 166
  Sagamore Cascades Trail, 170
  Tioga Point Trail, 149
Bog Meadow Trail, 42, 56–57
Boreas (Greek god), 12
Boreas River, Hewitt Eddy–Boreas River Trail, 27, 28, 35
Botheration Pond Trail, 60, 70–71
Brooktrout Lake Trail, West Canada Lakes via, 111, 125–128
Broomstick Lake Trail, 204, 220–222
Browns Tract Pond State Campground, 154–155, 156
Bug Lake, 167, 168
Bullhead Pond Trail, 96

C
Callahan Brook Trail, 111, 112–113
camping and campsites
  Alder Brook Trail, 187
  Baldface Mt. Trail, 106
  Beaver Lake Trail, 179
  Big Alderbed Lake Trail, 198
  Big Eddy and West Branch Gorge and Falls Trail, 242
  Broomstick Lake Trail, 220

Browns Tract Pond State Campground, 154–155, 156
Callahan Brook Trail, 112
Crotched Pond Trail, 105
Dry and Dexter Lakes Trail, 207
Durant Lake Public Campground, 141
East Canada Creek, 185
Eighth Lake, 163–164, 167
Falls Pond, 126
First Cedar Lake, 123
Forest Preserve regulations, 18–19
G Lake Trail, 189
Glasgow Mills and Hillabrandt Lake and Vlei Trail, 226
Goldmine Stream Falls Trail, 195
Good Luck Lake, 209, 211, 215
group camping permits, 19, 20
handicap accessibility, 59, 62
Helldiver Pond Trail, 178
Hewitt Eddy–Boreas River, 35
Hillabrandt Lake and Vlei Trail, 229
Horn Lake, 183
Hour Pond Trail, 72–73
Ice House Pond Trail, 178
Indian Lake, 95, 106, 182
John Pond Trail, 85
Kunjamuk Trail, 82
Lewey Lake Public Campground, 95, 103–104, 124
Limekiln Lake, 175
Little Holmes Lake, 231
Lost Ponds Trail, 179–180
Mason Lake Campsites, 112
Nine Corner Lake, 220
Northville–Placid Trail, Upper Benson to Piseco, 238, 239
Old Farm Clearing Trail, 69
Peaked Mt. Pond, 64
Puffer Pond from Kings Flow Trail, 78
Rock Lake, 139, 140
Ross Pond Trail, 99
Round Pond from Kunjamuk Trail, 83
Sargent Ponds Loop Trail, 146
Second Pond, 58
Seventh Lake Trail, 166
Shanty Brook and Mud Ponds, 50
Siamese Ponds Trail, 56
Sly Pond Trail, 180

Spectacle Lake from NY 29A Trail, 218
Squaw Lake Trail, 182
state and area campgrounds listed, 248
Stony Pond from NY 28N, 30
Upper Sargent Pond Trail, 145
Vanderwhacker Mt. Trail, 39
Wakely Dam, 151–152
West Canada Lakes via Brooktrout Lake
    Trail, 127
Woods Lake Trail, 237
see also lean-tos
Canadian Shield, 11–12
Canary Pond, elevation of, 239
canoeing. *See boating and canoeing*
Carroll Brook, 77, 79
Cartier, Jacques, 12
Cascade Pond Trail, 135, 136–137
Wilson Pond–Cascade Pond Connector
    Trail, 136, 137–138
Castle Rock
Blue Mountain Lake from South Castle
    Rock Trail, 136, 147–148
elevation of, 146
North Castle Rock Trail, 136, 146–147
South Castle Rock Trail, 136, 146
Cathead Mt., 236
Cathedral Pines Trail, 152, 153, 169
Cedar Lakes
Otter Brook Road to, 111, 128–129
Pillsbury Mt. to First Cedar Lake Trail,
    109, 111, 114–115
Center Pond Trail
Olmstedville–Minerva Section, 28,
    29–30
Siamese Ponds Wilderness Area, 76, 87
Champlain, Samuel de, 12
Chase Lake Trail, 204, 232–233
Chimney Mt., 75, 76
Chimney Mt. Trail, 75, 76–77
elevation of, 77
Christine Falls, 41
Cisco Creek Trail to the Kunjamuk River
    Trail, 90, 91–92
Clear Pond
bushwhack to, 84, 85
Clear Pond Trail, 75, 76, 86–87
Clockmill Corners, Rock Lake and
    Kennels Ponds from, 186, 199–201

Clockmill Pond Trail, 186, 198–199
Colvin, Verplank, 37, 144
compass, importance of carrying on trails,
    17, 20–21
Constable Pond–West Mt. Trail, 153,
    158–160
map, 162
County Line Brook Trail, 42, 46, 48
Crotched Pond Trail, 96, 105–106
Curtis Clearing Trail, 42, 54–56

D
Death Falls Trail, 152, 153, 169–170
Deep Lake, 125, 126
deer
hunting season for, 23
ticks and Lyme disease, 25
DEET, 25
Department of Environmental
    Conservation
hunting season information, 23
predecessor organizations, 27
regulations of, 18–19
website of, 18
Dexter Lakes. *See* Dry and Dexter Lakes
    Trail
Diamond Brook, 52
drinking water safety, 21, 23
Dry and Dexter Lakes Trail, 204, 205–208
Dug Mt. Brook Falls Trail, 96, 99–100
Dunning Pond
from Gilmantown Road, 236, 244
from NY 30, 236, 245–246
Durant (Gilborn), 151
Durant, W.W., 167, 170
Durant Lake, Wakely Dam to NY 28/30
    at, 111, 131–133
Durant Lake Public Campground, 142

E
Eagles Nest Lake, 168–169
East Branch Sacandaga River
Gorge and Square Falls Trail, 42, 51, 236
from Old Farm Clearing, 42, 53–54
to Old Farm Clearing, 42, 52–53
East Canada Creek, 185, 193, 196
East Shore Path (Limekiln Lake) and
    Snowmobile Trail, 153, 175–176

Echo Cliff Trail, 185, 186, 191
Eckford, Henry, 135, 143
Eighth Lake Public Campground,
    163–164, 167
Elizabeth Point Trail, 59, 60, 69–70
emergency procedures and contacts, 4, 25

F

falls. *See* waterfalls
Ferds Bog Trail, 152, 153–154
Ferris Lake Wild Forest, 203
Finch, Pruyn and Company, 141–142
fire safety, 19
fire towers
    Blue Mt., 144
    Kane Mt., 222, 223
    Pillsbury Mt., 113, 114
    Snowy Mt., 103
    Vanderwhacker Mt. Trail, 37, 39
    Wakely Mt., 131
First Cedar Lake, Cedar Lakes Trail from
    Pillsbury Mt. to, 109, 111, 114–115
Forest Preserve
    creation of, 11, 12–13
    land units and classifications in, 13
Forest Preserve Series guidebooks, of
    ADK, 11, 13–16, 252
forest rangers, contacting of, 20
Fourth Lake
    area map, 162
    –Black Bear Mt. Trail, 153, 161, 163
    and Third Lake Trail, 204, 215–217
Fox Lair Walk, 42, 50–51
French Louie, 109, 121, 122, 127
French Louie Trail, 114, 121

G

G Lake Trail, 185, 186, 189–190
Garnet Hill Lodge, 59, 64, 65, 67, 68, 69
garnet mines, 64, 68, 80
Giardia lamblia, 21
Gilborn, Craig, 151
Gilmantown Road, Dunning Pond from,
    236, 244
Glasgow Mills and Hillabrandt Lake and
    Vlei Trail, 204, 226–227
Goldmine Stream Falls Trail, 185, 186,
    194–196

Good Luck Lake
    and Cliffs Trail, 203
    from NY 10, 204, 208–210
    Short Path Trail, 204, 211–212
    from West Stoner Lake Trail, 204,
        213–215
Good Luck Mt. Cliffs Trail, 204, 210–211
Gore Mt., 66
    Gore Mt. Ski Area, 61, 62
    via the Schaefer Trail, 60–62
GPS devices, 21
Great Camps, Pigeon Lake Wilderness
    Area, and Moose River Recreation Area
    trails, 151–184
    Bear Pond, 153, 176
    Beaver Lake, 152, 153, 179
    Benedict Creek, 153, 176–177
    Black Bear Mt. Ski Trail, 153,
        164–165
    Cathedral Pines, 152, 153, 169
    Constable Pond–West Mt., 153,
        158–160
    Death Falls, 152, 153, 169–170
    East Shore Path and Snowmobile
        Trail, 153, 175–176
    Ferds Bog, 152, 153–154
    Fourth Lake–Black Bear Mt., 153,
        161, 163
    Helldiver Pond, 153, 178
    Ice House Pond, 153, 178
    Indian Lake, 153, 182
    Indian River (Horn Lake), 152, 153,
        182–184
    Lost Ponds, 153, 179–180
    Mitchell Ponds, 153, 177–178
    Muskrat Pond, 153, 182
    Old Black Bear Mt. Trail, 153,
        165–166
    Raquette Lake–West Mt., 152, 153,
        156–157
    Rocky Mt., 152, 153, 160
    Sagamore Cascades, 153, 170–171
    Sagamore Lake, 153, 172–173
    Seventh Lake, 152, 153, 166–167
    Shallow Lake, 152, 153, 154–155
    Short Trails on Indian River Rd.,
        153, 182
    Sly Pond, 152, 153, 180–181

Squaw Lake, 153, 182
Sucker Brook Bay, 153, 155–156
Uncas Rd.–Black Bear Mt., 152, 153, 163–164
Uncas Rd.–Mohegan Lake, 153, 173–174
Uncas Trail, 153, 167–169
Greene, Don, 60
Griffin Falls, 41, 43

H
Halfway Brook Trail, 59, 60, 64–65
Hayes Flow, 93
Hayes Flow Trail, 89, 90, 93–94
Helldiver Pond Trail, 153, 178
herd paths, 17
Hermitage Trail, 158
Hewitt Eddy–Boreas River Trail, 27, 28, 35
Hewitt Lake Club, 28
Hewitt Pond
  to Irishtown, 27
  to Stony Pond, 27, 28–29
Hillabrandt Lake and Vlei
  Glasgow Mills and, 204, 226–227
  from Stewart Landing, 203, 204, 229–230
Hochschild, Harold, 155
Holmes, Russell, 231
Holmes Lake, 232
Hooper Mine Trail, 59, 60, 68–69
Horn Lake, and Indian River Trail, 152, 153, 182–184
Hour Pond
  Hour Pond Trail, 60, 72–73
  –Peaked Mt. Connector Trail, 60, 73
Hoy, John, 172
Hudnut, Alexander, 50
Hudson, Henry, 12
Humphrey Mt. Trail, 76, 80–81
hunting seasons, 23

I
Ice House Pond Trail, 153, 178
Indian Lake
  Indian Lake Trail, 153, 182
  Stewart and Indian Lakes Trail, 204, 224–225
Indian Lake Islands Public Campground, 95, 106

Indian Lake Section trails, 95–107
  Baldface Mt., 95, 96, 106–107
  Big Bad Luck Pond, 96, 98
  Bullhead Pond, 96
  Crotched Pond, 96, 105–106
  Dug Mt. Brook Falls, 96, 99–100
  John Mack Pond, 95, 96, 103–104
  John Mack Pond–Long Pond Cross, 96, 104–105
  Ross Pond, 96, 98–99
  Snowy Mt., 95, 96, 103
  Watch Hill from Indian Lake, 96, 101–102
  Watch Hill from NY 30, 96, 100–101
  Whortleberry Pond, 96–98
Indian River (Horn Lake) Trail, 152, 153, 182–184
Indian River Rd., Short Trails on, 153, 182
insect-borne diseases, 25
International Paper Company, 43, 46
Irishtown
  Hewitt Pond to, 27
  Stony Pond from, 27, 28, 31–32
Irving Pond and Bellows Lake to Peters Corners Trail, 204, 230–232

J
Jessup River, Panther Pond and Jessup River Trail, 109, 111–112
Jockeybush Lake Trail, 204–205
John Mack Pond
  John Mack Pond Trail, 95, 96, 103–104
  –Long Pond Cross Trail, 96, 104–105
John Pond
  Crossover Trail, 76, 85–86
  John Pond Trail, 75, 76, 84–85
Johns Brook Lodge, 18, 251

K
Kamp Kill Kare, 151, 174
Kane Mt.
  East Trail, 204, 223–224
  South and North Trails, 203, 204, 222–223
Keelan, Brian and Eileen, 180
Kennels Ponds, from Clockmill Corners, 183, 199–201
Kenwell, Gerald, 179

Kenwell, Wellington Alexander, 179
King, Eliza Emilia (gravesite), 85
Kings Flow
    Kings Flow East Trail, 76, 79–80
    Puffer Pond from Kings Flow Trail, 76,
        77–78
Kings Pond, 122
Kunjamuk Cave Trail, 89, 90–91
Kunjamuk Mt. Trail, 76, 84
Kunjamuk River, 89
    Cisco Creek Trail to, 90, 91–92
Kunjamuk Section, 89
Kunjamuk Trail, 75, 76, 81–83
    Round Pond from, 76, 83–84

L
LaFrance, Ferdinand, 153
Lapland Lake Nordic Ski and Vacation
    Resort, 237
Last of the Mohicans (film), 221
lean-tos
    Brooktrout Lake, 122, 127
    Cascade Pond Trail, 137
    Cedar Lakes, 127
    Cedar River, 124
    Chase Lake, 232, 233
    Colvin Brook, 124
    East Branch Sacandaga to Old Farm
        Clearing, 52
    First Cedar Lake, 123, 124
    Hamilton Lake Stream, 240
    Holmes Lake, 232
    Hour Pond Trail, 73
    John Pond Trail, 84, 85
    Mud Lake, 239
    Northville–Placid Trail, Piseco to
        Wakely Dam, 118, 120–121
    Northville–Placid Trail, Upper Benson
        to Piseco, 238
    Old Farm Clearing to East Branch
        Sacandaga, 53
    O'Neil Flow, 142
    Pillsbury Lake to West Canada Creek
        Trail, 116
    Pillsbury Lake Trail, 114
    Puffer Pond from Kings Flow Trail, 78
    Puffer Pond Trail, 71–72
    regulations, 18, 19–20
    Sampson Lake, 117

Sargent Pond, 149
Sargent Ponds Loop Trail, 146
Seventh Lake Trail, 166
Siamese Ponds Trail, 56
Stephens Pond, 132, 133
Stony Pond, 29, 30, 32
T Lake Trail, 190
Third Cedar Lake, 122, 128
Tioga Point Trail, 149
Tirrell Pond, 141, 142, 143
West Canada Creek, 118, 121
West Canada Lakes via Brooktrout
    Lake Trail, 127
West Lake, 122, 125
Wilson Pond, 138, 139
see also camping and campsites
Leave No Trace principles, 19, 22
Lewey Lake and West Canada Lakes
    Section trails, 109–133
    Callahan Brook, 111, 112–113
    Cedar Lakes Trail, Pillsbury Mt. to First
        Cedar Lake, 109, 111, 114–115
    Mason Lake Campsites, 112
    Northville–Placid Trail, Piseco to
        Wakely Dam, 111, 118, 120–125
    Northville–Placid Trail, Wakely Dam to
        NY 28/30 at Lake Durant, 111,
        131–133
    Otter Brook Road to Cedar Lakes, 111,
        128–129
    Panther Pond and Jessup River, 109,
        111–112
    Pillsbury Lake, 111, 115–116
    Pillsbury Lake to West Canada Creek,
        111, 116–118
    Pillsbury Mt., 109, 111, 113–114
    Sprague Pond, 109, 111, 130–131
    Sucker Brook, 109, 111, 129–130
    Wakely Mt., 109, 111, 131
    West Canada Lakes via Brooktrout
        Lake, 111, 125–128
Lewey Lake Public Campground, 95,
    103–104, 124
Limekiln Lake, 175
    East Shore Path and Snowmobile Trail,
        153, 175–176
Linsey Marsh Trail, 28, 34–35
Little Holmes Lake, 231

Long Pond
  Long Pond Cross–John Mack Pond
    Trail, 96, 104–105
  and Rock Pond Trail, 89, 90, 92–93
Lost Ponds Trail, 153, 179–180
Lower Pine Lakes Trail, 89, 90, 91
Lyme disease, 25
Lyme Timber Company, 75, 81, 89, 113

M
maps
  ADK maps, 16
  GPS devices and, 21
  guidebooks and, 15
  importance of carrying on trails, 17,
    20–21
  National Geographic Trails Illustrated
    maps, 7, 15, 21
Mason Lake
  map, 110
  Mason Lake Campsites Trail, 112
Mays Pond Trail, 158
Meco Lake
  elevation of, 238
  Meco Lake Trail, 186, 193–194
Mitchell Ponds Trail, 153, 177–178
mobile phones, 18, 21
Mohegan Lake, and Uncas Rd. Trail, 153,
  173–174
Moose River Plains Wild Forest, 125, 128,
  178
Moose River Recreation Area, 109, 118,
  151–152. *See also* Great Camps, Pigeon
    Lake Wilderness Area, and Moose
    River Recreation Area Trails
Morehouseville Wilderness Access, 187
Morgan, J.P., 167, 173
mosquitoes, and West Nile virus, 25
Moxham, Robert, 37
Moxham Mt. Trail, 28, 36–37
Mud Lake, from Stewart Landing Trail,
  204, 227–229
Mud Ponds Trail, 42, 48–50
Muskrat Pond Trail, 153, 182
muzzle-loading season, 23

N
National Geographic Trails Illustrated
  maps, 7, 15, 21

Native Americans, 12
Nine Corner Lake Trail, 203, 204,
  219–220
Normans Cove, 106
North Creek Reservoir, 61
North Creek Ski Bowl, 60, 61, 62, 66
North Pine Lake Trail, 90, 91
Northville–Placid Trail
  map, 16
  Piseco to Wakely Dam, 111, 118,
    120–125
  start of, 235
  to Tirrell Pond, 136, 141–143
  Upper Benson to Piseco, 236, 237–241
  Wakely Dam to NY 28/30 at Lake
    Durant, 111, 131–133
NY 10 Corridor trails, 203–233
  Broomstick Lake, 204, 220–222
  Chase Lake, 204, 232–233
  Dry and Dexter Lakes, 204, 205–208
  Glasgow Mills and Hillabrandt Lake
    and Vlei, 204, 226–227
  Good Luck Lake and Cliffs, 203
  Good Luck Lake from NY 10, 204,
    208–210
  Good Luck Lake, from West Stoner
    Lake, 204, 213–215
  Good Luck Lake, Short Path, 204,
    211–212
  Good Luck Mt. Cliffs, 204, 210–211
  Hillabrandt Lake and Vlei from Stewart
    Landing, 203, 204, 229–230
  Irving Pond and Bellows Lake to Peters
    Corners, 204, 230–232
  Jockeybush Lake, 204–205
  Kane Mt., East Trail, 204, 223–224
  Kane Mt., South and North Trails, 203,
    204, 222–223
  Mud Lake from Stewart Landing, 204,
    227–229
  Nine Corner Lake, 203, 204, 219–220
  Spectacle Lake from NY 10, 204,
    212–213
  Spectacle Lake from NY 29A, 204,
    217–219
  Stewart and Indian Lakes, 203, 204,
    224–225
  Third and Fourth Lakes, 204, 215–217

NY 28
  Northville–Placid Trail, Wakely Dam to
    at Lake Durant, 111, 131–133
  Stony Pond from, 28, 30
NY 29, Spectacle Lake from, 214, 217–219
NY 30
  Dunning Pond from, 236, 245–246
  Northville–Placid Trail, Wakely Dam to
    at Lake Durant, 111, 131–133

O

Old Black Bear Mt. Trail, 153, 165–166
Old Farm Clearing
  from East Branch Sacandaga Trail, 42,
    52–53
  to East Branch Sacandaga Trail, 42,
    53–54
  Old Farm Clearing Trail, 60, 69
Olmstedville–Minerva Section trails,
  27–39
  Blue Ledges, 27, 28, 33–34
  Center Pond, 28, 29–30
  Hewitt Eddy–Boreas River, 27, 28, 35
  Linsey Marsh, 28, 34–35
  Moxham Mt. Trail, 28, 36–37
  Rankin Pond, 27, 28, 34
  Stony Pond from Hewitt Pond, 27,
    28–29
  Stony Pond from Irishtown, 27, 28,
    31–32
  Stony Pond from NY 28N, 28, 30
  Vanderwhacker Mt. Trail, 27, 28, 37, 39
Oregon Tannery ruins, 50
Otter Brook Road to Cedar Lakes Trail,
  111, 128–129
Ovitt, Steve, 60

P

Panther Pond and Jessup River Trail, 109,
  111–112
Peaked Mt.
  Hour Pond–Peaked Mt. Connector
    Trail, 60, 73
  Peaked Mt. Pond and Peaked Mt. Trail,
    59, 60, 62–64
permits, for group camping, 19, 20
Peters Corners, Irving Pond and Bellows
  Lake to, 204, 230–232

picnic sites
  Austin Falls Walk, 46
  Broomstick Lake Trail, 220
  Crotched Pond Trail, 105
  Elizabeth Point Trail, 69
  G Lake Trail, 189
  Glasgow Mills and Hillabrandt Lake
    and Vlei Trail, 226
  Hewitt Eddy–Boreas River Trail, 35
  Indian Lake Section, 95
  Jockeybush Lake Trail, 205
  Kane Mt., South and North Trails, 222
  Mason Lake Campsites, 112
  Sprague Pond Trail, 131
Pigeon Lake, 159
Pigeon Lake Wilderness Area. *See* Great
  Camps, Pigeon Lake Wilderness Area,
  and Moose River Recreation Area
Pillsbury Lake
  Pillsbury Lake Trail, 111, 115–116
  to West Canada Creek Trail, 111,
    116–118
Pillsbury Mt.
  Cedar Lakes Trail to First Cedar Lake
    Trail from, 109, 111, 114–115
  elevation of, 113
  Pillsbury Mt. Trail, 109, 111, 113–114
Pine Lake Campground, 222
Piseco
  Northville–Placid Trail from Upper
    Benson to, 236, 237–241
  Northville–Placid Trail to Wakely Dam
    from, 111, 118, 120–125
Piseco–Powley Road Vicinity trails,
  185–201
  Alder Brook, 186–187
  Bearpath Inn, 186, 192
  Big Alderbed Lake, 185, 186, 196–198
  Big Marsh Mt., 186, 190
  Black Cat Lake, 186, 200, 201
  Clockmill Pond, 186, 198–199
  Echo Cliff, 185, 186, 191
  G Lake, 185, 186, 189–190
  Goldmine Stream Falls, 185, 186,
    194–196
  Meco Lake, 186, 193–194
  Rock Lake and Kennels Pond from
    Clockmill Corners, 186, 199–201

Sand Lake, 186, 192–193
Sheriff Lake via Bearpath Inn, 186, 192
South Branch Trail, 186, 187–189
T Lake, 185, 186, 191
pit privies, 19
poison ivy, at Lost Ponds, 180
"posted" signs, 17
Powely, John, 196
Primitive areas, 13
Prospect House, 135
Puffer Pond
  from Kings Flow Trail, 76, 77–78
  Puffer Pond Brook Trail, 76, 78–79
  Puffer Pond Trail, 60, 71–72

Q
Queer Lake Trail, 158, 159

R
rabies, 24–25
Rankin Pond Trail, 27, 28, 34
Raquette Lake Railroad, 163, 167, 173
Raquette Lake–West Mt. Trail, 152, 153, 156–157
Raymond Brook Trail, 60, 66–67
Rock Lake
  elevation of, 238
  and Kennels Pond from Clockmill Corners Trail, 186, 199–201
  Rock Lake Trail, 135, 136, 139–140
Rock Pond Trail, 89, 90, 92–93
Rock River Trail, 136, 140
Rocky Mt. Trail, 152, 153, 160
Ross Pond Trail, 96, 98–99
Round Pond from Kunjamuk Trail, 76, 83–84

S
Sacandaga River. See East Branch Sacandaga River; West Branch Sacandaga River
safety issues
  bears, 23–24
  drinking water, 21, 23
  emergency procedures and contacts, 4, 25
  GPS devices, 21
  hunting season, 23
  insect-borne diseases, 25
  mobile phones, 18, 21
  rabies, 24–25
  waste disposal, 19, 21
Sagamore Camp, 174
Sagamore Cascades Trail, 153, 170–171
Sagamore Lake Trail, 153, 172–173
Sagamore Lodge and Conference Center, 151, 172
Sampson Bog, 121
Sampson Lake, 115, 117
Sand Lake Trail, 186, 192–193
Sargents Pond
  Sargent Ponds Loop Trail, 136, 148
  Upper Sargent Pond Trail, 136, 144–145
Savary, Peter (gravesite), 85
Sawyer Mt. Trail, 136, 140–141
Schaefer, Carl, Paul, and Vincent, 60
Schaefer Trail, Gore Mt. via, 60–62
Second Pond Trail, 42, 58
Seventh Lake Trail, 152, 153, 166–167
Shaker Mountain Wild Forest, 203
Shallow Lake Trail, 152, 153, 154–155
Shanty Brook and Mud Ponds Trail, 42, 48–50
Sheriff Lake via Bearpath Inn Trail, 186, 192
Siamese Pond Wilderness Area, trails from the east, 59–73
  Balm of Gilead Mt., 60, 67–68
  Botheration Pond, 60, 70–71
  Elizabeth Point, 59, 60, 69–70
  Gore Mt. via the Schaefer Trail, 60–62
  Halfway Brook, 59, 60, 64–65
  Hooper Mine, 59, 60, 68–69
  Hour Pond, 60, 72–73
  Hour Pond–Peaked Mt. Connector, 60, 73
  Old Farm Clearing, 60, 69
  Peaked Mt. Pond and Peaked Mt., 59, 60, 62–64
  Puffer Pond, 60, 71–72
  Raymond Brook, 60, 66–67
Siamese Pond Wilderness Area, trails from the north, 75–87
  Center Pond, 76, 87
  Chimney Mt., 75, 76–77
  Clear Pond, 75, 76, 86–87

Humphrey Mt., 76, 80–81
John Pond, 75, 76, 84–85
John Pond Crossover, 76, 85–86
Kings Flow East, 76, 79–80
Kunjamuk Mt., 76, 84
Kunjamuk Trail, 75, 76, 81–83
Puffer Pond Brook, 76, 78–79
Puffer Pond from Kings Flow, 76, 77–78
Round Pond from Kunjamuk Trail, 76, 83–84
Siamese Pond Wilderness Area, trails from the south, 41–58
  Auger Falls (east side), 41, 42, 43, 235
  Auger Falls (west side), 41–42, 45, 235
  Austin Falls Walk, 42, 45–46
  Bog Meadow, 42, 56–57
  County Line Brook, 42, 46, 48
  Curtis Clearing, 42, 54–56
  East Branch Sacandaga Gorge and Square Falls, 42, 51, 236
  East Branch Sacandaga to Old Farm Clearing (from south), 42, 52–53
  Fox Lair Walk, 42, 50–51
  Old Farm Clearing to East Branch Sacandaga (from north), 53–54
  Second Pond, 42, 58
  Shanty Brook and Mud Ponds, 42, 48–50
  Siamese Ponds, 42, 56
Siamese Pond Wilderness Area, trails from the west, 89–94
  Cisco Creek to the Kunjamuk River, 90, 91–92
  Hayes Flow, 89, 90, 93–94
  Kunjamuk Cave, 89, 90–91
  Lower Pine Lakes, 89, 90, 91
  Rock Pond and Long Pond, 89, 90, 92–93
Silver Lake, elevation of, 238
Silver Lake Wilderness Area trails, 235–246
  Big Eddy and West Branch Gorge and Falls, 236, 241–243
  Dunning Pond from Gilmantown Road, 236, 244
  Dunning Pond from NY 30, 236, 245–246
  Northville–Placid Trail, Upper Benson to Piseco, 236, 237–241
  Woods Lake, 235, 236–237

Sly Pond Trail, 152, 153, 180–181
Snowy Mt.
  elevation of, 103
  Snowy Mt. Trail, 95, 96, 103
South Branch Trail, 186, 187–190
South Castle Rock Trail, 136, 146
South Inlet Falls. See Sagamore Cascades Trail
South Pine Lake Trail, 90, 91
Spectacle Lake
  Dry and Dexter Lakes bushwhack to, 204, 205–208
  from NY 10, 204, 212–213
  from NY 29A, 204, 217–219
Speculator Tree Farm, 90–91
Sprague Pond Trail, 109, 111, 130–131
Spruce Lake, elevation of, 120
Square Falls and East Branch Sacandaga Gorge Trail, 42, 51, 236
Squaw Lake Trail, 153, 182
Stephens Pond, 132–133, 137
Stewart and Indian Lakes Trail, 203, 204, 224–225
Stewart Landing, Mud Lake from, 204, 227–229
Stoddard, S.R., 179
Stony Pond, 28
  from Hewitt Pond Trail, 27, 28–29
  from Irishtown Trail, 27, 28, 31–32
  from NY 28N Trail, 28, 30
Student Conservation Association, 103
Sucker Brook Bay Trail, 153, 155–156
Sucker Brook Trail, 109, 111, 129–130
swimming
  Baldface Mt. Trail, 106, 107
  County Line Brook footpath, 46
  Elizabeth Point Trail, 69
  Fox Lair Walk, 50
  Good Luck Lake, 215
  Jockeybush Lake Trail, 204, 205
  Long Pond, 93
  Nine Corner Lake, 220
  Panther Pond and Jessup River Trail, 111
  Ross Pond Trail, 98

T

T Lake Trail, 185, 186, 191
Third and Fourth Lakes Trail, 204, 215–217
Tioga Point Trail, 135, 136, 149
Tirrell Pond
  from Blue Mt. Trailhead Trail, 135, 136, 143
  Northville–Placid Trail to, 136, 141–143
Township 34 (Hochschild), 155
"trailless" routes, 17
trails, in general
  distance and time on, 17–18
  guidebook abbreviations and conventions, 15
  guidebook legend, 14
  maps and, 15–16
  markers and signs on, 16–17
  unmaintained, unmarked, 17

U

Uncas Camp, 151, 167, 173, 174
Uncas Rd.
  –Black Bear Mt. Trail, 152, 153, 163–164
  –Mohegan Lake Trail, 153, 173–174
Uncas Trail, 153, 167–169
unmaintained and unmarked trails, 17
Upper Benson, Northville–Placid Trail to Piseco from, 236, 237–241
Upper Sargent Pond Trail, 136, 144–145

V

Vanderbilt, Alfred G., 173
Vanderwhacker Mt.
  map, 38
  Vanderwhacker Mt. Trail, 27, 28, 37, 39

W

Wakely Dam, 151–152
  Northville–Placid Trail from Piseco to, 111, 118, 120–125
  Northville–Placid Trail to, at Lake Durant 111, 131–133
Wakely Mt. Trail, 109, 111, 131
waste disposal, 19, 21
Watch Hill
  Watch Hill from Indian Lake, 96, 101–102
  Watch Hill from NY 30, 96, 100–101

waterfalls
  Broomstick Lake Trail, 221
  Christine Falls, 41
  County Line Brook Falls, 46
  Death Falls Trail, 152, 153, 169–170
  Dug Mt. Brook Falls Trail, 99
  Dunning Pond from NY 30 Trail, 245, 246
  Goldmine Stream Falls Trail, 185, 186, 194–196
  Gore Mt. via the Schaefer Trail, 61
  Griffin Falls, 41, 43
  Jockeybush Lake Trail, 205
  Puffer Pond Trail, 71
  Sagamore Cascades Trail, 170
  Shanty Brook, 49
  Stony Pond from Irishtown, 32
  West Branch Sacandaga River, 241
  Whiskey Falls, 41
  see also Auger Falls; Austin Falls
West, Robert, 177
West Branch Sacandaga River, Big Eddy and West Branch Gorge and Falls Trail, 236, 241–243
West Canada Lakes Section. *See* Lewey Lake and West Canada Lakes Section trails
West Mt.
  Constable Pond–West Mt. Trail, 153, 158–160
  elevation, 151, 156
  Raquette Lake–West Mt. Trail, 152, 153, 156–157
West Nile virus, 25
West Stoner Lake, Good Luck Lake from, 204, 213–215
Whiskey Falls, 41
Whitney Lake, 115, 116, 117
Whortleberry Pond Trail, 96–98
Wild Forest areas, 13, 23
Wilderness areas, 13
William Blake Pond, 59, 64, 65, 68
Wilson Pond
  –Cascade Pond Connector Trail, 136, 137–138
  Wilson Pond Trail, 136, 138–139
Wolf Lake, 125, 126
Woods Lake Trail, 235, 236–237